RELIGION AND THE
SELF IN ANTIQUITY

Religion and the Self in Antiquity

EDITED BY

DAVID BRAKKE

MICHAEL L. SATLOW

STEVEN WEITZMAN

INDIANA UNIVERSITY PRESS

Bloomington and Indianapolis

This book is a publication of
Indiana University Press
601 North Morton Street
Bloomington, Indiana 47404-3797 USA

http://iupress.indiana.edu

Telephone orders 800-842-6796
Fax orders 812-855-7931
Orders by email iuporder@indiana.edu

Library of Congress Cataloging-in-Publication Data

Religion and the self in antiquity / edited by David Brakke, Michael L. Satlow, Steven Weitzman.
p. cm.
Includes index.
ISBN 0-253-34649-5 (cloth : alk. paper) — ISBN 0-253-21796-2 (pbk. : alk. paper)
1. Self—Religious aspects—History—To 1500—Congresses. 2. Self—Mediterranean Region—
History—To 1500—Congresses. I. Brakke, David. II. Satlow, Michael L. III. Weitzman, Steven, date
BL65.S38R45 2005
202'.2—dc22
2005008639

1   2   3   4   5   10   09   08   07   06   05

CONTENTS

Acknowledgments   vii

Introduction   1

Part I
SEEKING RELIGIOUS SELVES

1. Shifting Selves in Late Antiquity   PATRICIA COX MILLER   15
2. The Search for the Elusive Self in Texts of the Hebrew Bible
   SAUL M. OLYAN   40
3. Paul and the Slave Self   J. ALBERT HARRILL   51
4. Prayer of the Queen: Esther's Religious Self in the Septuagint
   ESTHER MENN   70
5. Giving for a Return: Jewish Votive Offerings in Late Antiquity
   MICHAEL L. SATLOW   91
6. The Self in Artemidorus' *Interpretation of Dreams*
   PETER T. STRUCK   109

Part II
SENSING RELIGIOUS SELVES

7. Sensory Reform in Deuteronomy   STEVEN WEITZMAN   123
8. Locating the Sensing Body: Perception and Religious Identity in Late
   Antiquity   SUSAN ASHBROOK HARVEY   140
9. Dialogue and Deliberation: The Sensory Self in the Hymns of Romanos the
   Melodist   GEORGIA FRANK   163

Part III
TEACHING RELIGIOUS SELVES

10. From Master of Wisdom to Spiritual Master in Late Antiquity
    GUY G. STROUMSA   183
11. The Beastly Body in Rabbinic Self-Formation
    JONATHAN SCHOFER   197

12. Making Public the Monastic Life: Reading the Self in Evagrius Ponticus'
    Talking Back   DAVID BRAKKE   222

13. The Student Self in Late Antiquity   EDWARD WATTS   234

Contributors   253
Subject Index   255
Source Index   261

ACKNOWLEDGMENTS

This book grew out of a conference on "The Religious Self in Antiquity" held at the Bloomington campus of Indiana University in September 2003. The conference received financial support from the President's Arts and Humanities Initiative, established by President Myles Brand, and from the Robert A. and Sandra S. Borns Jewish Studies Program, then directed by Alvin Rosenfeld. Richard Miller, the chair of the Department of Religious Studies at the time, supported our efforts, and staff members Jan Cobb, Patsy Ek, and Melissa Deckard helped to facilitate the conference. To all of these people and programs we express our gratitude.

The papers in this volume benefited immensely from the rich intellectual exchange that took place at the conference. Numerous faculty and graduate students participated in the discussions, but we thank especially Robert Ford Campany, Natalie Dohrmann, Constance Furey, Alan Segal, and Benjamin Sommer for their formal presentations and responses.

For assistance in the preparation of the book, we are grateful to Corrine Shirley, who did preliminary copyediting; to Michael Lundell and Robert Sloan of the Indiana University Press, who expressed interest in and support for the project from its beginning; to Betsy Garman, Elisabeth Marsh, and Jane Lyle of the Press, who guided the manuscript through publication; to Bradley Storin, who created the indexes; and to Elizabeth Yoder, whose copyediting expertise saved us from errors and infelicities.

Despite the generous funding awards that we received, the original conference would not have taken place nor would it have been as congenial and stimulating as it was without the crucial support of our late colleague in the Department of English, Albert Wertheim. In gratitude we dedicate this book to his memory.

Abbreviations of ancient and modern sources and the style of annotation follow Patrick H. Alexander et al., eds., *The SBL Handbook of Style: For Ancient Near Eastern, Biblical, and Early Christian Studies* (Peabody, Mass.: Hendrickson, 1999). Additional abbreviations of ancient sources follow Henry George Liddell and Robert Scott, with Henry Stuart Jones, eds., *A Greek-English Lexicon* (9th ed.; Oxford: Clarendon, 1968).

RELIGION AND THE
SELF IN ANTIQUITY

INTRODUCTION

What is the self and where does it come from? How one answers these questions depends on who is doing the asking. Psychologists trace the self's formation back to instinctual urges, unconscious conflicts, or biological interactions. Philosophers cast the self's emergence as a process of intellectual development, culminating in the emergence of the modern autonomous self, whose identification with external authorities and larger communities is seen as an entirely conscious and voluntary act. Anthropologists, followed by historians, have focused on the self as a cultural construction fashioned through discursive practice, an approach often in tension with the views of psychologists and philosophers.[1] The self presents itself as a different kind of problem to different kinds of scholars.

Our perspective as scholars of ancient religion impels us to focus on two aspects of self-formation. The first is the early history of the self. What can be recovered of ancient selves, or of ancient perceptions of the self, from surviving textual sources? Are there axial moments in antiquity when the self was reconceptualized in new ways, and what accounts for such changes? Does recent work on the body, gender, sexuality, the anthropology of the senses, and power—not to mention selfhood itself—sharpen our perception of how selves were perceived, constituted, or expressed in ancient cultures? Does this work draw us any closer to ancient selves, or does it push them farther away?

Second, we are interested in the role of religion in the history of the self. The self can be provisionally defined, in Stephen Greenblatt's words, as "a sense of personal order, a characteristic mode of address to the world, a structure of bounded desires."[2] Precisely because religion suffuses all these aspects of selfhood—certainly it did so in antiquity—the two topics are inseparable. In an ancient context, the self was a religious concept: for some, it was an entity separable from the body and yearning for contact with the divine, while for others it constituted an expression of the divine in its own right. Religion certainly entered the picture the moment the self reached out to others, mortal or immortal. What, then, can the study of religious ideas, texts, institutions, or practices tell us about the early history of the self? And conversely, what can the self tell us about the history of ancient religion?

Seeking a way to draw all these questions together, we organized a conference at Indiana University in September 2003 on the self in the ancient religions of the Mediterranean and the ancient Near East. We were and remain well aware of the fuzziness of the central terms and boundaries of the topic. Participants were initially bewildered by our use of the term *self*. We were no less uneasy with the contested word *religion*, an intrinsically slippery concept all the more difficult to pinpoint in ancient societies, which inextricably wove the worship of divine beings into their larger cultural tapestries. Despite or perhaps due to our hesitancy to sharply delimit the bounds of the conference, the contributions produced a shifting, complex, and multilayered set of conversations that were sharpened during the three days that we spent discussing them. The results can be seen in the revised essays in this volume. Not all of the papers discussed at the conference are included in this volume, and not all of the papers in the volume were discussed at the conference. Moreover, the conference and the authors benefited from thoughtful responses to sets of papers given by Robert Ford Campany, Natalie Dohrmann, and Constance Furey, which also do not appear here. Still, the essays in this book capture the fruitful dialogues of the conference.

Although this volume makes no bold theoretical claims about the nature of the self, neither are the individual essays simply narrow technical studies. Each essay participates in several simultaneous discussions—with the specialized scholarship of its field, with the other essays in this volume, and with broader intellectual issues shared with scholars across the humanities. This short introduction cannot do justice to the multitextured conversations that connect the essays, but we would like to provide some of our own, perhaps idiosyncratic, understandings of the more prominent questions and issues that they address.

Turning Points in the History of the Self

There is certainly no shortage of scholarly accounts of the self's histories. Most current histories of the self focus on the relatively recent past, the emergence of a "self-fashioning" self in the Renaissance, or the development of an autonomous self in the Enlightenment.[3] Each claims its period as an axial moment when the self was radically reconceptualized. The authors of such studies know, however, that there were selves before Western modernity supposedly invented the concept, if only because they are influenced by the seminal contributions of Marcel Mauss and Michel Foucault, whose work has encompassed non-Western or premodern cultures. Mauss is often credited with initiating the study of the self as a cultural construct, exploring the category of personhood as formulated in non-Western cultures like India and China. Foucault began his narrative of the history of self-formation with the effort to "care for the self"—to improve and police it—in Greco-Roman philosophy and late antique Christianity.[4] Charles Taylor also numbered among the sources of the modern self Plato and Augustine, the traditional (if not actual) markers of the beginning and end of Mediterranean antiquity.[5]

This book does not purport to be a history of the self or even the outline of such a history. Most of its essays focus on discrete moments or transitions spread across a broad swath of chronology and geography that encompasses not just Greco-Roman philosophers and Christian monks but also ancient Israelite sages, Roman slaves, and common Palestinian Jews. The result is more fragmented and less unidirectional than the narratives of Foucault, Taylor, and other historians of the self, but it is precisely for this reason that it can contribute to a more nuanced understanding than grand narratives allow, demonstrating that the history of the self begins before Plato, that it is not just an intellectual history, that it unfolds along multiple trajectories, and, most crucially from our perspective, that it is bound up with the history of religion.

Refining Foucault's initial contribution, several essays in this volume call for a rethinking of how the history of the self is emplotted by proposing new transitional moments, identifying new causal factors or catalysts, or including new actors. Patricia Cox Miller's essay argues, for example, that a basic transformation in the way the self is represented took place between the third and fifth centuries. She plots this transformation between two poles that, drawing from categories of the New Historicism, she designates as "a touch of the transcendent" and "a touch of the real." Exemplifying the first pole, third-century pagan and Christian thinkers such as Plotinus and Origen oriented themselves toward the transcendent divine, motivated by optimism that the self's divine core could be realized. In later antiquity, because "the high gods had become more remote," pagans and Christians turned to materially oriented practices, objects, and figures (e.g., theurgy, relics, and holy men) to mediate their relationship with divine power.

All the selves described in this book can be plotted along a spectrum between the transcendent and the material, developing different ways to mediate between them. Still, the particular historical shift that Miller so elegantly portrays is supported, at least in part, by two other essays that focus on the increasing importance of the senses in Christian religious experience in this period. Susan Ashbrook Harvey argues that, from the middle of the fourth century, Christians turned away from an austere distrust of the senses and embraced "sensory appreciation": the senses, connecting the self to the material world, increasingly became instruments for the reorientation of the self toward the divine. She ascribes this shift less to cosmic pessimism than to the public opportunities afforded to Christians after 313. The Christian poet Romanos (ca. 485–ca. 560), Georgia Franks claims, displays a similar valuation of the senses— a "touch of the real"—in his *kontakia,* chanted sermons given in churches, whose goal was to "educate" the senses in the self's quest for the divine.

Other contributions suggest still other ways to plot the history of the religious self in the ancient Mediterranean. Steven Weitzman argues that the engagement with sensory experience may predate Christianity and even Hellenistic philosophy by centuries, surfacing in Deuteronomy's retelling of biblical history. J. Albert Harill suggests that Roman Stoics came to a revised notion of the self by thinking about the selves of slaves. Guy Stroumsa constructs a different narrative of late antique religion by proposing two other categories of self-orientation, one focused on contemplation of the divine (the gnostic model), the other on bodily training *(askēsis)* in imitation of Christ. For both, however, the ultimate goal of the spiritual guide is to bring salvation, not knowledge: "*Sōtēria* is the goal, much more than *epistēmē.*" The desert monks, exemplified by Evagrius, turn to masters not as philosophical teachers but as guides to salvation. Still other essays by Esther Menn, Jonathan Schofer, and Michael Satlow try to draw Jews—in one case a Jewish woman—into a scholarly history of the self that has been dominated by Greek, Roman, and Christian males. The cumulative effect of these essays is to reshape the conventional history of the self, to identify new axial moments or rethink ones already recognized, and to enlarge the roster of players involved.

The narratives of Miller and Stroumsa also articulate a number of broad questions. What inclines some selves toward the transcendent and others toward the material? Is the pull between these poles unique to late antiquity or can it be detected earlier, and what prompts a move in one or the other direction? Are there connections between how ancient pagans, Christians, and Jews navigate between these poles? What roles do shifting political, intellectual, or religious currents play in inclining a self toward either the transcendent or the material? At the same time, they raise difficult questions about the very enterprise of constructing a history of the self. Can such a history really be written? Where would it begin and end? What are its geographical parameters? Which selves are to be included?

Seeking Selves in Antiquity

Following Foucault, the narratives described above approach the "self" as a discursive structure that orders and shapes a societal understanding of the individual. Yet the dilemma of this academic approach is that it obscures those very individuals. Is there any room in a view of the self as socially constructed for *real* selves, that is, for individuals to express themselves in all the quirky and messy ways that we feel intuitively that they do? The "self" may be a social construct, but surely real individual selves existed and acted in antiquity. Methodologically, the question is how the historian can recover an individual self accessible only through its linguistic expressions and embedded in remote cultural settings. After all, the language and concepts that I have at my disposal to articulate my notion of "myself" to some extent predetermine how and even whether I am going to articulate that notion. Considering the gendered self, Judith Butler has stated this point most baldly: "Subjected to gender, but subjectivated by gender, the 'I' neither precedes nor follows the process of this gendering, but emerges only within and as the matrix of gender relationships themselves."[6] At first glance this observation appears to pose for the historian a dilemma with only two alternatives: Does a text that purports to describe an author's inner life give access to a real self, or is that self a fiction—not what generates the text, but what the text generates?

So when Jeremiah curses the day he was born (Jer 20:14–18) or when Paul declares himself a slave to the law of sin (Rom 7:25) or when Esther, in the Greek additions to the Septuagint, declares herself to be a slave of God (Esth 14:17, 18 LXX), how are we to understand these assertions? Saul Olyan's answer is, cautiously indeed. As much as they may seem to reflect the interior life of emoting selves, self-referential and internally focused biblical texts such as Jeremiah's confessions draw on preexistent tropes. It is only where these texts depart from literary convention, Olyan argues, that we can hope to detect the real self behind the literary persona of a real self. J. Albert Harrill similarly observes that Paul's public "I" makes more sense when seen as a dramatization of a stock type than as a reflection of his own inner life. Arguing that Paul's "slave self" is "a technique of 'speech-in-character' familiar from Greco-Roman rhetoric and literature," Harrill suggests that Paul adopts this persona as something to "think with," to reflect on "community, social categorization, hierarchy, and one's relation to the divine." Harrill's insistence that we read the character of the "I" against the public scripts for that character—in this case we can understand Paul's slave only against the background of Roman slave ideology—has implications for Esther Menn's discussion of the Esther of the Septuagint. Unlike the Esther of the Hebrew Bible on which she is based, this Greek Esther declares herself a slave of God, the only true sovereign. Obviously, in a story that revolves around a Persian king who holds the power of life and death over her and her people, this creates a complex and tense literary effect. Esther's slave "I" is not the same as Paul's, a function not only of differing public slave scripts but also, as Menn emphasizes, of public gender scripts.

All the ancient selves appearing in this book, not just the biblical ones, are linguistic constructions, known only as they are described or as they express themselves in texts. For example, David Brakke shows that Evagrius' *Talking Back* contains, not the reflections of a monastic self, but a prescriptive guide that externalizes and scripturalizes experiences that we are tempted to attribute to an interior self; and Michael Satlow unpacks the religious meaning of Jewish votive inscriptions in late antiquity, whose expressions are couched in conventional language. Together these essays sensitize us to the opacity of our evidence, which, even when it seems to reveal a self, inevitably makes those disclosures in ways shaped by shared perceptions about what selves are supposed to be like. Alternatively, the papers may be seen as calling into question the very metaphor of disclosure, which positions individual selves behind a text that either reveals or conceals them, or both. Rather, the text may be better understood as the product of a cultural process in which linguistic conventions, social institutions, and individual agency, as well as individual experience, collude in creating and re-creating selves.

Caring for the Self

Foucault emphasized the efforts the ancients devoted to shaping their selves, and his profound influence on the study of the self is most evident in discussions on the "care of the self," the focus of Pierre Hadot's scholarship as well. Ancient philosophy, Hadot has argued, is in fact best seen as a regimen for the self, a rigorous training *(askēsis)* for the entire self, not just its cognitive parts.[7] Technologies of the self, as Foucault would refer to these forms of self-discipline, are inextricably linked to understandings of the human body. Thus, Peter Brown showed that early Christian thinkers, despite their shared theological commitments, differed widely in their anthropological assumptions and displayed great diversity in their approaches to caring for the self.[8] Greenblatt traces the idea that selves could be fashioned, and self-fashioned, to the sixteenth century; but as several essays in this volume confirm, the effort to reshape the self—to alter its appetites and perceptions, or reposition it in relation to the world—began long before the Renaissance.

The senses play an especially important role in earlier technologies of the self because of their role in mediating between the self and the external world. Weitzman demonstrates that far prior to the earliest Greek philosophical reflections on the nature of the self, the author of Deuteronomy 1–11 had already broached the topic. Weitzman reads these chapters as "a sustained history of the senses in Israel's religious life, the ways in which its eyes, ears and mouth threatened its covenant with God, and the solution that Moses contrives to counter this threat." Not a sustained treatise on the self but an attempt to "work through the problems that sensory experience poses to Israel's religious life," Deuteronomy seeks to educate the senses, to instill a discipline that will allow its readers to recognize when the senses threaten their relationship to God, and to turn to a text, a transcription of hearing, as the foundation of religious experience.

Touched by the material, Christians of late antiquity reengaged sensory experience in more sophisticated ways, differing in whether and how it might connect human beings to the divine. Many Christians, such as Augustine, Romanos, and Ephrem, attempted to cultivate their senses as a way to understand God. Ephrem, the focus of Harvey's study, valued the purity of sensory experience and its potential for direct contact with the divine over rational inquiry into God's ways: God's fullness must be experienced rather than known. Romanos, according to Frank, shares this optimism about the physical senses, "those conduits to the interior life."

The monks for whom Evagrius was writing appear to side with Deuteronomy's misgivings about the senses, although they formulated those misgivings very differently. According to Brakke, Evagrius assumes that the boundaries between the self, the demons, and God are blurry; demonic forces constantly threaten the embodied monk. "The monk's goal," Brakke writes, "was to ward off these adversaries, to shake off their thoughts as so many raindrops that obscure the self's vision, and ultimately to contemplate God in a state beyond thoughts or images." The answer to the "problem" of the senses is, as in Deuteronomy, memory, as transmitted by the appropriate scriptural verses. Evagrius instructs monks to counter the demons that assault their senses with Scripture. Ultimately, however, the late antique monk goes where the author of Deuteronomy never imagined possible: to the pure, unmediated contemplation of God.

Also at the boundary between the self and the world is the body, the self's material extension. As Daniel Boyarin has emphasized, the rabbis of late antiquity were concerned about carnality and the problems it posed, especially sexual appetite.[9] Looking particularly at one (probably late antique) rabbinic text, *The Fathers According to Rabbi Nathan,* Jonathan Schofer explores this concern for the body and its role in self-formation. Schofer argues that this text, wrestling with the status of the embodied human suspended between heaven and earth, creates "portraits of the self as both animal/beastly/porous and divine/angelic/cosmic at the same time." The result is a vision of the "beastly body," an embodied self whose body is celebrated as God's creation.

Several chapters focus on forms of self-education, ways of retraining or disciplining the self. Watts's essay reminds us that the education of the self was socially located, situated in specific educational contexts. Students of philosophy in late antiquity formed a distinct social class, complete with its own customs, deportment, ways of thinking, and dress. The "student self" was constituted through external markers, distinctive curricula, and a value placed on communal loyalty. The educational system, in fact, "encouraged students to develop a distinct personal identity that was shaped by the rituals and rhythms of both the specific teaching circle to which the student belonged and the larger intellectual community in which they functioned." Self-formation, Watts shows, had an institutional as well as an intellectual/spiritual component.

These essays not only complement each other but also, when read against each other, raise provocative questions about the relationship between "self"-perception and practice. What prompted Deuteronomy to offer ritual practice as a solution to the senses' failings? What role did the vision of the self and bodily prescriptions of *The Fathers of Rabbi Nathan* really play in the formation of the rabbinic "student self" or "sage self"? How did particular constructions of the self serve the institutional needs of the school, the church, or the monastery?

Weitzman's essay most pointedly raises another related issue that runs through many of the essays in this volume, the role of memory, especially textual memory, in shaping the self. Memory, as understood by Deuteronomy, trumps the senses. None of the other cases discussed in this volume go quite that far, but memory—and the texts that encode that memory—nevertheless play significant roles in self-formation. Evagrius suggests hurling scriptural verses at errant sensory experiences, while Romanos, Augustine, and Ephrem evoke Scripture in order to educate the senses. The rabbis, like the philosophers, were writing guides for self-formation, to be read and enacted. Even recovering the meaning of dreams, according to Peter Struck's reading of Artemidorus, was a textual practice. Texts obscure the real selves of antiquity, but they can also speak to how they were refashioned precisely because of the emergent roles of writing and reading in the self's formation and education. The production and recitation of texts were central aspects of the ancient technology of the self.

The Self Seeking the Divine

Just before our conference met, another volume appeared that engages, from a more broadly comparative perspective, some of the issues with which we are concerned here: *Self and Self-Transformation in the History of Religion.*[10] Its editors, David Shulman and Guy Stroumsa, propose two more axes along which we can plot the self, a typology that complements Miller's distinction between the touch of the real and the touch of the transcendent but that helps to identify a different set of issues. One axis might be characterized as horizontal: we draw lines between ourselves and other human beings. At the most basic level, this involves knowing where "I" stop and someone else begins. In a more intricate way we fashion multiple group selves: ethnic, gender, and class identities. I can simultaneously be a Roman self, which makes me not a Greek self; a male self rather than a female self; and a student self, which sets me between the sage and the *paganus* (peasant). On the horizontal axis we place ourselves on a map of human relations.

At the same time, we plot ourselves along a vertical axis. Are we closer to the heavens or to the earth, to the angels or to the animals? This question vexed religious thinkers in antiquity in part because, despite the apparent abstruseness of the issue, the stakes were high. As the essays in *Self and Self-Transformation* argue, notions of the self lead directly to understandings of the possibilities for self-transformation. How firmly are we held along that vertical axis? Can I climb it ontologically, if only a little, to become more like a divine being? And conversely, can I slip down it if I am not careful? Can my senses, to return to Harvey's essay, lead me to a spiritual self-transformation, so that I do not merely feel closer to God, but actually *become* closer to God? Or do they tie me so tightly to the material world that I cannot expect to draw nearer to God while in the body?

Several of our essays focus on how selves maneuver along the vertical axis between human beings and the divine. Among the thinkers discussed in this volume, Artemidorus, Struck argues, provides one of the more nuanced, even prescient, visions of the self. Dreams provide a natural, if unexpected, entry into this anthropological and ontological issue. To interpret dreams correctly, Artemidorus reasons, one must first understand whence they are coming and how humans perceive them. Church fathers, rabbis, and later Freud were well-attuned to this problem. According to Struck, Artemidorus fashioned a "divinatory self," a soul that acts "not merely as a passive recipient of a perception" sent by an outside divine agent, but one that "takes an active role in deciding what images will be produced from any given dream." The soul, in other words, "has a volition independent from the individual person." Artemidorus's self is thus a split or multiple self, with a transcendent aspect that enhances this self's possibilities for self-transformation.

Linked to this anthropological issue is also a cosmological one. The anthropological question concerns the pliability of the human self; the cosmological question concerns the permeability of the heavens. The classical theological formulation of the problem is that of immanence and transcendence: is the divine close or near? Can human beings even apprehend the divine? The Hebrew Bible is famously schizophrenic on this issue, sometimes understanding God as quite immanent and at other times as impossibly distant. Nor can Plato quite make up his mind. In some passages he posits the ineffability of the divine, and in others he states that there is a bit of the divine, the soul, in all of us, waiting to be released from its bodily prison. This latter position, especially as the Neoplatonists and the Stoics developed it later, combines anthropology and cosmology: the individual must first effect a self-transformation in order to lead to an ascent. Origen and other Christian thinkers, as Miller notes, were much taken with this notion. Jews, or at least the rabbis that we know about from textual sources, were not.

Menn calls attention to the role of prayer in positioning the one who prays in relation to the divine addressee. Esther's prayer "identifies her as fundamentally a relational self, although the self's relationality is not dependent on the immediate presence of any human community or individual." By making herself "fully transparent before an Other whom she addresses directly and incessantly," Esther puts herself into a personal and intimate relationship with God. This God, Esther's personal confidant, is not the detached transcendent "First Mover" of Aristotle. God, even in silence, is immanent and maintains somewhat permeable boundaries. At the same time, the relationship is by no means equal. It is one of utter and complete subservience to God, like an ideal subject to a king.

Jewish votive inscriptions of late antiquity, Satlow argues, reveal a very different understanding of the relationship between individuals and their God. Like Esther's prayer, these inscriptions (really commemorations of communal, particularly synagogue, gifts) are in some sense addressed to the deity. Unlike her prayer, though, they are meant to be displayed before other humans, adding a horizontal dimension. More strikingly, they are as devoid of humility as Esther's prayer is replete with it. Using vow terminology, these inscriptions imply a belief that humans can barter with God, that God, in Plato's language, can "be bribed." "Unlike their pagan neighbors," Satlow writes, "Jews may not have brought statuary of healed body parts to their synagogues (or did they?), but they did make deals with God to heal them, and rewarded him with a plaque if, and when, he fulfilled his end of the bargain." Here is an active agent in negotiation with the divine, not merely a slave or subject.

Read individually, these essays provide new knowledge and insight into specific topics. Read together, though, they are much more powerful. There are, to be sure, many differences among the essays. By most scholarly standards their geographical and chronological range is large; they focus on very different types of evidence; and they differ, and sometimes disagree, in both method and conclusions. Perhaps as is fitting, they are as splintered as the self that they study.

But at the same time they are bound together in a series of shifting and overlapping conversations that in our view get to the very heart of the humanities. For lying behind the many humanistic and social scientific disciplines by which we order our quest for knowledge is the ultimate goal of understanding what it means to be human. When ancient Israelites, Greeks, Romans, Jews, and Christians sought to understand and cultivate the self, their project was a practical one: to enhance the self's potential, to correct its deficiencies, to bridge between the self and the (divine) other. Our project is not as practical, but that is not to say that it does not address deep and enduring human concerns. "The questions I ask of my material, and indeed the very nature of this material," Greenblatt acknowledges, "are shaped by questions that I ask myself."[11] These essays show that the ancients, despite the chronological, geographical, and cultural chasm that separates us from them, still offer a rich set of intellectual resources for thinking through shared problems.

NOTES

1. For an important attempt to understand ancient Greek concepts of the self in dialogue with modern psychological and philosophical positions, see Christopher Gill, *Personality in Greek Epic, Tragedy, and Philosophy: The Self in Dialogue* (New York: Oxford University Press, 1996).

2. Stephen Greenblatt, *Renaissance Self-Fashioning: From More to Shakespeare* (Chicago: University of Chicago Press, 1980), 1.

3. See, for example, Greenblatt, *Renaissance Self-Fashioning;* and Dror Wahrman, *The Making of the Modern Self: Identity and Culture in Eighteenth-Century England* (New Haven, Conn.: Yale University Press, 2004).

4. Marcel Mauss, "Une catégorie de l'esprit humain; La notion de personne, celle de moi," in Marcel Mauss, *Sociologie et anthropologie* (Paris: Quadrige/Presses Universitaires de France, 1950); M. Foucault, *The Use of Pleasure* (trans. Robert Hurley; New York: Random House, 1985), esp. 39–68; and Luther Martin et al., eds., *Technologies of the Self* (Amherst: University of Massachusetts Press, 1990).

5. Charles Taylor, *Sources of the Self: The Making of the Modern Identity* (Cambridge, Mass.: Harvard University Press, 1989).

6. Judith Butler, *Bodies That Matter: On the Discursive Limits of "Sex"* (New York and London: Routledge, 1993), 7.

7. Pierre Hadot, *Philosophy as a Way of Life* (ed. Arnold Davidson; trans. Michael Chase; Cambridge, Mass.: Basil Blackwell, 1995).

8. Peter Brown, *The Body and Society: Men, Women, and Sexual Renunciation in Early Christianity* (Lectures on the History of Religions, n.s. 13; New York: Columbia University Press, 1988).

9. Daniel Boyarin, *Carnal Israel: Reading Sex in Talmudic Culture* (The New Historicism: Studies in Cultural Poetics; Berkeley: University of California Press, 1993).

10. D. Shulman and Guy Stroumsa, *Self and Self-Transformation in the History of Religions* (Oxford: Oxford University Press, 2002), 11.

11. Greenblatt, *Renaissance Self-Fashioning*, 5.

Part I

SEEKING RELIGIOUS SELVES

—1—

Shifting Selves in Late Antiquity

Patricia Cox Miller

Introduction: What Is a Self?

"Pleasures and sadnesses, fears and assurances, desires and aversions and pain—whose are they?"[1] Although Plotinus had struggled with this poignant question for many years—and indeed, had found an answer to it—he was still, at the end of his life, trying to articulate a vision of an authentic self, free from the emotional entanglements of the embodied human being, entanglements that distracted the self from its genuine powers of self-discernment.[2] This worry about self-identity—"But we . . . who are 'we'?"[3]—arose at least in part from Plotinus's recognition of the soul's tendency toward fragmentation—its false tendency, that is, to define itself in terms of its attachment to cares and concerns of the moment.[4]

This concern about fixating distractions that alienate and diminish the self was not limited to the Platonic tradition to which Plotinus adhered. Almost a century earlier, the Stoic Marcus Aurelius had asked himself, "To what use am I now putting the powers of my soul? Examine yourself on this point at every step, and ask, 'How does it stand with that part of me called the master-part? Whose soul inhabits me at this moment? Is it a little child's, a youngster's, a woman's, a tyrant's, that of a beast of burden, or a wild animal?' "[5] Characterizing Marcus as "criticizing himself relentlessly, like a bug under glass," Carlin Barton has argued that the "result of such a severe internalized critic" was "self-splitting," and that "the shared, blurred social identity that ideally molded and formed the personality was experienced as a loss of identity, an unsightly chaos of the self."[6]

Worry about such a chaos of the self could also be found in Christianity. For Origen of Alexandria, an older contemporary of Plotinus, the "inner man" was unfortunately rent by demonic presences. Frequently interpreting images of beasts from scriptural passages as figures for emotions, Origen interpreted them as fixating prisons—"serpent-man" and "horse-man"—and as grotesque masks.[7] When caught in the grip of negative emotions and false attachments, he wrote, "we wear the mask [*persona*] of the lion, the dragon, the fox . . . and the pig."[8] An unsightly chaos indeed.

Although Plotinus, Marcus Aurelius, and Origen did not share the same thought-systems regarding the composition and destiny of the soul, all three did reflect in similar ways about the phenomenon of the self in disarray. Yet this is only part of the story, since they also expressed a certain optimism about the self that was both personal and cosmic. This is a topic to which I shall return. For the moment, however, I want to observe that these Graeco-Roman portraits of a self divided against itself, bewildered as to its identity, seem strikingly "modern." However, it is important not to confuse the ancient terminology of "soul" with modern concepts of "self," especially the self of Freudian psychoanalysis in which, as Gregory Jay has explained, "human identity turns out to be a speculation *par excellence*, an image formed as a reflective compromise between wishes and defenses that engage in a ceaseless struggle for ascendancy."[9] This staging of the self in terms of ambivalence, that is, in terms of a constant conflict between desire and repression, makes any attempt to formulate a stable *auto*biography impossible. "In autobiography psychoanalytically read," Jay continues, "the undecidable question, as Jacques Lacan pronounces it, is 'Who speaks?'"[10] In light of such a definition, it is somewhat problematic to use the word "self" for ancient understandings of human identity expressed as "soul."

Plotinus, for example, did not think that the question, "Who speaks?" was finally undecidable. At the end of the very treatise that he opens by asking to whom the emotions belong, he again asks a series of self-definitional questions: "What is it that has carried out this investigation? Is it 'we' or the soul? It is 'we,' but by the soul. And what do we mean by 'by the soul'? Did 'we' investigate by having soul? No, but in so far as we *are* soul."[11] Despite his worries about the soul's proclivity for errancy, Plotinus believed that the soul was a principle of self-cohesion anchored in a stabilizing transcendent reality.[12] Origen too, despite his bestial scripting of the soul's debased desires, did not understand human identity to be a compromise formation premised on ceaseless struggle; instead, he located the true self in an inner *logos*, incorporeal and changeless, through which a sustaining relation to the divine mind is established.[13]

Nonetheless, given the marked tendency of classical and Graeco-Roman authors to view soul as the locus of human identity,[14] I think the term "self" can be used to characterize what ancient thinkers meant by "soul" as long as it is used to describe, not actors in an unconscious script, but an orientation to context. When conceptualized as such, the self-as-soul is not a "thing" that one "has." As Frederick Schroeder has observed about confusion over what the modern term "self" designates, "the ancients were perhaps wiser in not rendering the equivalent Greek pronoun *autos,* or the Latin *ipse,* a substantive."[15] Given the virtual equivalence of *autos* and *psyche,* especially (but not only) in Platonic traditions,[16] *soul* is likewise not a substantive. In other words, as a term that describes the self, "soul" is a placing function that serves to orient the self in a network of relationships that are both material and spiritual.

The Self and Images of Place

The admittedly broad topic that this paper addresses is a shift in the ways in which the self was represented in Neoplatonism and Christianity, moving from Plotinus and Origen in the third century, to theurgists and theorists of relic-worship in the late fourth and fifth centuries. I intend this comparison of ways of thinking about the self, somewhat distant in time from each other, to serve as what Simon Goldhill, in another context, calls "paradigmatic moments." As he explains, "These moments are not chosen because of any commitment to Foucauldian 'rupture' but in order to maximize difference for the sake of rhetorical clarity."[17] My argument focuses on the orienting function of soul insofar as it comes to expression in images of the self in relation to place; for as Jonathan Smith has observed, a total worldview is implied by an individual's or a culture's imagination of place: "It is through an understanding and symbolization of place that a society or individual creates itself."[18]

Furthermore, the shift that occurs in such images of self-placement will be plotted along a continuum whose two poles I designate as "a touch of the transcendent" and "a touch of the real."[19] What I mean to designate by these phrases, appropriated from the New Historicism, is an aesthetics of self-identity that "places" the self by using cosmic imagery—"a touch of the transcendent"— which gives way to an aesthetics of self-identity that "places" the self by using material imagery—"a touch of the real." The word "touch" is important to this distinction because the distinction is not an absolute one but rather a matter of shifting emphasis concerning the relation between, and reconciliation of, idea and materiality, or the abstract and the concrete.

It is this shift from a transcendent to an earthy aesthetic that I will explore as a shift in ancient senses of the self, drawing on an approach advocated by New Historicists Gallagher and Greenblatt. Describing their interpretive procedure as routing "theoretical and methodological generalizations through dense networks of particulars," they defend their use of anecdotes in historical explanation in terms of their reluctance "to see the long chains of close analysis go up in a puff of abstraction."[20] In addition to the appeal to anecdotes, they borrow from the poet Ezra Pound "the method of the Luminous Detail' whereby we attempt to isolate significant or 'interpreting detail' from the mass of traces that have survived in the archive."[21] In this essay I will follow in their footsteps, using "luminous details" to anchor my presentation of the imagination of "place" as a useful way to tap into ancient senses of "self."

PLOTINUS AND THE TOUCH OF THE TRANSCENDENT: THE TRANSPARENT SPHERE

Greco-Roman authors were alert to the dangers involved in sight.[22] The eye could wither, devour, de-soul, or bewitch another, but it could also bewitch or consume the self.[23] Nowhere is the self-consuming function of the eye more striking than in the myth of Narcissus, to which Plotinus alluded in the course of a discussion about how the soul can "see" intelligible beauty and, ultimately, the Good. Arguing that bodily beauty is a seductive image, Plotinus warns that the person "who clings to beautiful bodies and will not let them go" will, like Narcissus, sink down—but in soul, not body—into "dark depths where intellect has no delight," consorting with shadows in Hades (*Enn.* 1.6.8.4–16). The tragedy of Narcissus, described by modern interpreters as an arresting self-fascination or as a conflictual splitting of the subject,[24] was for Plotinus a cautionary tale about the fate of the soul that mistakes sensory for spiritual (i.e., noetic) realities. When the self is placed with respect only to the material world, it gropes blindly after shadows. Thus Plotinus, like modern interpreters of Narcissus, also used this story to picture the problem of misdirected sight, that is, a form of attention that fixates and fragments the soul into a congeries of its own grasping desires.

Plotinus often linked this kind of woeful particularity to human physicality. Forgetfulness, for example, is due to the "moving and flowing" nature of the body (*Enn.* 4.3.26.54); the soul's "fellowship" (*koinōnia*) with the body is "displeasing" because the body hinders thought and fills the soul with negative emotions (*Enn.* 4.8.2.43–45). This only happens, however, to the soul that "has sunk into the interior of the body" and has forgotten that the body belongs to it, and not the reverse (*Enn.* 4.8.2.46–49). There is a question about the extent to which sheer physicality was really the issue in Plotinus's presentation of the difficulties faced by the soul, since he admitted that "it is not evil in every way for soul to give body the ability to flourish and to exist, because not every kind of provident care for the inferior deprives the being exercising it of its ability to remain in the highest" (*Enn.* 4.8.2.23–27).

Nonetheless, to the extent that the soul becomes "mixed up" with bodily stuff, it loses its proper focus and becomes "isolated and weak and fusses and looks towards a part and in its separation from the whole it embarks on one single thing and flies from everything else."[25] Even though, as Stephen Clark has argued, for Plotinus the soul is not a "ghost in a machine," the real split being not between body and soul but between two kinds of consciousness,[26] still there is a tension in Plotinus's thought regarding the self in its earthy context. His frequent use of the place-markers "there" and "here" to designate a metaphysical world of intelligible reality ("there") and its shadowy reflection in the material cosmos ("here"), when read anthropologically as the "there" of the soul's true home and the "here" of its cramping particularity, seems undeniably dualistic. Taking seriously Plotinus's language of "ascent," Stephen Halliwell sees "an ambivalence in his system of thought as a whole, an ambivalence that keeps Plotinian philosophy caught between ultimately irreconcilable ideals of 'flight' from the merely physical and, on the other hand, a commitment to finding the echo of higher realities in what it continues to regard as the rich and multiform 'tapestry' of life itself."[27]

Other interpreters, however, suggest that Plotinus's "here" and "there" should not be distinguished so sharply as a spiritual flight from the merely physical: as A. H. Armstrong has observed, "in the end we are left with the very strong impression that for Plotinus there are not two worlds but one real world apprehended in different ways on different levels."[28] Even when Plotinus occasionally imagined a time before time, as it were, when disembodied souls were "united with the whole of reality," he was quick to redirect attention to human life as it is lived now: "We were parts of the intelligible, not marked off or cut off but belonging to the whole; and we are not cut off even now" (*Enn.* 6.4.14.18–22). The task of the soul is to learn how to direct its attention to the whole—to detach itself, as Sara Rappe has argued, from "the narrow confines of a historical selfhood."[29] What the Plotinian self needs, in other words, is a touch of transcendence that, as Rappe continues, "does not consist in a denial of the empirical self [but] allows the larger selfhood of soul to emerge from behind the veil of the objective domain."[30]

In order to perform its proper placing function with regard to spiritual reality, the soul must direct its vision inward: "Shut your eyes, and change to and wake another way of seeing, which everyone has but few use" (*Enn.* 1.6.8.26–28). Thus centered, the self expands. Plotinus developed techniques for achieving this kind of awareness, the so-called "spiritual exercises." Perhaps the most famous of these is his image of the transparent sphere, which I will read as an image that pictures selfhood in terms of place:

> Let there, then, be in the soul a shining imagination of a sphere, having everything [in the visible universe] within it. . . . Keep this, and apprehend in your mind another, taking away the mass: take away also the places, and the mental picture of matter in yourself, and do not try to apprehend another sphere smaller in mass than the original one, but calling on the god who made that of which you have the mental picture, pray him to come. And may he come, bringing his own universe with him, with all the gods within him, he who is one and all, and each god is all the gods coming together into one. (*Enn.* 5.8.9.8–17)

In this image, according to Frederic Schroeder, "Plotinus is presenting us with a noetic universe in which there is no fixed point of observation: all is transparent to all."[31] It is a picture of intense inward concentration that opens the soul outward as it is filled with the "real beings" of the noetic world.[32] Both the image and the self disappear into their own luminosity, as knower and known become one.[33]

By engaging the image of the transparent sphere, the soul achieves self-knowledge, a knowledge that is distinct from the kind of objectivizing self- and world-awareness that Plotinus linked with discursive thought.[34] The sensible world is not so much abandoned as it is turned into light—a process of subtraction that adds insofar as the soul is oriented in a nexus of relationships rather than in an "opaque" world of discrete objects. In order to be free from the attractive tug of particularity, especially in its material forms, the soul "must see that light by which it is enlightened: for we do not see the sun by another light than his own. How then can this happen? Take away everything!" (*Enn.* 5.3.17.37–39)

What kind of self emerges in the light of the transparent sphere? When Plotinus directs the eyes of the soul inward, the vision that emerges is starkly different from the internalized self-watcher of Marcus Aurelius. A certain cosmic optimism pervades his thought, as "the levels of reality become levels of inner life, the levels of the self."[35] As "our head strikes the heavens" and becomes the transparent sphere, the illusions of personality and individuality vanish, revealing a "self" that is essentially divine (*Enn.* 4.3.12.5).[36] Thus centered in the divine, the Plotinian self is, in Rappe's words, "infinitely expansive"; "no longer circumscribed by its historical, temporal, and emotional limitations, the Plotinian self embraces a vast domain whose boundaries extend to the fullness of what is encountered in every knowing moment."[37] Skittish to the end concerning the dangers posed by materiality, and especially by the human body, Plotinus offered a self touched by transcendence, a "self glorified, full of intelligible light—but rather itself pure light—weightless, floating free, having become—but rather being—a god."[38]

ORIGEN AND THE TOUCH OF THE TRANSCENDENT: THE DIVINE LIBRARY

As for Plotinus, so also for Origen, human corporeality could be troubling, a mark of a self in disarray. Commenting, for example, on Matthew 7:6 ("Do not give what is holy to dogs; and do not throw your pearls before swine"), Origen remarked, "For I would say that whoever is constantly muddied with bodily things and rolls around in the filthy things of life and has no desire for the pure and holy life, such a person is nothing but a swine."[39] Origen sometimes thought of human embodiment as the result of spiritual defect; the body in itself is not only "dead and completely lifeless" but is also "opposed and hostile to the spirit."[40]

Yet despite his sometime disparagement of the body, Origen seemed more concerned with how the soul orients itself with regard to the Pauline concept of "the flesh," understood as a willful attachment to false values that drag the soul in different directions.[41] The soul takes on the qualities of what it contemplates: hence, Origen's sense of the human dilemma as one of divided consciousness, which he frequently pictured as a kind of doubleness, an "outer man which looks at things in a corporeal way," and an "inner man" who sees spiritually.[42] In several of his writings, Origen developed this concept of doubleness at length, arguing that the empirical perceptions of human beings have as analogues the spiritual senses— having a nose for righteousness, an eye of the heart, the touch of faith, and so on through the five senses.[43] As David Dawson has argued, the doctrine of the spiritual senses rests on "an intrinsic connection between the visible and the invisible," and "although the bodily realm always informs one's love for God, it should not become the object of that love."[44]

However, choosing an object for that love is just the problem. As Origen explained in his *Commentary on the Song of Songs,* "it is impossible for human nature not to be always feeling the passion of love for something."[45] Unfortunately, he continued, people misuse the god-given faculty of love by pursuing worldly ends—money, fame, sex, careers. This picture of a perverted self is very much like the restless and "fussy" self envisaged by Plotinus, a self that is placed only in relation to the material world and its enticements. Human love must be directed to the good—"and by that which is good," Origen concluded, "we understand not anything corporeal, but only that which is found first in God and in the powers of the soul."[46]

Unfortunately, the powers of the soul are not easy to harness. Frequently relying on scriptural animal imagery in order to picture the soul as a kind of menagerie, Origen argued that consciousness is multiple; it has "secret recesses" *(arcanae conscientiae)* and can "admit . . . controlling influences of spirits either good or bad."[47] The key to redirecting these inner powers is self-inspection, a probing of the false *personae* that make the soul "dingy and dirty."[48] Thus, Origen called for a kind of reflexive self-seeing that is transformative: "If we are willing to understand that in us there is the power to be transformed from being serpents, swine, and dogs, let us learn from the apostle that the transformation depends on us. For he says this: 'We all, when with unveiled face we reflect the glory of the Lord, are transformed into the same image.' "[49]

That the self is capable of such metamorphosis is due in part to its ability to read Scripture properly so as to discern the spiritual metanarrative encrypted within it. Proper reading was, for Origen, allegorical reading, which spiritualizes the material realities of the text, its "sensible aspect," and at the same time spiritualizes the reader, who learns how to distinguish between "the inner and the outer man."[50] Learning how to make this distinction is crucial, because an allegorical reading of the biblical text "reveals a surprising and total isomorphism with the very structure of spiritual reality,"[51] a reality that is not only cosmic but also central to authentic self-identity as Origen understood it. In a passage of his *Commentary on John* concerning "elevated interpretation," Origen wrote that "the mind that has been purified and has surpassed all material things, so as to be certain of the contemplation of God, is divinized by those things that it contemplates."[52] As Robert Berchman has argued, the purpose of this form of textual contemplation is "to foster the potential of intellectual self-awareness and so orient the self upon a path of self-knowledge that eventually leads to consciousness of the *Logos.*"[53]

As book becomes spirit, so person becomes book: one of Origen's most powerful images of the self in relation to Scripture is presented in the *Homilies on Genesis* as one of the figural meanings of Noah's ark:

> If there is anyone who, while evils are increasing . . . can turn from the things which are in flux and passing away, . . . and can hear the word of God and the heavenly precepts, this man is building an ark of salvation within his own heart and is dedicating a library, so to speak, of the divine word within himself. . . . From this library learn the historical narratives; from it recognize "the great mystery" which is fulfilled in Christ and in the Church.[54]

This "library of divine books" is the "faithful soul" who, by internalizing the word, begins to realize a touch of transcendence in the self. As Dawson has observed, "the allegorical reader's necessary departure from Scripture's literal sense parallels her resistance to the fall of her soul away from contemplation of the *logos* into body, history, and culture. But the equally necessary reliance of the allegorical story on the literal sense parallels the reader's salvific use of her soul's embodiment (by virtue of the prior, enabling self-embodiment of the divine *logos*)."[55] Although by directing the attention of the soul away from temporal reality and toward the divinity within Origen envisioned the self's proper place as a cosmic one, this does not mean that embodied life has no value. When the soul is "placed" in the context of a divine library, it is also placed with regard to the incarnation, as Dawson indicates briefly in the quotation above.

The full import of the image of the divine library can be seen in a remarkable passage from the *Philocalia,* in which Origen argues that "the word is made flesh eternally in the Scriptures in order to dwell among us."[56] That dwelling is not only the literal presence of the book *among* us but also the transfigured presence of Christ *in* us. Scripture embeds the incarnation in the world, but it also transfigures that world, as Origen went on to say: "Those who are capable of following the traces of Jesus when he goes up and is transfigured in losing his terrestrial form will see the transfiguration in every part of Scripture" and will be transfigured themselves, since they have the key to the wisdom hidden in the text.[57] No longer divided, then, the Origenian self is as expansive and as embracing of a transcendent structure of reality as the Plotinian self.

Origen's connection of the incarnation with Scripture and, by extension, with the reader whose self encompasses a divine library, would seem to dignify the body. Indeed, Dawson argues vigorously that Origen's "celebration of allegorical transformation of identity is a spiritualization, not a rejection, of the body."[58] Such a spiritualized view of human materiality, however, is hard to reconcile with a valorization of the embodied human being, the historical self. As Peter Brown remarks, for Origen "the present human body reflected the needs of a single, somewhat cramped moment in the spirit's progress back to a former, limitless identity."[59] And, even though "body" would remain for Origen a marker of identity, it did so only as it was transformed into a spiritual body.[60] Origen may have had a "heady sense of the potency and dynamism of body," as Caroline Walker Bynum argues, but as she goes on to observe, his theory of the body "seemed to sacrifice integrity of bodily structure for the sake of transformation; it seemed to surrender material continuity for the sake of identity."[61] Thus, although Origen shared with Plotinus a sense of a self touched by transcendence,[62] he went one step further in spiritualizing the self by allowing even the body an eventual touch of transcendence.

From the Touch of Transcendence to the Touch of the Real

As I noted earlier, the ways of conceiving of the self that are the focus of this discussion can be located along a continuum, with the views of Plotinus and Origen representing a paradigmatic moment when the self is oriented toward the spiritual, sometimes at the expense of the material world. The later Neoplatonists and Christians to whom attention will now shift also privileged spiritual knowing as a defining feature of the self, but they did so with greater emphasis on, and valuation of, the material realm. Whereas Plotinus and Origen directed the gaze inward in order to orient the self "outward" to a transcendent spiritual structure, later thinkers did the reverse, directing the gaze outward in order to achieve inner vision.

The focus will continue to be on images in texts that can be read as pictures of how a particular author orients the self. As with Plotinus and Origen, the soul is placed by such textual imagery, but that imagery also recommends a form of practice—spiritual exercises in Plotinus's case, and introspective reading and interpretation in Origen's. However, unlike the rather intellectual and even ethereal images and practices seen so far, those to which I now turn—the animation of statues and the devotion to relics—involve a kind of material engagement not characteristic of the earlier forms of self-construal.

The shift in sensibility that reconfigured the relationship between materiality and meaning was part of a wider cultural phenomenon, as several studies have shown. Beginning in the fourth century, there was an increase in appreciation for color, glitter, and spectacle, from public ceremonies to personal clothing.[63] This heightened appeal to the eye, variously characterized as a new theatricality and "a peculiarly expressionistic manner,"[64] can also be seen in poetry and sculpture—a "jeweled style" based on a preference for effects of visual immediacy achieved by an emphasis on the part at the expense of elaborations of organic wholes.[65] Petitioning the visual imagination of the spectator also marked the biographical literature of this period, as authors invited readers to "see" holiness in the bodies of their heroes.[66] Indeed, an increase in the ability to "see more than was there,"[67] as one scholar has put it, seems characteristic of the cultural scene that also witnessed a new appreciation for the role both of "things" and of the material imagination in understandings of self-identity.

PROCLUS AND THE TOUCH OF THE REAL: ANIMATED STATUES

Although, in the wake of Plotinus, achievement of a "self glorified, full of light" (*Enn.* 6.9.9.56) continued to be the goal of later Neoplatonists, the means for achieving that goal, as well as the cosmology and psychology upon which those means were premised, had changed. The earlier tendency to suppress materiality as fundamental to self-identity was revised when the orienting function of the soul shifted with regard to the spiritual value of the sensible world. This shift toward a sacramental view of the world—a view, that is, that invests the sensible world with divine presence rather than seeing the sensible as a shadowy reflection of the divine—was already evident in the psychology of Iamblichus, whose views of the soul Proclus largely followed.

Unlike Plotinus, who argued that part of the embodied soul never descended but remained always in the intelligible realm, thus linking human identity permanently to a kind of transcendent consciousness, Iamblichus thought that the soul descended entirely.[68] No part of the Iamblichean "I" is untouched by embodiment.[69] This has been viewed as a kind of demotion and even self-alienation of the soul, and indeed Iamblichus argued that the soul could not recover its own divinity by itself but needed help from the gods.[70] Embodiment, however, was part of a larger cosmogonic process: reading the *Timaeus*'s description of the creation of Forms and matter as simultaneous rather than as sequential, Iamblichus argued that "the separation of corporeality from its principles was an impossibility that could occur only in abstraction, not in actuality."[71] Thus, even though the embodied soul suffered dividedness—in Iamblichus's words, "the sameness within itself becomes faint"—the material world provided it with resources for the recovery of its divine nature, since traces of the divine were infused throughout the world.[72]

Theurgy, a ritual process whose goal was self-unification and illumination by the gods, was based on this view of the material world as theophany.[73] According to Iamblichus, divine power was immanent in the world.[74] It was present in the form of divine "tokens" (*synthēmata* and *symbola*), those "godlike stones, herbs, animals, and spices" that the theurgist combined and consecrated in order to "establish from them a complete and pure receptacle [for the gods]."[75] By this ritual use of matter, an altered sense of self-identity was actualized, as the divine in the self was united with the god by the god's own action: theurgical "ascent" was not an escape from the material world, but rather a deification of the soul through a unifying process that eventuated in what

Iamblichus called "putting on the form of the gods."[76] Shaw has put the matter succinctly: "Theurgic rites transformed the soul from being its own idol, in an inverted attitude of self-interest, into an icon of the divine, with its very corporeality changed into a vehicle of transcendence."[77]

This theurgical view of the self was inherited and developed further by Proclus, whose view of the religious import of materiality was equally, if not more emphatic than that of Iamblichus. Because, as Proclus argued, "all things are bound up in the gods and deeply rooted in them," everything in the sensible world is linked by lines of sympathy with the god appropriate to it (*Inst.* prop. 144).[78] Indeed, according to the principle expressed in Proposition 57 in his *Institutio theologica*, whereby the earlier members of a causal series have greater power and so extend throughout all the levels of being that they illuminate, the divine is directly present in matter.[79] "Some things," remarked Proclus, "are linked with the gods immediately [*amesōs*], others through a varying number of intermediate terms, but 'all things are full of gods,' and from the gods each derives its natural attribute" (*Inst.* prop. 145).

Despite this rather ecstatic affirmation of "the touch of the real," Proclus, like Iamblichus, had a diminished view of the human capacity to realize its connection with the divine world by using its own powers. No part of the soul remains above, and it does not have the intelligible realm within.[80] Indeed, its knowledge "is different from the divine sort" due to our intermediate position in the cosmos (*in Prm.* 948).[81] Contact with higher levels of reality can only be made through their effects, and even those effects—the tokens or traces of the divine sown in the material world—are irradiations from the divine and not the gods themselves.[82] In one sense, then, the Proclean self had no choice but to remain "someone," having lost Plotinus's heady view of the possibility of coming to identify with the divine.[83] In another sense, however, that same self was oriented in a world dense with divine power, and in a religious tradition that provided the techniques for making contact with that power. The network of relationships in which Proclus's theurgical self was placed continued, as in earlier Neoplatonism, to be both spiritual and material, but it now presupposed a realignment of perception and the senses with regard to the divine. Seeing more than was (visibly) there, the theurgist looked out at the physical world in order to fill the self with divine images.

In terms of orienting the self in the world theurgically, Proclus is probably best known for the practice of the animation of statues, a practice that Iamblichus eschewed.[84] Proclus thought that statues were, in effect, aesthetic elaborations of the gods: "Through their shapes, signs, postures, and expressions," as Shaw notes, "theurgic statues revealed the properties of the gods."[85] Furthermore, when the material *symbola* proper to a specific god were inserted into hollow cavities in the statue, the statue was "animated" or activated with the divine power channeled through the levels of being by those *symbola*, revealing divine wisdom in the form of oracles and enabling human participation in that wisdom.[86] The religio-aesthetic basis for this practice was as follows: "A theurgist who sets up a statue as a likeness of a certain divine order fabricates the tokens of its identity with reference to that order, acting as does the craftsman when he makes a likeness by looking to its proper model" (*in Prm.* 847).

This way of conceiving of animated statues, which shifts the relation of the spiritual and the material in a positive direction by affirming the likeness between them, brought a touch of the real into the area of human identity as well. Passages in Proclus's writings suggest that the animated statue functions as an image of the self in both implicit and explicit ways. The implicit connection between statue and human being is in Proclus's discussion about the three ways in which the cosmos, considered as the entire visible order, is related to the Forms. Defining these three modes as participation, impression, and reflection, Proclus offered the following example of "the three kinds of participation interwoven with each other":

> The body of a good and wise man . . . appears handsome because it participates directly in the beauty of nature and . . . by receiving reflections from the beauty of soul it carries a trace of ideal beauty, the soul serving as connecting term between his own lowest beauty and Beauty itself. So that the reflection reveals this species of soul as being wise . . . or a likeness of some other virtue. And the animated statue . . . participates by way of impression in the art which turns it on a lathe and polishes and shapes it . . . while from the universe it has received reflections of vitality which even cause us to say that it is alive; and as a whole it has been made like the god whose image it is. (*in Prm.* 847)

In this passage the human being, body and soul, is placed in apposition with the animate statue; at the very least, they are analogous as icons of a sacralized world.

Elsewhere, however, Proclus brought statue and human being together more explicitly: "The theurgist, by attaching certain symbols to statues, makes them better able to participate in the higher powers; in the same way, since universal Nature has, by creative corporeal principles, made [human] bodies like statues of souls, she inseminates in each a particular aptitude to receive a particular kind of soul, better or less good."[87] Here human body and statue relate in the same way that the human soul and *symbola* do. In another passage, this time from his fragmentary *Commentary on the Chaldean Oracles*, Proclus united divine tokens, human souls, and bodies in a single image: "The soul is composed of the intellectual words [*noeroi logoi*] and from the divine tokens [*theia symbola*], some of which are from the intellectual ideas, while others are from the divine henads. And we are in fact icons of the intellectual realities, and we are statues of the unknowable *synthēmata*" (5.8–11).[88]

The Proclean "we" is as full of divine energy as an animated statue; indeed, it is itself a "statue" capable, when guarded by ritual, of being illuminated by the divine.[89] The qualifier regarding ritual is important. Since for Proclus the self was always in a world marked by division, it could not activate its own channels of connection to the divine apart from the material world and the ritual procedures whereby elements of the world provided pathways of spiritual communication. This was, of course, a "spiritualized world," as Rappe notes; but it was a *world* nonetheless.[90] Proclus's image of the self as an animated statue is a view of the self touched by the real, oriented to the divine world in such a way that materiality took on new meaning. This expression of self-identity addressed the human being's lowered cosmic status with a kinetic sense of the tangible presence of the transcendent.

VICTRICIUS OF ROUEN AND THE TOUCH OF THE REAL: SPIRITUAL JEWELS

Origen had written in *Contra Celsum* that "in order to know God we need no body at all."[91] A century later, many Christians disagreed. Indeed, the fourth-century literature that describes desert ascetics provides ample testimony to a (literally) visual organization of meaning whereby observers of ascetic practitioners claimed to see with their own eyes men whose bodies were illuminated with flashes of angelic light.[92] As Peter Brown has observed, underlying the conviction that holiness could be seen was "the notion that body and soul formed a single field of force, in which what happened in the one had subtle and lasting effects on the other. . . . Somehow, the body itself was the companion of the soul in its effort to recover the 'image of God.' "[93]

This alignment of the body with spiritual attainment signaled a shift away from Origen's perceived tendency to privilege mind as the most essential aspect of human identity. In late-fourth-century views of both the creation of Adam and the resurrection, body was an integral, if troubling, part of the human being.[94] Viewed as embodied from the beginning, the self was now in greater need of mediating channels to establish connection with the divine, since a gulf had opened between the uncreated God and the embodied created order.[95] Origen's view of the soul's contemplative ability to bring itself into accord with an inner *logos* gave way, especially in ascetic thought, to concentration on the salvific role of the incarnate Christ in making possible a restoration of humanity's relationship with the divine.[96] Curiously, as the body became more central to human identity, it became more dangerous, needing a fully divine Christ to assume it so as to make possible its divinization.

The thought of Athanasius is a case in point. In his view, Adam and Eve, having at first lived a life of ascetic self-control in Eden, became distracted by the body and turned their attention toward it and away from God.[97] Now corrupted, "the body took center stage," as Brakke remarks, and he summarizes the function of the incarnation as follows: "According to Athanasius, the incarnation of the word made a successful ascetic life possible once again. . . . When the Word of God assumed a human body, and perfectly guided it, he divinized this body and made it incorruptible; through their 'kinship of the flesh' to the

Word's body, individual human beings can restore a proper relationship between their own body and soul and thus live a virtuous life."[98]

Those who came closest to this divinization of the flesh were those who,
like the exemplary St. Antony of the *Life of St. Antony*, practiced ascetic self-
discipline. In the wake of Athanasius' hagiographical master-text, such holy
persons—whether alive or dead—not only gave "human density" to the need to
connect heaven and earth but also came to be seen as conduits of spiritual
power.[99] If the fourth century witnessed the rise of the holy man and the boom
in hagiographical literature devoted to this figure, it also witnessed the bur-
geoning of another form of visible holiness, the cult of the saints and their
relics. Like the body of the theurgist, the living body of the ascetic holy man and
the dead body of the saintly martyr were seen as vehicles of transcendence, their
"matter" charged with religious meaning.

The view of ascetic practice as the highest form of Christian spirituality
and the veneration of relics were connected, since it was precisely ascetics like
Ambrose, Jerome, Gregory of Nyssa, and Victricius who promoted the cult of
relics.[100] As forms of spirituality aimed at overcoming human instability, asceticism and the cult of relics were united by the need for a tangible locus of
sanctity.[101] They also shared similar views of the nature of divine presence in the
world insofar as both demanded sensory expression—whether in a living or a
dead body—for their abstract belief in conduits of divine power. Treading a fine
line between the touch of the real and the touch of the transcendent, they
espoused a spirituality that embraced earthly contact while avoiding idolatrous
materialism.[102]

As one who developed a "radically incarnational theology" of relics, Victricius of Rouen, bishop from 385–410 C.E., is the only known theoretician of
the cult of relics.[103] As his treatise *De laude sanctorum* shows, the performative
as well as the religio-aesthetic dimension of "matter" was a feature of the
Christian cult of relics as it was of the Neoplatonic animation of statues.[104] As
part of his argument that "the truth of the whole corporeal passion [of the
martyr] is present in fragments of the righteous," Victricius wrote that a proper
understanding of relics called for an imaginative use of sight as well as language:
one must interpret the "blood and clay" before one with "the eyes of the heart,"
not allowing "bodily sight" to be a barrier.[105] This would seem to be a reversion
to Origen's doctrine of the spiritual senses were it not for the fact that Victricius
and his congregation were in fact literally looking at fragments of human
bodies. Victricius hoped to accomplish a retraining of physical sight such that
one could apprehend how "an animate body" *(animatum corpus)* had been
converted by God "into the substance of his light."[106] Victricius shared with
Proclus an ability to see more than was there as he developed this strategy for
retrieving what was visually intractable, the presence of divine power in an
earthly object.

It is difficult not to notice the similarity between the theurgist's *agalma empsychon,* the animated statue, and the relic venerator's *animatum corpus,* the animated body. Writing about Augustine's worry that agency might be attributed to the martyrs themselves rather than to God, Clark notes that "invocation of martyrs could too easily be assimilated to theurgy (which used 'sympathetic' physical objects to invoke divine powers) or, worse, to sorcery."[107] Assimilation of the two is understandable, since both were material objects that centered divine power, giving it a place from which it could be communicated to human beings and thus drawing them into the network of relationships that they activated. Unlike animated statues, however, whose function was to impart divine wisdom, the major performative function of relics was healing: because martyrs are "bound to the relics by the bond of all eternity," they bring "heavenly brilliance" into human life in the very concrete form of physical restoration.[108]

Although Victricius mentioned healing, recitation of miraculous cures was not part of his sermon. His main interest lay in explaining how such tiny bodily fragments could be so powerful. His argument hinged on his view of the consubstantiality of all bodies. Since the saints are entirely united to Christ and thus to God, and since God cannot be divided, the whole is present in every part: "Nothing in relics is not complete," and "unity is widely diffused without loss to itself."[109] Bringing out the full incarnational thrust of his argument, Victricius stated that not only the souls but also the bodies of the martyrs are united with Christ: "They are entirely with the Savior in his entirety . . . and have everything in common in the truth of the godhead."[110] Much like the theurgical view of the diffusion of the transcendent in special material objects, Victricius's position was premised on the belief that "God is diffused far and wide, and lends out his light without loss to himself."[111]

Having established that "the martyr is wholly present—flesh, blood, and spirit united to God—in the relic," as Clark observes, "Victricius preempts a shocked reaction: is he really saying that these relics are just what God is, the 'absolute and ineffable substance of godhead' (8.19–21)? His answer, apparently, is 'yes.'"[112] Yes, but with an important qualifier: the martyr "is the same by gift not by property, by adoption not by nature."[113] Relics, that is, retained enough of the human so that they could function as condensations of the ideal self that ascetics like Victricius hoped to achieve. Not only are the martyr-saints advocates, judges, and associates of their venerators, they are also teachers of virtue who "remove the stains of vice" in the human, body and soul.[114] Perhaps the most astonishing aspect of Victricius's view of relics is their ability to remake human identity in their own image. When Victricius says, "I touch fragments," he is touching the fiery rays of his own transformation.[115]

In the presence of relics, one of the things that their venerators "see" is that the martyrs are "dwellers in our hearts" *(habitatores pectoris nostri).*[116] Relics put one in touch with models of human identity toward which the soul strives. Victricius was fairly straightforward about this. In the following passage, in which he imagined the ceremonial entry of the relics into Rouen as a Christian *adventus,* he wrote:

> There is no lack of things for us to admire: in place of the royal cloak, here is the garment of eternal light. The togas of the saints have absorbed this purple. Here are diadems adorned with the varied lights of the jewels of wisdom, intellect, knowledge, truth, good counsel, courage, endurance, self-control, justice, good sense, patience, chastity. These virtues are expressed and inscribed each in its own stone. Here the Savior-craftsman has adorned the crowns of the martyrs with spiritual jewels. Let us set the sails of our souls towards these gems.[117]

One feature of this passage that deserves mention first is its description of the ritualistic character of the entry of relics into the city. Underlying Victricius's imaginative portrayal is an important feature of the cult of relics: human body-parts did not become the animate bodies that were relics apart from ritual practice, and in highly elaborate and aesthetically enhanced places that evoked the visionary atmosphere in which relics took their proper place.[118] Spectacle was as much a part of the cult of relics as it was of theurgical animation of statues.

Participants in such spectacles were confronted with spiritual objects to which they were not only related (as Victricius insisted, there is only "one mass of corporeality"[119]) but in which they could see the "spiritual jewels," as it were, of their own selves, body and soul, touched by transcendence. When Victricius urged his congregation, whom he had extolled from the outset for its ascetic valor, to "set their souls towards these gems," he offered those spiritual jewels as an image for how soul "places" the self in regard to its own ethical ideals, since the gems represent virtues whose realization was the goal of the ascetic life. As an image of self-identity in the context of relic-veneration, "spiritual jewels" flirts with erasing the boundary between the material and the spiritual; however, the inescapable "touch of the real" in this form of devotion ensured that "body" would remain as a locus of religious meaning.

Conclusion

Two paradigmatic moments in the history of self-understanding in late antiquity have been presented in this paper, each represented by striking images drawn from texts by the Neoplatonic and Christian thinkers upon whom the discussion has focused. My wager has been that these images—Plotinus's transparent sphere, Origen's divine library, Proclus's animated statues, and Victricius's spiritual jewels—can function as expressions, in condensed form, of their authors' views of self-identity. Following Jonathan Smith's argument that a worldview as well as a view of the self can be discerned through a culture's or an individual's imagination of place, I chose these particular images not only because of their vividness as figures or metaphors of place, but also because they reveal how each author thought that the self could best orient itself with respect to the spiritual and material aspects of human life. These "luminous details" are active in that they recommend a way of being-in-the-world religiously.

Each of these images not only envisions a place but also recommends a practice whereby proper placement can be achieved. Both Plotinus and Origen drew on images of actual places—a globe teeming with life, and a library of sacred books—that are metaphors of interior dispositions from beginning to end. They turned these figures of place into images of a self transformed by the knowledge that the empirical, historically conditioned world is not the locus of true identity and can even hinder connection with the divine realm. Moreover, both are spiritual exercises that teach the reader how to turn vision inward; both model a form of intense inner concentration that opens the self out to structures of spiritual reality that are the soul's true home.

By contrast, the images in the texts of Proclus and Victricius both begin and end in actual places—temples with animated statues, cathedrals and mar-tyria with relics.[120] In a sense, they provide snapshots of the self engaged in forms of practice that orient the soul to sources of divine power. But they are also figurations of self-identity and not simply descriptions of ritual behavior, since animated statue and relic are used to describe not only the object of practice but also the identity of the practitioner. In these images as well as the earlier ones, an imagination of place implies a view of the self.

When compared, these two sets of images and the cultural preferences that they imply demonstrate a shift in conceptions of the self with respect to mate-riality, broadly construed to include the physical world as well as the human body. By plotting this shift as a movement from a religious orientation of the self that emphasized "the touch of transcendence" to one that emphasized "the touch of the real," I have not wanted to suggest that views of the self in the earlier era of the third century were somehow more spiritual than they were in the later era. Orienting the self in relation to the divine remained a constant. Rather, the shift involved a change in views of the soul's ability to make contact with the god or gods.

One way to describe the change is to consider how these two groups of authors thought about loss. For Plotinus and Origen, so confident that intense inner contemplation could bring about realization of the self's divine core, distraction was a major problem; loss of attention diminished the soul's con-sciousness of its expansive identity, and this loss was often attributed by them to the particularity of the material world and the body's involvement with it. For Proclus and Victricius, living in an age when the high gods had become more remote, loss was expressed as a loss of immediacy and as a diminished view of the human capacity to make contact with the divine by using its inner powers. This loss of cosmic optimism concerning the makeup of the self, together with the felt need for figures who could mediate divine presence, eventuated in a new appreciation precisely for particularity. Now the sensible world, including human sense-perception, the body, and objects in the material realm, could be viewed not as distractions but as theophanic vehicles. This was the basic shift, and it entailed a re-formation of the viewing subject, who was newly dependent on rituals of transformation in order to see spiritual animation in the world and the self. Perhaps not surprisingly, when the tendency to suppress materiality as a locus of meaning was revised, the fully embodied "I" could see both more, and less, than in an earlier age.

NOTES

1. Plotinus, *Enneads* 1.1.1.1–3 (A. H. Armstrong, LCL). All translations of Plotinus's *Enneads* are from this translation unless otherwise noted.

2. See *Enn.* 1.1.4 on "mixture" and "being interwoven."

3. *Enn.* 6.4.14.17. See Pierre Hadot, *Plotinus or the Simplicity of Vision* (trans. Michael Chase; Chicago: University of Chicago Press, 1993), 31–32, with reference to "the divisive alienation of [the] conscious self."

4. See, for example, *Enn.* 4.3.8.15–16.

5. Marcus Aurelius, *Meditations* 5.11 (trans. Maxwell Staniforth; London: Penguin Books, 1964), 83, slightly emended.

6. Carlin A. Barton, "Being in the Eyes: Shame and Sight in Ancient Rome," in *The Roman Gaze: Vision, Power, and the Body* (ed. David Fredrick; Arethusa Books; Baltimore: Johns Hopkins University Press, 2002), 227.

7. For the images of serpent- and horse-man, see Origen, *Hom. Ezech.* 3.8 (*Homilien zu Samuel I, zum Hohelied und zu den Propheten* [ed. W. A. Baehrens; GCS 8; Leipzig: J. C. Hinrichs, 1925], 355–57).

8. Origen, *Hom. Luc.* 8.3 (*Homélies sur S. Luc* [ed. and trans. Henri Crouzel, François Fournier, and Pierre Périchon; SC 87; Paris: Cerf, 1962], 166–68).

9. Gregory Jay, "Freud: The Death of Autobiography," *Genre* 19 (1986): 104.

10. Ibid., 105.

11. *Enn.* 1.1.13.1–3; italics added by Armstrong.

12. See, for example, *Enn.* 4.8.8.1–6; 4.8.1.1–11, and passages like 6.5.12.13–29 in which Plotinus argues that the "All" is continuously present, even when we turn away from it.

13. See John David Dawson, *Christian Figural Reading and the Fashioning of Identity* (Berkeley: University of California Press, 2002), 79, for discussion.

14. For a survey of ancient conceptions of the soul, see Kevin Corrigan, "Body and Soul in Ancient Religious Experience," in *Classical Mediterranean Spirituality: Egyptian, Greek, and Roman* (ed. A. H. Armstrong; World Spirituality 15; New York: Crossroad, 1986), 360–83; see also Frederick M. Schroeder, "The Self in Ancient Religious Experience," in Armstrong, ed., *Classical Mediterranean Spirituality,* 337–59, especially with regard to the Platonic tradition, in which soul is the locus of human identity (350).

15. Schroeder, "Self in Ancient Religious Experience," 337.

16. Ibid., 348.

17. Simon Goldhill, "Refracting Classical Vision: Changing Cultures of Viewing," in *Vision in Context: Historical and Contemporary Perspectives on Sight* (ed. Teresa Brennan and Martin Jay; New York: Routledge, 1996), 18.

18. Jonathan Z. Smith, *Map Is Not Territory: Studies in the History of Religions* (Leiden: Brill, 1978; repr. Chicago: University of Chicago Press, 1993), 143.

19. Catherine Gallagher and Stephen Greenblatt, *Practicing New Historicism* (Chicago: University of Chicago Press, 2001), 31. Gallagher and Greenblatt define "the touch of the real" as their commitment to particularity in historical explanation: "We wanted the touch of the real in the way that in an earlier period people wanted the touch of the transcendent" (31). While they do not specify who those earlier people were, their sense for what they are moving away from—"the touch of the transcendent"—is captured in such phrases as "a unitary story, a supreme model of human perfection" (5) and "the path to a transhistorical truth" (7), and in this sentence: "The task of understanding then depends not on the extraction of an abstract set of principles, and still less on the application of a theoretical model, but rather on an encounter with the singular, the specific, and the individual" (6). Though I have adapted these phrases for my own purposes, the distinction they make between the transhistorical and the particular will continue to inform my use of them.

20. Gallagher and Greenblatt, *Practicing New Historicism,* 19.

21. Ibid., 15.

22. See Carlin A. Barton, *The Sorrows of the Ancient Romans: The Gladiator and the Monster* (Princeton, N.J.: Princeton University Press, 1993), 90–95; Barton, "Being in the Eyes," 216–35.

23. On the aggressive eye as well as the self-bewitching eye, see Plutarch, *Mor.* 680C–682B, *Quaest. conv.* 5.7; on Narcissus and the self-consuming eye, see Barton, *Sorrows of the Ancient Romans,* 92, and John Elsner, "Naturalism and the Erotics of the Gaze: Intimations of Narcissus," in *Sexuality in Ancient Art: Near East, Egypt, Greece, and Italy* (ed. Natalie Boymel Kampen; Cambridge Studies in New Art History and Criticism; Cambridge: Cambridge University Press, 1996), 248–61.

24. For the "eye" of Narcissus as self-consuming, see Barton, *Sorrows of the Ancient Romans,* 92; on self-splitting, see Elsner, "Naturalism and the Erotics of the Gaze," 255, discussing the presentation of Narcissus in Callistratus, *Descriptiones* 5.3: "The terrifying confrontation with the self's gaze as if it were other causes a psychic move whereby Narcissus looks at himself as another would look at him"—i.e., he objectivizes himself, much like Plotinus's self thrown into a world of objects.

25. *Enn.* 1.6.5.50–58 (on being mixed); 2.3.9.31–32 (on person as compound being); 4.8.4.15–18 (on being isolated).

26. Stephen R. L. Clark, "Plotinus: Body and Soul," in *The Cambridge Companion to Plotinus* (ed. Lloyd P. Gerson; Cambridge: Cambridge University Press, 1996), 280, 284.

27. Stephen Halliwell, *The Aesthetics of Mimesis: Ancient Texts and Modern Problems* (Princeton, N.J.: Princeton University Press, 2002), 322.

28. A.H. Armstrong, preface to *Enn.* 6.7 (LCL 7:79). For discussion of reality as a "structure of dependence" and as a continuous whole, see Dominic J. O'Meara, "The Hierarchical Ordering of Reality in Plotinus," in Gerson, ed., *Cambridge Companion to Plotinus,* 66–81, citing especially such passages as *Enn.* 5.2.2.24–29: "The whole is continuous with itself, but with one part differentiated from another, and the prior does not perish in the posterior" (76).

29. Sara Rappe, "Self-Knowledge and Subjectivity in the *Enneads,*" in Gerson, ed., *Cambridge Companion to Plotinus,* 266.

30. Ibid.

31. Frederic Schroeder, "The Vigil of the One and Plotinian Iconoclasm," in *Neoplatonism and Western Aesthetics* (Studies in Neoplatonism 12; ed. Aphrodite Alexandrakis, assoc. ed. Nicholas J. Moutafakis; Albany: SUNY Press, 2002), 67.

32. Earlier in *Enn.* 5.8, Plotinus describes the real beings of the noetic world as follows: "They see themselves in other things; for all things there are transparent, and there is nothing dark or opaque" (*Enn.* 5.8.4.4–7).

33. See Schroeder, "The Vigil of the One," 68, and Robert M. Berchman, "Aesthetics

as a Philosophic Ethos: Plotinus and Foucault," in *Neoplatonism and Contemporary Thought, Part Two* (Studies in Neoplatonism 11; ed. R. Baine Harris; Albany: SUNY Press, 2002), 190, both describing the iconoclastic aspect of such an exercise.

34. See Sara Rappe, "Self-Perception in Plotinus and the Later Neoplatonic Tradition," *American Catholic Philosophical Quarterly* 71 (1997): 433–51, on the problem of "being aware that one is aware": "To be aware that one is engaged in the act of knowing an object is to be distracted by a different object of awareness as well as to be excessively removed from the object with which one is engaged" (440). See also idem, "Metaphor in Plotinus' *Enneads* v 8.9," *Ancient Philosophy* 15 (1995): 155–72, esp. 161–63.

35. Hadot, *Plotinus*, 27.

36. Trans. Hadot, *Plotinus*, 27. See *Enn.* 4.8.1.1–6, describing entering into the self as coming to identity with the divine. See also Hadot, "Neoplatonist Spirituality," in Armstrong, ed., *Classical Mediterranean Spirituality*, 241: Plotinus "shows the soul trying to renounce its individuality, trying not to be 'someone,' in order to become the whole."

37. Rappe, "Self-knowledge and Subjectivity," 266, 270.

38. *Enn.* 6.9.10.3 (body as hindrance); *Enn.* 9.9.57–59 (self glorified).

39. *Dial.* 13.3–6 (Origen, *Entretien d' Origène avec Heraclide* [ed. and trans. Jean Scherer; SC 67; Paris: Cerf, 1960], 82).

40. *Princ.* 3.4.1 (Origen, *Traité des Principes Tome III* [ed. and trans. Henri Crouzel and Manlio Simonetti; SC 268; Paris: Cerf, 1980], 200).

41. See the discussion of Gal 5:17 (on flesh warring against spirit) in Origen, *Princ.* 3.4.4; see also *Hom. Gen.* 1.15 (*Homélies sur Genèse* [ed. and trans. Louis Doutreleau; SC 7; Paris: Cerf, 1944], 68) on the "insolence" of the "flesh" and its connection to "carnal vices." For a discussion of flesh as "the force that attracts the soul towards the body," see Henri Crouzel, *Origen: The Life and Thought of the First Great Theologian* (trans. A. S. Worrall; San Francisco: Harper & Row, 1989), 89.

42. See Origen, *Comm. Jo.* 32.27.338 (*Origen* [trans. Joseph W. Trigg; The Early Church Fathers; London: Routledge, 1998], 237) on the mind being "divinized by those things that it contemplates"; on being subjected to "the passions of the mind," see *Princ.* 3.4.4; on the inner and outer man, see *Hom. Gen.* 1.2, 1.13, 1.15; *Hom. Luc.* 39.5 (of the two images in the human being, one is earthly, the other in the image and likeness of God); *Comm. Cant.*, prologue 2.4; *Hom. Ezech.* 3.8; *Dial.* 16.

43. See Origen, *Comm.Cant.* 1.4; *Cels.* 1.48; *Dial.* 16–22. For discussion, see John Dillon, "Aisthêsis Noêtê: A Doctrine of Spiritual Senses in Origen and in Plotinus," in *The Golden Chain: Studies in the Development of Platonism and Christianity* (Collected Studies 333; Aldershot: Variorum, 1990), 443–55.

44. Dawson, *Christian Figural Reading*, 56, 63.

45. *Comm. Cant.* prol. 2 (GCS 8:72; trans. R. P. Lawson, *Origen: The Song of Songs: Commentary and Homilies* [ACW 26; Westminster, Md.: Newman, 1957), 36).

46. Ibid. (GCS 8:72; ACW 26:36).

47. *Princ.* 3.3 (SC 268:198). For a discussion of Origen's use of animal imagery as a way of characterizing the soul's many dimensions, see Patricia Cox, "Origen on the Bestial Soul: A Poetics of Nature," *VC* 36 (1982): 115–40.

48. These false *personae* are "the masks of the lion, the dragon, and the fox" referred to in Origen, *Hom. Luc.* 8.3 (ed. and trans. Crouzel et al., SC 87:166–68). In *Hom. Luc.* 8.2 (Crouzel et al., SC 87:166), Origen explains that the human soul was "created as the image of an Image that already existed. . . . Each one of us shapes his soul into the image of Christ and makes either a larger or a smaller image of him. The image is either dingy and dirty, or it is clean and bright and corresponds to the form of the original" (*Homilies on Luke* [trans. Joseph T. Lienhard; FC 94; Washington, D.C.: Catholic University of America Press, 1996], 34).

49. *Dial.* 14 (SC 67:84).

50. *Comm. Cant.* prol. 2 (GCS 8:66). See *Comm. Jo.* 1.8.44–45: Origen argues that it

is necessary to "differentiate the sensible aspect of the gospel from its intelligible and spiritual aspect. And now our task is to change the sensible gospel into the spiritual, for what is interpretation of the sensible gospel unless it is transforming it into the spiritual?" (*Commentaire sur Saint Jean Tome I* [ed. and trans. Cécile Blanc; SC 120; Paris: Cerf, 1966], 82; trans. Trigg, *Origen*, 113).

51. Dawson, *Christian Figural Reading*, 61.

52. *Comm. Jo.* 32.27.338 (trans. Trigg, *Origen*, 237). See Dawson, *Christian Figural Reading*, 54, for discussion of the link between allegorical reading and the spiritual transformation of the interpreter in Origen's thought.

53. Robert Berchman, "Self-knowledge and Subjectivity in Origen," forthcoming in *Origeniana Ottava: Origene e la Tradizione Alessandrina* (ed. L. Perrone; Leuven: Peeters, 2004); I thank Prof. Berchman for allowing me to use his manuscript prior to publication.

54. *Hom. Gen.* 2.6 (SC 7:108; trans. Ronald E. Heine, *Origen: Homilies on Genesis and Exodus* [FC 71; Washington, D.C.: Catholic University of America Press, 1982], 86–87). Note should be made here of Origen's argument in *Princ.* 4.2.4, where another way of envisioning the relation between human beings and Scripture is outlined: as Mark Julian Edwards observes, "the division of the person into body, soul and spirit was the charter for his [Origen's] own ascription of a threefold meaning to the text" (*Origen Against Plato* [Aldershot: Ashgate Publishing Limited, 2002], 89).

55. Dawson, *Christian Figural Reading*, 54.

56. Origen, *Philoc.* 15.19.15–16: *aei gar en tais graphais ho logos sarx egeneto, hina kataskēnōsē en hēmin* (*The Philocalia of Origen: The Text Revised with a Critical Introduction and Indices* [ed. J. Armitage Robinson; Cambridge: Cambridge University Press, 1893], 85).

57. *Philoc.* 15.19.25–28 (Robinson, *The Philocalia of Origen*, 85). See the discussion by Jean Daniélou on Origen's equation of touching the flesh of the Word with allegorical interpretation in his *Hom. Lev.* 4.8 (*Origène* [Le génie du christianisme; Paris: La Table Ronde, 1948], 182–83). See also Trigg, *Origen*, 103–04: "the person thus transformed [by participation in Christ] becomes, like John the Evangelist, another Jesus, not differing from Christ and knowing the Father as the Son does."

58. Dawson, *Christian Figural Reading*, 65.

59. Peter Brown, *The Body and Society: Men, Women, and Sexual Renunciation in Early Christianity* (Lectures on the History of Religions, new ser. 15; New York: Columbia University Press, 1988), 167.

60. See Origen, *Princ.* 3.6.6 (Crouzel et al., SC 268: 246).

61. Caroline Walker Bynum, *The Resurrection of the Body in Western Christianity, 200–1336* (New York: Columbia University Press, 1995), 68. See also Dawson, *Christian Figural Reading*, 78–80, who discusses a passage from Origen's *Fr. Ps.* 1 in which Origen distinguished between the body's material substratum, always in flux, and a corporeal form *(eidos)* that endures and accounts for continuity of personal identity. He comments, following Bynum, that "despite Origen's insistence that the body is intrinsic to personal identity, his recourse to the category of 'form' to distinguish the body from mere materiality-without-identity still leaves hanging the pertinence of flesh or physicality to personal identity" (80).

62. See Berchman, "Self-knowledge and Subjectivity in Origen," who refers to Origen's goal of achieving "a self that is beyond itself." His point is that "complete self-knowledge requires a grasp of first principles, and this kind of knowledge is an uncovering of self-knowledge through a two-fold process of gradual detachment from the objects of everyday consciousness, and an immersion in the sources of consciousness itself."

63. The "power of pomp and glitter" in architecture, language, and costume is discussed by Ramsay MacMullen, "Some Pictures in Ammianus Marcellinus," *Art Bulletin* 46 (1964): 435–55. See also the major study of Sabine MacCormack, *Art and Cere-*

mony in Late Antiquity (The Transformation of the Classical Heritage 1; Berkeley: University of California Press, 1981).

64. MacMullen, "Some Pictures," 437 (theatricality); John Matthews, *The Roman Empire of Ammianus* (Baltimore: Johns Hopkins University Press, 1989), 460 (expressionistic manner).

65. See Michael Roberts, *The Jeweled Style: Poetry and Poetics in Late Antiquity* (Ithaca, N.Y.: Cornell University Press, 1989). In discussing late ancient mosaics, for example, Roberts refers to "the liberation of the individual stone and its investment with light and color" (72) and to the "verbal dazzle" (75) of poetry, in which individual words were used as though they possessed "a physical presence of their own, distinct from any considerations of sense or syntax" (58). Part of his point is that, with the loss of organic relationship in poetry and the arts, the eye of the spectator is focused on the part, and the relationships among such parts must be reconstituted or imagined by the spectator.

66. For discussion of Eunapius's *Vitae philosophorum et sophistarum* and the *Historia monachorum* in this light, see Patricia Cox Miller, "Strategies of Representation in Collective Biography: Constructing the Subject as Holy," in *Greek Biography and Panegyric in Late Antiquity* (ed. Tomas Hägg and Philip Rousseau; The Transformation of the Classical Heritage 31; Berkeley: University of California Press, 2000), 209–54; on visual imagination and Christian holiness, see, inter alia, Georgia Frank, *The Memory of the Eyes: Pilgrims to Living Saints in Late Antiquity* (The Transformation of the Classical Heritage 30; Berkeley: University of California Press, 2000) for discussion of such phenomena as "embracing with the eyes" (14) and "the readable body" (150).

67. John Onians, "Abstraction and Imagination in Late Antiquity," *Art History* 3 (1980): 1–24. Onians adduces many examples of fourth- to sixth-century descriptions of material objects (marble walls, church floors) in which the authors purport to see something not literally there (e.g., Sidonius Apollinaris's description of a marble wall as a field of grass [*Ep.* 2.10.13–15, 20–21], and Paul the Silentiary's description of marble strips in the floor of Hagia Sophia as the four rivers of Paradise [*Narratio de S. Sophia* 26]).

68. For Plotinus, see *Enn.* 4.8.8.1–6, and for discussion, Dominic O'Meara, *Plotinus: An Introduction to the Enneads* (Oxford: Clarendon, 1995), 102–03.

69. See Gregory Shaw, "After Aporia: Theurgy in Later Platonism," *Journal of Neoplatonic Studies* 5 (1996): 3–41, esp. 18–19.

70. E. R. Dodds, ed. and trans., "Introduction," *Proclus: The Elements of Theology* (Oxford: Clarendon, 1963), xx: "the humbler cosmic status assigned by Iamblichus and most of his successors to the human soul" (note: all translations of *Institutio theologica* are from this volume). See Polymnia Athanassiadi, "Dreams, Theurgy and Freelance Divination: The Testimony of Iamblichus," *JRS* 83 (1993): 120, n. 59, on Iamblichus's "more pessimistic view of humanity" when compared with Plotinus; see Shaw, "After Aporia," for a more nuanced view: "According to Iamblichus, all souls had to mediate [between immortal and mortal, as part of their role in cosmogenesis], and in the case of human souls their mediation included the experience of suffering, dividedness, and mortality. Since the soul's original nature was immortal and coordinate with the gods it meant that—as human—the soul was alienated not only from the divinity of the gods but from its own divinity as well. And this alienation was not an accident or a temporary condition that could be rectified when the soul corrected the 'error' of identifying with the body: *the experience of self-alienation constituted the soul's very essence as human*" (20–21, italics in original).

71. Gregory Shaw, *Theurgy and the Soul: The Neoplatonism of Iamblichus* (University Park: Pennsylvania State University Press, 1995), 35.

72. Priscianus, *De anima* 223.32, quoting Iamblichus (trans. Shaw, "After Aporia," 25). On the presence of the divine traces in the cosmos, see Iamblichus, *Myst.* 1.21 (*Les mystères d'Egypt* [ed. and trans. Édouard des Places; Collections des universités de

France; Paris: Les Belles Lettres, 1966], 76–77; all subsequent translations are from this text unless noted otherwise).

73. Shaw, *Theurgy and the Soul*, 157; Anne Sheppard, "Proclus' Attitude to Theurgy," *CQ* 32 (1982): 220; Robert M. Berchman, "Rationality and Ritual in Neoplatonism," in *Neoplatonism and Indian Philosophy* (ed. Paulos Mar Gregorios; Studies in Neoplatonism: Ancient and Modern 9; New York: State University of New York Press, 2002), 229-68.

74. Iamblichus, *Myst.* 5.23 (Des Places, *Mystères*, 178; trans. Shaw, *Theurgy and the Soul*, 165).

75. Ibid. (Des Places, *Mystères*, 178; trans. Y. Lewy, *Chaldean Oracles and Theurgy: Mysticism, Magic, and Platonism in the Later Roman Empire* [Cairo: L'Institut français d'archéologique orientale, 1956], 496).

76. Iamblichus, *Myst.* 4.2 (Des Places, *Mystères*, 148): *to tōn theōn schēma peritithesthai.*

77. Gregory Shaw, "Theurgy: Rituals of Unification in the Neoplatonism of Iamblichus," *Traditio* 41 (1985): 21. See also Sara Rappe, *Reading Neoplatonism: Non-discursive Thinking in the Texts of Plotinus, Proclus, and Damascius* (Cambridge: Cambridge University Press, 2000): "The human soul, through its realization of unity with the divine, thereby sacralizes its own world and thus 'saves' the world of matter" (177); and Berchman, "Rationality and Ritual," 238: "The soul's purification and ascent not only begins but ends [*sic*] in the sensible realm."

78. See Sheppard, "Proclus' Attitude to Theurgy," 220: "In Proclus' metaphysical system everything in both the natural and the intelligible world belongs both to a particular level of being and to a particular 'chain' (*seira* or *taxis*) by which it is inherently related to other members of the same 'chain' on other levels."

79. See John Dillon, "Origen's Doctrine of the Trinity and Some Later Neoplatonic Theories," in *Neoplatonism and Christian Thought* (ed. D. J. O'Meara; Studies in Neoplatonism 3; Albany: SUNY Press, 1982), 22. See also *Institutio theologica*, props. 140, 142–43, 145. Proclus developed a very complex view of a multiple spiritual realm, anchored by first principles (the henads identified with Greek gods) that activate the chains of *sympatheia* that permeate the cosmos. For discussion, see R. T. Wallis, *Neoplatonism* (2d ed.; London: Gerald Duckworth & Co. Ltd., 1995), 147–48.

80. Proclus, *Inst.* prop. 211; *in Prm.* 948 (*Proclus' Commentary on Plato's Parmenides* [trans. John Dillon; Princeton: Princeton University Press, 1987]; all subsequent translation are from this volume).

81. See *Inst.* prop. 190, on the soul's position between the indivisible and the divided realms as, in Dodds' words, "a frontier between two worlds," following the Neoplatonic understanding of the creation of the soul in the *Timaeus* (Dodds, *Proclus*, 297).

82. See *Inst.* prop. 145: "All things are dependent from the gods, some being irradiated by one god, some by another, and the series extend downwards to the last orders of being"; and Wallis, *Neoplatonism*, 153, for discussion.

83. See n. 36 above for Hadot's view of Plotinus's renunciation of being "someone" in order to become the whole.

84. Iamblichus, *Myst.* 3.30 (Des Places, *Mystères*, 143); see Athanassiadi, "Dreams, Theurgy, and Freelance Divination," 123, 128, for discussion.

85. Shaw, *Theurgy and the Soul*, 167, n.9.

86. Proclus, *in Ti.* 3.155.18: once the *symbola* that participate in the god activate the statue, the statue "foretells the future" (*prolegein to mellon*) (text in E. R. Dodds, *The Greeks and the Irrational* [Berkeley: University of California Press, 1966], 292). See also Michael Pselles, quoting from Proclus's (now mostly lost) *Eclogae de philosophia Chaldaica*: "The practitioners of the telestic science fill the cavities of the statues with substances belonging to the potencies presiding over the statues: animals, plants, stones, herbs, seals, engravings, sometimes also sympathetic spices . . . and they vivify the

images and move them with a secret power" (*Ep.* 187, trans. in Yochanan Lewy, *Chaldean Oracles and Theurgy: Mysticism, Magic and Platonism in the Later Roman Empire* [Recherches d'archéologie, de philologie et d'histoire 13; Cairo: L'Institut français d'archéologie orientale, 1956], 496). On the animation of statues in Chaldean theurgy, see Sarah Iles Johnston, *Hekate Soteira: A Study of Hekate's Role in the Chaldean Oracles and Related Literature* (American Classical Studies 21; Atlanta: Scholars Press, 1990), esp. ch. 6 ("Theurgy and Magic") and ch. 8 ("The Epiphany of Hekate").

87. Proclus, *in Ti.* 1.51.25–31 (*Proclus: Commentaire sur la Timée* [trans. A. J. Festugière; 5 vols.; Paris: J. Vrin, 1966–68], 1:85).

88. Proclus, *Eclogae de Philosophia Chaldaica* (ed. H. Jahn; Halle: Preffer, 1891); trans. Rappe, *Reading Neoplatonism*, 176.

89. See Rappe, *Reading Neoplatonism*, 176–78, for the importance of ritual.

90. Ibid., 178; see also 192: "Theurgic rite involves the creation of a ritual cosmos, which is then sacralized through its capacity to draw down the power of the gods."

91. Origen, *Cels.* 7.33 (SC 150:88; trans. Henry Chadwick, *Contra Celsum* [Cambridge: Cambridge University Press, 1965], 421).

92. For discussion of the "angelic" bodies of desert ascetics in such texts as Palladius's *Historia Lausiaca,* Theodoret's *Historia religiosa,* the *Historia monachorum in Aegypto,* and others, see Patricia Cox Miller, "Desert Asceticism and 'The Body from Nowhere,'" *JECS* 2 (1994): 137–53.

93. Peter Brown, "Asceticism: Pagan and Christian," in CAH 13: *The Later Empire, A.D. 337–425* (ed. Averil Cameron and Peter Garnsey; Cambridge: Cambridge University Press, 1998), 625.

94. Views of the body as integral to human identity were developed in the contexts of the Arian and Origenist controversies; for the former, see David Brakke, *Athanasius and Asceticism* (Baltimore: Johns Hopkins University Press, 1998), 145–61; for the latter, Elizabeth A. Clark, *The Origenist Controversy: The Cultural Construction of an Early Christian Debate* (Princeton, N.J.: Princeton University Press, 1992), 86–104 (on Epiphanius), 121–51 (on Jerome). On the resurrection of the body and the late-fourth-century linking of bodily integrity with material continuity, see Bynum, *Resurrection of the Body,* 59–94.

95. On the new sense of the instability of the created order, as well as the intensifying of the difference between creator and created, see J. Rebecca Lyman, *Christology and Cosmology: Models of Divine Activity in Origen, Eusebius, and Athanasius* (Oxford Theological Monographs; Oxford: Clarendon, 1993), 141–46, esp. 146 on Athanasius: "Indeed, as *treptos* rather than *autexousios,* human nature is alienated more profoundly from history or the world, as well as from eternal divine nature, than it is in Irenaeus or, ironically, even Origen. The body, if the locus of transformation, has become to an even greater extent the principal distraction."

96. See Brown, *Body and Society,* 236: "Theologians of ascetic background, throughout the fourth and fifth centuries, would not have pursued with such ferocious intellectual energy the problems raised by the Incarnation of Christ, and the consequent joining of human and divine in one single human person, if this joining had not been sensed by them as a haunting emblem of the enigmatic joining of body and soul within themselves."

97. Athanasius, *C. Gent.* 2.20–21; 3.3–5, 16–17 (*Athanasius: Contra Gentes and De Incarnatione* [ed. and trans. R. W. Thomson; OECT; Oxford: Clarendon, 1971]). For discussion, see Brakke, *Athanasius and Asceticism,* 146–47; Lyman, *Christology and Cosmology,* 141–43.

98. *Athanasius and Asceticism,* 149, 239.

99. Peter Brown, "Arbiters of Ambiguity: A Role of the Late Antique Holy Man," *Cassiodorus* 2 (1996): 140.

100. David G. Hunter, "Vigilantius of Calagurris and Victricius of Rouen: Ascetics,

Relics, and Clerics in Late Roman Gaul," *JECS* 7 (1999): 401–30; see also Peter Brown, *The Cult of the Saints: Its Rise and Function in Latin Christianity* (Haskell Lectures on History of Religion, new ser. 2; Chicago: University of Chicago Press, 1981), 66–67.

101. On localizing the holy, see Brown, *Cult of the Saints,* 86–105.

102. Like an animated statue, the body of a holy man or a relic is a *vehicle* for divine power, not the divine itself; on the relation between spirit and matter in relics, see Patricia Cox Miller, "'The Little Blue Flower Is Red': Relics and the Poetizing of the Body," *JECS* 8 (2000): 213–36.

103. The quotation is from Hunter, "Vigilantius," 428.

104. Dated c. c.e. 396, this sermon was given on the occasion of the arrival of Ambrose's gift of relics; for an account of Victricius's life, see the preface to the edition of *De laude* in *Foebadius, Victricius, Leporius, Vincentius Lirinensis, Evagrius, Rubricius* (ed. R. Demeulenaere; CCSL 64; Turnhout: Brepols, 1985: 53–93; the text has recently been translated, with an introduction, by Gillian Clark, "Victricius of Rouen: Praising the Saints," *JECS* 7 (1999): 365–99.

105. *Laud.* 10.1–5 (CCSL 64:84; Clark, "Victricius of Rouen," 391).

106. *Laud.* 9.15–16 (CCSL 64:83; Clark, "Victricius of Rouen," 389).

107. Clark, "Victricius of Rouen," 371–72.

108. *Laud.*11.46–50 (CCSL 64:88) (healing and bond of eternity); 1.30 (CCSL 64:70) (heavenly brilliance) (Clark, "Victricius of Rouen," 395, 377). For many examples of these healings at martyrs' shrines, see Ramsay MacMullen, *Christianity and Paganism in the Fourth to Eighth Centuries* (New Haven, Conn.: Yale University Press, 1997), 120–34; as he notes, martyria served as hospitals (121).

109. *Laud.* 9.30–31; 7.12 (CCSL 64:83–84, 79; Clark, "Victricius of Rouen," 386, 385).

110. *Laud.* 7.39–40 (CCSL 64:80; Clark, "Victricius of Rouen," 386).

111. *Laud.* 8.15–16 (CCSL 64:81; Clark, "Victricius of Rouen," 388).

112. Clark, "Victricius of Rouen," 367.

113. *Laud.* 8.21–22 (CCSL 64:82; Clark, "Victricius of Rouen," 388).

114. *Laud.* 8.25–40; 12.1–8 (CCSL 64:82, 88–89; Clark, "Victricius of Rouen," 388, 395–96).

115. *Laud.* 11.27 (CCSL 64:87; Clark, "Victricius of Rouen," 394): "I touch fragments; I affirm that in these relics is perfect grace and perfect virtue." Victricius's sermon is studded with references to fire, light, brilliance, and radiance, reminiscent of the divine and illuminative fire in theurgy (see Shaw, *Theurgy and the Soul,* 150).

116. *Laud.* 1.18 (CCSL 64:70; Clark, "Victricius of Rouen," 377).

117. *Laud.* 12.25–33 (CCSL 64:89; Clark, "Victricius of Rouen," 396–97).

118. Ritual practices included processions like the one described by Victricius in *Laud.* 3.11–42 (CCSL 64:73–74), candle-lit processions, sermons like Victricius's own, prayers; martyria were often decorated with paintings and mosaics; for discussion of the aesthetic contexts of relics, see Miller, "'The Little Blue Flower is Red.'"

119. *Laud.* 7.1 (CCSL 64:79; Clark, "Victricius of Rouen," 385).

120. There is little information about where the animation of statues took place, although temples seem a likely choice in light of Eunapius's account of the theurgist Maximus's animation of a statue of Hekate in a temple in Pergamum (*VS* 475). The ritual may also have taken place in private homes; see Archer St. Clair, "Imperial Virtue: Questions of Form and Function in the Case of Four Late Antique Statuettes," *DOP* 50 (1996): 156–57, for discussion of private lararia containing statues with hollowed-out heads, perhaps for the deposit of theurgical substances.

—2—

The Search for the Elusive Self in Texts of the Hebrew Bible

SAUL M. OLYAN

Four decades ago, in a discussion of Jeremiah's confessions, John Bright stated: "Although it is true that other prophets frequently speak in the first person and tell of their experiences, there is no real parallel to these little self-revelations in which Jeremiah lays bare before us his most intimate feelings."[1] Bright's assertion, not uncommon for its time, presupposes our ability as scholars to access the "inner life" of an individual from antiquity through our reading of ancient texts attributed to that individual. In a word, Bright seems to assume that the personal, the private, the truly subjective is within our reach because it is clearly and directly communicated through the written word. The confessional passages of Jeremiah, with their rich and highly charged emotional language, are, suggests Bright, a window through which we might know Jeremiah the historical personage intimately.

From our vantage point, Bright's confidence in our ability to gain unproblematic access to the inner life of a particular ancient individual seems misplaced. We cannot know that the confessions—in whole or in part—are the product of the historical Jeremiah. And even if we were to assume for the sake of argument that they are Jeremianic compositions, the very written word that Bright assumed would provide us with a window into the personal and subjective has turned out to be a far more complex phenomenon than he and his contemporaries imagined. In fact, few today would assume that scholars possess the power of direct access to the inner life of ancient individuals through extant texts, and there is good reason for such skepticism. In every instance, we are dependent on *representations* of the subjective experience intended for public reception of some kind.

The very act of writing for an audience produces a public construction of a subject's emotional life that is not at all the equivalent of that life. In comparison with the inner life of an individual, a textual representation is far less complex and interesting, given all that must by definition be left out due to the limits of linguistic representation, the constraints on the writer's own self-knowledge and memory, and whatever audience-oriented motivations the writer might have.[2] Jeremiah's confessions, whatever their authorship, are formulated to communicate a particular impression of the prophet and his inner life to a particular audience for a particular purpose. Our image of Jeremiah is completely dependent on these textual representations of his anger, his suffering, his insecurity, his piety, his rebellion against Yhwh.[3] Apart from what they might communicate to us, we can know nothing of Jeremiah and his subjective experience. And the same is true of other biblical personages whose inner life is represented with even less richness of detail.

So does this mean that our efforts to access the inner life of the ancients are by definition doomed to complete failure? Are there any aspects of the individual subjective experience that might be grasped by the contemporary scholar through analysis of ancient textual materials? Though I am deeply skeptical about our ability to gain unproblematic entry into the inner life of ancient persons, or even that of contemporary individuals, I do believe that we can find evidence of individual voices in the texts we study. Though these distinct voices are public constructions, their artistry points nonetheless to aspects of the individuality, subjectivity, and uniqueness of the particular persons behind the voices.[4] The identification and querying of individual creative voices in the biblical text represents a necessary first step—and perhaps the only step possible—in the search for the self in ancient texts and will be the focus of this investigation. I shall discuss several sixth-century texts in which a creative individual voice emerges clearly, question what we might learn about the program and possible motivations of the author behind that voice, and then consider the implications of my findings for the larger project of retrieving ancient selves.[5]

Let us begin with the move of the author of Isaiah 40–55 to envision the return of exiles from Babylon to Jerusalem after 539 B.C.E. as a new exodus. Though the concept of a new exodus is not wholly novel in the biblical tradition, Second Isaiah develops and deploys it in creative ways and to an unprecedented degree concerning specifically the Babylonian exiles.[6] At several points in the text, Second Isaiah speaks of the anticipated return of exiled Judeans, drawing innovatively upon the language and imagery of the pentateuchal exodus narrative. His skilful and subtle use of allusion[7] is especially evident in Isaiah 43:16–21, the first of three passages of interest to us:

> Thus says Yhwh,
> Who sets a way in the sea,
> A path in the mighty waters,

Who brings forth chariotry and horses,
Warrior and soldier together.
They lie down, they shall not arise,
They are extinguished, quenched like a wick.
Do not remember the first things,
And the ancient things do not consider carefully.
I am about to do a new thing.
It's happening now, do you not know it?
Indeed, I shall set a way in the desert, rivers in the waste.
The beasts of the fields will honor me, the jackals and ostriches.
For I have placed water in the desert, rivers in the waste,
To water my people, my chosen,
The people whom I formed for myself,
That they might recount my praises. (my translation)

This passage begins with a clear allusion to the exodus from Egypt, with the author drawing on both the Priestly prose narrative of Exodus 14 and the old poem of Exodus 15:1b-18. Though the terms "way" and "path" are not drawn directly from the P narrative of Exodus 14, the idea of such a route through the sea certainly is, as are the pair "chariotry" and "horses" *(rekeb wāsûs)* (cf. Exod 14:23). At the same time, the poet draws upon the countertradition in Exodus 15, most significantly in the final statement of the pericope, in which Yhwh speaks of "the people whom I formed for myself," an unmistakable allusion to Exodus 15:16: "the people whom you created."[8] Thus, multiple exodus textual traditions are brought to bear on the poet's contemporary situation, and the anticipated return of the exiles to Jerusalem is subtly cast as a new exodus through the simple move of describing them as "the people whom I formed for myself," alluding directly and unmistakably to the Song of the Sea, and through the paralleling of "a way in the sea" *(bayyām derek)* and "a way in the desert" *(bammidbār derek).*[9] Furthermore, the surpassing nature of the "new thing" that Yhwh is about to do is conveyed by the command not to remember or dwell upon the past, even though the past has been made to inform the present in a creative and innovative way.[10] To forget about the exodus from Egypt is a rather jarring recommendation in a biblical context suffused with exodus language and imagery, and it underscores nicely the novel and exciting nature of what Yhwh is about to do for the exiles.

Isaiah 51:9–11 is a second instance of the use of exodus imagery to provide a casting for events after 539. In this text, the poet utilizes not only the exodus tradition but also the conflict myth that informs it,[11] when he calls upon Yhwh to act again for his people's benefit:

Awake, awake, dress on strength, O Arm of Yhwh!
Awake as in ancient days, generations of antiquity!
Was it not you who cut up Rahab, who pierced the dragon?

Was it not you who dried up sea, the waters of the great deep?
Who set a way (in) the depths of the sea for the redeemed to pass?
The ransomed of Yhwh will return,
They will come to Zion with a cry of joy,
Eternal rejoicing will be upon their heads,
Joy and rejoicing shall meet (them),
Sorrow and groaning will flee.

After having alluded to Yhwh's cosmic victory over the sea dragon Rahab, the text shifts to the victory over Egypt at the Sea of Reeds and the passing of Israel, described as "the redeemed," through the sea. The text then moves seamlessly from the exodus to the anticipated return of the exiles from Babylon to Jerusalem. The return to the land is cast as a new exodus through the lining up of the two events in the text, and especially through the use of the term "ransomed of Yhwh" (*pedûyê yhwh*) to describe the people in exile, an expression close in meaning to "redeemed," (*gěʾûlîm*) and one used of Israelites in an exodus context in texts such as Deuteronomy 7:8; 2 Samuel 7:23 and Micah 6:4.[12] Just as Yhwh defeated the mythic foe and redeemed his people in Egypt, providing a way through the sea, so Yhwh has ransomed them now and will bring them to Zion from Babylon. The anticipated new exodus is by implication an event at least on par with both the mythic victory over the sea dragon and the original exodus from Egypt. Yhwh's redemptive activity known from the past continues in the present.

The third and last text concerning the new exodus that I shall discuss is Isaiah 52:11–12:

Depart, depart, go forth from there!
Do not touch anything unclean!
Go forth from its midst, purify yourselves,
O bearers of the vessels of Yhwh.
For you will not go forth in haste (*beḥippāzôn*),
You will not go in flight,
For Yhwh is going before you,
The god of Israel will be your rearguard.

The connection of the return from Babylon to the exodus is established in this text very subtly through the use of the rare expression "in haste" (*beḥippāzôn*), which, aside from this passage, occurs only in an exodus context, playing a central role in the Passover legislation in Exodus 12:11 and Deuteronomy 16:3. In Exodus 12:11, we are told that Israelites should eat the Passover sacrifice "in haste," meaning with loins girded, shoes on, and rod in hand; in Deuteronomy 16:3, unleavened bread is to be eaten with the Passover sacrifice for seven days, "for in haste you went forth from the land of Egypt." But in Isaiah 52:12, in contrast to the original exodus, the people will not go forth in

haste, suggesting that the new exodus will be superior to the old because it will
not be characterized by the element of rushed flight that is central to the various
extant traditions of the exodus from Egypt.[13] This strikes me as a rather sharp
and perhaps unprecedented critique of the original exodus, zeroing in on what
the prophet apparently sees as its great fault: its haste. Such an implicit criticism
of Yhwh's past salvific work is an effective way to exalt his anticipated act of
redemption, emphasizing the uniqueness of what is to come. The prophet
seems to imply that with the new exodus, Yhwh will perfect his liberating
activity on behalf of Israel.

Pentateuchal exodus materials—narrative, poetic, and legal—were drawn
upon by Second Isaiah to construct a vision of Yhwh's anticipated acts of
salvation on behalf of the exiles in Babylon. The prophet's descriptions of this
new "exodus" are not only shaped by the account of the exodus from Egypt, but
the two events are compared and contrasted, with the new exodus cast as
superior to the old at several points. The prophet's artistry is particularly evident in the way he draws upon resonant language (e.g., "in haste") or arranges
materials to create a series of parallels between "then" and "now" that establish
a strong linkage between the fate of the Israel of the past and that of the Israel of
the present. The new exodus texts of Second Isaiah are a striking instance of the
way in which an individual creative voice might be recovered through the critical study of the biblical text. Though we do not know the name of the prophet,
and his locus is not entirely clear, there is little dispute about the dating of his
oracles (c. 539 or soon after), or the authorship of the three passages themselves.[14] But does such an analysis bring us closer to the prophet's inner life? We
certainly learn that the prophet is a literate, close reader of the exodus tradition
and one unafraid to marshal, manipulate, and even critique it in the service of
his particular program: the exhortation of the exiles to prepare for a return to
Jerusalem. He dares to make apparently unprecedented and even outrageous
claims about the surpassing nature of the new exodus and the inferiority of the
old. And it is possible that the prophet's intrepid assertion of the superior
nature of Yhwh's anticipated act of redemption served as a model for others
several decades later who would make similar claims about the superiority of
the new temple in Jerusalem (e.g., Hag 2:9). But we cannot know what motivated the prophet's daring declarations, nor can we know anything about the
thought processes that led Second Isaiah to make them. Did he believe in the
surpassing nature of Yhwh's new act of redemption, or was he using hyperbole
in a calculated way as a tool to encourage the people to abandon mourning and
prepare for a return to Zion? Did he really think that the exodus of old was a
flawed liberation because the people had to leave quickly? Unhappily, these
questions, intriguing as they are, must remain unanswered, given the limits of
our knowledge of the prophet's thoughts and motivations. I simply cannot
think of a way to gain access to such information.

Jeremiah 31:27–28 is another case in which we can identify a distinct, individual creative voice in the biblical text. These verses are part of a larger collection of hopeful oracles found in Jeremiah 30–31 concerning the future of Israel and Judah.[15] Though it is clear that verses 27–28 postdate the disasters of 587, we cannot speak with any confidence about the identity or locus of the person responsible for their composition, though it seems quite likely that the author had some connection to what survived of Jeremiah's circle and was writing at a time of hope in some kind of restoration, possibly around 539. This anonymous author, with consummate exegetical skill, produced an oracle of Yhwh that radically reinterprets the last verse of Jeremiah's call narrative in light of the two verses following it:

> "Behold, the days are coming"—oracle of Yhwh—"when I shall sow the House of Israel and the House of Judah (with) human seed and the seed of beasts. And just as I watched over them [*šāqadtî ʿălêhem*] to uproot and to pull down, to throw down, to destroy and to do evil, so I will watch over them [*ʾešqōd ʿalêhem*] to build and to plant," oracle of Yhwh. (Jer 31:27–28)

In the final verse of Jeremiah's call narrative (1:10), the prophet, exalted by Yhwh, is given power over nations and kingdoms to act destructively and constructively: "See, I have appointed you today over nations and over kingdoms, to uproot and to pull down, to destroy and to throw down, to build and to plant." The two following verses represent a shift to the first of a series of symbolic visions: "The word of Yhwh came to me as follows: 'What do you see, Jeremiah?' And I said, 'I see a rod of almond [*šāqēd*].' And Yhwh said to me, 'You see well, for I am watching [*šōqēd ʾănî*] over my word to accomplish it.'" Through the use of a pun, the almond rod is made to symbolize Yhwh's attentiveness to the accomplishment of his oracles, an ominous promise in the literary context, given the condemnation and images of destruction that immediately follow. The author of Jeremiah 31:27–28 has taken the series of infinitives of the last verse of Jeremiah's call narrative, illustrative of Jeremiah's power over nations and kingdoms, detached them from their original context, and understood them, not in relation to the prophet's international exaltation by Yhwh, but as a series of promises concerning Israel and Judah, past and future.[16] The influence of 1:11–12 is evident in the use of the rare verb *šqd*, "to watch over," applied to the people of Israel and Judah in 31:28. Whereas in 1:11–12 Yhwh is watching over his word to accomplish it, in 31:28 he has watched over the people to punish them through destruction ("to uproot and to pull down . . . ") and will watch over them now to prosper them ("to build and to plant"). The author's creativity is especially evident in his understanding of the last two infinitives in the series in Jeremiah 1:10 as a promise of future restoration and flourishing after destruction has been accomplished. Yhwh has promised to accomplish his word, and building and planting, like destroying, are understood as part of that word with respect to Israel and Judah.[17]

As with the new exodus material in the work of Second Isaiah, one can identify striking elements of the author's originality and artistry from the text, but it is not possible to speak confidently of the motivations underlying the author's claim regarding Yhwh's past promises to the people. It is not even possible to be certain that "to build and to plant" is intended by the author to be a reference to a return to Judah and Jerusalem. Israel and Judah will prosper and increase in the future, says the author, because Yhwh has promised it, but he does not suggest where this will happen. Even if we were to assume that the author understood sowing human and animal seed and building and planting as references to a return and rebuilding of Jerusalem and Judah, and that the text was produced in the period just after 539, we cannot speak of what in particular the author sought to accomplish through the casting of this oracle of Yhwh. Did he, like Second Isaiah, wish to exhort the people for the sake of stimulating a return to the land? Was he trying to raise money for the venture?[18] Was it some combination of motivations such as these, or was there another motivation underlying the author's exegesis? As with Second Isaiah, our ability to answer such questions is constrained by our ignorance of the author's thoughts and motivations. And our uncertainty about the author's historical context and even his understanding of "to build and to plant" and the sowing of human and animal seed further complicates any interpretation we might develop of his possible motives and interests. Again, we are stymied by our own ignorance and have no way to escape from it.

Yet another example of an individual creative voice in the biblical text is the author of Ezekiel 47:22–23, a passage that envisions a re-division of the land of Israel into inheritance portions as a component of the restoration of the people after their return from exile.[19] The verses read as follows:

> You shall assign it (by lot) as inheritance portions for yourselves and for the resident aliens who reside in your midst who have fathered children in your midst. They shall be for you like the natives among the children of Israel; with you they shall receive inheritance portions in the midst of the tribes of Israel. In the tribe with which the alien resides, there you shall assign his patrimonial share.

This passage, apparently from an innovative voice within the Holiness School, is remarkable in its radical re-envisioning of Israelite social structure. For now the resident alien who has fathered children in Israel, formerly excluded from the lineage-patrimony system, will have a share in that system, receiving a patrimonial land grant just as native Israelites do. As a result, the status category "resident alien" is all but eliminated from the social system, except, presumably, for that minority of aliens who have not fathered children in Israel. No earlier text dealing with resident aliens goes this far to assimilate them. Other Holiness passages, which go to lengths to emphasize the cultic equality of the native Israelite and the circumcised resident alien (e.g., Exod 12:48), never advocate the outright elimination of the social category "resident alien." Yet recognizable Holiness idiom is deployed by the author of Ezekiel 47:22–23 to go beyond previous Holiness views on this subject.

The voice of Ezekiel 47:22–23 is certainly distinct, creative, even radical in its vision. Yet, as with the previous texts examined, we are only able to guess what might have motivated the individual responsible for the text in question to re-envision Israelite society in such a fundamental way. Was it concern to eliminate the social disadvantages of resident aliens as a group? Was the author's vision motivated by a desire to increase the size of Israel by adding to the people resident aliens who had married Israelite women?[20] Did some other, now wholly obscure motivation inspire this innovative program? Unhappily, no satisfactory answer to these questions is ever likely to emerge from our wrestling with this text, given the nature and limitations of the data. We can state with confidence that the author wished to change the status of resident aliens who had fathered children in Israel, but we cannot say what motivated this desire on the author's part.

What can be concluded from this brief survey? I have argued that we cannot even begin to speak about the self in antiquity without first identifying distinct individual voices in the texts that survive. Happily, such voices sometimes stand out on account of their creativity, as in the three sixth-century examples discussed. Though the voices speaking are public constructions, their artistry points nonetheless to aspects of the individuality that lies behind them. Second Isaiah emerges from a consideration of his deployment and manipulation of the exodus tradition as an intrepid commentator on contemporary events and past traditions. His daring assertions about both the original exodus and the anticipated return from Babylon suggest a bold character behind the public voice. Yet the aims and interests that lie behind Second Isaiah's audacity remain obscure to us. When he claims that the new exodus will surpass the old, is he using hyperbole to achieve his programmatic ends, or is this really what he believes? If we are to speak in a serious way about the self, the inner life, the subjective experience of an ancient personage such as Second Isaiah, we must be able to answer a question such as this. Yet we cannot offer anything more than pure speculation about Second Isaiah's thought processes, his fears, even his strategy to achieve his program. And Second Isaiah is exceptional in that we can place him with some confidence in a particular historical period. Most scholars agree that he was writing from Babylon, and we know something about his program from the extensive textual materials that are almost universally attributed to him by scholars.

The same is not true of the author of Jeremiah 31:28. When and where he is writing is somewhat less evident, and we cannot even say whether he expected and supported a return of Judeans to their land or some other kind of restoration, let alone speak of his motivations. The radical social visionary of Ezekiel 47:22–23, like Second Isaiah, has a clear enough program, but again, we cannot know what motivated his advocacy of a near total dissolution of the social category "resident alien." So at best we are left with suggestive hints about our writers' motivations, aims, inner conflicts, personalities. Given the limitations of what we are able to discover about the inner life of the ancient persons whose creative expression has been under consideration here, all talk of accessing the self in texts of the Hebrew Bible must remain tentative at best.

NOTES

1. John Bright, *Jeremiah* (AB 21; Garden City, N.Y.: Doubleday, 1965), lxv.

2. For a recent, helpful assessment of the historian's task in dealing with emotions and their textual representation, see Barbara H. Rosenwein, "Worrying About Emotions in History," *American Historical Review* 107 (2002): 821–45. On 839, n. 70, Rosenwein speaks of the difficulties confronting anyone—including contemporary anthropologists and psychotherapists—seeking access to the inner life of another. With respect to the textual representation of emotions, she writes that "even the most seemingly intimate diary can give us only an approximation of the emotional life of its subject. We cannot know for sure (and often neither can the diarist) if the feelings expressed are purely conventional, idealized, manipulative, or deeply felt."

A recent work of theoretical importance on the emotions is William M. Reddy, *The Navigation of Feeling: A Framework for the History of Emotions* (Cambridge: Cambridge University Press, 2001), initially brought to my attention by Rosenwein. Drawing on the insights of recent work in cognitive psychology and anthropology of the emotions, the author builds on his own previous research, constructing a bold, broadly interdisciplinary theory of emotions intended to accommodate cultural variation, historical change, and the one aspect of emotional expression that he believes is universal: that "emotion and emotional expression interact in a dynamic way" (xii). At various points, Reddy emphasizes our inability to render complex emotions in words because of their complexity, because of the poverty of language, and because rendering complex emotions in words may affect the emotions themselves, transforming them (e.g., 90, 102, 108).

A recent, theoretically sophisticated discussion of the representation of the self from the perspective of qualitative sociology is Lynn Davidman, *Motherloss* (Berkeley: University of California Press, 2000), 43–55. Davidman emphasizes the important role played by normative social discourses as well as the limits of memory in the construction of biographical narratives by her interviewees. I am grateful to Lynn Davidman for reading a draft of this paper and making suggestions toward its improvement.

3. It ought to be noted that the writer of Jeremiah's confessions draws heavily on topoi of various sorts, even at points that seem uniquely personal at first blush. Jeremiah's talk of his pain, his shame, and his persecution at the hands of his enemies; his call to Yhwh to deliver him from pursuers; and his wish that his tormentors be punished, are all motifs found in the psalms of complaint and related material. Even his self-cursing in Jer 20:14–18 finds a close thematic (though not idiomatic) parallel in Job 3, suggesting that a shared literary topos underlies the two texts. Yet there are also some elements in the confessions that appear to be unrelated to literary topoi, e.g., Yhwh's periodic role in the confessions as an adversary of Jeremiah. On this in particular, see further the discussion of Robert C. Culley, "The Confessions of Jeremiah and Traditional Discourse," in *"A Wise and Discerning Mind": Essays in Honor of Burke O. Long* (ed. S. M. Olyan and R. C. Culley; BJS 325; Providence, R.I.: Brown University Press, 2000), 80–81. The presence of topoi in Jeremiah's confessions is indicative of the degree

to which an ancient "autobiographical" narrative—like the contemporary narratives addressed by Davidman—may be shaped by normative social discourses.

4. I want to emphasize that I do not simply equate the individual voices extant in these texts with the individuals responsible for constructing those voices. My authorial voice in this paper may reflect aspects of my character or self, but it remains a purposefully fashioned public representation; it is to a large degree the voice I want to present to my peers.

5. Though some might challenge the very notion of a "self" in antiquity, biblical texts do bear witness to the idea of an individual having an inner life of thoughts and feelings not immediately accessible to other persons. This is implied in 1 Kgs 8:39, which states that Yhwh alone knows the mind (literally, the heart) of all humans. Ps 139:1–6, 23, is similar in its thrust, stating that Yhwh knows a petitioner's thoughts even before they are spoken. I am indebted to Ross Kraemer for reminding me of this material.

6. Scholars have long recognized the importance of the new exodus as a motif in Second Isaiah. Works of interest on this topic include Walther Zimmerli, "Der 'neue Exodus' in der Verkündigung der beiden grossen Exilspropheten," in *Gottes Offenbarung: Gesammelte Aufsätze zum Alten Testament* (TB 19; Munich: C. Kaiser, 1963), 192–204, esp. 197–201; Bernard W. Anderson, "Exodus Typology in Second Isaiah," in *Israel's Prophetic Heritage: Essays in Honor of James Muilenburg* (ed. Bernard W. Anderson and Walter J. Harrelson; New York: Harper, 1962), 177–95; Carroll Stuhlmueller, *Creative Redemption in Deutero-Isaiah* (AB 43; Rome: Pontifical Biblical Institute, 1970), 59–98; and Patricia T. Willey, *Remember the Former Things: The Recollection of Previous Texts in Second Isaiah* (SBLDS 161; Atlanta: Scholars Press, 1997), 72–74, 132–37, and passim. Scholars have seen some precedent for Second Isaiah's new exodus motif in earlier materials such as Hosea and Jeremiah (e.g., Hos 11:10–11; Jer 16:14–15). Though texts such as these allude to the earlier exodus tradition in their new exodus formulations, the new exodus itself is not as well developed or as creatively deployed as it is in Second Isaiah. As Stuhlmueller observes, Second Isaiah's "references [to a new exodus] . . . are numerically more impressive and theologically richer than those of any prophet before him" (66).

7. The theme of allusion in Second Isaiah is explored insightfully in Benjamin D. Sommer, *A Prophet Reads Scripture: Allusion in Isaiah 40–66* (Contraversions; Stanford, Calif.: Stanford University Press, 1998). Sommer argues that the prophet's originality is found in his allusive deployment of older traditions (166).

8. Michael Fishbane, *Biblical Interpretation in Ancient Israel* (Oxford: Clarendon, 1985), 364 has anticipated me in noting the direct relationship between Isa 43:21 and Exod 15:16.

9. Stuhlmueller draws attention to Second Isaiah's frequent use of "way" *(derek)* in descriptions of the new exodus (40:3; 42:16; 43:16, 19; 49:9, 11; 51:10). See *Creative Redemption,* 67.

10. Others have pointed this out (e.g., Claus Westermann, *Isaiah 40–66: A Commentary* [OTL; Philadelphia: Westminster, 1969], 127; Stuhlmueller, *Creative Redemption,* 70).

11. On the relationship of Exodus 15:1b–18 and P's sea splitting motif to the conflict myth, see Frank Moore Cross, *Canaanite Myth and Hebrew Epic: Essays in the History of the Religion of Israel* (Cambridge: Harvard University Press, 1973), 112–44.

12. On the roots *pdh* and *gʾl* and their relationship, see J. J. Stamm, "*gʾl* to redeem," *TLOT* 1:293.

13. See also Exod 12:33 (J) in addition to Exod 12:11 (P) and Deut 16:3. Anderson, anticipating me, makes a similar observation ("Exodus Typology," 191), and many others have noted the allusion to the Passover legislation in Isa 52:12. A useful recent discussion of Pentateuchal allusions in Isa 52:11–12 is to be found in Willey, *Remember the Former Things,* 132–37.

14. Scholars are divided on the question of the locus of Second Isaiah. Though a majority believes Second Isaiah was active in Babylon, a number of recent works argue for a locus in Judah. For the latter, see, e.g., Hans M. Barstad, *The Babylonian Captivity of the Book of Isaiah: "Exilic" Judah and the Provenance of Isaiah 40–55* (Oslo: Novus Forlag, 1997).

15. On the relationship of these verses to what precedes and follows them, see the discussion of William McKane, *A Critical and Exegetical Commentary on Jeremiah* (2 vols.; ICC; Edinburgh: T. & T. Clark, 1996) 2:812–17.

16. McKane, op. cit., 814, notes a number of the scholars who have recognized a relationship between 1:10–12 and 31:28. Several have also noticed the transfer of agency from the prophet in 1:10 to Yhwh in 31:28.

17. On the late-seventh- and sixth-century exegetical "career" of Jer 1:10 more generally, see Saul M. Olyan, "'To Uproot and to Pull Down, to Build and to Plant': Jer 1:10 and Its Earliest Interpreters," in *HESED VE-EMET: Studies in Honor of Ernest S. Frerichs* (ed. J. Magness and S. Gittin; BJS 320; Atlanta: Scholars Press, 1998), 63–72.

18. On the fundraising dimension of the first return, see Ezra 1:4, 6.

19. On the unit Ezek 47:13–48:29, of which 47:22–23 is a component part, see W. Zimmerli, *Ezekiel 2: A Commentary on the Book of the Prophet Ezekiel ch. 25–48* (ed. Paul D. Hanson and Leonard J. Greenspan; trans. James D. Martin; Hermeneia; Philadelphia: Fortress, 1983), 526–27. As Zimmerli notes, vv. 22–23 are likely an expansion on the text (p. 526). I treat Ezek 47:22–23 from a different perspective in *Rites and Rank: Hierarchy in Biblical Representations of Cult* (Princeton, N.J.: Princeton University Press, 2000), 73–74.

20. This is the implication of the qualification "who have fathered children in Israel."

—3—

Paul and the Slave Self

J. ALBERT HARRILL

Several essays in this volume reflect on the accessibility of the "self" in ancient religious sources by introducing the notion of voice. Saul Olyan, for example, examines Second Isaiah, Jeremiah, and Ezekiel as case studies to argue against the "recovery" of an ancient religious self—the motivations and personal intentions of a Hebrew prophet's "inner life"—by simply collecting passages together that speak in the first person singular. What at first sounds to us like the clear, unmediated, and authentic voice of the prophet becomes in the end a literary construction. The textual "I," therefore, is not a secure index of the self within language. The value of such close readings of religious sources is that they offer historical explanations, which may close some possibilities in interpretation but also open the way for others. Although the first person singular may not always refer to the writer, making the distinction between the discursive "I" and the authorial "self" nonetheless brings greater methodological clarity to the use of evidence.

This finding connects to the thesis of my essay here. In the New Testament, we find a comparable case study of another biblical "I." Paul writes:

> So I find it to be a law that when I want to do what is good, evil lies close at hand.
> For I delight in the law of God in my innermost self [*kata ton esō anthrōpon*],
> but I see in my members another law at war with the law of my mind, making
> me captive to the law of sin that dwells in my members. Wretched man that I
> am! Who will rescue me from this body of death? Thanks be to God through
> Jesus Christ our Lord! So then, with my mind I am a slave to the law of God, but
> with my flesh I am a slave to the law of sin. (Rom 7:21–25, NRSV)

This statement appears in one of the most important—and controversial—passages on the self in the Christian Bible: Romans 7. The traditional reading, which goes back to Augustine, credits Paul with centering his attention on the split internal to the individual and the resulting incapacity of the self to carry out its own will. Augustine first took the passage to depict the introspective conscience of the unregenerate human and later came to identify Paul's words, assumed to be autobiographic, with his own agonizing struggle against sin, described in the *Confessions*. Interpreting his own conversion retrospectively in light of the Platonic myth of the soul (its alienation from the good and its return), Augustine created from Romans 7 a normative model of the religious self that in Western culture has become the archetype for inquiry into the individual, influencing Thomas Aquinas, Martin Luther, John Calvin, and the Protestant Reformation, as well as Søren Kierkegaard and Sigmund Freud.[1] Biblical scholars advancing this psychologizing model of the self assume that the mythic picture of bondage and helplessness in Romans 7 is direct testimony of Paul's interior, subjective religious life. The claim is that the voice is both personal and realistic.[2]

Viewing Paul's letters from the perspective of Greco-Roman literary conventions, however, sharpens the problem of this psychologizing approach to the ancient Christian self. One of the successes of modern biblical criticism is the discovery that there is little indication that Paul understood himself or the typical convert to be a person who had previously agonized under a subjective sense of incapacitating guilt. In the rare places where Paul speaks about his former life in Judaism, he does so with pride (Gal 1:13–14; Phil 3:4–6).[3] It is therefore unlikely that the first person singular in Romans 7:7–25 is Paul voicing his inner struggle of his preconversion experience, or that it includes the apostle at all.[4] The subject is the fictive "I," specifically, a technique of "speech-in-character" familiar from Greco-Roman rhetoric and literature.[5]

Speech-in-character *(prosōpopoiia)* is the introduction of a character whose speech represents, not that of the author, but that of another person or invented persona.[6] The technique played a central role in the preliminary exercises of rhetoric in formal Roman education, which closely followed Greek teaching methods. The teacher *(grammaticus* or *rhetor)* would ask the student to compose poetry or prose, for the purposes of recitation, by imagining what a certain type of person would say to another in a given situation. The identification of the speaking voice and characters formed particular reading habits, attuning the student's ear to standard interpretive conventions of oral speech used in written texts and teaching him to ask in every passage, "Who is speaking?" a critical skill in an ancient culture where readers faced texts containing dialogues that had no punctuation, no word division, and nothing to indicate change of speakers. Importantly for our study of Romans 7, the exercise figured prominently for training in letter writing.

The technique of speech-in-character is commonplace in Greco-Roman literature. The best evidence comes from Cicero, Quintilian, and the extant handbook *progymnasmata* ("preliminary rhetorical exercises").[7] Aelius Theon of Alexandria, a rhetor of the first century c.e., explains in his handbook that speech-in-character consists of both cases in which one invents through conventional diction the character *(ēthos)* of a known person *(prosōpon)*, and cases in which one invents both the *ēthos* and the person. In the latter case, the student conforms the words of the invented persona—the self—to fit the moral habits and inner dispositions of a recognizable stock type, often taken from Greco-Roman drama, such as a husband, soldier, braggart, barbarian, or the slave.[8] While to me the argument that Paul employs this latter case of speech-in-character to invent both the *ēthos* and persona of the "I" in Romans 7 is convincing, what remains unclear in this reading is why a *slave* is chosen for the persona.[9]

Paul writes, "I delight in the law of God in my innermost self [*kata ton esō anthrōpon*], but I see in my members another law at war with the law of my mind, making me captive to the law of sin that dwells in my members" (Rom 7:22). As many commentators have shown, Paul refers to the Greek philosophical idea of an "inner" versus an "outer" human being, an idea of the self that originated from Platonic tradition, going back to the ninth book of the *Republic*.[10] Scholarship emphasizes that although the Platonic tradition identifies the "inner human being" with the *psychē* ("soul"), *nous* ("mind"), or *pneuma* ("spirit"), Paul considers the "inner human being" not to have a higher status than the "outer human being," but thinks that both are two aspects of the same *anthrōpos,* a non-dualistic entity.[11] What commentators overlook in their analysis of "Pauline anthropology" is that Paul does not describe a generic or "typical" *anthrōpos,* but one pointedly characterized as enslaved, having specific connotations in the slaveholding culture of Roman imperial society. In the rush to analyze the Platonic "background" of Pauline theology, there has been no serious inquiry into why Paul chooses the persona of the slave as his model of the *anthrōpos* containing both an "outer" and "innermost self."

At first glance, the slave seems an unlikely model of the *anthrōpos,* if we follow the formal definitions of the slave in Greek philosophy. Aristotle and his epigones claim the slave not to have the very "inner self" that Paul's speech-in-character requires. Aristotle writes that because the slave is deficient in many human essentials such as emotion, virtue, reason, and deliberative powers, the slave is only a partial (outer, bodily) self whose actions are incomplete. Since the slave's actions are incomplete, the slave is and ought to be an "animate tool" *(empsychon organon)* of someone else.[12] After arguing the inherent naturalness ("goodness") of slavery, Aristotle raises the subsequent, independent question of whether some slaves are "natural" slaves. His comments on this second topic are, to be sure, scattered and inconsistent, but his overarching theme is clear: the relationship of master and slave in the family is the paradigm that grounds and naturalizes all human relationships of domination.[13] Later Hellenistic and

Roman writers, particularly among the Peripatetic school, develop Aristotelian ideas of the natural slave into a coherent theory with detailed elaboration and systemization in technical handbooks on physiognomics.[14] In this theory, the slave's body, by virtue of its very anatomy, is biologically built for servitude. The natural slave is a deficient *anthrōpos,* without the faculty of reason, a human subspecies assimilated to irrational beasts requiring taming and domestication.

Greeks in general defined the slave, like the animal, in terms of its body alone. A common word in Greek for "slave" was simply "body" *(sōma);* other ancient terms (in Greek or Latin) included "boy" *(pais, puer),* "rogue" (that is, someone who needs a whipping: *mastigia; verbero),* "garbage" *(katharma),* and "man-footed creature" *(andrapodon),* the last term derived from a common word for cattle *(tetrapodon).*[15] The somatic vocabulary reflects a cultural habit that tended to define the slave by its (my use of neuter is pointed) outer corporality alone—a mere "body." The semantic and philosophical evidence, therefore, makes Paul's case of a speech-in-character, in which an invented slave persona communicates thoughts from his "innermost self" (and not, as we would expect, its flesh or bodily members), curious. Significantly, the passage in Romans 7 expresses no need to argue that "the slave" has an innermost self. It just presumes that a slave character would naturally have one and proceeds with the speech. If Paul expected that his encoded Gentile readers (Rom 1:5–6, 13; 15:15–16) would immediately associate the speech-in-character with a recognizable stock type whose special trademark was the innermost self and would thereby catch his wider meaning about baptism, "the slave" seems a poor choice. In classical Greek philosophy, ideology, and even vocabulary, the slave has neither a self nor an interior experience.[16] The passage does not make sense in the philosophical history-of-ideas context of standard biblical commentary.

Examining Romans 7 in a context wider than Greek philosophy, we find that Paul's choice of an enslaved *anthrōpos* to depict the inner and outer aspects of the religious self becomes more intelligible. Key is attention to different social constructions of the slave in classical culture, focusing on Roman and not Greek (Athenian) ideologies of slavery. The focus on Roman sources serves as a methodological control against exclusive reliance on Aristotle or Plato to interpret the passage and its ideas of slavery. In contrast to Aristotelian ideas of the slave being only an outer "body" without interior rationality or agency, the main Roman (Stoic) ideology required the ideal slave to possess reason and virtue *(logos* and *aretē).*[17]

Roman law recognized the slave to have inner subjectivity and moral agency. Influential on this principle were Stoic ideas of common humanity, organic cosmology, and fate.[18] A condition of fate and not of nature, slavery in Roman legal categorization belonged to the law of nations *(ius gentium),* by which contrary to nature *(contra naturam)* one person is subjected to the power *(dominium)* of another. Remarkably, this case is the only one in the entire extant corpus of Roman private law in which the *ius gentium* and the *ius naturale* are in conflict.[19] The legal material reveals also the enormous importance of slaves in commercial and other acquisitions. The centrality of trusted managerial slaves on rural estates, which Roman agricultural writers emphasize, parallels the urban household situation envisioned in the legal texts.[20] Partly because masters employed their slaves as de facto agents, Roman law lacked a concept of agency in the modern sense of a free person representing another—one reason why a slave was often more useful to his master in business transactions than a free client. The importance in the Roman economy and society of trusted slaves who often worked independently and in locations outside the master's hometown rests on an ideology that the master did not need to supervise every decision a slave agent made. The Roman notion of mastery defined the ideal slave, not in terms of obedience to individual commands of the master, but in terms of having accepted the master's wishes so fully that the slave's innermost self could anticipate the master's wishes and take the initiative. Romans did not want automatons for their slaves.[21]

Roman moral philosophy used the slave automaton and the comedy of its ineffectiveness to teach the art of authority. The *Life of Aesop* offers an illustration. Although the legendary figure of Aesop originates from the early Greek period, the extant biography was written no earlier than the time of the Roman empire. The *Life of Aesop* is a romance based on themes found in the fables, a repository of slave-savant anecdotes about Aesop and his hapless master, Xanthos, a so-called philosopher.[22] A recurring theme of the biography is Aesop's philosophical game of cat and mouse with his master. Xanthos looks for excuses to beat his slave. Aesop, in turn, evades punishment by his ingenious "misunderstandings" of the orders, repeatedly receiving opportunities to lecture his master on the meaning of self-control and proper household authority. This willful misbehavior frustrates Xanthos (and his wife) so completely that Xanthos finally orders Aesop to act like an automaton, to do nothing more or less than what his commands literally tell. Of course, this move only leads to further situation comedy as Aesop takes his master exactly at his word. Going to the baths, Xanthos instructs Aesop, "to pick up the oil flask." Aesop picks up the flask but not the oil. Xanthos orders the slave home to "cook lentil" for a dinner party. Aesop tosses a single legume into the cooking pot. Xanthos tells Aesop to give his dinner guests "something to drink, right from the bath." Aesop returns with a pitcher full of bathing swill. Succeeding in driving Xanthos nearly mad, Aesop explains that his demonstrations are the same a philosopher would use with students: "You shouldn't have been so precise in laying down the law, and I would have served you properly. But don't feel sorry about it, master. The way you decreed the law to me will be useful to you, for it will teach you not to make mistakes in the classroom. Statements that include or exclude too much are no small mistakes." The moral is that one's subordinate has a self. When they want subordinates to act as automatons —that is, without a self—masters have only themselves to blame for the resulting chaos in the household (and in the classroom). To be properly served, the master needs the slave to have agency and to take some initiative from interior subjectivity. The farcical comedy of the *Life of Aesop* teaches the moral philosophy of proper mastery.[23]

That mastery was *auctoritas,* which routed power through patterns of personalized influence (rather than through abstract institutions such as bureaucracy, wage labor, or public office). The Latin term—whose force was something like "influence" or making known one's will based on mutuality—was, as the Greek senator and historian Dio Cassius remarked, quintessentially Roman and untranslatable (Dio 55.3.5). *Auctoritas* denoted a quality of actual power in the individual person (the *auctor*), granted by the willing compliance of subordinates and the esteem of one's colleagues, in contrast to the transactional power from governmental magistracies, social status, or family name. The value was deeply moral, belonging to the cultural milieu of aristocratic competition in Rome's conflict culture. Roman government was based on the concept.[24]

The emperor Augustus had underscored the term as the central characteristic of his rule, asserting that he "surpassed all others in *auctoritas* while possessing no more official power *(potestas)* than those who were colleagues of his in each magistracy" (*Res Gestae* 34.3).[25] Spectacles of Augustan providential "realities" of power *(imperium)* for awe and emulation filled public space throughout the Roman world, in monumental architecture, art, coinage, epic literature, and the imperial cult. Augustus, whose very name carried religious and divine connotations, was proclaimed the ultimate guarantor *(auctor)* of peace and stability after decades of civil war. By deliberately emphasizing *auctoritas* as his governing concept in the restoration of the *res publica,* Augustus made clear his intention to provide leadership higher and more moral than that of just a functionary or magistrate. He played upon culturally charged themes in both public and private discourse.[26] In that discourse, an aristocratic adult male achieved honor *(dignitas)* and mastery *(auctoritas)* from the successful domination of others. Rome's fundamentally hierarchical society envisaged slavery as the absolute in a continuum of domination and subordination.[27]

This personalized view of power recognized subjectivity in the slave. *Auctoritas* was achieved in specific, concrete events in which the slave expressed acceptance of the master's point of view so fully as to anticipate the master's wishes. Rather than merely following individual orders in mechanical fashion, the good slave *(servus frugi)* completed and developed what the master had only suggested or even unconsciously desired—a task that in the practice of Roman slaveholding encouraged the actual slave to develop moral intuition.[28] This social construction imagined the slave with an internal faculty of assent, a function of reason. The ideology reflects the Stoic philosophy of *prohairesis* that detached an essential self from the outer body (the flesh) and identified it with an interior moral subject understood to be personal and individualized.[29] The Stoics stressed the importance of the self to such an extent that some scholars are tempted to say that they even discovered the concept.[30]

Personalization of the slave with this kind of subjective self is a central tenant in the Roman discourse of authority. Ancient authors discuss the hard work and constant maintenance that such mastery over a self requires. Epictetus warns his aristocratic students—teenaged masters themselves, and future householders—against allowing their happiness to depend upon the constant obedience of their slaves. "Nothing is got without a price," lectures the Stoic teacher. "And when you call your slave boy, bear in mind that it is possible that he may not heed you, and again, that even if he does heed, he may not do what you want done."[31] In actual practice, mastery does not always work. Slaves do not always conform their innermost self to the master's will. Additionally, the moralist Plutarch recounts the "famous case" of a slave resisting mastery to illustrate a lesson about foolish chatter. Ironically, the case involves an orator. Plutarch writes:

> Pupius Piso, the orator, not wishing to be troubled, ordered his slaves to speak only in answer to questions and not a word alone. Subsequently, wishing to pay honour to Clodius when he was a magistrate, Piso gave orders that he be invited to dinner and prepared what was, we may suppose, a sumptuous banquet. When the hour came, the other guests were present, but Clodius was still expected, and Piso repeatedly sent the slave who regularly carried invitations to see if Clodius was approaching. And when evening came and he was finally despaired of, Piso said to his slave, "See here, did you give him the invitation?" "I did," said the slave. "Why hasn't he come then?" "Because he declined." "Then why didn't you tell me at once?" "Because you didn't ask me that."[32]

The anecdote resembles the episode discussed above in the *Life of Aesop* and is further evidence that the "automaton slave" is a stock comic type. Plutarch goes on to contrast the backtalk of such a "typical Roman slave" with the poetic line an Athenian slave would say to his master: *houtōs men Rōmaikos oiketēs, ho d' Attikos*, the moral of the story being that people often talk in habituated banter rather than from intelligence.

Cicero provides an additional example. He pleads:

> What law, what decree of the senate, what edict of the magistrates, what pact or agreement or even, if I may speak of the civil law, what will, what judgments or stipulations or formulae of agreement and contract could not be weakened and pulled apart, if we wanted to twist the substance to suit the words and leave unaccounted for the intentions, reasoning, and *auctoritas* of those who wrote the document? By god, everyday household language will make nonsense, if we try to pounce on each other's words; ultimately there would be no household authority [*imperium domesticum*] if we allowed our slaves to obey us in accordance with our words, and not comply with what we understand from the words.[33]

Cicero uses the private discourse of household mastery to illustrate by analogy the public discourse of *auctoritas*. He and the other authors above show the prevalence of *auctoritas* in Roman culture across the board, from education and moral philosophy to law, rhetoric, and religious/political ideology.

This cultural context is critical for the interpretation of Romans 7 because Paul uses the ideology of *auctoritas*, with its model of the slave self, to influence his Roman audience. Establishing this thesis requires locating Roman cultural influence not only on Paul himself but also on early Christians broadly, since Paul's encoded audience, though Gentile, is not "Pauline" in the sense of having the apostle as their founder. Paul had not visited Rome and had not established any of the congregations in that city (see Rom 1:10–15). Comprehensive examination of the Roman imperial context of early Christianity is beyond the scope of my exegetical study and hardly needs repeating. As a prelude to the exegesis of Romans 7, one example of what I find to be the best source outside of the Pauline material must suffice: the Parable of the Talents/Pounds.[34]

In Matthew's version, a man "going on a journey" summons three slaves and entrusts talents to each "according to his ability" (Matt 25:15). Predictably, and almost as a setup, the slave having the least ability, and so entrusted only with a single talent (his inherent character flaws made explicit in the narrative's introduction), fails to prove his usefulness and worth. While the slave complies with the literal commands, he is worthless because he has not internalized the master's will, as the ideology of *auctoritas* requires. Ironically, the paralysis causing the slave to act like an automaton stems from fear of merciless punishment for failure to obey, his master being characterized as a "harsh man" (25:24–25). The slave hides the money in a hole, whereas his more able fellows go out and trade with the talents to make more (25:16–18). The master, in Matthew's reasoning, rightly rewards the entrepreneurship of the good slaves, who receive more responsibility in the household and "enter into the joy of their master" (25:21–22), and punishes the bad. "You wicked and lazy slave!" the master yells at the terrified piece of chattel, "You knew, did you not, that I reap where I did not sow, and gather where I did not scatter? Then you ought to have invested the money with the bankers, and on my return I would have receive what was my own with interest" (25:26–27). The master then gives the slave the beating of his life: "As for this worthless slave, throw him into the outer darkness, where there will be weeping and gnashing of teeth," the master employing domestic torturers used regularly for such purpose (25:30).[35]

The author of Matthew makes explicit his contrast of the "good slave" (who shows loyalty to an absent master) and the "bad slave" (who does not), two stock types in tales of *apsente ero* ("when the master's away") familiar from ancient comedy. This contrast echoes what Cicero and Plutarch say above and is a further example story (moral *exemplum*) of the distinctively Roman ideology of *auctoritas*—personalized power channeled through the master's ethos. The bland moralistic division into good and bad, which the slave parables of the

Synoptic Gospels advance, makes the connection to Roman slaveholding ideology (and its stock of comic slave types) even more likely.[36]

The principal concept of *auctoritas* influenced Paul's gospel as well. As did Augustus, Paul claims that the root of his authority is, quite simply, his deeds. Paul connects his authority to apostolic activity (converting Gentiles and establishing congregations) and not to official rights (*exousia;* "power") granted by the title or office of "apostle" (2 Cor 3:1–3; 1 Cor 9:4–6, 12, 18; cf. 1 Cor 8:9).[37] Part of the historical meaning of Paul's letter to the Romans, as Stanley Stowers has shown, comes from imagining how readers in Paul's day would have received this gospel in the context of the Augustan revolution and its developing ideology of declining morality, divine wrath, and hopes of a golden age (compare Rom 1:18–32). Paul's message appealed, not because it introduced new moral values into the wider "pagan" culture, but because it played on politically and culturally charged themes that all readers met daily on the images of coins, in public monuments, and in everyday discourse, transcending ethnic boundaries of Jewish, Greek, and Roman.[38] I argue that Paul integrated the current moral value of *auctoritas* and its particular model of the slave into his gospel to urge a new social allegiance in dialogic relation to the old, pre-converted self.[39] In Romans 7, the Apostle Paul uses the specifically Roman cultural imagination of the slave to help himself and his Gentile audience think through what happens to the religious self, the *anthrōpos*, before and after the ritual of baptism. In other words, to borrow Lévi-Strauss's famous formulation, Paul found slaves "good to think with."[40]

Romans 7 and the Slave Self

Convincing to me is the thesis of Stowers that the *anthrōpos* in Romans 7:7–25 refers to a Gentile, and not a "universal," self. The subject of Romans 7:7–25 is a representation of the Gentile situation described at the outset of the letter (Rom 1:18–32), punished by God for idolatry with slavery to the passions (*epithymiai*). In this way, Paul's speech-in-character appropriates the caricature, in Hellenistic Judaism, of Gentiles as morally degenerate. The perspective is not philosophical anthropology (the human essence) but what we would call ethnic cultural stereotype. Yet, as Stowers continues, the persona Paul so carefully constructs is more specific than "Gentiles." That *anthrōpos* represents someone caught between two cultures, torn between the passions of an idolater and the law of the one true God.[41] Paul, then, depicts the religious quest of his encoded reader—the Gentile attracted to Judaism, who undergoes (and should undergo) an agonizing crisis of identity, especially when confronted with the Pauline gospel.

The importance of these exegetical issues lies in the fact that they raise directly the question of what interpretative categories we should use for an adequate reading of Paul's letter. Whereas Stowers focuses on the moral philosophy of self-mastery, and others examine the presence of Platonic themes, my aim is to relocate the issue of the religious self in Romans 7 from a predominately philosophical question to one that stems from considerations of mastery and slavery in Roman ideologies of power. I take the prevailing metaphor in the passage seriously. I am challenging New Testament scholarship that downplays or dismisses outright the importance of the slave language.[42]

Paul incorporates Roman slaveholding ideology, the cultivation of the interior motivation of the slave by *auctoritas,* into his discussion of baptism (Rom 6:6–14) and into his speech-in-character (Rom 7:14–25). The opening chapters establish interior motivation as a central theme in Paul's definition of the religious self. First, a set of antitheses (concerning God's impartiality) underscores the point: "visible" *(en tō phanerō)* versus "in secret" *(en tō kryptō);* "on the fleshly surface" *(en sarki)* versus "from the heart" *(kardias);* "literal" *(en grammati)* versus "spiritual" *(en pneumati)* (Rom 2:28). Next, Paul reassures his readers that Christ had redeemed them from a curse: by agreeing to go to and die on a cross, Christ had displayed trust *(pistis)* in God and his promises, and in so doing had generated a proper relationship with God on the model of Abraham's faithfulness to God and the covenant (Rom 3:21–33). The term *pistis* ("faith") here carries the sense of faithfulness or trust ("obedience"), not "belief" as in the traditional theological reading.[43] Paul then encourages his readers to think about their participation in the Christ event during the ritual of baptism, knowledge being an explicit warrant for the exhortations: "We know that our old self was crucified with him, so that the body of sin might be destroyed, and we are no longer enslaved to sin [*douleuein hēmas tē hamartia*]" (6:6).[44] Paul asks rhetorically:

> Do you not know that if you present yourselves to anyone as obedient slaves [*doulous eis hypakoēn*], you are slaves of the one whom you obey, either of sin, which leads to death, or of obedience [*hypakoēs*], which leads to (God's) righteousness [*dikaiosynēn*]? But thanks be to God that you, having once been slaves of sin [*douloi tēs hamartias*], have become obedient from the heart [*hypēkousate de ek kardias*] to the standard of the teaching to which you were entrusted, and that you, having been set free from sin [*eleutherōthentes de apo tēs hamartias*], have become slaves of (God's) righteousness [*edoulōthēte tē dikaiosynē*]. (6:16–18)

The slave speech-in-character of chapter 7 follows, leading into chapter 8 where Paul expresses apocalyptic knowledge that "creation itself will be set free from its slavery to decay and will obtain freedom" (Rom 8:21). The whole section (Romans 6–8) argues against Gentile adherence to the law by pairing the law with slavery under sin.

In this context, sin is not something the self does (as in a "crime"), but is a personalized demonic power that victimizes the self by residing in the self's fleshly "members" (where sinful passions are located) when the self hears the holy law.[45] The Gentile self remains devoted to the Mosaic Torah but is nonetheless powerless to achieve what it wants, even doing the very opposite of what it avoids (7:18–19). The conflict is not between two different selves, nor two selves at different levels—such as the "rational self" *(nous)* and "irrational self" *(sōma)* in the Platonic tradition—as though one were under the power of sin and the other not. Both "innermost self" and "members" are two facets of the same self that is "sold under sin" (6:14).

Paul does not, then, simply repeat Platonizing concepts of the self but thinks in terms of a whole *anthrōpos* (both *nous* and *sōma,* but without the *sarx*) that will be saved. To be sure, there is an apocalyptic dualism, but not in anthropology. Paul speaks about two different laws—the holy law of God, and a demonic law (an anti-Torah, not just "another law") called the "law of sin," which resides in the outer members of the religious self. The speech-in-character declares allegiance and delight in the first (7:22) and then reports discovery of the second (7:23). The eschatological hope of salvation is not *release of the soul* from the body but *redemption of the self* (the pneumatic *sōma*) from the "law of sin and death" (8:2) for enslavement to God, where it belongs.[46] The problem is not slavery per se, but slavery to the wrong master.

The slavery is also partial and chaotic. The demonic power of sin possesses external "members" but not the "innermost" part of the religious self, which still delights in the law of God. For this reason, Paul reminds his readers that baptism does not bring a complete end of sinning (in the judicial sense of committing crimes and vice; hence, the moral exhortation in Romans 14–15) or manumission from sin itself (in the personalized sense of a demonic power). The apocalyptic drama imagined has the religious self caught in the eschatological tension of "already and not yet," forced to work against its will like a captured war slave, but already experiencing partial effects of God's redemption because of baptism.[47]

Paul's letter to the Romans participates in and is implicated in the particularly Roman ideology of *auctoritas.* The apocalyptic drama personalizes God's power and authority over sin and other demonic war enemies. Gentile converts are captives of sin, slaves whom God has now "bought [back] with a price" (see 1 Cor 6:20; 7:23). In Paul's gospel, Christ had demonstrated *pistis* ("faithfulness"; "trust"; "obedience") to God. Converts must likewise accept God's point of view so fully as to anticipate the divine personal will and to make it effective in the world, even when the eschaton is not yet present. This theme corresponds to the classical Roman topos of the "faithful slave" who acts and dies on behalf of her or his master *(de fide servorum).*[48] Baptism celebrates the concrete ritual moment in which the catechumen moves away from identification of the subject (or "I," the normative locus) with him- or herself and toward identification of that subject with Christ. Comparable to the Stoic theory of *oikeiōsis* ("appropriation," or "taking as one's own"), this transference of subjectivity is believed by Paul to be a direct consequence of a transformation in

the individual self. The Pauline view of God's mastery recognizes the subjectivity and agency of the converted religious self and sees that true authority
consists, not in obeying individual commands—as in the automaton who mis-
understands and who obeys only literal instructions of the law—but in total
directness toward God.[49]

Paul's overarching combat language echoes themes not only in Jewish
apocalyptic eschatology but also in Roman military culture that symbolized
slavery with the language of "death" and "life." The classic statement comes
from Roman law and its discussion on the etymological root of the Latin word
for slave: "slaves [servi] are so called because commanders generally sell the
people they capture and thereby save [servare] them instead of killing them.
The word for property in slaves [mancipia] is derived from the fact that they are
captured from the enemy by force of arms [manu capiantur]" (Digesta 1.5.4.2–
3). In Pauline understanding, catechumens present themselves as if they were
brought from death to life (6:13; note the baptismal cry in 8:15; cf. 7:25), baptism
being the analogue to Christ's death and resurrection. The theme of "being
dead to" also confirms for ancient studies the interpretive value of modern
definitions of slavery as a "social death."[50] In addition, Paul's theological statements on baptism connect directly to his paraenesis later in the letter, a central
plank of which is obedience to Rome's governing authorities (Rom 13:1–7). The
paraenesis further confirms Paul's full participation and deep implication in
the Augustan imperial ideology of auctoritas.[51]

Before making broad claims from first-person narratives about the accessibility
of the self in religious sources, we must do close reading of the texts. Often
those texts present voices that prove, in the end, not to be reflective of the
authorial self but to be artificial and literary. In Paul's case, slavery served as a
way of thinking about community, social categorization, hierarchy, and one's
relation to the divine. The subject of Paul's speech-in-character (Rom 7:14–25)
presents for an ancient Roman audience a recognizable stock voice of the slave
self. Presenting pietas as his gospel defines it, the apostle uses the slave, and
especially the topos of the faithful slave (de fide servorum), to "think with."

Paul offers the slave experience of disassociation in the change of owners as
a metaphor for the situation of Gentile converts. The metaphor also corresponds to the Stoic philosophy of prohairesis (volition) that urged the integrity
of the individual self in the face of moral slavery to the passions. Paul could not
have been unaware that Gentile converts could not completely forget their
former life in paganism. Using stereotypes about slaves familiar from wider
"pagan" culture, Paul aims to help his encoded Gentile readers move into a
dialogic relation with their old, preconverted selves. The juxtaposition of two
worldviews—the bad enslavement under sin and the good enslavement under
God's auctoritas—allows each worldview to throw light on the other. This
finding confirms that the juxtaposition of one culture over against another is a

fundamental feature of self-definition in Paul.[52] Of course, the slave is a common representation of the other, and of a person caught between two cultures.

The specific persona is a captured slave who undergoes an agonizing crisis of identity because he is alienated from his rightful owner. Every facet of the *anthrōpos*, both inner and outer, responds. Like all slaves, the persona is answerable to his new master (the demonic power sin) with his body. The slave cannot control or prevent the violence inflicted on his body; he can only learn to withstand it in a known passive strategy of disguised resistance common for all slaves, a "hidden transcript" of slave resistance that the "public transcript" of *auctoritas* creates.[53] The persona is compelled to follow the new master, but in his external bodily members alone and only in habitual, mechanical obedience to individual commands (to the law of sin) like an automaton. The subject of the slave's self takes solace in not letting sin have *auctoritas* over him. A passive commodity of sin, the persona delights in a different law (the holy law of God) inwardly. Its innermost self perseveres unwaveringly in total directness toward his true master (God), as a good and faithful slave should, even when the master is not yet present. Paul thinks of "the slave" in terms of *auctoritas,* the quintessentially Roman idea of personalized power. The religious self, though captured, retains its subjective agency.

Paul, in the final analysis, does not present a polemical argument against slavery as an ideology or institution in the Roman world. Rather, slavery provides a powerful and compelling idiom through which to articulate Christian community formation and self-definition precisely because early Christians shared with wider "pagan" society the same set of cultural assumptions, literary tropes, and social stereotyping of the slave. As a metaphor for the transformation of the religious self by baptism "from death to life" existing within the eschatological tension of the parousia being not yet present, the experience of enslavement is perfect for an ancient audience. Like a slave, the convert experiences the violent psychological force of personal upheaval, the social dishonor of turning away from one's family and traditional culture, and the natal alienation of losing one's whole past identity—getting a new name, having to learn a new language and worldview, and forming new (fictive) kinship relations.[54]

The implications of this exegesis, however, are limited for the wider question of whether we can know anything about the private, hidden, or unconscious selves that lie behind public constructions of ancient self-identity.[55] The extent to which Paul's statements can reasonably be said to provide a context for the idea of the self in early Christianity is hindered in part because the modern idea of self—as a unique individual, a possessor of a "real" or an "authentic" personality rather than a "bearer of character-traits that are assessed in reference to general moral norms"—has no obvious equivalents in ancient Greek (or Latin). The term "self" is also normatively and sometimes politically charged in modern discourse, particularly in reference to freedom and slavery. The definition of a slave as a "person" or "self" often leads too quickly into assertions about the recognition of moral and political rights for slaves and evidence of criticism of the institution of slavery.[56] Ideas such as that of "personality" and "self" need to be taken as part of a whole context, in the specific cultural milieu under study, and not just in isolation.[57]

The findings do, however, draw attention to the notion of voice as a literary construction. For our study of Paul, the most obvious connection to the larger question of the religious self in antiquity lies in the analytic categories of the "public transcript" (the voices of masters) and the "hidden transcript" (the voices of slaves). These categories, however, should not be taken as absolutely separable in the Pauline material. No evidence survives from antiquity that reflects the voices of slaves or their point of view that can then act as a method-ological control on the evidence generated by Roman slaveholding society.[58] The so-called hidden transcript of "playing the automaton" would not have been very hidden to Paul's Roman audience. The act was well-known in the ancient comedy of the "bad slave," which slaveholders created for their "public transcript" of domination, as Plutarch and the *Life of Aesop* above prove.[59]

In the end, Paul's representation of "the slave" consists of a bland moral polarity of good and bad and is an artificial construction serving Roman slaveholding ideology. The apostle's speech-in-character uses such stereotyping to influence the congregation, which would have only strengthened beliefs that his Gentile readers already had about the morality of control, domination, and abuse of human chattel. We learn, therefore, how Paul uses voice as an essential tool in his construction of the slave self.

NOTES

I am grateful to David Brakke, Natalie Dohrmann, Martin Rese, and Lawrence Wills for comments and suggestions on previous drafts.

1. Stanley K. Stowers, *A Rereading of Romans: Justice, Jews, and Gentiles* (New Haven, Conn.: Yale University Press, 1994), 1–4, 258–59; J. Louis Martyn, "A Formula for Communal Discord as a Clue to the Nature of Pastoral Guidance," in *Putting Body and Soul Together: Essays in Honor of Robin Scroggs* (ed. Virginia Wiles, Alexandra Brown, and Graydon F. Snyder; Valley Forge, Penn.: Trinity Press International, 1997), 207; Eugene TeSelle, "Exploring the Inner Conflict: Augustine's Sermons on Romans 7 and 8," in *Engaging Augustine on Romans: Self, Context, and Theology in Interpretation* (ed. Daniel Patte and Eugene TeSelle; Romans through History and Cultures; Harrisburg, Penn.: Trinity Press International, 2002), 111–46; Paula Fredriksen, "Paul and Augustine: Conversion Narratives, Orthodox Traditions, and the Redemptive Self," *JTS* n.s. 37 (1986): 3–34.

2. Most recently, Gerd Theissen, *Psychological Aspects of Pauline Theology* (trans. John P. Galvin; Philadelphia: Fortress, 1987), 177–265.

3. Wayne A. Meeks, *The First Urban Christians: The Social World of the Apostle Paul* (New Haven, Conn.: Yale University Press, 1983), 186; the fundamental article is Krister Stendahl, "The Apostle Paul and the Introspective Conscience of the West," in *Paul among Jews and Gentiles and Other Essays* (Philadelphia: Fortress, 1976), 78–96.

4. The particular identification of the *egō* does not matter to my argument; my point is that the persona is enslaved. The literature is extensive, and commentaries sometimes claim that the identity of the *egō* remains an open question: whether personal for Paul, typical for all human beings (as Adam's voice), or fictive as a rhetorical figure. However, most scholarship today agrees that the *egō* cannot be the personal voice of Paul's *preconversion* experience. A minority view claims that Paul speaks at least partly autobiographically, out of his personal *postconversion* experience; see James Dunn, "Rom. 7,14–25 in the Theology of Paul," *TZ* 31 (1975): 257–73; idem, *Romans 1–8* (WBC 38A; Dallas: Word Books, 1988), 382–83. A good survey of the exegetical issues and history of research for the nonspecialist is Jan Lambrecht, *The Wretched "I" and Its Liberation: Paul in Romans 7 and 8* (Louvain Theological and Pastoral Monographs 14; Louvain: Peeters, 1992), 29–91.

5. Werner Georg Kümmel, *Römer 7 und das Bild des Menchen im Neuen Testament: Zwei Studien* (TB 53; Munich: C. Kaiser, 1974), 1–160; Stanley K. Stowers, "Romans 7.7–25 as a Speech-in-Character *(prosōpopoiia),*" in *Paul in his Hellenistic Context* (ed. Troels Engberg-Pedersen; Studies of the New Testament and its World; Edinburgh: T. & T. Clark, 1994), 180–202; idem, *Rereading Romans*, 264–73.

6. This paragraph and the next follow the excellent discussion in Stowers, *Rereading Romans*, 16–21 (and idem, "Speech-in-Character," 180–91), with further literature cited there.

7. Sources: George A. Kennedy, *Progymnasmata: Greek Textbooks of Prose Composition and Rhetoric* (SBLWAW 10; Atlanta: SBL, 2003), 47–49, 115–17, 164–66, 213–17.

8. The slave's stock type, like that of the others on the speech-in-character list, is informed by comic figures in ancient drama. Aelius Theon, *Progymnasmata* 8 (115–18); Michel Patillon with Giancarlo Bolognesi, eds., *Aelius Théon: Progymnasmata* (Budé; Paris: Belles Lettres, 1997), 70–71; see also James R. Butts, "The Progymnasmata of Theon: A New Text with Translation and Commentary" (Ph.D. diss., Claremont Graduate School, 1986), 445–64; Kennedy, *Progymnasmata*, 48 and 214 (slave speech-in-character); W. Martin Bloomer, "Schooling in Persona: Imagination and Subordination in Roman Education," *Classical Antiquity* 16 (1997): 57–78.

9. For a persuasive reply to objections, see Stanley K. Stowers, "Apostrophe, *Prosôpopoiia* and Paul's Rhetorical Education," in *Early Christianity and Classical Culture: Comparative Studies in Honor of Abraham J. Malherbe* (ed. John T. Fitzgerald, Thomas H. Olbricht, and L. Michael White; NovTSup 105; Leiden: Brill, 2003), 351–69.

10. Hans Dieter Betz, "The Concept of the 'Inner Human Being' *(ho esō anthrōpos)* in the Anthropology of Paul," *NTS* 46 (2000): 315–413; Theo K. Heckel, *Der Innere Mensch: Die paulinische Verarbeitung eines platonischen Motivs* (WUNT 2/53; Tübingen: Mohr Siebeck 1993), 153–97 (see Stanley K. Stowers, review of Heckel, *Innere Mensch, JBL* 114 [1995]: 342–44).

11. Betz, "Concept of the 'Inner Human Being,'" 334.

12. Aristotle, *Pol.* 1.1–7 (1252a–56a); *Eth. nic.* 8.11.6–7 (1161b); Eugene Garver, "Aristotle's Natural Slaves: Incomplete *Praxeis* and Incomplete Human Beings," *Journal of the History of Philosophy* 32 (1994): 173–95. See also P. A. Brunt, "Aristotle and Slavery," in idem, *Studies in Greek History and Thought* (Oxford: Clarendon, 1993), 343–88; Nicholas D. Smith, "Aristotle's Theory of Natural Slavery," in *A Companion to Aristotle's Politics* (ed. David Keyt and Fred D. Miller Jr.; Oxford: Blackwell, 1990), 142–55.

13. Page duBois, *Slaves and Other Objects* (Chicago: University of Chicago Press, 2003), 189–205.

14. J. Albert Harrill, "Invective against Paul (2 Cor 10:10), the Physiognomics of the Ancient Slave Body, and the Greco-Roman Rhetoric of Manhood," in *Antiquity and Humanity: Essays in Ancient Religion and Philosophy Presented to Hans Dieter Betz on his 70th Birthday* (ed. Adela Yarbro Collins and Margaret M. Mitchell; Tübingen: Mohr Siebeck, 2001), 192–201.

15. Keith Hopkins, "Novel Evidence for Roman Slavery," *Past and Present* 138 (1993):

23; Keith Bradley, "Animalizing the Slave: The Truth of Fiction," *JRS* 90 (2000): 110–11; Jennifer A. Glancy, *Slavery in Early Christianity* (New York: Oxford University Press, 2002), 3–38.

16. For Gentiles as the exclusive "encoded readers" of Romans, see Stowers, *Rereading Romans,* 21–22, 287–89 and passim. For the classical Greek ideology on slavery, see the literature on Aristotle cited above; Peter Hunt, *Slaves, Warfare, and Ideology in the Greek Historians* (Cambridge: Cambridge University Press, 1998), 19–25 and passim; and Vincent J. Rosivach, "Enslaving *Barbaroi* and the Athenian Ideology of Slavery," *Historia* 48 (1999): 129–57.

17. In contrast to Platonism and its dualistic metaphysics and anthropology, Stoicism had a monistic metaphysics and anthropology that understands the self as a unity; see Brad Inwood, "Hierocles: Theory and Argument in the Second Century AD," *Oxford Studies in Ancient Philosophy* 2 (1984): 163, 176–77.

18. C. E. Manning, "Stoicism and Slavery in the Roman Empire," *ANRW* 36.3: 1518–43; Brent D. Shaw, "The Divine Economy: Stoicism as Ideology," *Latomus* 44 (1985): 16–54.

19. Justinian, *Institutiones* 1.3.2; *Digesta* 1.5.4.1; W. W. Buckland, *The Roman Law of Slavery: The Conditions of the Slave in Private Law from Augustus to Justinian* (1908; repr. New York: AMS Press, 1969), 1.

20. Jesper Carlsen, *Vilici and Roman Estate Managers until AD 284* (Analecta Romana Instituti Danici Supplementum 24; Rome: Bretschneider, 1995).

21. Kathleen McCarthy, *Slaves, Masters, and the Art of Authority in Plautine Comedy* (Princeton, N.J.: Princeton University Press, 2000), 24 n. 39; Alan Watson, *Roman Slave Law* (Baltimore: Johns Hopkins University Press, 1987), 102–14; Barry Nicholas, *An Introduction to Roman Law* (3d ed; Oxford: Clarendon, 1962), 201–4.

22. Jeffrey Stuart Rusten, "Aesop," *OCD,* 29; Lawrence M. Wills, "The Depiction of Slavery in the Ancient Novel," in *Slavery in Text and Interpretation* (ed. Allen D. Callahan et al.; Semeia 83/84; Atlanta: Scholars Press, 1998), 124–25.

23. Lloyd W. Daly, *Aesop without Morals: The Famous Fables, and a Life of Aesop* (New York: Thomas Yosloff, 1961), 54–53; Hopkins, "Novel Evidence," 18–21; William Fitzgerald, *Slavery and the Roman Literary Imagination* (New York: Cambridge University Press, 2000), 27.

24. J. E. Lendon, *Empire of Honour: The Art of Government in the Roman World* (Oxford: Clarendon, 1997), 61, 129–30, 275.

25. The Greek version of the *Res Gestae* renders *potestas* as *exousia* ("power") and *auctoritas* as *axiōma* ("authority"), the latter Greek word also a common translation for Latin *dignitas;* P. A. Brunt and J. M. Moore, *Res Gestae Divi Augusti: The Achievements of the Divine Augustus* (New York: Oxford University Press, 1967), 49; J. P. V. D. Balsdon, "Auctoritas, Dignitas, Otium," *CQ* 10 (1960): 44.

26. Karl Galinsky, *Augustan Culture: An Interpretive Introduction* (Princeton, N.J.: Princeton University Press, 1996), 10–41 and passim; Andrew Feldherr, *Spectacle and Society in Livy's History* (Berkeley: University of California Press, 1998), 6–7, 13–14 and passim.

27. In this context belongs the use of the gladiator's oath *(auctoramentum gladiatorum)* as a literary topos of *auctoritas;* Seneca, *Ep.* 37.1–2, Petronius, *Sat.* 117; cf. Plautus, *Most.* 780; Carlin A. Barton, *The Sorrows of the Ancient Romans: The Gladiator and the Monster* (Princeton, N.J.: Princeton University Press, 1993), 14–15, 21.

28. McCarthy, *Slaves, Masters, and the Art,* 21–24. The Roman comic complement of the *servus frugi,* the good ("useful") slave, is the *servus callidus,* the trickster ("clever") slave whose subjective agency is out of control. See John Wright, *Dancing in Chains: The Stylistic Unity of the Comoedia Palliata* (Papers and Monographs of the American Academy in Rome 25; Rome: American Academy in Rome, 1974), 161.

29. Epictetus, *Diatr.* 4.11.26–27; Seneca, *Ben.* 3.20; *Marc.* 24.5; see A. A. Long, "Representation and the Self in Stoicism," in *Psychology* (vol. 2 of *Companions to Ancient*

Thought; ed. Stephen Everson; Cambridge: Cambridge University Press, 1991), 102–20; and Fitzgerald, *Slavery,* 91.

30. Troels Engberg-Pedersen, "Stoic Philosophy and the Concept of the Person," in *The Person and the Human Mind: Issues in Ancient and Modern Philosophy* (ed. Christopher Gill; Oxford: Clarendon, 1990), 122.

31. Epictetus, *Ench.* 12.2 (Oldfather, LCL).

32. Plutarch, *Mor.* 511D-E, *Garr.* 18 (Babbitt et al., LCL).

33. Cicero, *Caecin.* 51–52 (trans. McCarthy, *Slaves, Masters and the Art,* 23 n. 36).

34. The original version of the parable is lost and comes from the Sayings Source (known as Q). Biblical scholars make this determination because the parable appears only in Matthew ("Parable of the Talents"; 25:14–30) and Luke ("Parable of the Pounds"; 19:12–27), two early Christian sources without a known literary relationship. I do not argue that Q originated from Rome; the parable is illustrative only as a general example of Gentile Christianity in non-Pauline circles.

35. Roman masters, weary of the effort, often hired the services of professional torturers; see Moses I. Finley, *Ancient Slavery and Modern Ideology* (enl. ed., ed. Brent D. Shaw; Princeton, N.J.: Markus Wiener, 1998), 163; and K. R. Bradley, *Slaves and Masters in the Roman Empire: A Study in Social Control* (New York: Oxford University Press, 1987), 118–23. For "righteous" punishment as a theme in Matthew's slave parables, see Glancy, *Slavery,* 112–22. Compared with Matthew's account, Luke's version portrays less violence in regard to the slave: the Lukan master, though angry, gives the slave no more than a stern talking to (Luke 19:23).

36. See McCarthy, *Slaves, Masters, and the Art,* 26–28, 71–73 and passim; with Keith Bradley, *Slavery and Society at Rome* (Key Themes in Ancient History; Cambridge: Cambridge University Press, 1994), 122–25

37. For helpful analysis using modern sociological categories of power and authority, see John Howard Schütz, *Paul and the Anatomy of Apostolic Authority* (SNTSMS 26; Cambridge: Cambridge University Press, 1975), 12–13, 204–5, 224–25 and passim.

38. Stowers, *Rereading Romans,* 124; cf. Bernard Frischer, *The Sculpted Word: Epicureanism and Philosophical Recruitment in Ancient Greece* (Berkeley: University of California Press, 1982), 277.

39. See M. M. Bakhtin, *The Dialogic Imagination* (ed. Michael Holquist; Austin: University of Texas Press, 1981), 12; McCarthy, *Slaves, Masters and the Art,* 6.

40. Claude Lévi-Strauss, *Totemism* (Boston: Beacon Press, 1963), 89 (in reference to animals); and Elizabeth A. Castelli, "Romans," *A Feminist Commentary* (vol. 2 of *Searching the Scriptures;* ed. Elisabeth Schüssler Fiorenza; New York: Crossroads, 1994), 294–95 (in reference to women).

41. The specific persona is a Gentile attracted to Judaism, what modern scholars would call a "godfearer" (Stowers, *Rereading Romans,* 34, 42–43, 108–9, 260, 273–79). Central to Paul's argument is the Greco-Roman model of self-division *(akrasia),* its classic expression being Medea's great monologue (Euripides, *Med.* 1021–80); on this monologue, see Christopher Gill, *Personality in Greek Epic, Tragedy, and Philosophy: The Self in Dialogue* (Oxford: Clarendon, 1996), 216–26. On the slave persona in Roman literary imagination as a topos for the acrastic self, see Fitzgerald, *Slavery,* 22–23.

42. For Stowers (*Rereading Romans,* 180, 257, 271), the slave language is "only a metaphor" (like "The ship mastered the storm") and simply a shorthand expression for "being overrun by one's passions." According to Troels Engberg-Pedersen (*Paul and the Stoics* [Louisville: Westminster John Knox, 2000] 234–37, 291–92), the slave language has little relation to Paul's central message; Paul distances himself from the metaphor and even "apologizes" for using it.

43. The exegetical debate on the "faith of Christ" question has too long a history to repeat here. See Stowers, *Rereading Romans,* 194–26 and literature cited there; see also Jouette M. Bassler's review of Stowers, *Rereading Romans, JBL* 115 (1996): 365–68.

44. Cf. 2 Cor 4:16–18; Margaret E. Thrall, *A Critical and Exegetical Commentary on the Second Epistle to the Corinthians* (2 vols.; ICC; Edinburgh: T. & T. Clark, 1994), 2.347–56. The different context of the usage in 2 Corinthians 4 should not override or otherwise control interpretation for Romans 7.

45. Leander E. Keck, "The Absent Good: The Significance of Rom 7:18a," in *Text und Geschichte: Facetten theologischen Arbeitens aus dem Freundes- und Schülerkreis Dieter Lührmann zum 60. Geburtstag* (ed. Stefan Maser and Egbert Schlarb; Marburger theologische Studien 50; Marburg: Elwert, 1999), 68–69. On the Roman literary image of the slave as the "limbs" or "members" of the master's body, see Fitzgerald, *Slavery*, 49.

46. Paul W. Meyer, "The Worm at the Core of the Apple: Exegetical Reflections on Romans 7," in *The Conversation Continues: Studies in Paul and John in Honor of J. Louis Martin* (ed. Robert R. Fortna and Beverly R. Gaventa; Nashville, Tenn.: Abingdon, 1990), 78–79; Martyn, "Formula for Communal Discord," 209–10; Betz, "Concept of the 'Inner Human Being,'" 338–40; Keck, "Absent Good," 70; Dale B. Martin, *The Corinthian Body* (New Haven, Conn.: Yale University Press, 1995), 123–28.

47. On the apocalyptic drama and eschatological tension, see Keck, "Absent Good," 74–75; cf. Dunn, *Romans*, 396, 406–411. Otto Michel (*Der Brief an die Römer*, 5th ed. [KEK 4; 14th ed.; Göttingen: Vandenhoeck and Ruprecht, 1978], 230) connects the "sold under" language in Paul to LXX usage as a term for debt bondage.

48. E.g., Valerius Maximus 6.8.1–7. To Valerius, such faithfulness was not just an instance of *fides*, but of *benevolentia* and *pietas* as well; see Bradley, *Slaves and Masters*, 36. On this topos in early Christianity, see J. Albert Harrill, "The Domestic Enemy: A Moral Polarity of Household Slaves in Early Christian Apologies and Martyrdoms," in *Early Christian Families in Context: An Interdisciplinary Dialogue* (ed. David Balch and Carolyn Osiek; Religion, Marriage, and Family; Grand Rapids, Mich.: Wm. B. Eerdmans, 2003), 231–54. On the related Stoic theme of attaching one's "self" *(autos)* in total directedness toward the divine as a "slave of Zeus" *(tou Dios diakonos)*, see Epictetus 3.4.20; 3.24.65; 4.1.98–102; 4.1.131; 4.12.11–12 (cf. 4.1.175–76; Seneca, *Ep.* 61.3).

49. Engberg-Pedersen, *Paul and the Stoics*, 225–46 and passim. Engberg-Pedersen confuses his otherwise clear and excellent analysis by his assumption that the fearful slave (acting like an automaton) is the representation for all "obedient slaves" in classical antiquity.

50. J. Albert Harrill, *The Manumission of Slaves in Early Christianity* (HUT 32; Tübingen: Mohr Siebeck, 1995), 1, 15–17, 32; Orlando Patterson, *Slavery and Social Death: A Comparative Study* (Cambridge, Mass.: Harvard University Press, 1982), 35–76 and passim.

51. Paul's advice in Rom 13:1–7 presupposes Christians sharing in the special relationship of Jewish communities to Roman rule. Paul reuses a traditional piece of Jewish paraenesis that was formed in the Greek synagogue to address *auctoritas* directly: Jewish rights under Roman rule come with mutual obligations on the part of subordinates; see Wayne A. Meeks, "Corinthian Christians as Artificial Aliens," in *Paul Beyond the Judaism/Hellenism Divide* (ed. Troels Engberg-Pedersen; Louisville, Ky.: Westminster John Knox, 2001), 137; idem, *First Urban Christians*, 208 n. 192, and literature cited there.

52. E.g., Paul defining "Gentiles" as captives to their appetites over against Jewish freedom from such captivity; see Stowers, *Rereading Paul*, 273–76 and passim.

53. See James C. Scott, *Domination and the Arts of Resistance: Hidden Transcripts* (New Haven, Conn.: Yale University Press, 1990), 2–4, 79 and passim.

54. I integrate the "social death" definition of a slave by Patterson (*Slavery*, 13 and passim) into my exegesis here.

55. *Pace* Gary W. Burnett, *Paul and the Salvation of the Individual* (BibInt 57; Leiden: Brill, 2001), 173–214, whose reading of Rom 7:7–25 is by the author's own admission straightforward and simple.

56. E.g., Wolfgang Waldstein, "Zum Menschsein von Sklaven," in *Fünfzig Jahre*

Forschungen zur antiken Sklaverei an der Mainzer Akademie, 1950–2000: Miscellanea zum Jubiläum (ed. Heinz Bellen and Heinz Heinen; Forschungen zur antiken Sklaverei 35; Stuttgart: Franz Steiner, 2001), 31–49. On the fallacy of "discovering" human rights and humanity in slavery from juridical definitions of the slave as a legal personality, see Patterson, *Slavery,* 22–23.

57. Amélie Oksenberg Rorty, "Persons and *Personae,*" in *The Person and the Human Mind: Issues in Ancient and Modern Philosophy* (ed. Christopher Gill; Oxford: Clarendon, 1990), 1–36; Christopher Gill, "The Character–Personality Distinction," in *Characterization and Individuality in Greek Literature* (ed. Christopher Pelling; Oxford: Clarendon, 1990), 2; Gill, *Personality in Greek Epic,* 2; Luther H. Martin, "The Anti-individualistic Ideology of Hellenistic Culture," *Numen* 41 (1994): 124. The ancient Greeks and Romans expressed the *grammatical* meaning of "self" by the use of the reflective pronouns *autos* and *ipse,* not in itself evidence of a "technology of the self" in classical antiquity. The latter pronoun in Latin was also a common poetic expression for "the master," making the slave a metonym for the master's self; Fitzgerald, *Slavery* 18–22.

58. See Harrill, *Manumission of Slaves,* 18–20; cf. A. A. Long, *Epictetus: A Stoic and Socratic Guide to Life* (Oxford: Clarendon, 2002), 11–12.

59. The *Metamorphoses* of Apuleius provides a further example of a Roman author using the "public transcript" of ancient slavery to invent a slave self who is initially alienated from his true master (the goddess Isis); see discussion in Bradley, "Animalizing the Slave"; and Fitzgerald, *Slavery,* 94–95.

—4—

Prayer of the Queen: Esther's Religious Self in the Septuagint

ESTHER MENN

The prayer of Queen Esther in the Septuagint version of the book of Esther provides a telling site for investigation of the concept of the religious self in antiquity. This well-crafted prayer is clearly a secondary composition by a Hellenistic Jewish author, probably living in Palestine sometime in the late second or first century B.C.E. After carefully considering the sparer version of the narrative circulating in his time, which may not have even mentioned the name of God if it closely resembled what ultimately came to be known as the Masoretic Text, this anonymous author creatively imagined the words that its female protagonist might have addressed to her deity before risking her life in an attempt to save her people. The invention of a prayer for the queen there-fore also meant the simultaneous invention of a particular religious self-understanding for her, in keeping with what the author's Hellenistic Jewish community was capable of imagining for a woman in Esther's unique position.

Esther's prayer, which appears in the Septuagint version as the second half of Addition C,[1] cannot tell us anything about the religious self of the historical Esther, if there ever was such a figure, or even much about the religious self of the literary character minimally sketched by the original author in the earliest Hebrew version. But Esther's prayer in the Septuagint can certainly reveal central aspects of what it meant for the author's religious community to be Jewish, and for this reason alone it is worthy of careful exploration.

The Septuagint is not the only version of the narrative that secondarily attributes a prayer to Esther. The two Targums, the Babylonian Talmud, and midrashic collections including *Esther Rabbah* and the *Midrash on the Psalms* all interject distinctive prayers through which the Jewish queen directly discloses an illuminated interiority building on, but far exceeding, the intimations of her inner life in the Masoretic Text. The reasons for this virtually universal practice of supplementing the original narrative with a prayer attributed to Esther are not difficult to imagine. The introduction of her prayer fills a gaping void of religiosity left by the Hebrew version of the narrative and transforms her character into an exemplar of conventional piety. The descriptions in chapter 4 of fasting by Mordecai and the rest of the Jewish community as well as by Esther and her maids no doubt also motivated the introduction of the motif of prayer, since fasting and prayer are commonly associated practices in early Judaism. Ultimately, a specific detail in the biblical text itself was identified as an indication that the queen prayed before taking action: the unnamed "king" approached by Esther in 5:1 came to be regarded as an allusion to the divine Sovereign whom Esther first approaches in prayer.

In every version of the narrative that includes some form of the queen's petition, Esther's prayerful articulation of her self-understanding corresponds with the portrayal of her character in the larger text into which it is embedded. Comparative study of Esther's many prayers in ancient Jewish literature would therefore reveal a fascinating variety of conceptions of the religious self in the Hellenistic, Roman, and Byzantine periods as these conceptions came to be applied to this single female figure responding to the particular circumstances of her life and times in the Persian court.

Esther's prayer in the Septuagint is an excellent focus for this initial study of the queen's religious self in Jewish antiquity. For one thing, it appears to be the oldest of Esther's prayers preserved in any extant literature. The colophon concerning the translation of the Esther scroll into Greek suggests that this prayer may have been composed already in the late second or first century B.C.E.[2] Esther's prayer in the Septuagint is also exceptionally well-developed and reveals a number of aspects of her identity, since it appears at a critical turning point when the Jewish queen emerges from her characteristic silence and compliance to deliver the Jews from annihilation. This version of her prayer is also thematically coherent, presenting an overarching understanding of Esther's religious self as a humble subject of the divine King who claims the complete loyalty of the entire Jewish people. This essay will explore this conception of the religious self, reflecting on how the genre of prayer suggests a relational self that opens toward a transcendent God.

Esther in Prayer: Interiority as an Opening of Oneself toward God

As a genre of speech addressed to God, prayer in and of itself contributes to a definition of the religious self. At first glance, it might appear that such a conventional component of Second Temple literature as prayer would be unlikely to yield insight. Examples of penitential and petitionary prayers abound, including those offered by Daniel (Dan 9:3–19), Ezra (Ezra 9:5–15), Tobit and

Sarah (Tob 3:1–6, 12–15), and particularly Judith (Jud 9:9–14), whose willingness to risk her life for the deliverance of her people most closely echoes Esther's
situation. But perhaps it is the ordinariness of Esther's prayer that makes it all
the more revealing about certain presuppositions concerning the self.

In the Septuagint, Esther's prayer constitutes her longest speech and therefore her deepest self-disclosure. For the sake of comparison, it is worth noting
that in the Masoretic Text, Esther is as efficient in her speech as she is effective in
her action, speaking only after first being addressed—to voice her sense of
danger and then of resolve to Mordecai (MT Esth 4:11, 16), and to appeal
diplomatically to the king on behalf of her people (MT Esth 5:4, 7–8; 7:3–4, 6;
8:5–6; 9:13). By contrast, the praying Esther of the Septuagint is a loquacious
self, who initiates a lengthy discussion about many facets of her being. Through
eavesdropping on Esther's prayer we come to know her thoughts on her people's identity and current situation, on her pending action and the fear that it
raises, on her own conflicted and wretched life in the Persian court, and on her
desperate trust in God to come to her assistance. Were one of us rewriting the
story today, we might, in order to disclose Esther's perspective on her situation,
interject an extended soliloquy; or a confessional conversation with Mordecai,
the seven maids, or one of the ever-present eunuchs; or, in keeping with a key
motif of the scroll, we might include a letter sent out by courier. Instead of any
of these, in the Septuagint we find Esther's prayer.

What might it mean for the understanding of the religious self that in the
Septuagint Esther's interiority is made known most fully in the form of prayer?
Esther's prayer reveals an interiority that neither remains contained and autonomous nor discloses itself to any human confidant, but rather opens most
completely to a transcendent and silent partner. Esther keenly feels her own
loneliness in the Persian court (LXX Esth 14:3, 14), separated from the fasting
community outside and anticipating her solitary approach before the forbidding king. Her prayer nevertheless identifies her as fundamentally a relational
self, although the self's relationality is not dependent on the immediate presence of any human community or individual. Precisely at her moment of
greatest isolation, Esther makes herself fully transparent before an Other whom
she addresses directly and incessantly, with names implying a depth of famil-
iarity, such as "my Lord," "our King," "Helper," and "Lord God of Abraham," as
well as with names acknowledging divine grandeur, such as "King of gods" and
"Master of all dominion."

There is a poignancy to Esther's self-revelation in prayer that we might
easily miss, since we know that the story ends with "light and gladness" (Esth
8:16) and since the Septuagint takes pains to identify God's providential hand in
all things (LXX Esth 10:9–12). During and immediately after Esther's prayer,
however, there is an absence of response to her radical self-disclosure. When
she prays, Esther orients a vulnerable and dependent self entirely toward a
silent God whom she names as her only helper, even though his providential

care has not been much in evidence in her own life and that of her community. Esther's solitary condition is emphasized in her prayer, when before the God who "alone" may be recognized as Israel's King, she confesses that she too is all "alone." The adjective "alone" thus creates an identification between the two parties bound together through prayer, despite the fact that Esther is alone in her frightening responsibility to intervene on behalf of her people, and the divinity is alone in his unique status as the divine Monarch who has the ability to lend assistance.

The Religious Self as Subject of the Divine King

Turning from the genre of prayer to the particular contents of Esther's prayer in the Septuagint, we find that Esther discloses her core identity as a humble subject of Israel's divine Monarch. The rhetoric of Esther's prayer in the Septuagint emphasizes that God, and no mere human such as Artaxerxes (as the Persian ruler is identified in the Septuagint), is the true King whose benefactions and decrees claim the loyalty of the Jews.

Already in her initial address, Esther acknowledges the Lord God of Israel as the sole Ruler of her people. Her first words confess her allegiance in no uncertain terms: "My Lord, you alone are our King" (LXX Esth 14:3). With this assertion of divine rule, Esther echoes the opening invocation of Mordecai's prayer, set immediately before hers in Addition C: "Lord, Lord, you reign as King over all things, for the universe is in your power" (LXX Esth 13:9). Implicit in Mordecai's invocation is a contrast between the 127 provinces comprising the Persian king's exaggerated empire in the book of Esther and the yet vaster expanse of the divinity's cosmic reign that dwarfs all human pretensions. When Esther's own prayer continues with her petitions for divine presence within the context of her people's affliction and for courage to face her own daunting task, she again addresses the deity in royal terms as "King of gods and Master of all dominions" (LXX Esth 14:12). Again at the conclusion of her prayer, Esther repeats her acknowledgment of God's universal and magnanimous rule, as the one "whose might is over all" (LXX Esth 14:19), enabling him to hear the voice of the despairing and to save them from harm intended by evildoers. Esther's most frequent term of address, "Lord," which she uses a total of seven times in her prayer, similarly stresses her identification of God as King, since this term, although no doubt also standing in as a cipher for the personal, unspoken name of God in the Septuagint, is also a decidedly political term in the Hellenistic context. These exalted titles confirm what Mordecai's prayer has already suggested, that the contested office of kingship extends far beyond the realm of human governments to encompass cosmic dimensions and that no rival deities or powers can usurp the divine throne.

The Esther of the Septuagint understands the present threat to Jewish survival as primarily an assault on the divine King's authority by idol-worshipping nations, who with their misplaced allegiance seek to wrongfully "praise worthless idols and magnify a king of flesh forever" (LXX Esth 14:10). While the deification of the Persian king implied in Esther's charge does not emerge as an issue in the Hebrew text, this charge seems to address the religious challenge of emperor worship within the later Hellenistic context of the Septuagint and its Additions. Esther's dismissive reference to the pretensions of a "king of flesh" is the only time in her prayer that she refers to her husband with the title "king," although at one other point she does employ animal imagery typically associated with royalty when she calls him the "lion" (LXX Esth 14:13).

Royal titles and imagery in Esther's prayer are otherwise reserved for the divine Monarch whose reign is under attack. As Esther describes the situation to her sole Sovereign, Israel's enemies "have joined hands with the hands of their idols to remove the boundary set by your mouth" (LXX Esth 14:8–9). In a narrative filled with illustrations of a human monarch's commands and laws, the reference to what God's mouth has ordained once again appropriates royal language for Israel's deity. The implication is that God's divine decree, and not the decree of any human king, should remain unalterable (cf., MT Esth 8:8), and that any scheme challenging it amounts to rebellion. Similarly, when Esther beseeches God not to "surrender your scepter to what has no being" (LXX Esth 14:11), she employs the imagery of the golden scepter that Artaxerxes extends to touch her neck in the next scene (LXX Esth 15:11; cf., 4:11; 8:4). Counter to the surrounding narrative, Esther's prayer asserts that only Israel's divine Monarch rightly retains the royal token of the scepter and the attributes of authority and clemency that it symbolizes. The alarming imagery of the nullified divine decree and the illicitly transferred scepter emphasizes that not only is Israel threatened in the current situation, but so is God's own honor and power.

This threat is highlighted through references to the theme of praise due to a monarch by his subjects. Just as the subjects of a human monarch offer their praise and homage, so Israel's mouths rightly praise God and they offer their worship at the temple with its altar for sacrifices (LXX Esth 14:9). By contrast, as noted previously, the other nations open their mouths to "praise worthless idols and magnify a king of flesh forever" (LXX Esth 14:10). They even threaten to stop Israel from their rightful praise and worship of their divine King (Addition C 14:10). Esther's direct invocation of her divine Monarch and her use of royal imagery to describe his power serve to usurp and nullify the Persian king's authority. Esther's identity, as well as that of her entire people, is detached from their condition as subjects of a human monarch, although paradoxically the most pressing reality of their existence involves the potential catastrophic effects of his edict. The communal identity of the Jewish people as subjects of the divine King challenges the power of the human king and his allies, both human and divine.

The metaphor of divine kingship becomes especially vital in Esther's prayer in the Septuagint due to the prominence of the motif of kingship in the

Esther narrative itself. From the first chapter with the Persian king's extravagant display of wealth and glory, to the concluding chapter with its briefer notice of his power and might, the entire book revolves around the royal court. In the Septuagint, the new preface provided by Mordecai's symbolic dream in Addition A similarly begins with a temporal reference to the second year of the "reign" of Artaxerxes the Great. At certain points, the Greek version exceeds the MT in its elaborate description of royal splendor, as when Esther first glimpses the king upon approaching him in violation of the law: "[The king] was seated on his royal throne, clothed in the full array of his majesty, all covered with gold and precious stones. He was most terrifying" (LXX Esth 15:6; cf., MT Esth 5:1b). Symbols of monarchic rule abound in both the Hebrew and Greek versions. Besides the king's throne and costly clothing in the passage just cited, these symbols include luxurious palace furnishings, drinking vessels, and extensive harems; crowns and signet; as well as the golden scepter and royal decree appropriated as expressions of divine sovereignty in Esther's prayer. The presentation of God as Monarch in Esther's prayer therefore has organic connections with the body of the narrative, polemically dismissing the apparent power of even the most powerful of human rulers.

Something akin to this polemical message emerges already from the Hebrew version, although it is expressed in a quite different manner. In the Masoretic text kingship is satirized and qualified through humor. For example, the exaggerated displays of wealth and magnanimity that open the book ultimately serve not so much to illustrate the human king's power as to highlight his actual impotence. Unable to influence effectively even the behavior of his own wife, the king's recourse is to establish as official policy what she has already determined. Ahasuerus adopts Vashti's willful refusal to appear before him as his own decision that she never again appear before him, apparently to his later regret (Esth 2:1).

Even this seemingly trivial matter concerning his own queen's insubordination, however, is not handled independently by the king as a family matter, but rather is decided on the advice of numerous counselors expert in Persian law. This incident in the opening chapter therefore also illustrates the king's ridiculous inability to rule without the assistance of the eunuchs, advisors, and other officials omnipresent in the court. Indeed, in subsequent chapters of the book, Ahasuerus appears altogether too ready and eager to hand over his signet and the power to legislate that it symbolizes to those near to him (Esth 3:10).

Despite his dependence on the counsel of others, however, Ahasuerus's commands and decrees are never based on rational considerations, but rather emerge from more immediate responses, such as his emotions of anger or pleasure. The result is the promulgation of ludicrous and outrageous laws. The king's decree about gender relations, for example, that "every man should be master in his own house," merely imposes a commonplace assumption of Persian culture as official policy. This transformation from custom to law, however, emerges from the king's own humiliating inability to assert the minimum standard of dominance henceforth legally required from all men. This failure within his own household makes suspect Ahasuerus's ability to rule over the broader realm of the Persian empire. His eventual willingness to comply with Queen Esther's every wish up to "half of the kingdom," even after she appears before him without permission, pointedly illustrates the limits of the king's law. Similarly, the pernicious law providing for the destruction of "a certain people" (never further defined as the Jews in Haman's proposal to the king) is aimed primarily against Mordecai, ironically the very person whom the king himself proposes to honor as a reward for revealing the eunuchs' assassination plot (Esth 6:3; 7:9). This genocidal law, besides being immoral and horrific, is therefore also revealed to be at cross-purposes with the king's own self-interests.

Taken together, the various passages in the Hebrew version of Esther treating the theme of royal power contribute to what might be considered a carnivalesque critique of kingship. By contrast, the interjection of Esther's prayer in the Septuagint suspends the humor of the larger narrative to develop in more explicit terms the serious polemic concerning human government implied previously through the indirect means of irony and satire. Perhaps writing with the memory of a similar period of crisis under the Seleucids such as that precipitated by Antiochus IV (Epiphanes), the author of Esther's prayer considered it necessary to assert the serious theological nature of the situation faced by Esther, Mordecai, and the rest of the Jews living under foreign rule.

Redefining the Subject Self

The identification of Israel's God as sole Monarch of the Jewish people has consequences for the concept of the self that is articulated through the character of Esther in the Septuagint. Esther emphasizes her self-understanding primarily as a humble subject of the divine King by twice identifying herself as the deity's female slave ("your slave," *hē doulē sou*, LXX Esth 14:17, 18). This repeated identification emphasizes that Esther owes her primary allegiance to God and not to the many others who claim her devotion and obedience within the layered hierarchical structures of her world. Esther's reiterated self-identification as God's slave also appears in the final section of her prayer, when she discusses her refusal to participate in the revelries and observances typical of palace life, including eating at Haman's table, honoring the king's feast, and drinking the wine of libation. Instead of enjoying the luxurious and possibly idolatrous benefits offered by the court, Esther finds joy only in the Lord God of Abraham, whose might is over all. This context for Esther's identification of herself as God's slave accentuates the opposition between earthly and heavenly sovereigns as competing claimants for her personal allegiance and obedient behavior.

Esther as a subjected self is certainly not an entirely novel introduction into the Septuagint. Especially in the first part of the basic narrative (until the end of chapter 4), Esther's behavior reveals a docile young woman who readily complies with the instructions, commands, and laws of her superiors. She may be understood as a subordinate within multiple hierarchical relationships. Even without her additional subjection to the divine King in her prayer in Addition C, Esther is already at least thrice-ruled. She is at once a Persian subject (one of the many girls brought from all the provinces of the kingdom to Susa for the royal harem), a member of a soon-to-be-persecuted minority (sentenced not only to loss of liberty but also of life itself through Haman's law), and a woman within a family network that includes a male guardian representing her origins and within a marriage with the most powerful of all men, the king (who himself promulgated a decree about husbands' mastery of wives). This focus on the Jewish queen and the complex concept of the subordinated self developed in this narrative contrasts sharply with the focus of contemporary philosophical treatises on the self that employ the metaphor of the sovereign king, exemplified in the Graeco-Roman writings of the Cynics and Stoics.

As we know, however, Esther's position and character encompass more than mere subordination. In the course of the narrative, the Jewish queen of the Persian empire reveals herself as a diplomatic negotiator and an effective administrator, whose success demonstrates the weakness and navigability of the empire's hierarchies as well as the alternating currents of power dynamics within family, marriage, and the multicultural context of a world empire. Esther's paradoxical position as both subject and ruler, as both outsider and insider, contributes greatly to her achievement.

Closer examination of Esther's situation within the royal court further illustrates the paradox of her position and focuses on the particular relationship between subject and king that is redefined in the Septuagint prayer. Despite multiple layers of gender and ethnic subjection, Esther is at the same time in a unique position as Persian queen. Through a royal marriage based on the king's love, favor, and devotion (Esth 2:7), Esther enjoys an intimate, if asymmetrical, parity with the highest human authority of the empire. She is therefore both outsider to power, with her status as wife bound by law to honor her husband and with her undisclosed minority identity, and insider, with her proximity to the king himself. Esther has a layered identity that bridges the demarcation of those who command and those who are commanded, which on the surface seems clear but which comes to be subverted in the course of the book. It is Esther's unique status that Mordecai stresses when he points out her placement in the palace (Esth 4:13) and her royal standing that makes her the most likely to succeed in petitioning the king (Esth 4:15). Esther's distinctive position is also indicated when she dons her royal apparel (literally her "royalty") before entering the inner court before the king, signaling that she is part of his regal world (5:1). Her status as insider will again be emphasized when she twice invites the king and Haman to dine with her, since royal banquets with their power to reinforce hierarchy and bestow honor characterize life at the Persian court.

Despite her special status, however, Esther considers the king's decree, with its threat of death for all who disobey, as applicable to herself as much as to his other subjects (Esth 4:11). Nor does Esther appear to have immunity from the royal law contrived by Haman condemning the Jews to death (Esth 4:13–14). Just as within her family she complied with the instructions of Mordecai (Esth 2:10, 20), and within the harem with the advice of the king's eunuch in charge of the women (Esth 2:15), Esther initially intends to comply with the law prohibiting her unbidden entry (Esth 4:11). Her timidity and eagerness to please appear to mark her identity at the court. The remainder of the book will proceed to unravel this portrayal of Esther as compliant subject and therefore to critique the assumptions that it is based upon, depicting a much more complicated negotiation of power structures and hierarchical relationships, for the joy and light of a diaspora people. In fact, one substantive impact that the book makes is to challenge the whole notion that oppressive hierarchies are as stable and strong as they might appear to be. Rather, fate and chance, along with human agency of those in pivotal positions of privilege and access, make all the difference between death and life, between darkness and light, between sorrow and joy for the Jewish minority population.

In any event, Esther's primary self-understanding as a subject of the divine King in her prayer in the Septuagint further qualifies her placement within the multiple human hierarchies of the surrounding narrative. The important transformation of the treatment of Esther as subject-self in the Septuagint involves no liberation from subservience, but rather an additional layer of subjection and a corresponding shift in her identity as a subject with the explicit identification of God as the only King of her people. This trumping of all other subjections in the Septuagint explains her determination and strength to approach her terrifying husband unbidden, to reveal her Jewish identity and accuse her people's foe, and to exact her requests from the Persian king. Paradoxically, Esther's humility as the female slave of the divine King in the Septuagint becomes the source of her power to confront competing pretenders to authority, both human and divine. Esther's prayer makes clear that it is not her unique status as Persian queen that contributes to her heroic success in delivering her people, but rather her humble subjection and unswerving loyalty to a power greater even than that of the Persian king. Toward the end of her prayer, Esther's status as a subject of the divine King similarly explains how she has been able to live day by day as a Jew in the foreign court with at least a limited amount of integrity and happiness.

Presenting Oneself Before the King

Esther reveals her identity as a subject of the divine Monarch in Addition C even before she verbally invokes the God of Israel as her only King. The queen's attention to her clothing, hair, and body in preparation for her prayerful appearance before the universal Sovereign concretely dramatizes her self-understanding as his obedient subject and defines her body as the site for declaring her undivided allegiance:

> Then Queen Esther, seized with deadly anxiety, fled to the Lord. She took off her splendid apparel and put on the garments of distress and mourning, and instead of costly perfumes she covered her head with ashes and dung, and she utterly humbled her body; every part that she loved to adorn she covered with her tangled hair. She prayed to the Lord God of Israel: "O my Lord, you only are our King." (LXX Esth 14:1–2)

Esther's preparation to approach the divine King in prayer replicates with telling variations a simple type scene developed in several distinctive ways elsewhere within the Hebrew narrative and corresponding passages of the Greek translation. This type scene depicts a queen (or potential queen) attending to dress or other physical aspects of the self in anticipation of an audience before the Persian king. A summary review of the three exemplars of this type scene in the Hebrew book and its Greek parallels will establish a backdrop for viewing Esther's climactic preparation to approach the divine King in prayer secondarily introduced into the Septuagint in Addition C, and for exploring the importance of the body for the religious self in this Hellenistic version of the narrative.

Paradoxically, the first exemplar of this type scene in the Masoretic Text, which for convenience we can call "Vashti's refusal," reveals not its basic contours but the shock of its disruption. On the seventh and final day of his banquet in Susa, the drunken monarch commands his seven eunuchs "to bring Queen Vashti before the king, wearing the royal crown, in order to show the peoples and officials her beauty" (MT Esth 1:11). In defiance of this directive, as well as of the conventions of the type scene as developed twice later in the Hebrew narrative, "Queen Vashti refused to come at the king's command" (MT Esth 1:12). With this refusal, the queen also rejects her husband's proposal that she prepare to appear before him by donning the emblem of her royal position. In the Septuagint, a slightly different order of events further complicates the relation of this episode to the basic type scene, since Vashti does not yet possess the crown at this point in the narrative. Vashti's failure to fulfill the basic conventions of the type scene in its first exemplar results in her elimination as an active character in the narrative. An unexpected opening is thereby made for Esther, whose compliance with the conventions of the type scene in the second and third exemplars preface her successful audiences with the king.

The second exemplar of this type scene, which may be labeled as the "harem regimen," is in marked contrast to the first, in that it reinforces the typical pattern through its en masse execution. When a new queen is sought to replace the recalcitrant Vashti, each and every one of the countless virgins brought from all parts of the Persian kingdom to the royal harem in Susa

undergoes extensive beauty treatments in anticipation of her single-night audience with the king. In the Masoretic Text, the procedures entail "twelve
months under the regulations for the women, since this was the regular period
of their cosmetic treatment: six months with oil of myrrh and six months with
perfumes and cosmetics for women" (MT Esth 2:12). After this beautification
program, each girl is "given whatever she asked for to take with her from the
harem to the king's palace," suggesting attempts to win the king's favor by
sexually entertaining him (MT Esth 2:12–13), noticeably absent in the Septuagint version of the scene (LXX Esth 2:13). This variation protects the character of Esther and the other gathered virgins, who earlier in the chapter are
described not only as "beautiful," but also as "virtuous" (LXX Esth 2:2). As
Esther prepares to go before the king in the Septuagint, she neglects "none of
the things that Gai, the eunuch in charge of the women, had commanded"
(LXX Esth 2:15), thus illustrating her characteristic trait of obedience. Participation in the "harem regimen" results in Esther's winning of the king's love and
favor, and thereby the royal crown (Esth 2:17).

As the new queen, Esther no doubt comes into the presence of her royal
husband frequently, including upon the occasion of the banquet held on her
behalf, called "Esther's feast" in the Masoretic Text (MT Esth 2:18) and identified
as their marriage celebration in the Septuagint (LXX Esth 2:18). Esther's preparation for an audience with the king is not subsequently depicted, however, until
much later in the narrative, after Mordecai urges her to intercede for the Jewish
people and she reveals her resolve to risk her life in this endeavor. Immediately
before Esther approaches the king, she once again attends to personal appearance, in the third and final exemplar of the type scene in the Hebrew version
of the narrative: "On the third day, Esther dressed in royal garb and stood in the
inner court of the king's palace, opposite the king's hall" (MT Esth 5:1). This brief
description of Esther's donning of royal clothing visually symbolizes her elevated position within the court and her relationship with the king that promise
to gain her a positive reception. This brief though highly charged description of
Esther's preparation for her audience with the king in the Masoretic Text is
much more fully elaborated in the Septuagint. The royal clothing that she puts
on is designated as "her glory" (LXX Esth 15:1), in keeping with the development
and critique of the theme of regal glory throughout the Septuagint version of the
narrative. "Majestically adorned" (LXX Esth 15:2), Esther requires the assistance
of two maids to walk, one to lean upon and one to follow, carrying the train of
her garment (LXX Esth 15:4). As she approaches the king, she appears "radiant
with perfect beauty," looking "happy, as if beloved" (LXX Esth 15:5).

Following "Esther's dressing" for her climactic approach before the king in
the third exemplar of the type scene, she again wins the monarch's favor and
even surpasses her earlier achievement of securing her position as queen. When
the king invites her to ask for up to half of his kingdom, a way is opened for her
to intervene on behalf of her people. Esther's voluntary donning of royal garb

and appearing unbidden before the king in this third exemplar of the type scene in the Hebrew narrative contrasts with Vashti's earlier refusal to wear the crown and appear before the king when commanded. The first queen's noncompliance creates a crisis in her husband's surprisingly fragile government and marital relations that the routine regulations set for all the women of the harem are intended to resolve. Together "Vashti's refusal" and the "harem regimen" work to establish Esther in her unique position as the Jewish queen of Persia. The third exemplar, "Esther's dressing," accentuates the royal status that enables the queen to affect a resolution to the crisis of impending genocide.

But in the expanded Septuagint version of the narrative, "Esther's dressing" to approach the Persian king is postponed, as an additional exemplar of the type scene with a significant variant is interjected in Addition C. In the Septuagint, before "Esther's dressing" for her audience with her husband, she first attends even more fastidiously to the details of her clothing, hair, and body in anticipation of her approach before her divine King in prayer:

> Then Queen Esther, seized with deadly anxiety, fled to the Lord. She took off her splendid apparel and put on the garments of distress and mourning, and instead of costly perfumes she covered her head with ashes and dung, and she utterly humbled her body; every part that she loved to adorn she covered with her tangled hair. She prayed to the Lord God of Israel: "O my Lord, you only are our King." (LXX Esth 14:1–2)

A number of unique features distinguish this additional fourth exemplar of the type scene, referred to henceforth as "Esther's humiliation," from the others that we have examined. Most immediately obvious is Esther's very different treatment of her body, which dramatizes the queen's distress and humility rather than her beauty and position. Of even greater import is Esther's identification of the only King that she recognizes as the Lord God of Israel, not only through her spoken invocation but also through her careful preparation to come into his presence in prayer. Especially telling in this connection is the description following the conclusion of this scene of the simple clothing in which she had worshipped as "the garments of a household servant" (LXX Esth 15:1), which confirms her identity as a subject of the divine King. Also significant is that Esther's approach of this transcendent King is not in the least coerced or hesitant, as when she is brought to the palace along with the other Persian virgins or when at Mordecai's urging she finally agrees to speak to her husband despite the risk to her own life. Rather, she hastens to this King, and her flight indicates her confidence that he will provide refuge and help in her time of danger. The fact that in the Septuagint this additional exemplar of the "preparing to meet the king" type scene is the longest and most detailed, and that it is immediately followed by Esther's longest speech in the entire book, shifts the weight of the narrative toward this particular royal audience between the queen and her divine Monarch.

Earlier, in mentioning some of the factors that may have prompted or at least supported the inclusion of Esther's prayer at this particular point in the Septuagint narrative, it was noted that the "king" before whom Mordecai urges Esther to plead (MT Esth 4:8) and before whom Esther approaches (MT Esth 5:1) is never further identified by name. This lack of specificity is not particularly problematic in a narrative whose cast of characters includes only a single monarch. The lack of the king's name, however, made it possible for later readers to conclude that it must be the divine King that Esther must first approach with her supplication, since her prayer will affect the outcome of her subsequent audience with the human king. Other details of the original biblical narrative also seem to support the insertion of this extra exemplar of the type scene depicting "Esther's humiliation" before her audience with the divine Monarch.

Since the other Jews, including Mordecai and all those living in all the provinces of the Persia spontaneously began mourning and fasting in sackcloth and ashes (Esth 4:1–3), it is no wonder that the Septuagint portrays Esther adopting this general practice of her people, especially since she indicates that she and her attendants would be participating along with all the Jews of Susa in the three-day fast before she went to the king (Esth 4:16). The brief notice of "Esther's dressing" in royal garb (Esth 5:1) before approaching the human king in the Hebrew narrative itself suggests that Esther must have previously taken off her ceremonial clothing, since she needed to put it on again. The Septuagint builds on these suggestive details of the original narrative when it describes "Esther's humiliation" in preparation for her prayer before the divine King.

With respect to its extended attention to the preparation of the body, the additional fourth exemplar of the type scene in the Septuagint recalls most vividly the virgins' cosmetic procedures before their private audiences with the Persian king (Esth 2:12). Despite this similarity in focus, however, the attitudes toward feminine beauty and the treatments of the physical self portrayed in the "harem regimen" and in "Esther's humiliation" could not be more different. This contrast marks the Septuagint interpolation as a critique or even a reversal of Esther's participation in the earlier scene in the harem. Unlike the previous scene, where Esther anonymously submits to the procedures prescribed for all the young women gathered for the king's pleasure, here the queen acts in solitude and on her own initiative to remove all traces of her association with the Persian court.

A particularly graphic contrast between the "harem regimen" and "Esther's humiliation" may be seen in the different valences given to sensuous ointments in the two exemplars of the type scene. In the Septuagint Addition C, Esther employs defiling ashes and foul-smelling dung instead of "costly perfumes," a phrase that appears to summarize the longer list of "oil of myrrh" and "spices and ointments for women" used in the harem (LXX Esth 2:12; cf., LXX Esth 2:9). Rather than cultivating feminine beauty in an effort to curry the human king's favor, Esther's extreme humiliation of her body in Addition C demonstrates her disdain for status based on physical attractiveness and indicates her intentional choice to participate within an alternative reality. The larger context of the three-day fast by the Jews of Susa further stresses the severe physical denial involved in this scene. Esther's vow that she and her maids in the palace would refrain from eating and drinking both night and day along with the other Jews (Esth 4:16) contrasts to the comfort and luxury of the king's harem, where Esther's servings of food were quickly provided for her by a doting eunuch, along with her ointments (Esth 2:9). In this scene, Esther rejects what is typical and desirable in the Persian palace to prepare herself for an audience in the divine court.

The Septuagint scene of "Esther's humiliation" proves to be much more encompassing than the "harem regimen," however, in that besides topical applications it also details matters of clothing, adornment, and coiffure. Esther sheds the glorious regalia and jewelry that symbolize her royal position to put on humble garments appropriate for distress and mourning and to cover her neck and shoulders with tresses of disheveled hair. Besides distancing herself from the Persian court, Esther's change of appearance therefore also establishes her alliance with Mordecai and the rest of the Jewish community outside the palace walls, who take to wearing sackcloth and ashes upon hearing the king's decree (Esth 4:1–3). The importance of this response to the impending calamity is indicated by Mordecai's refusal to change his clothing even when urged by Esther (Esth 4:4). Although "no one was allowed to enter the courtyard clothed in sackcloth and ashes" (LXX Esth 4:2), Esther's change of attire within the palace penetrates that cloistered guard and forms a link with those who mourn and fast outside.

Esther's debasement of her own body in Addition C raises the larger issue of the value of physicality for the concept of the religious self in the Septuagint version of the narrative. Details appearing later in Esther's prayer, such as her denigration of the king of "flesh" whom the nations wrongly extol (LXX Esth 14:10), might suggest an extremely negative perspective of the corporeal aspects of human existence. Yet it is highly significant that far more attention is paid to Esther's physical condition and appearance in the Septuagint than in the Hebrew narrative, through such means as the insertion of this scene of "Esther's humiliation" in Addition C and as the elaboration of the description of her dress and demeanor as she approaches the human king in Addition D. With such emphasis, the body can hardly be inconsequential for human identity. Nor, upon closer examination, is it entirely negative in its valence.

In the Septuagint, the human body and in particular Esther's female body becomes the contested site for human allegiance in a fundamental conflict between two competing kingdoms, those ruled by pagan gods and royalty, and that ruled by the one God. It is for this reason that the Greek Esther, as other Hellenistic Jewish heroines from the same period like Judith and Aseneth, display such attentiveness to their bodies, stripping themselves of fine clothing and jewels, loosening and tearing their hair, and disciplining their bodies through fasting and other ascetic practices. The almost voyeuristic scenes in Hellenistic Jewish literature depicting these women's radical alteration of their clothing, appearance, and comportment dramatize their protest and rejection of the values held dear by the foreign political worlds in which they move and occupy exalted positions, and their rightful alignment and devotion to the one true God.

"Esther's humiliation" of her body in the Septuagint goes beyond a simple donning of sackcloth and ashes for the purpose of mourning the impending death of her people or of fasting to affect providential intervention, as seems to be the case for Mordecai and the other Jews in the Persian empire. Rather, Esther's severe treatment of her body is part of a more fundamental denouncement of the foreign kingdom with its worship of pagan gods, which for all appearances defines her everyday reality. In addition to expressing an emphatic rejection of the false empire, Esther's physical humiliation in the Septuagint also has a positive value. The queen's body becomes the tangible means of her self-identification as a subject of an entirely different Monarch as well as of her embrace of membership in an alternative community of those who similarly owe their exclusive allegiance to the one God.

Esther's Communal Self: Memory and Identity

The self that Esther reveals through her prayer to the "Lord God of Israel" (LXX Esth 14:3) is therefore to a large extent a communal self, defined by her identity as part of a family within one of the tribes of the people Israel (LXX Esth 14:5). Following a short introduction that deals with the immediate risk to her own life (LXX Esth 14:3–4), the first major part of Esther's prayer concerns the plight of her people (LXX Esth 14:5–11). Certainly the theme of Esther's identification with her community and their dire situation in the Persian empire is also a critical part of the Masoretic Text, especially beginning at the end of the fourth chapter, where Esther instructs Mordecai to gather the Jews in Susa for a fast in support of her determination to plead their cause before the king, and continuing through the rest of the book as she reveals her identity, advocates for her people, and establishes the holiday of Purim as a memorial for their deliverance. Before that turning point in the Masoretic Text, however, any distinctive Jewish identity that Esther may have had in her early years under Mordecai's supervision, including her Hebrew name Hadassah, remains completely hidden in the Persian court, in compliance with her uncle's order (MT Esth 2:10). Apparently Esther has so successfully assimilated that her ethnicity has remained unnoticed in the palace, and when she sends clothes to Mordecai as he laments the king's decree in sackcloth (MT Esth 4:1–8), she reveals either complete isolation and ignorance of events critical to her own people or a naïve attempt to keep her uncle's Jewish identity a secret so as to spare him from perishing along with the others. In any event, in the Masoretic Text there is nothing comparable to the disclosure of Esther's thoughts about her connections to the Jewish people that we find in the Septuagint.

In her prayer, Esther draws on collective memory to define the moment in which she and the rest of the Jewish people find themselves and to establish the basis of her appeal for divine assistance. Memory, as a part of communal identity, is of course also one of the main purposes of the Esther scroll, which establishes the celebration of Purim to remember the deliverance of the Jews from their enemies (Esth 9:20–22, 26–29). In the Septuagint, however, Esther reaches farther back to recall traditions about her people that she had heard repeated within her family and her tribe from the time she was born (LXX Esth 14:5). Esther's recourse to memory in her prayer complies with Mordecai's earlier appeal to her in the Septuagint version of the narrative: "Remember the days when you were an ordinary person, being brought up under my care. . . . Call upon the Lord; then speak to the king on our behalf, and save us from death" (LXX Esth 4:8).

Whereas in the Masoretic Text the only explicit reference to Israelite history recalls the end of national existence with the trauma of exile (MT Esth 2:6), in Esther's prayer in the Septuagint she recounts a history that is ancient, long, and ongoing. The formative identity that Esther shares with the rest of her people stretches back to God's election of Israel from the nations and continues through their captivity because of idolatry:

> You, O Lord, took Israel out of all the nations, and our ancestors from among
> all their forebears, for an everlasting inheritance, and that you did for them all
> that you promised. And now we have sinned before you, and you have handed
> us over to our enemies because we glorified their gods. (LXX Esth 14:5–7)

Esther's recapitulation of her people's story, although schematic, follows a basic Deuteronomistic pattern and contains several important scriptural allusions, including the election of Israel from the nations as an everlasting inheritance, the promises to the ancestors, and the deliverance of the people to enemies because of idolatry. Her recitation thus exemplifies the scripturalization of communal memory typical of prayers in the Second Temple period.[3] A detail in the shorter Greek version known as the A-Text, where Esther learns of her people's history from reading a written document that she calls "my father's book" (AT Esth 14:5), confirms the importance of scripture as a source of communal memory and identity.

As Esther culminates her account of Israel's history with the agony of the present crisis, she continues to obliquely draw on scriptural memory:

> You are righteous, O Lord! And now they are not satisfied that we are in bitter
> slavery, but they have covenanted with their idols to abolish what your mouth
> has ordained, and to destroy your inheritance, to stop the mouths of those

who praise you and to quench your altar and the glory of your house, to open
the mouths of the nations for the praise of vain idols, and to magnify forever a
mortal king. (LXX Esth 14:7–10)

In calling the condition of the exile "bitter slavery," Esther recalls Israel's op-
pression in Egypt. The description of exile as slavery is repeated in LXX Esther
7:4, where Esther informs the king, "For we have been sold, I and my people, to
be destroyed, plundered, and made slaves—we and our children—male and
female slaves" (cf., MT Esth 7:4) Esther's reference of a threat to the altar and
the temple, while jarring in the literary setting of the Persian court (although
not in the Hellenistic context in which the additions were written), brings to
mind the sanctuary in Jerusalem with its priests, sacrifices, and divine presence
that figure so centrally in the biblical tradition. In all these details, we see that
Esther's understanding of her identity as part of the Jewish people is embedded
in a memory steeped in scripture, even though by comparison with some of the
prayers offered in other versions of the story, especially the second Targum of
Esther, the biblical references are quite general and sparse.

Identity in Opposition

In her prayer, Esther's identity as a member of the Jewish people includes a clear
opposition between Israel and the other nations of the world. These nations are
defined as Israel's enemies (LXX Esth 14:6), whose worship of worthless gods
(LXX Esth 14:10) has led Israel into sinful idolatry with its disastrous consequences (LXX Esth 14:7). Hand in hand with their idols, these nations seek to
destroy Israel, and this plot also targets Israel's deity, since the existence of this
nation as his own inheritance has been ordained by decree of his mouth (LXX
Esth 14:8–9) and its destruction will terminate the people's worship and praise
(LXX Esth 14:9). As Esther's prayer continues, she voices her fear that the other
nations will mock Israel's downfall, and she pleads that their own plan of
destruction be turned against them (LXX Esth 14:11). These expressions contrasting Israel and its divine Monarch with the other nations of the world, their
king, and their idols are concentrated in a section (LXX Esth 14:6–12) that is
lacking from the Old Latin version and from Josephus's paraphrase of Esther's
prayer in *Jewish Antiquities*, indicating that they may not have originally been
part of Addition C, but rather were a later addition.

The stark division of the world into two enemy camps, comprised of the
Jews and their divine King and of the Gentiles and their idols and mortal king,
is distinctive to the Septuagint and forms a central aspect of Esther's religious
identity in this work. The continuation of Esther's prayer eliminates any ambiguity concerning the distinction between Jews and non-Jews. It comes as no
surprise that in her prayer Esther describes Haman as the "man who is fighting
against us" (LXX Esth 14:13) and asks that his scheme be turned against him
(LXX Esth 14:11), since the plot elements to which these phrases allude are also

present in the Masoretic Text. What is of considerable significance is that as Esther reflects on her own personal situation as part of a mixed marriage, the Persian king is transformed from merely a foolish and malleable despot into a wicked, uncircumcised foreigner for whom Esther feels nothing but contempt. As she reminds God, "You have knowledge of all things, and you know that I hate the splendor of the wicked and abhor the bed of the uncircumcised and foreigners" (LXX Esth 14:15). Circumcision as the missing mark of Jewish identity becomes the symbol of what remains fundamentally wrong with her marriage, even though Addition D incongruously portrays the interaction between the couple as mutually affectionate once God changes the king's anger to gentleness. Esther's expression of loathing addresses what otherwise might appear as a shocking violation of prohibitions against intermarriage elsewhere in the Bible, since she makes clear in her prayer that if she had any choice in the matter she would not be married to an uncircumcised foreigner.

Esther also has strong feelings about the crown that the king gave her because he loved her and found her more desirable than all the other virgins (Esth 2:17): "You know my necessity—that I abhor the sign of my proud position, which is upon my head on days when I appear in public. I abhor it like a menstrual rag, and I do not wear it on the days when I am at leisure" (LXX Esth 14:16). This graphic comparison expresses Esther's shame over the public exposure required in her official capacity, which is depicted as a period of unavoidable impurity. While Esther may not be able to avoid the marital bed or her public appearances as queen, there are certain areas over which she maintains more control: "Your servant has not eaten at Haman's table, and I have not honored the king's feast or drunk the wine of libation" (LXX Esth 14:17). Esther's fastidiousness concerning diet in her Septuagint prayer is in marked contrast to the Masoretic Text, where she appears to routinely receive her portions of food from a solicitous eunuch (MT Esth 2:9). Her concern for eating only proper foods recalls similar scruples held by other Second Temple figures, including Daniel's refusal of the king's rich food and drink (Dan 1:8–16), Judith's care to eat only her own provisions (Jud 12:2–4), and Eleazar's refusal to eat pork with its more serious consequence (2 Macc 6:18–31). The behavior that Esther reports here may indicate the observance of dietary laws, but it is significant that in each instance what is emphasized is the separation that she maintains between herself and Haman, the king, and the false gods of the pagans. Esther's absolute sense of distance from life in the palace and her identification with her ancestral people is summarized when she reveals: "Your servant has had no joy since the day that I was brought here until now, except in you, O Lord God of Abraham" (LXX Esth 14:18).

The Religious Self Defined by Different Laws

The ideal of separation from other peoples in the king's vast empire, while an important component of Esther's critical attitude toward her marriage and royal position as well as of her refusal to eat and drink with the rest of the court, does not completely exhaust the significance of her conduct as described in her prayer in the Septuagint. Esther's refusal to participate in the feasting and festivities that are featured so prominently in the narrative proves to be an especially illuminating case in this regard. Within Esther's prayer, her principled abstention is a positive expression of her authentic self that she affirms whole-heartedly. Esther's consistent behavior with regard to what she eats and drinks contrasts with the other accommodations that she is forced to accept, such as the crown that she unwillingly wears in public and her marriage with the uncircumcised king whose bed she abhors. Scattered glosses throughout the Septuagint version of Esther create a larger context in which her care in dietary matters may be viewed as participation in a community ethos of obedience to divinely mandated laws.

In the Masoretic Text, Haman portrays the Jews scattered and separated throughout the kingdom as a single people united by their observance of distinctive laws: "Their laws are different from those of every other people, and they do not keep the king's laws" (MT Esth 3:8). One wonders, however, to what extent Haman's words are intended as an accurate description of Jewish practice in the Persian empire and to what extent they serve his own rhetorical purposes before a monarch who considers his royal decrees as irrevocable (MT Esth 8:8). Haman's charge is brought into question at many points in the narrative, for example, when the Jews scrupulously do obey the king's decrees in order to act in unison to defend themselves (Esth 8:7–14; 9:13–15). In fact, Esther's hidden identity in the palace appears to depend precisely on her lack of any distinctive ethnic or religious behavior based on special laws. While it is true that Mordecai's identity as a Jew is revealed in the context of his refusal to obey the king's command that all bow to Haman after his inexplicable promotion (Esth 3:1–6), the reason for Mordecai's refusal is not clear and might be attributed to a personal feud between these descendants of the ancient enemies Saul and Agag. More generally, Haman's second charge, that the Jews fail to keep the king's laws, is qualified by the text's portrayal of these royal edicts as ridiculous, arbitrary, and even pernicious. As discussed above, the king's laws consist of outrageous measures advocated by his subordinates that happen to please the monarch at the moment but that he seems to forget in the next, including the obedience of all women to their husbands because of his own wife Vashti's refusal, and the destruction of all Jews because of Mordecai's offense. The considered disregard and overturning of these laws that Esther exemplifies cannot therefore be attributed to some antimonarchic principle characteristic of all Jews, who instead operate under separate laws, as Haman accuses.

But if the Masoretic Text raises more questions about the Jewish community's relation to the laws of the majority government than it solves, the Septuagint, by contrast, seems to reiterate and confirm what Haman says about the distinctive laws of the Jews. In Addition B of the Septuagint, which purports to be a copy of the king's letter authorizing the slaughter of the Jews, Haman's accusation of this people before the king in Esther 3:8 is expanded. In addition to disregarding the king's laws and following their own, the Jews become a troublesome and hostile nation, whose existence causes instability and prevents the unification of the nation (LXX Esth 13:4). As the king's letter further explains, "We understand that this people, and it alone, stands constantly in opposition to every nation, perversely following a strange manner of life and laws" (LXX Esth 13:5). Esther herself is instructed by Mordecai upon becoming queen not only to keep the identity of her people a secret but also "to fear God and keep his laws, just as she had done when she was with him. So Esther did not change her mode of life" (LXX Esth 2:20).

Ultimately, the king himself recognizes the legitimacy of the Jews' distinctive way of life, and in addition to ordering them to defend themselves, he also "ordered the Jews to observe their own laws" (LXX Esth 8:11). In Addition E, the copy of the king's second letter denouncing Haman, the king furthermore acknowledges that the Jews are not evildoers, "but are governed by most righteous laws and are children of the living God, most high, most almighty, who has directed the kingdom both for us and for our ancestors in the most excellent order" (LXX Esth 16:15). The posting of the king's letter is intended to "permit the Jews to live under their own laws" (LXX Esth 16:19). Esther's abstention from feasting and drinking in the Persian court therefore fits into the additional emphasis on the distinctive way of life and laws of the Jews celebrated in the Septuagint. One assumes that Esther's behavior as depicted in her prayer in Addition C therefore expresses solidarity with her community in following the righteous laws of God and not the laws of Persia. In making this choice, Esther again defines her primary religious identity as a subject of her people's true sovereign.

The praying Esther of the Septuagint, even though much more fully described, is in some respects actually less complex than the minimally portrayed Esther of the Masoretic Text with her fluidity within the Persian culture and her emergent identification with her own people. Esther's prayer in the Septuagint draws her character into a more clear-cut definition of what it means theologically and practically to be a member of a Jewish minority community within the cosmopolitan world of the Hellenistic empire. Our exploration of the Jewish queen's prayer has revealed an ideal concept of the religious self that is characterized by an exclusive orientation toward a transcendent deity who is regarded as the only legitimate Monarch. Esther's identity as a subject of the divine King means a rejection of the worldly values and idolatrous ways of the human royal court. The queen's severe treatment of her body becomes a mark of her loyalty to her deity and of her solidarity with her people, who worship the same all-powerful God.

Esther's identity in her Septuagint prayer is solidly communal in nature, including a collective memory consisting of a scripturalized past, a principled separation from non-Jews (or at least maintenance of a critical attitude when compelled to be in close contact, as in her marriage), and a commitment to obeying the laws of the divine King along with the rest of the Jewish people. Because Esther's identity in the Septuagint is bound together on so different many levels with that of the larger Jewish community, her solitude in the palace and her contemplation of her people's destruction become all the more desperate. As a communally defined self in complete isolation at the moment when she prays, Esther's plight is severe, and her core identity appears to be radically jeopardized. The threat to Esther's self in her prayer in the Septuagint therefore expresses the severity of the threat to the Jewish community within the foreign empire.

Yet, despite the presentation of these aspects of Esther's identity through her prayer in the Septuagint, the larger narrative context will not easily allow such a clear-cut definition of the religious self to stand. It is precisely because of the actual tensions between the ideal presented in her prayer and the reality of the life that she leads in the Persian court that the Jewish queen is able to succeed in delivering her people from annihilation. It is precisely because she does share the foreign king's bed, because she does wear royal garb and navigate the culture of the palace, and because she does eat and drink with the king and Haman that she is able to play the remarkable role for which she continues to be remembered year by year. Moving from the ideal of the religious self portrayed in Esther's prayer to the messier reality of her life in the rest of the narrative, we would have to address the positive aspects of ambiguity, conflict, and historical contingency that form part of Esther's religious self—but that is the subject of another exploration.

NOTES

1. The Septuagint contains six supplemental Additions (known as A, B, C, D, E, and F) to the main narrative that are lacking in the Hebrew.

2. This colophon credits Lysimachus, son of Ptolemy, a resident of Jerusalem, with the translation of the Greek version of Esther that was brought to Egypt during the fourth year of the reign of Ptolemy and Cleopatra. Since three kings of Egypt named Ptolemy were married to queens named Cleopatra, the fourth year mentioned could be 114–13, 78–77, or 49–48 B.C.E. The appearance of the colophon after Addition F suggests that Lysimachus had before him a Hebrew text containing all of the Septuagint additions, although this cannot be ascertained with certainty.

3. See Judith Newman, *Praying by the Book: The Scripturalization of Prayer in Second Temple Literature* (Atlanta: Scholars Press, 1999).

—5—

Giving for a Return:
Jewish Votive Offerings in Late Antiquity

MICHAEL L. SATLOW

When the otherwise unknown Maximos made a donation to the synagogue in Hammath Tiberias in the fourth or fifth century c.e., he—like many other Jews who made such gifts throughout the circum-Mediterranean—commemorated it with an inscription. Like a significant minority of such Jews, he noted that his contribution was made "in fulfillment of a vow." In fact, the tabular mosaic that contains his inscription notes five other gifts in fulfillment of vows. Though written in Greek, the names of these donors reflect Greek, Latin, and Semitic origins. This was far from atypical; from the fourth century on, Jewish men and women, from a variety of origins, began to mark the fulfillment of their vows with public inscriptions in the synagogue.

Although donation inscriptions in general have received extensive scholarly attention, the religious aspects of these votive inscriptions have largely gone unnoticed. The argument of this paper is that the Jewish votive inscriptions from late antiquity represent a distinctive religious *mentalité* that imagines God as an immanent being to be bartered with; they reflect selves in active negotiation with the divine. Yet while they reflect personal sentiments, they are also public documents written and displayed according to conventional norms. As texts that are personal but not private, they lie at the intersection of individual religious sentiments and their public representation. Additionally, these inscriptions give us a window, however opaque, into the religious lives of a group of people typically ignored in the richer literary remains examined by most of the other papers in this volume.

Let us momentarily return to Maximos. His votive inscription appears in a mosaic located in one of the most lavishly decorated synagogues yet found in the land of Israel. The elaborate floor mosaic was apparently installed in the fourth century or later, as part of an extensive renovation of the Hammath Tiberias synagogue.[1] Measuring about ten meters square, the mosaic almost covers the entire floor of the main room. Of the three surviving sections (out of four), it is the central one that most concerns us. Positioned between the central entrance to the synagogue and the ark, it is divided into three panels. The top panel (closest to the ark) contains a central picture of the tabernacle or ark surrounded by an assortment of implements related to the temple (e.g., incense shovel, seven-branched candelabra). The panel below it is a zodiac, with a picture of a figure (Helios? God?) in the middle. The lowest panel—directly in front of the entrance—is laid out as a table, flanked by lions, containing eight Greek inscriptions:

> Maximos vowing, fulfilled (it). Long may he live.
>
> Aboudemos vowing, fulfilled (it).
>
> Zoilos vowing fulfilled (it). Long may he live.
>
> Ioullos the supervisor completed the whole work.
>
> Sever[os] disciple of the most illustrious patriarchs fulfilled (it). Blessings upon
>   him. Amen.
>
> Kalinikos vowing fulfilled (it). Long may he live.
>
> [Profutouros vow]ing fulfilled (it). Long may he live.
>
> Siortasis vowing fulfilled (it). May he be saved.[2]

Of these eight inscriptions, seven record donations given in fulfillment of a vow. The donors have Greek, Latin, and Aramaic names, and several receive a blessing for a "long life." Siortasis receives a wish for "salvation" (*sōzestō*), perhaps here meaning good health.

For a late antique synagogue from the land of Israel, the quantity of such inscriptions is somewhat unusual, but the wording and ideas that they reflect are not. Two of the Greek inscriptions found at the synagogue in Sepphoris appear to share the vow terminology as well as the wishes for salvation.[3] Greek inscriptions in Palestinian synagogues sometimes mention "thanksgiving offerings" (*eucharizō*).[4] One inscription from a fragment of a screen in a synagogue from Ashkelon, for example, reads: "God help *kura*[5] Domna daughter of Julianus [?], and *kuros* Mari(n) son of Nonnus, having made a thanksgiving offering (*eucharizō*). *Kuros* . . . grandson of Helikias made a thanksgiving offering to God and to this holy place, gift for the sake of salvation."[6] Another fragmentary inscription from Gaza begins: "[For the salvati]on of Jacob, Leaz[ar, and Mar]eina, having made a thanksgiving offer[ing to God and] to this holy place."[7] Some of the other Greek terminology found in the Hammath Tiberias, such as "salvation" and "be remembered for good," recurs in synagogues throughout Palestine.[8]

Synagogue inscriptions throughout Palestine also sometimes contain Aramaic and Hebrew forms of this terminology. A fragmentary Aramaic inscription from Tiberias notes a man who "gave a freewill offering."[9] An expansive Hebrew inscription from the mosaic floor of the synagogue at Horvat Susiya reads: "Remember for good the holy, *mari,* Rabbi Isi the Kohen, honored, *berebi,* who made this mosaic and plastered its walls in fulfillment of what he vowed at the feast of Rabbi Yohanan the Kohen the scribe *berebi,* his son. Peace on Israel. Amen."[10] Joseph Yahalom and Gideon Forester have suggested that among Palestinian synagogue inscriptions the root *ḥzq* has a similar meaning to *ndb;* if so, the corpus of such inscriptions increases substantially.[11]

Vow terminology in synagogue inscriptions is not confined to Palestine. The synagogue at Sardis, dating perhaps from the fourth century but probably later, is one of the most majestic synagogues from late antiquity yet found. Out of 79 Greek inscriptions that were able to be reconstructed from its remains, 34 record donations made in fulfillment of a vow.[12] Usually these inscriptions record the donations of relatively small items. Two out of the six fragmentary Hebrew inscriptions from this synagogue contain the word "vow" *(ndr),* although the contexts are missing.[13]

Inscriptions with vow terminology are in fact common throughout synagogues in the Diaspora.[14] Inscriptions that record gifts given to synagogues in fulfillment of vows were found in Greece, the Balkans, Egypt, and Asia Minor.[15] An inscription from Delos records a thanksgiving offering.[16]

These inscriptions are only the most explicit of a much larger class of Jewish dedicatory inscriptions from synagogues. Many more inscriptions give simple notice of a gift: "Peace on all Israel, amen, amen, selah. Pinhas bar Baruch, Yose bar Shmuel, and Yudan bar Hezakaya," reads one Hebrew mosaic from Geresh;[17] "Remember for good Leazar the Kohen and his son who gave one *terimisis* from his property," according to an Aramaic inscription from Eshtamoa;[18] "Hanariah son of Jacob" reads a simple Greek mosaic inscription in a *tabula ansata* at Gaza;[19] "Aurelios Alexandros, also called Anatolios, citizen of Sardis, Councillor, mosaicked the third bay," reads a Greek inscription from Sardis.[20] The language changes slightly, but nearly all commemorate the generosity of an individual or family to the synagogue.

The practice of making votive gifts to the synagogue apparently continues well into late antiquity. A Roman law from the *Codex theodosianus* provides a tantalizing witness to the pervasiveness of the practice. On February 15, 423, the emperors Honorius and Theodosius II decreed that the synagogues of the Jews should be protected from future seizure and damage, adding: "Votive offerings *(donaria)* as well, if they are in fact seized, shall be returned to them provided that they have not yet been dedicated to the sacred mysteries *(sacris mysteriis);* but if a venerable consecration does not permit their restitution, they shall be given the exact price for them."[21] Apparently, Christians looted the synagogues before torching them, and they occasionally reconsecrated the synagogues' votive objects for use in their churches. The law does not tell us of what these *donaria* consisted.[22]

This brief survey points to the ordinariness of these votive inscriptions. Written in Greek, Hebrew, and Aramaic, in the land of Israel and abroad, these inscriptions all testify to the same phenomenon. Jews in late antiquity throughout the pan-Mediterranean and Near East gave (often small) donations to the synagogues, and in return were honored with a (usually simple) inscription. Men, women, and families all participated in this activity.

Nothing in rabbinic literature predicts either the quality or quantity of these inscriptions. Indeed, the rabbis rarely mention votives, and when they do, it is almost entirely within an academic or historical (i.e., the biblical or second temple periods) context. Rather, these inscriptions are the work of those whom the rabbis derisively call the ʿame haʾarets, "the people of the land." Recent scholarship has tended to emphasize the gap between the rabbis and other Jews, even those living in the very centers of rabbinic activity in the land of Israel in the third through fifth centuries C.E.[23] The "people of the land," not the rabbis, built and directed the central Jewish civic and religious institutions throughout Palestine and beyond.[24] Not the uneducated and unsophisticated boors portrayed by the rabbis, they built synagogues (18 in Sepphoris alone!), adorned them with intricate and expensive mosaics, organized administrative structures for running them, and created a system of communal support to finance them.[25] Centuries after the destruction of the temple, they may have continued to practice purity rituals and to esteem the priests as religious leaders.[26] They apparently recited the Torah in their synagogues, presumably subscribing to some of its fundamental myths. But unlike the rabbis, they appear to have put neither Torah study nor adherence to its *mitzvot*—as defined by the rabbis—at the heart of their religious life. Jewish inscriptions from antiquity, for example, almost never mention scholarly qualities or adherence to the Torah as admirable character traits.[27] These votive inscriptions thus represent "popular religion," by which I mean simply a pervasive religious sentiment not necessarily reflected in what would later become the "canonical" texts.[28]

The religious sentiment underlying these votives, in short, was that of divine immanence. These short inscriptions help to create and reinforce the relationships between the donors and their God. The Jewish votive inscriptions that explicitly use vow terminology fall roughly into two groups. One uses the language of freewill and thanksgiving offerings.[29] These inscriptions appear to thank God for particular perceived acts of divine intervention. God has helped the donor weather an illness or perhaps even find a lost coat, and the donor repays God with a gift to the "holy place." Alternatively, they may serve more as down payments against which one plans to draw future divine favor. In either case, they establish a cycle: the donor gives a gift in order that God might continue to give. God is thus drawn into a continuing relationship with the donor.

The second type of explicit votive offerings employs actual "vow" terminology (*ndr/euchē*). According to some literary sources, vows were conditional: if you do x for me, I will do y for you.[30] Unlike the unconditional vows found in modern Jewish liturgy (e.g., "I vow to give money in memory of x"), these vows demanded that God fulfill the condition, and do so prior to the gift. They appear to have been popular among Jews in late antiquity.[31]

The conditional vow implies a distinctly mutual relationship with the divine in which one barters with, rather than beseeches, the divinity. This implication was not lost on Greek philosophers. Plato argued against those who thought that they could "bribe" the gods (*Leg.* 905d–907d). For Theophrastus, veneration of the gods should not resemble a "gift on a contractual basis."[32] The rabbis of late antiquity rarely discuss votives to the synagogue, but given their general opposition to vows and insistence on the awe and respect owed to God, I suspect that they would ally themselves with Plato and Theophrastus against the authors of these votive inscriptions.[33]

Anthropological models of exchange provide a perspective that can help to make sense of the personal goals of those who make votive offerings. Gifts, like sacrifices, serve many different purposes simultaneously. For our purposes, I would emphasize the role of exchange in perpetuating relationships. Building on the work of Marcel Mauss, Maurice Godelier suggests that gift-giving creates social relationships by forming inerasable debts.[34] When social actors exchange gifts, the result is not a cancellation of the debt but a deepening of the social bond. This especially applies when "the thing or the person given is not alienated. To give is to transfer a person or thing whose 'usage' is ceded, but not its ownership."[35] "The giving of gifts and counter-gifts creates a state of mutual indebtedness and dependence which presents advantages for all parties. To give therefore is to share by creating a debt or, which amounts to the same thing, to create a debt by sharing."[36]

Although Godelier uses this model for an entirely different purpose, this insight does help to explain votives. A votive is a gift to a god. It is set aside for the god's use, but ultimately it "belongs" to the temple, synagogue, or priest. Most importantly, while paying back a debt, it in fact creates a new one. Cristiano Grottanelli has used this line of analysis to argue that ancient Greek and Punic votive inscriptions set up a continual cycle of gift-giving between humans and the gods.[37]

These somewhat theoretical observations about the function of votive offerings help to explain the distinctive religious *mentalité* underlying these late antique Jewish inscriptions. The inscriptions show religious selves in negotiation with the divine, who is brought into a continuing relationship with the donor. Yet this is only one part of the story. These particular Jewish votive inscriptions were written within a specific historical context. Why did Jews begin to commemorate their vows with synagogue inscriptions specifically in late antiquity? And what is the significance of the public form of these inscriptions? These two historically specific questions largely overlap.

Although Jewish votive inscriptions appear with frequency only in late antiquity (see below), Jewish votive *institutions* have a long history. The Torah prescribes an elaborate system of votives to the sanctuary. Leviticus 7, for example, delineates a tripartite hierarchy of sacrifices. The guilt and sin offerings are most holy and most highly regulated; they must be eaten by male priests in a sacred area (vv. 1–10). The "sacrifice of well-being," if a "thanksgiving offering," is eaten by the one who brought it on the same day it is offered (vv. 11–15). Finally, the vow and freewill offerings can be eaten over the course of two to three days (vv. 16–18).

These three types of voluntary offerings—thanksgiving, vow, and freewill— reappear regularly throughout the Bible, in legal as well as narrative contexts.[38] Priestly sources elsewhere govern the kinds of animals that may be offered for a vow or freewill offering (Lev 22:21–23) and the way in which they are to be offered (Num 15:2–13). Vows, the Bible frequently exhorts, are to be "paid" to God.[39]

Freewill offerings appear also in narrative sections of the Bible. The paradigmatic account is Moses' fundraising campaign for the building of the tabernacle: "This is what the Lord has commanded: Take from among you gifts to the Lord; everyone whose heart so moves him shall bring them—gifts for the Lord" (Exod 35:4–5). The people responded in force: "Everyone whose spirit moved him came, bringing to the Lord his offering for the work of the Tent of Meeting. . . . Men and women, all whose hearts moved them, all who would make an elevation offering of gold to the Lord, came" (Exod 35:21–22). Nor did they cease:

> But when these continued to bring freewill offerings to him morning after morning, all the artisans who were engaged in the tasks of the sanctuary came, each from the task upon which he was engaged, and said to Moses, "The people are bringing more than is needed for the tasks entailed in the work that the Lord has commanded be done." Moses thereupon had this proclamation made throughout the camp: "Let no man or woman make further effort toward gifts for the sanctuary!" (Exod 36:3–7)

The story of the people's generosity almost certainly served as the paradigm for the author of David's speech to the people in 1 Chronicles 29.[40] This speech culminates a long discussion of David's preparation for building the temple (1 Chr 22–29), a scene virtually irreconcilable with the parallel narrative of David's life in 2 Samuel. After David made these preparations, even drawing up the plans that Solomon was to use for the temple (1 Chr 28:11–12), he assembled the people and, much like Moses before him, called for the people to give freely. And like their literary progenitors, the heads of the tribes and the people responded (vv. 9, 17). Unlike the story in Exodus, however, David never tells the people to cease their gifts.

Although these are highly crafted ideological stories, they probably do reflect real practices. The psalmist strikes a deal with God: If God defeats the psalmist's enemies, he will reciprocate with a freewill offering (Ps 54:8). On their return from Babylon, the heads of the clans are said to have given freewill offerings to rebuild the temple (Ezra 2:68). Ezra receives a royal decree in which Artaxerxes states that he and his counselors gave gold and silver as a freewill offering to the God of Israel (7:15), to be supplemented by the freewill offerings of the Israelites and the priests (7:16). The authenticity of this decree is somewhat suspect, but it nevertheless suggests not only that Israelites gave freewill offerings to the temple and understood these offerings as gifts for God, but also that they were common enough that the practice was institutionalized.[41]

Jacques Berlinerblau argues that the "Israelite vow was accessible to women, heterodox elements and non-privileged economic strata."[42] For Berlinerblau, this accessibility points to the "popular" character of the biblical vow, the fact that those outside "official Yahwism" made vows and offerings to God that were outside of official control. Try as they might to control votives, religious "authorities" were incapable of taming this well-entrenched popular practice.[43] Berlinerblau correctly cautions against the traditional, and traditionally vague, dichotomy between "official" and "popular" religion and focuses on the tension between spontaneous and institutionalized religious expression and its control. The biblical "vow" and "freewill offering" are inherently supererogatory and individually determined. At the same time, the biblical authors did attempt to domesticate (if not quite institutionalize) them, suggesting that there were appropriate gifts, times, and places for these offerings. Leviticus 27, for example, deals with the ways in which vows of persons or goods to the temple should be assessed; it no doubt represents an attempt to standardize and control a rather chaotic stream of votive offerings.

"Great wealth," Emil Schürer asserted, "must finally have flowed into the Temple from voluntary donations."[44] While such an assertion is not implausible, the evidence for it is scattered and difficult to evaluate.[45] The book of Judith regards votive offerings as unremarkable. Judith (4:14) portrays the priests, praying for success in the approaching war, offering first the standard whole-offering, and then the votive offerings of individuals. Later, upon their salvation, the people offer additional votives (16:18).[46]

According to Pseudo-Hecataeus, as preserved by Josephus, the Jerusalem temple contained "not a single statue *(agalma)* or votive offering *(anathēma)*, no trace of a plant in the form of a sacred grove or the like" (*Contra Apionem* 1.199).[47] Bezalel Bar-Kochva suggests that Pseudo-Hecataeus is referring to the pre-Herodian temple, for which references to votive offerings are sparse.[48] Whatever the precise meaning of Pseudo-Hecataeus's comment, beginning in the first century c.e. the literary references to votives in the Jerusalem temple increase. Josephus mentions several rulers who made such offerings.[49] He also mentions a golden vine at the entrance to the temple; according to the Mishnah, "anyone who made a free-will offering of a [golden] leaf, or berry, or cluster, would bring and hang [it] on the [vine]" (*A.J.* 15.394–395).[50] Elsewhere, the Mishnah makes several other references to the extensive votive offerings made to the temple.[51] Luke 21:5 also alludes to beautiful, publicly visible votive offerings at the Jerusalem temple. Upon the fall of the temple, Josephus reports, Jews grieved over the looting of the votive offerings (*A.J.* 17.265).[52] Although there is no epigraphical evidence for votives to the Jerusalem temple, inscriptions do testify to votives in the Samaritan temple on Mt. Gerizim.[53]

Jews outside of the land of Israel also made votive offerings. Onias modeled his temple in Egypt after the Jerusalem temple, even adorning it with similar votive offerings (Josephus, *B.J.* 7.428). The Jews of Babylonia were accustomed to depositing their money for votives at a central city, Nisibis, from which it was periodically sent to the Jerusalem temple (*A.J.* 18.312–13). Seleucid kings after Antiochus Epiphanes "restored to the Jews of Antioch all such votive offers as were made of brass, to be laid up in their synagogue" (*B.J.* 7.44–45 [Thackeray, LCL]). As the Jewish community in Antioch grew, they offered elaborate and expensive votive offerings to "the temple" *(to hieron);* whether that means the synagogue, the temple in Jerusalem, or a Jewish temple in Antioch is unclear (*B.J.* 7.45).

In a different context, Philo testifies to the importance placed on votives. For Philo, the Nazirite vow is the "great vow," an offering of the self to God (*Spec.* 1.247).[54] Thus, commenting on Genesis 31:13 in which God reveals himself to Jacob as the one to whom Jacob vowed at Beth-El, Philo says, "Now a vow is in the fullest sense a dedication, seeing that a man is said to give a gift to God when he renders to Him not only his possessions but himself the possessor of them" (*Somn.* 1.252 [F. H. Colson and G. H. Whitaker, LCL]). Creatively linking murder to sacrilege, Philo elsewhere compares a human to a votive offering (*Decal.* 133). The heavenly temple has stars for its votives (*Spec.* 1.66). Philo, however, is not unaware of earthly votaries. He devotes a long passage to explicating Leviticus 27 and declares the Jews "not a whit behind [in piety] any other either in Asia or in Europe, in its prayers [or] its erection of votive offerings."[55]

According to Josephus, the Essenes "send votive offerings to the Temple" (*A.J.* 18.19). The Dead Sea scrolls appear to take for granted freewill offerings to the temple, although there are very few mentions of the practice in the scrolls.[56] One sapiential text advises men to annul the binding oaths of their wives but gives them discretion in dealing with their wives' "ordinary" vows and freewill offerings.[57]

Throughout the second temple period, Jews in the land of Israel as well as the Diaspora had a strong tradition of offering votives. These votives were primarily given to the temple in Jerusalem but might also have occasionally made their way to competing temples or even to synagogues. As with the votive offerings from late antiquity, we have little knowledge of the substance of the vows. Nor do we know what people vowed, although it seems likely that Jews did not donate statuary. It is reasonably clear, however, that Jews, like the Israelites before them, used votives to express a popular piety. By making vows that resulted in their bringing gifts to the temple, to be housed in God's holy residence, these donors established some form of commerce with God.

Despite the antiquity of Jewish votive practices, their epigraphical commemoration, although not completely unattested during the second temple period, flourishes only from the fourth century onward. The extant Jewish inscriptions from the Second Temple period are for the most part qualitatively different from those that date from the fourth century or later. For example, the most famous synagogue inscription from the second temple period, the Theodotus inscription from Jerusalem, is entirely factual. It records Theodotus's genealogy, the fact that he built the synagogue, and the functions of the synagogue (e.g., reading Torah).[58] The earliest surviving synagogue inscriptions date from third century B.C.E. Egypt and all honor the Ptolemaic royal family. Such communal honors appear in other pre-70 C.E. synagogues but are rare in later inscriptions.[59] This is not to say that vow or gift terminology was completely absent from earlier synagogue inscriptions from the Diaspora.[60] In 41 C.E., for example, a man dedicated a prayer house in Bosphorus (Gorgippia) in accordance with a vow.[61] Nearly all of the other diaspora synagogue inscriptions with this terminology, however, date from the third century C.E. or later.

Between the destruction of the Jerusalem temple in 70 C.E. and the spread of votive inscriptions in the fourth century, there is scant evidence of Jewish votive practices. A Tannaitic source refers to "a non-Jew who dedicated a beam to a synagogue."[62] A perhaps later rabbinic source asserts that the non-Jew Antoninus (Caracalla?) gave a menorah to a Palestinian synagogue.[63] To my knowledge, only a single rabbinic source—from any time period—mentions the possibility of a Jew making a gift for the synagogue, and this source is theoretical.[64]

If, for the sake of argument, we assume that the near absence of evidence for Jewish votive offerings from archaeological and literary sources between the first and fourth centuries C.E. is not a function of spotty source preservation but reflects a genuinely new development, then the reemergence of Jewish votive practices in the fourth century requires explanation. It cannot be a mere continuation of previous Jewish practices.

In fact, the emergence of these votive inscriptions is consistent with other developments in the fourth-century synagogue. Whatever the synagogue was in the second and third centuries, it does not appear to have been seen as a replacement for the Jerusalem temple. New Testament and early Christian writings from this period do not ascribe any special sanctity to the synagogue. Tannaitic sources do not appear overly troubled by the loss of the temple; the synagogue barely entered into their discussion of their response to the temple's loss.[65] Synagogue architecture from this period, especially in the land of Israel, tended to be modest, often containing benches that surrounded a common space.[66] The elaborate edifices, partitioned space, and mosaic floors common to the fourth- and fifth-century synagogues are rare or absent in this period. To the extent that these synagogues were seen as "holy spaces," non-Jews, and perhaps Jews as well, may have thought that the Torah scrolls generated the holiness.[67] There was nothing intrinsically holy about the synagogue space itself, as there was with the Jerusalem temple.

Both the literary and archaeological evidence change dramatically beginning in the fourth century. Amoraic rabbinic literature ascribes sanctity to the synagogue.[68] Christian literature, most notably the sermons of John Chrysostom, indicates that at least some Christians in fourth-century Antioch saw the synagogue as "holy space."[69] Synagogue architecture in the land of Israel became more elaborate. In fact, from the fourth century onward, synagogue architecture began to mimic church architecture, at least in Palestine.[70] The space within fourth- and fifth-century synagogues was divided hierarchically, limiting access to the Torah shrine (aedicule).[71] Richly ornate mosaics, some of which contain zodiacs that portray in their centers what appears to be Helios, cover the floors of many of these synagogues. Pictures of items meant to evoke the temple service frequently surround these zodiacs.[72] These mosaics frequently contain the inscriptions that I have been discussing, and that, for the first time, begin to refer to the synagogue as a "holy place."[73]

Patricia Cox-Miller, in this volume, notes a shift among late antique pagans and Christians toward a "touch of the real," that is, increased importance given to materiality. I would suggest that the developing Jewish understanding of the synagogue as a locus of holiness conforms to this shift. For Jews, the synagogue began to take on some of the characteristics of the holy space of the Jerusalem temple.[74] Joan Branham has termed this evolving concept of sacred space in the synagogue "vicarious sacrality" in order to signal the second-order nature of synagogue sacrality, which was derived from the temple.[75] Jewish votive practices that centered on the temple in Jerusalem could now be adapted for the sacred space of the synagogue; there was a way, once again, to render material gifts to God.

Jewish votive institutions were ancient, but their epigraphical commemoration marks an essentially a new and different institution. Whereas in the temple, the votives were sacrifices and moveable property, the bulk of late antique Jewish votives appear to be donations to support the building of synagogues. If there ever was an epigraphical component to votive offerings to the temple, it was secondary to the gift, whereas for the late antique votives a permanent written notice appears to have been critical. The public notice became an essential component of the personal sentiment.

Jewish votive commemorations closely parallel those of contemporary non-Jews. For example, the sacred precinct of Zeus Madbachos and Salamanes on a mountain peak at Djebel Shêkh Berekât in north central Syria, dating from the first and second century, contains a variety of Greek inscriptions very similar to the synagogue inscriptions. Several of the Greek inscriptions on the walls of the *temenos* record gifts made by families to the "ancestral gods," Zeus Madbachos and Selamanes, "in fulfillment of a vow" (*euchēn*). One family, for example, gave a long stretch of the wall "in fulfillment of a vow."[76] Although this inscription dates to 86 c.e., the custom continued for at least forty years.[77]

Many other inscriptions throughout north central Syria attest to the practice of relatively small familial gifts made in fulfillment of a vow, usually to sacred sites. An inscription on a lintel over a temple in Dmêr records a gift made by a man in fulfillment of his own and his children's vow, "for the salvation" of "our lords and emperors."[78] The Synod of Concord in Mushennef, according to a vow, honored King Agrippa with the construction of a house for Zeus and Athena.[79] A stele from the late second century c.e. fulfills a vow,[80] and a fragmentary inscription apparently records a vow made "to god," followed, perhaps, by the god's name.[81] Churches too contained such inscriptions. A circular medallion on a column from a church in Kasr il-Benât prays for Christ's help for Kyrios, who built the church in fulfillment of a vow,[82] and a lintel over a church chapel might record a vow of first fruits.[83]

Non-Jewish inscriptions from Dura-Europos in both Greek and Aramaic attest to the same phenomenon. The temple of Atargatis, which contains a Greek inscription recording a gift of *phalloi* to the goddess "for the sake of his and his children's salvation," also contains an Aramaic "good memorial" to a man who vowed one hundred denars to the god Shamash for eternal life.[84] A Greek inscription at the temple of Zeus Megistos records its construction in fulfillment of a vow.[85] Several other inscriptions, in both Greek and Palmyrene, exhort the reader to "remember" the benefactor.[86]

The phenomenon attested by these inscriptions is not, of course, unique to Syria. In Sardis a man consecrated a stele and gave of his own funds to celebrate the gods in fulfillment of his vow should he marry "the woman whom I want" (245 c.e.).[87] Around the same time Victor, from Caesarea Maritima, dedicated what appears to be an altar to the god Zeus Dolichenos "in fulfillment of a vow."[88] Perhaps a little earlier, also in Caesarea, a comic actor fulfilled a vow by making a dedication in the theatre.[89] A second-century inscription on an altar in Beth Shean dedicates a "thanksgiving offering" to Dionysius.[90] Moments of healing were commonly commemorated by a votive, often to the temple of Asclepius.[91] Christians too made small dedications to God, sometimes in fulfillment of a vow. Throughout Italy, Latin and Greek inscriptions record relatively small gifts to churches, many made in fulfillment of a vow.[92]

These non-Jewish inscriptions throw into sharper focus the public function of these inscriptions. On the one hand, as many scholars have noted, the Jewish synagogue inscriptions are examples of *euergesia,* a social institution through which the community honors, usually with an elaborate inscription, benefactors to communal and civic projects. There can be little question that one function of these inscriptions is to encourage individual donations to the synagogues.[93] Yet on the other hand, in language, form, and function these synagogue inscriptions are more similar to non-Jewish votive inscriptions than they are to traditional *euergesia* decrees.[94] In contrast to pagans and Christians, who produced scores of *euergesia* inscriptions honoring benefactors, Jews produced very few inscriptions in which it is clear that the community is honoring a benefactor.[95] Those inscriptions that exhort a reader (e.g., "remember for good") are not addressed to the community as much as they are addressed to God.[96] They are permanent markers of personal piety. And in this respect they are functionally equivalent to Roman votive inscriptions. "The underlying point of these texts," Mary Beard writes of Roman votive texts,

> was not . . . to record that yesterday you had performed a sacrifice because this or that god or goddess had miraculously found your lost coat. It was rather to make a permanent statement of your own (enduring) position in relation to a deity—a relationship that went much further than the particular needs of a particular occasion. Inscribed votive texts enacted that crucial conversation of an *occasional* sacrifice into a *permanent* relationship.[97]

Similarly, through votive inscriptions in the synagogue, Jews of late antiquity transformed their small, ad hoc vows into statements of their enduring relationships with God.

Jews throughout antiquity used votive inscriptions to create intimate relationships with their God, and in so doing, they gained the added advantage of currying favor with their readers. A gift to a synagogue, memorialized in mosaic or stone, was not merely a gift to the community meant to gain honor and social standing (although it was certainly this), but it was also an expression of piety that, like the votive offerings to the Jerusalem temple, created and reinforced a personal relationship to the divine. Such commerce makes sense only in "a world full of gods," that is, in the presence of a divine so immanent that it cared about an individual's health, or the wedding of a man's son.[98] Unlike their pagan neighbors, Jews may not have brought statuary of healed body parts to their synagogues, but they did make deals with God to heal them, and they rewarded him with a plaque if and when he fulfilled his end of the bargain.

NOTES

1. See Moshe Dothan, *Hammath Tiberias* (2 vols.; Jerusalem: Israel Exploration Society, University of Haifa, and Department of Antiquities and Museums, 1983–2000). Dothan labels this stratum IIa, dated to the end of the third or beginning of the fourth century (1:66–67). The second volume of the report, however, suggests a later dating (2:93).

2. Ibid., 1:54–50 (= Lea Roth-Gerson, *The Greek Inscriptions from the Synagogues in Eretz-Israel* [Jerusalem: Yad Yitzhak ben Zvi, 1987] [in Hebrew], no. 16).

3. The inscriptions have not yet been published, but are mentioned in Ze'ev Weiss and Ehud Netzer, *Promise and Redemption: A Synagogue Mosaic from Sepphoris* (Jerusalem: Israel Museum, 1996), 42.

4. For *euchesthai*, see also Roth-Gerson, *Greek Inscriptions*, no. 26 (Caesarea). *Eucharistein:* Roth-Gerson nos. 3 (Ashkelon); 21 (Gaza); 23 (Gaza).

5. This term and its male counterpart, *kuros,* appear to be titles of respect but might also refer to a married state.

6. Roth-Gerson, *Greek Inscriptions,* no. 3, my translation.

7. Ibid., no. 23, my translation.

8. Salvation: Roth-Gerson, *Greek Inscriptions,* nos. 2 (Ashkelon), 7 (Bet Shean), 28 (Caesarea), 30 (Katzin). Remember: Roth-Gerson, *Greek Inscriptions,* nos. 1 (Ashdod); 4 (Bet Alpha); 7 (Bet Shean).

9. Joseph Naveh, *On Stone and Mosaic: The Aramaic and Hebrew Inscriptions from Ancient Synagogues* (Jerusalem: ha-Ḥeverah le-Ḥakirat Ereṣ Yisrael ve-ʿAtiqoteiha, 1978) (in Hebrew), no. 25.

10. Ibid., no. 75.

11. Joseph Yahalom, "On Joseph Naveh, *On Stone and Mosaic,*" *KS* 53 (1978): 354 (in Hebrew); Gideon Foerster, "Synagogue Inscriptions and their Relation to Liturgical Versions," *Cathedra* 19 (1981): 12–40, at 31–32 (in Hebrew). The following inscriptions from Naveh's corpus would be added: nos. 21 (Avlin), 60 (Naaran), 69 (Jericho—a communal inscription), 76 (Susiyah).

12. John Kroll, "The Greek Inscriptions of the Sardis Synagogue," *HTR* 94 (2001): 5–55, nos. 1, 4–10, 18–20, 22, 25, 26, 29, 31–37, 42, 48, 50, 51, 54, 57, 61, 62, 66–68, 78.

13. Frank Moore Cross, "The Hebrew Inscriptions from Sardis," *HTR* 95 (2002): nos. 4, 5.

14. For a general survey of Jewish epigraphy in antiquity, see Margaret Williams, "The Contribution of Jewish Inscriptions to the Study of Judaism," in *CHJ* 3:75–93. On votive inscriptions in Jewish Diaspora communities, see Lea Roth-Gerson, "Similarities and Differences in Greek Synagogue Inscriptions of Eretz-Israel and the Diaspora," in *Synagogues in Antiquity* (ed. A. Kasher, A. Oppenheimer, and U. Rappaport; Jerusalem: Yad Izhak ben Zvi, 1987), 138–41 (in Hebrew).

15. These inscriptions are collected in Baruch Lifshitz, *Donateurs et fondateurs dans les synagogues juives, répertoire des dédicaces grecques relatives à la construction et à la réfection des synagogues* (Paris: J. Gabalda, 1967). The following numbers refer to this collection. Delos: no. 4, 5, 7; Stobi: no. 10; Smyrna: no. 14; Tralles: no. 30; Acmonia: no. 34; Amastris: no. 35; Apamea: nos. 40, 41, 42, 44, 45, 46, 47, 51, 52, 53, 54, 55, 56, 57; Lapethos: no. 83; Egypt: no. 97.

16. Lifshitz, *Donateurs et fondateurs,* no. 6.

17. Naveh, *On Stone and Mosaic,* no. 50.

18. Ibid., no. 74.

19. Roth-Gerson, *Greek Inscriptions,* no. 22

20. Kroll, "The Greek Inscriptions," no. 3.

21. *Codex theodosianus* 16.8.25 (trans. Amnon Linder, *The Jews in Roman Imperial Legislation* [Detroit, Mich.: Wayne State University Press, 1987], 288, no. 47).

22. A potshard found in the synagogue excavation at Hammath Tiberias, dating to the seventh century or later, "appears to be a dedicatory inscription referring to a pledge or donation to the synagogue by a single individual. . . . The pledge or donation would appear to be from a small donor able to offer part of his income, probably from agriculture, for the upkeep of the synagogue" (Dothan, *Hammath Tiberias* 2:102–3).

23. Cf. Shaye J. D. Cohen, "The Place of the Rabbi in Jewish Society of the Second Century," in *The Galilee in Late Antiquity* (ed. Lee I. Levine; New York: Jewish Theological Seminary of America, 1992), 157–73. For a review of some of this scholarship, see Seth

Schwartz, "Historiography on the Jews in the 'Talmudic Period,'" in *The Oxford Handbook of Jewish Studies* (ed. Martin Goodman, Jeremy Cohen, and David Sorkin; Oxford: Oxford University Press, 2002), 79–114, esp. 98–102.

24. Cf. Aharon Oppenheimer, *The Am Ha-aretz: A Study in the Social History of the Jewish People in the Hellenistic-Roman Period* (Leiden: E. J. Brill, 1977), 18–22, 188–95.

25. The number of synagogues for Sepphoris is recorded in *y Kil.* 9:4, 32b. Remains of three or four have been found to date. Cf. Zeev Weiss, "Sepphoris," in *NEAEHL* 4:1327–28.

26. See, in general, Oppenheimer, *The Am Ha-aretz;* Seth Schwartz, *Imperialism and Jewish Society, 200 B.C.E. to 640 C.E.* (Princeton, N.J.: Princeton University Press, 2001), 272–74. On the possible continuing vitality and influence of priests in late antiquity, see Joseph Yahalom, "The Sepphoris Synagogue Mosaic and Its Story," in *From Dura to Sepphoris: Studies in Jewish Art and Society in Late Antiquity* (ed. Lee I. Levine and Ze'ev Weiss; Journal of Roman Archaeology Supplementary Series 40; Portsmouth, R.I.: Journal of Roman Archaeology, 2000), 83–91; Rachel Elior, "From Earthly Temple to Heavenly Shrines; Prayer and Sacred Song in the Hekhalot Literature and its Relation to Temple Traditions," *JSQ* 4 (1997): 217–67.

27. I am not arguing that Galilean Jews were "lax" in their observance of Jewish law, although there are ancient accusations of this. Cf. Martin Goodman, "Galilean Judaism and Judaean Judaism," in *CHJ* 3: 596–617, esp. 606–13; and for a different view, Lawrence H. Schiffman, "Was There a Galilean Halakhah?" in *The Galilee in Late Antiquity,* 143–56. My point is that whatever their actual level of observance, these Jews rarely advertised or commemorated such study. Cf. Pieter W. van der Horst, *Ancient Jewish Epitaphs: An Introductory Survey of a Millennium of Jewish Funerary Epigraphy (300 B.C.E.–700 C.E.)* (Kampen: Koks Pharos, 1991), 65–68.

28. The term "popular religion," of course, is potentially loaded. For a summary of the state of research on "popular religion" and its application to the Bible, see Jacques Berlinerblau, *The Vow and the 'Popular Religious Groups' of Ancient Israel: A Philological and Sociological Inquiry* (JSOTSup 210; Sheffield: Sheffield Academic Press, 1996), 13–45. Saul Olyan gestures in this direction in *Asherah and the Cult of Yahweh in Israel* (SBLMS 34; Atlanta: Scholars Press, 1988), 1–22. Plato's most extended polemic on "popular" religious practice is book 10 of the *Leges.* Cf. P. A. Meijer, "Philosophers, Intellectuals, and Religion in Hellas," in *Faith, Hope and Worship: Aspects of Religious Mentality in the Ancient World* (ed. H. Versnel; Studies in Greek and Roman Religion 2; Leiden: Brill, 1981), 216–63. Cf. Natalie Zemon Davis, "Some Tasks and Themes in the Study of Popular Religion," in *The Pursuit of Holiness in Late Medieval and Renaissance Religion* (ed. Charles Trinkaus with Heiko A. Oberman; Leiden: E. J. Brill, 1974), 307–36.

29. The inscriptions use the terms *euchē* and *eucharistō.* The former commonly translates *ndr* in the LXX, and the latter never appears in the Torah. The language of the inscriptions thus appears to derive more from contemporary usage than from the LXX, although there is some overlap.

30. Cf. Moshe Benovitz, *Kol Nidre: Studies in the Development of Rabbinic Votive Institutions* (BJS 315; Atlanta: Scholars Press, 1998), 9–40. Benovitz's focus here is on the prohibitive, rather than conditional, vow.

31. Cf. Saul Lieberman, "Oaths and Vows," in *Greek in Jewish Palestine* (New York: Jewish Theological Seminary of America, 1942), 115–43. Lieberman writes, "Generally speaking, popular oaths and vows are an expression of piety. . . . But the natural tendency to swear was carried to excess; the populace swore always and everywhere" (115). For Lieberman, the Jews of antiquity were running amok, "turning to the strangest and most varied objects to serve vicariously as surety for their veracity." Only the "learned Rabbis" were able "to keep the unbridled zeal of the populace in check." Despite Lieberman's own contempt for the "populace" and overestimation of rabbinic authority, he may well be correct that at least in rabbinic eyes vowing was a popular religious activity.

32. Theophrastus, frg. 8, cited in Meijer, "Philosphers, Intellectuals and Religion in Hellas," 253.

33. On the rabbinic opposition to vows, see Lieberman, "Oaths and Vows." The rabbinic understanding of the divine needs to be revisited. For some polemical comments, see Solomon Schechter, *Aspects of Rabbinic Theology* (New York: Schocken, 1961; repr. Woodstock, Vt.: Jewish Lights, 1993), 21–45; Ephraim E. Urbach, *The Sages: Their Concepts and Beliefs* (trans. Israel Abrahams; Cambridge, Mass.: Harvard University Press, 1987), 37–134. When the rabbis construct parables, they are fond of equating God with either a king or a father, both of which are understood hierarchically. Cf. Ignaz Ziegler, *Die Königsgleichnisse des Midrasch beleuchtet durch die römische Kaiserzeit* (Breslau: S. Schottlaender, 1903); Alon Goshen-Gottstein, "God and Israel as Father and Son in Tannaitic Literature" (Ph.D. diss., Hebrew University, 1987) (in Hebrew).

34. Marcel Mauss, *The Gift: Forms and Functions of Exchange in Archaic Societies* (trans. Ian Cunnison; New York: W. W. Norton, 1967); Maurice Godelier, *The Enigma of the Gift* (trans. Nora Scott; Chicago: University of Chicago Press, 1999), 41–49.

35. Godelier, *The Enigma of the Gift*, 48.

36. Ibid.

37. Cristiano Grottanelli, "Do ut des?" *Scienze dell'Antichità: Storia Archeologia Anthropologia* 3–4 (1989–1990): 45–54. See also Robert Parker, "Pleasing Thighs: Reciprocity in Greek Religion," in *Reciprocity in Ancient Greece* (ed. Christopher Gill, Norman Postlethwaite, and Richard Seaford; Oxford: Oxford University Press, 1998), 105–25; and Jan-Maarten Bremer, "The Reciprocity of Giving and Thanksgiving in Greek Worship," in the same volume, 127–37.

38. There are certainly distinctions between these offerings, but the inscriptions of late antiquity appear to treat them all as equivalent.

39. Cf. 2 Sam 15:7; Isa 19:21; Ps 22:26, 50:14, 56:13, 61:9, 65:2, 66:13, 76:12, 116:14, 18; Job 22:27; Eccl 5:3; Jonah 2:10. This terminology is not used in the Pentateuch.

40. On the connection of these texts, see Sara Japhet, *I & II Chronicles: A Commentary* (OTL; Louisville, Ky.: Westminster John Knox Press, 1993), 503.

41. On the authenticity of the decree, see the discussion by Lester L. Grabbe, *Judaism from Cyrus to Hadrian* (2 vols.; Minneapolis: Fortress Press, 1992), 1:32–36.

42. Berlinerblau, *The Vow*, 166.

43. Ibid., 150–65.

44. Emil Schürer, *The History of the Jewish People in the Age of Jesus Christ* (rev. and ed. Geza Vermes, Fergus Millar, and Martin Goodman; 3 vols.; Edinburgh: T. & T. Clark, 1973–87), 2:274. Later, Schürer asserts that "many though these public sacrifices were, their number was insignificant compared to private sacrifices" (2:308).

45. Cf. Lester L. Grabbe, *Judaic Religion in the Second Temple Period: Belief and Practice from the Exile to Yavneh* (London: Routledge, 2000), 137–38: "Some aspects of this system remain elusive even now" (137).

46. Judith tends to use the term *hekousios*, the Septuagintal term for *nedavah*. Cf. Lev 7:16; Num 15:3, 29:39; Deut 12:6. In Lev 22:18 and 21 the Septuagint uses more general terminology, as it does throughout Exodus 35–36. Note that Judith herself dedicates Holophernes's possessions to the temple, including the net that she used to slay him, which is described as an *anathēma* (16:19).

47. Cf. Josephus, *A.J.* 8.195, which condemns Solomon for setting up offerings that resembled animals. The Bible does not condemn Solomon for this act. Josephus similarly condemns Herod (*A.J.* 17.151).

48. Bezalel Bar-Kochva, *Pseudo-Hecateaeus, "On the Jews": Legitimizing the Jewish Diaspora* (Berkeley: University of California Press, 1996), 166. The only explicit evidence for votive offerings in the second temple prior to the Herodian renovation is 1 Macc 1:21–22. Cf. Josephus *A.J.* 12.35, 50, 58, 85, 249; 2 Macc 9:16.

49. Josephus, *C. Ap.* 2.48 (referring to Ptolemy Euergetes); *B.J.* 2.312–14 (Berenice

discharging a vow); *B.J.* 5.205, 562–63 (Alexander, the brother of Philo, and from Augustus and other Roman nobles. Cf. Philo, *Legat.* 157); *A.J.* 19.294–295 (Agrippa I. Cf. Philo, *Legat.* 297). Cf. Philo, *Legat.* 319; Josephus, *A.J.* 13.78; *B.J.* 2.413, 4:181; 3 Macc 3:17.

50. Cf. Josephus, *B.J.* 5.210–212; *m. Mid.* 3:8 (*Mishnah* [ed. Chanoch Albeck and Henoch Yalon; 6 vols.; repr. Jerusalem and Tel Aviv: Bialik Institute and Dvir, 1988], 5:328).

51. See, for example, *m. Šeqal.* 6:5–6 (Albeck and Yalon, 2:203–4).

52. Cf. Josephus, *B.J.* 6.335.

53. Joseph Naveh and Yitzhak Magen, "Aramaic and Hebrew Inscriptions of the Second Century B.C.E. at Mount Gerizim, *Atiqot* 32 (1997): 9*–17*.

54. Cf. Josephus, *A.J.* 4.72–73.

55. Leviticus 27: Philo, *Spec.* 2.32–38, 115. Votive offerings: Philo, *Legat.* 280 (F. H. Colson, LCL).

56. CD 16:13 (= 4Q271 4 ii 13).

57. Q416 2 iv 7–9 (= 4Q418 10 9–10).

58. Roth-Gerson, *Greek Inscriptions,* no. 19.

59. See Lifshitz, *Donateurs et fondateurs,* nos. 92 (= Jean Baptiste Frey, *Corpvs inscriptionvm ivdaicarvm. Recueil des inscriptions juives qui vont du IIIe siècle avant Jésus-Christ au VIIe siècle de notre ère* [2 vols.; Rome: Pontificio istituto di archeologia cristiana, 1936] 2:1440. Hereafter abbreviated *CIJ*); 93 (= *CIJ* 2:1441); 94 (= *CIJ* 2:1442); 95 (= *CIJ* 2:1443); 96 (= *CIJ* 2:1444); 99.

60. See Lee I. Levine, *The Ancient Synagogue: The First Thousand Years* (New Haven, Conn.: Yale University Press, 2000), 74–123. It is interesting to note that Samaritan inscriptions found near the site of the Delos synagogue, and a long and significant inscription from Acmonia, have a more traditional *euergesia* form, in which the community honors the benefactors. On Delos, see Levine, *Ancient Synagogue,* 102 (and references); on Acmonia: Lifshitz, *Donateurs et fondateurs,* no. 36, and discussion in Levine, *Ancient Synagogue,* 111–12.

61. *CIJ* 1:690.

62. *t. Meg.* 2(3):16 (*The Tosefta: The Orders of Zeraim, Moed, Nashim, Nezikin* [ed. S. Lieberman; 4 vols.; New York: Jewish Theological Seminary of America, 1955–88], 2:352).

63. *y. Meg.* 3:2, 74a.

64. *t. Meg.* 2(3):14 (ed. Lieberman 2:352).

65. Shaye J. D. Cohen, "The Temple and the Synagogue," *CHJ* 3:313–18.

66. Levine, *Ancient Synagogue,* 42–73.

67. Steven Fine has argued that it was primarily the presence of biblical scrolls that gave the synagogue its designation as "holy space." See Steven Fine, *This Holy Place: On the Sanctity of the Synagogue during the Greco-Roman Period* (Notre Dame, Ind.: University of Notre Dame Press, 1997), 35–59. Martin Goodman similarly asserts that sanctity was thought to flow from the Torah scroll, but he goes further than Fine, arguing that this sanctity derives from a certain correspondence drawn between Torah scrolls and idols. See Martin Goodman, "Sacred Scripture and the 'Defiling of the Hands,'" *JTS* 41 (1990): 99–107.

68. Fine, *This Holy Place,* 61–94; Levine, *The Ancient Synagogue,* 184–88.

69. See especially John Chrysostom, *Adversus Judaeos* 6.7.2 (PG 48:914). Cf. Robert L. Wilken, *John Chrysostom and the Jews: Rhetoric and Reality in the Late 4th Century* (Berkeley: University of California Press, 1983), 79–83; Shaye J. D. Cohen, "Pagan and Christian Evidence on the Ancient Synagogue," in *The Synagogue in Late Antiquity* (ed. Lee I. Levine; New York: Jewish Theological Seminary of America, 1987), 159–81.

70. Yoram Tsafrir, "The Byzantine Setting and Its Influence on Ancient Synagogues," in *The Synagogue in Late Antiquity,* 147–57; Levine, *Ancient Synagogue,* 296–302.

71. Levine, *Ancient Synagogue,* 330. On the division of space within late antique synagogues and how it evokes the sacred space of the Jerusalem temple and contemporary churches, see Joan R. Branham, "Sacred Space under Erasure in Ancient Synagogues and Early Churches," *The Art Bulletin* 74 (1992): 375–94.

72. Cf. the third-century frescos from Dura Europos, which focus on biblical scenes. See Erwin R. Goodenough, *Jewish Symbols in the Greco-Roman Period* (ed. and abridged Jacob Neusner; Princeton, N.J.: Princeton University Press, 1988), 195–221. Goodenough atomizes the frescos to interpret the symbolism of each visual component. My observation is much more basic: at Dura the frescoes are biblically based and have narrative structure, whereas many of the later synagogue mosaics do not draw directly on the Bible, nor do they tell a story.

73. Aramaic inscriptions with "holy space": Naveh, *On Stone and Mosaic,* nos. 16 (Kfar Hanina), 26 (Hammat Tiberias), 46 (Bet Shean), 60 (Naaran), 64 (Naaran), 65 (Naaran). Greek *(hagios topos):* Roth-Gerson, *Greek Inscriptions,* nos. 3 (Ashkelon; reconstructed), 10 (Garash), 17 (Hammat Tiberias), 21 (Gaza), 23 (Gaza).

74. Cf. Shaye J. D. Cohen, "The Temple and the Synagogue," *CHJ* 3:298–325, esp. 317–23. Note the strong conclusion of Schwartz, *Imperialism and Jewish Society,* 259: "Thus, the ancient synagogues as a group seem to embody a different notion of sanctity from that evident in rabbinic texts. The synagogue seems often to have constituted an unearthly realm, a reflection of the heavenly temple, an inherently sacred space, and the community that built and maintained and attended the synagogue regarded itself as a holy congregation, an Israel in miniature."

75. Joan R. Branham, "Vicarious Sacrality: Temple Space in Ancient Synagogues," in *Ancient Synagogues: Historical Analysis and Archaeological Discovery* (ed. Dan Urman and Paul V. M. Flesher; 2 vols.; StPB 47; Leiden: E. J. Brill, 1995), 2:319–45.

76. William Kelly Prentice, *Greek and Latin Inscriptions* (Publications of an American Archaeological Expedition to Syria in 1899–1900 3; New York: Century, 1908), no. 100.

77. An inscription from 120 C.E. records a gift of 1500 drachmae, by a son in fulfillment of his father's vow. Ibid., no. 104. Cf. no. 107.

78. Ibid., no. 358.

79. Ibid., no. 380.

80. Ibid., no. 347.

81. Ibid., no. 410b.

82. Ibid., no. 76.

83. Ibid., no. 334.

84. For the *phalloi,* see R. N. Frye, J. F. Gilliam, H. Ingholt, and C. B. Welles, "Inscriptions from Dura-Europos," *YCS* 14 (1955): 127–213, no. 1. The dedication to Shamash is no. 3. This dedication is followed immediately by a shortened Greek version, which mentions a gift to the god Helios but does not mention the vow.

85. Ibid., no. 6.

86. Ibid., nos. 8, 14, 22, 26, 29; Comte du Mesnil du Buisson, *Inventaire des inscriptions palmyréniennes de Doura-Europos* (Paris: Paul Geuthner, 1939), nos. 19, 22, 41, 43, 50.

87. L. Robert, *Nouvelles inscriptions de Sardes* (Paris: Librairie d'Amérique et d'Orient A. Maisonneuve, 1964), no. 2.

88. Clayton Miles Lehmann and Kenneth G. Holum, *The Greek and Latin Inscriptions of Caesarea Maritima* (The Joint Expedition to Caesarea Maritima Excavation Reports 5; Boston: American Schools of Oriental Research, 2000), no. 124.

89. Ibid., no. 126.

90. Leah Di Segni Campagnano, "A Dated Inscription from Beth Shean and the Cult of Dionysos Ktistes in Roman Scythopolis," *Scripta Classica Israelica* 16 (1997): 139–61.

91. William Henry Denham Rouse, *Greek Votive Offerings: An Essay in the History of Greek Religion* (Cambridge: Cambridge University Press, 1902), 187–239; F. T. van Straten, "Gifts for the Gods," in *Faith, Hope and Worship*, 65–151.

92. See the comprehensive study of Jean-Pierre Caillet, *L'Évergétisme monumental Chrétien en Italie et à ses marges* (Collection de l'école française de Rome 175; Palais Farnèse: École française de Rome, 1993). The inscriptions below refer to the numbering of Caillet. Vows: pp. 22, 37 ("for the salvation of them and their children"), 88, 89, 90, 92, 94, 131, 148, 204, 206, 207, 209, 210, 216, 223, 224, 225, 228, 229, 231, 233, 238, 239, 245, 246, 247, 248, 249, 250251, 252, 253, 254, 277, 279, 301, 311, 314, 315, 327, 349, 388, 389.

93. Nearly all modern scholarly discussions of these inscriptions put them into a context of *euergesia*. Clearly these inscriptions do delimit an institution that encourages individuals to contribute to the synagogues. Rather than see these inscriptions as a Jewish expression of *euergesia*, though, I am arguing that they are better seen as votives. The social result is much the same (i.e., donations to the synagogues) but the strategy (i.e., God's providence rather than social honor) differs. For inscriptions that bless in general all who contribute or might contribute to the synagogue, see Naveh, *On Stone and Mosaic*, nos. 39, 43, 46, 57, 69, 70, 83, 84; Roth-Gerson, *Greek Inscriptions*, nos. 12, 25.

94. There are, to be sure, differences in the language of Jewish and non-Jewish inscriptions, but these seem to me to be relatively minor. Cf. Lea Roth-Gerson, "Similarities and Differences." Jews did sometimes (as in the case of one of the Hammath Tiberias inscriptions) mark their inscriptions as ethnically distinct through the symbolic use of Hebrew. Cf. Hayim Lapin, "Palestinian Inscriptions and Jewish Ethnicity in Late Antiquity," in *Galilee through the Ages: Confluence of Cultures* (ed. Eric M. Meyers; Winona Lake, Ind.: Eisenbrauns, 1999), 239–68.

95. Tessa Rajak, "Jews as Benefactors," in *Studies on the Jewish Diaspora in the Hellenistic and Roman Periods* (ed. Benjamin Isaac and Aharon Oppenheimer; Teʿuda 12; Ramat-Aviv: Tel-Aviv University, 1996), 17–38, especially at 37–38.

96. This becomes clearer when compared to contemporary non-Jewish inscriptions. For example, one Palmyrene inscription from Dura Europos begins, "Remember Malkho bar Wahballat before Yarhibol," suggesting that the Jewish remembrance formula is a kind of shorthand, implying "before God." For the inscription, see Buisson, *Inventaire*, no. 15. Cf. Naveh, *On Stone and Mosaic*, 7–9; Foerster, "Synagogue Inscriptions," 21; Buisson, *Inventaire*, 45–46. Some of the Aramaic inscriptions from Hatra similarly specify the god before whom the benefactor is to be remembered. See A. Caquot, "Nouvelles inscriptions araméennes de Hatra," *Syria* 29 (1952): 89–118. The following numbers refer to Caquot: 2, 13, 16, 17, 23, 24, 25, 26. A. D. Nock has argued that the Greek equivalent (*mnesthē*) similarly "is directed to a deity and not to the general public" ("Liturgical Notes," *JTS* 30 [1929]: 393). Cf. Foerster, "Synagogue Inscriptions," 18–21, for a similar point about the Jewish inscriptions that use this phrase. For a general discussion of the vocabulary of Greek votive inscriptions, see Maria Letizia Lazzarini, "Iscrizioni Votive Greche," *Scienze dell'Antichità: Storia Archeologia Antropologia* 3–4 (1989–90): 845–59, esp. 849–50.

97. Mary Beard, "*Ancient Literacy* and the Function of the Written Word in Roman Religion," in *Literacy in the Ancient World* (ed. Mary Beard et al.; Journal of Roman Archaeology Supplementary Series 3; Ann Arbor, 1991), 35–58, at 48 (original emphasis).

98. For a vivid (although polytheistic) evocation of this worldview, see Keith Hopkins, *A World Full of Gods: The Strange Triumph of Christianity* (New York: Free Press, 1999), esp. 7–45. More sober is H. S. Versnel, "Religious Mentality in Ancient Prayer," in *Faith, Hope and Worship*, 1–64.

—6—

The Self in Artemidorus' Interpretation of Dreams

PETER T. STRUCK

Those looking for an ancient Greek religious self find a few obstacles in the way. Taking a cue from the French philosopher of hermeneutics Paul Ricoeur and his observations in *Soi-même comme un autre,* we might begin by pointing out that Greek uses a single word, *autos,* to mark both the ideas of "same" and "self." Latin, like English, splits *autos* into two pieces: the pair *idem* and *ipse* answer to the English same and self, respectively. Latin *idem* marks a sense of identity in the context of comparison, where one thing, "thing-A," is claimed to be identical with another, "thing-B." *Idem* also indicates the notion of sameness over time, a permanence or continuity. This second sense could be called another form of comparison, in this case of thing-A at one time with thing-A at an earlier time. By contrast, the Latin notion of *ipse* does not at all hinge on comparison. It intensifies—"thing-A and I really mean the actual thing-A." And it separates what it refers to from everything else, particularly in the case of agency—"thing-A itself did the action (and not something else)." So *ipse* insists on a kind of autonomy that is absent from the notion of *idem. Ipse*-identity also admits change over time, which *idem* does not. In fact, *ipse* assumes an ongoing interaction with what is outside, in the form of agency, which again is part and parcel of it (see *Oxford Latin Dictionary* ad loc. 7).

In Greek, *autos* handles both the functions of *self* and *same*. It separates them, rather more subtly that either English or Latin do, by means of its grammatical construction with the article.[1] While *autos* meaning "self" is common in Greek literature—the philosophers leave behind a particularly rich array of considerations of things "in themselves"—one does not find it used in the sense in which it appears in a phrase like "the religious self." The Greek idea "self" is a deictic pointer, intensifying, by isolating, what it points to. (It has affiliations with the class of demonstrative pronouns.[2]) To nominalize such an idea is to open an entirely new question. In fact, Greek *cannot* nominalize the idea of "self" without an insurmountable confusion of the rules of grammatical construction mentioned above: "the self" in Greek will be impossible to disambiguate from "the same [unexpressed thing]," and even if one could get Greek to say "the self," it would likely sound as curious and as flat as a nominalized demonstrative ("the this" or "the that"). Of course, none of these considerations exactly prevents us looking for a "religious self" in a Greek context, but they do give us some pause. Considering "the self" in Greek antiquity will require an importation of non-native categories and a search for plausible "local" correlatives. This search will at the same time necessitate some reflection on the modern notion of "self."

Another note of caution comes from the observation that the idea of a specifically "religious self" seems already to have configured religion as an individual, private, or personal matter. It will be most at home in a tradition that can imagine such a configuration comfortably. But the truism still has some truth to it: most of Greek and Roman religion is not at all adequately characterized as a private matter. Certain soteriological cults in late antiquity (the Hermetic traditions and the Neoplatonists, for example) do some heavy intellectual lifting to reshape traditional pagan praxis into meditative cults that would be able to welcome a personalized religious life, but the bulk of Greek and Roman religious activity is based on public piety, communal acts of worship. So to speak of a religious self within the whole context of Greek and Roman antiquity, one would have to consider a slightly oxymoronic but still intelligible "public self" (something I will not do here), which would open up a rich discussion of various modes of performing selfhood in the public arena. This would be a complex but likely very rewarding study.

However, Artemidorus' text on dream interpretation, the only surviving example of a well-attested genre of ancient dream books, evades nearly all these difficulties and allows us to talk, without too much background noise, of a "religious self."[3] First, if we understand by a "self" a kind of close-up picture of individuals as agents negotiating their way through the intimate details of their lives, Artemidorus provides something of a goldmine.[4] No other text comes close to matching the sheer mass of intimate detail he provides on the lives of ordinary Greek citizens of the Roman empire. One thinks of Artemidorus in the hands of Foucault and Winkler, who have made noteworthy advances in our understanding of the sexual mores of the day. Also, Simon Price has revealed the text as an irreplaceable corrective on Freudian overreaching and as offering real insight into the ways in which ancient selves are not exactly Freudian selves.

Further, and more specific to the topic at hand, Artemidorus offers help to those trying to conceive of a specifically religious self in the late classical world. His text concerns an area of Greek and Roman religion that offers the best counterargument to the truism about it being unremittingly public. The widespread practice of divination by dreams reminds us that not quite every aspect of the religious life of Greeks and Romans was performed in the light of day. As opposed to cultic worship, nearly always a public act, divination, on the whole, is often a quite personal and private affair. Through divination, a kind of mirror image of prayer, Greeks and Romans were used to hearing their gods talk to them personally, even on a daily basis. And while the gods famously respond at times of grave public moment, the overwhelming majority of such consultations are more adequately reflected by the petitions, found on stellae and lamellae, asking for a cure for a toothache, an opinion on the likely success of a business arrangement, or advice in affairs of the heart.

Of the hundreds of divinatory technologies in regular use in the ancient period, dreaming was among the most popular, and no other technique was more personal and intimate. Price is surely correct in pointing out that the content of Artemidorus' dreams (both manifest and latent) points outward toward a public life (as opposed to the Freudian idea that the latent content always points inward toward the drama of an individual psyche). Nevertheless, the "dream space" itself, in Patricia Cox Miller's memorable phrase, is an interior one. Dreams offer private interactions with the divinity in a world that is most emphatically one's own. Whatever personal dimension there is to Greek and Roman religion will surely be on display here.

Finally, Artemidorus is writing at a time when philosophical views more congenial to the idea of a personalized sense of religious life have gained rather wide currency. His is a different thought-world from Homer's famously exteriorized one, or even from that of classical Athens. Beginning in about the third century B.C.E., the Stoics made available a novel set of ideas that not only removed certain earlier barriers to conceiving of religion in a private dimension but even seemed to welcome such a view. Best known for the popularity of their moral precepts in elite Roman circles, these thinkers advanced new ideas about the divine that, judging from their marked prominence in Cicero's theological works, were widely popular by the first century B.C.E. and continued so into Artemidorus' day. One is not able to discern in Artemidorus a committed Stoic; however, this is no impediment to the claim that the common sense of his day was shaped by Stoicism and that their views are discernable behind his expositions of divination. In addition, an obvious point is worth making: his interest in defending divination puts him squarely in their camp and outside of other philosophical schools that held a currency in his day. Neither the Epicureans, nor the Academics, nor the Peripatetics display any significant support for the practice in the existing evidence, and some display outright contempt.

Artemidorus' Cultural Anthropology

As has been well-noted in the contemporary scholarship, Artemidorus is a lavish resource for those interested in daily life. So if we understand the study of the "self" to be a study of the experiential lives of individuals, as opposed to larger historical, sociological, philosophical, or intellectual currents, Artemidorus offers much information. While it will not be breaking much new ground, it is advisable to make a quick overview of the kinds of information Artemidorus offers on the daily lives of selves. He follows an empiricist impulse in much of his work and assimilates what must have been many hundreds (perhaps thousands) of examples from real dreamers who marked certain outcomes after particular dreams. He presents his work as a kind of summary of his observations distilled into rough principles about what a certain image in a dream might portend, usually with a detailed breakdown of different semantic values for variants on the image and/or for different kinds of dreamers, along with occasional brief explanations of why the image carries the value it does. A section from book 2 is typical:

> Cormorants, gulls, and other sea birds portend extreme danger for those who are at sea but they do not portend death. For all these birds submerge beneath the sea but they do not drown. But for all other men, they signify courtesans and contentious wives or rapacious and ruthless swindlers and people who earn their living either directly or indirectly from the sea. They also predict that lost objects will not be found, since sea birds gulp down whatever they catch. (2.17)[5]

The division between sailors and all others is in keeping with his general habit of meticulously dividing the dreaming subject into different categories and subcategories for whom the dream image means different things. Cabbages are especially inauspicious for inn-keepers, vine-dressers, and all theatrical artists (1.76). Harps and lyres are good signs for people involved in marriages and partnerships, since they signify harmony, but bode ill for dealings with non-partners, since they signify tension (1.56). Dreaming of being an *ephebe,* a young Greek male in a formal period of training for full citizenship, has fully eleven separate meanings: for a slave it means freedom; for a craftsman or orator it means a year-long unemployment, since that is the customary period during which an ephebe is required to keep his hand under his cloak (but in places where the custom is three years of hand-cloaking, the dream bodes three years of unemployment); for a man, it predicts no travel for a year; for the unwed, it predicts marriage (with a division of different kinds of wives based on the color of the ephebe's cloak); for a man who wants children, it means his son will one day be an ephebe; for an old man, it prophesies death; for criminals, it portends arrest; for law-abiding citizens, it means assistance. It is inauspicious for the athlete, since it predicts that he will be disqualified for being over age; specifically for the wrestler, it means that he will be late for his match (1.54).

Artemidorus' level of attentiveness to the specific cultural coordinates of the dreamer is remarkable, and it generates an encyclopedia of data about the concerns, tastes, and whims of his subjects. He systematizes the coordinates by which individual selves can be specified in several theoretical grids that he lays down in the opening sections of books 1 and 4. He mentions that in getting to know a dreamer, it is important to know "who the dreamer is" (presumably the name), his occupation, his birth status, his amount of wealth, the condition of his bodily health, and his age (1.9). We could also add to this list gender, which is among the most prominent dividing lines between dreaming subjects, though overlooked in the formal statement of criteria. These criteria show Artemidorus' specifications for personal identity to be not unexpected or remarkable, though the catchall of "who the dreamer is" might have registers that are not obvious.

He presents several other lists to divide dream content that provide a few more interesting markers of his notion of the individual self. For example, dreams can be classified as having relevance to one's private affairs, the affairs of other people, oneself and others simultaneously, the city as a whole, or the cosmos as a whole (1.2). This suggests a self that is located by a few classes of experience: one's private experience, dealings with others, political affiliation to a city, and status as an existing thing in a large cosmic order. The final criterion is quite interesting, suggesting a consciousness of a whole order of things that is somehow relevant to understanding such a common experience as a dream— more on this in a moment. Also the localization of political identity to a city affiliation is noteworthy. It is quite in keeping with very old Greek ideas indeed, and it does not even recognize an imperial dimension to politics. This absence could be a deliberate erasing or a mere reflection of limited imperial intrusion into the core notions of identity of Artemidorus and the Hellenized subjects of his study, despite total political dominance.

More interesting, perhaps, is Artemidorus' list of the six basic criteria, which he calls the "elements" *(stoicheia)*, by which all dream content is to be evaluated. These are nature, law, custom, *technē*, words, and time (1.3, 4.2, cf. 1.8). The general principle for interpreting dreams is that if a dream accords with these six criteria for a dreamer, then it is auspicious; if it is in discord, it is inauspicious. In regard to the first element, things deemed "unnatural" portend bad things, and those deemed "natural" portend good things. Nature is most often invoked in instances that have to do with the anatomy of the human body.[6] Law is a relatively straightforward category and measures whether certain acts depicted in dreams are in accord with the laws of the dreamer's state. It does not come up often in the interpretations of individual dreams, perhaps because it is simply understood. But it might also be enlisted as evidence that Greek citizens in the Roman Empire in the second century (whom Artemidorus assumes to be pagan) did not feel themselves defined by their legal status in draconian ways. Perpetua's fantasies of torture under the boot of the Romans are not echoed in a systematic way in Artemidorus. Dreams of execution by the state appear in the text, but as a smallish subcategory of dreams about various forms of death (2.54).[7] And in place of Perpetua's grisly spectacle of victimhood, Artemidorus records what it means to dream of fighting as a gladiator: generally, it means a lawsuit is coming, but it can mean, interestingly, marriage to a woman whose character will correspond to the weapon used (2.32). Lawsuits are represented in the text, but as a nuisance to the businessman rather than as an oppressive specter (2.29).

The category of "custom" *(ethos)*, meaning the way people traditionally do things in any given context, is a pivotal one that comes up dozens of times in the text. For example, dressing in a ridiculous fashion is inauspicious to all except jesters, for whom it is customary (3.24). Some customs are considered universal, for example to venerate the gods, to nurture children, to yield to women in sex, to be awake during the day and asleep at night, to eat, to sleep, and to live in shelter (1.8). In book 4, this list is expanded to include the mystery religions, initiation rites, festal assemblies, national games, military service, agriculture, settlement of cites, marriage, and the education of children (4.2). All the rest are considered local and particular, and these can only be learned by careful study (4.4).

The category of *technē* is perhaps the second-most often invoked, after custom. It subsumes all consideration of arts, crafts, or professions, and of the six "elements." The category of words is the least explained of the elements. But when one turns to the actual interpretations of dreams, where puns, anagrams, and numerological considerations of letter values are common, one suspects that this is what is meant by this element.[8] For example: "A weasel signifies a cunning, treacherous woman and a lawsuit. For the word lawsuit [*dikē*] has the same numerical value as the word weasel [*galē*]. . . . It also signifies profits and success in business. For some people call it a fox [*kerdō*, which is a pun for *kerdos* = 'profit']" (3.28). Finally, there is the category of time, which seems to be imbedded in a tense-based system of past, present, or future (4.2), so that if something that is part of one's past is dreamt of as being in the past, this is auspicious, but if it is dreamt of as being in the present, this is inauspicious. This element, which carries a built-in impediment to predictive dreaming, is the least often invoked of the six.

This list of elements adds a few bits of understanding to our picture of the self (considered in general). First and foremost, the self is part of a culture, especially a local one, that determines the values of various acts and experiences. Second, the self is an occupied self; it is engaged in and with the various arts, crafts, and techniques by which human beings manipulate their environments. Next, the self is a natural self that must answer to certain necessities and limitations, mainly having to do with its bodily abilities. The self is also embedded in language, which makes its presence felt when it calls attention to itself in the form of puns. And finally, the self is subject to legal limitation and to the passing of time. Overall, the self is an embedded self, subject to large structures that order its experiences and give meaning to them. We will see that this view of the self in general is thoroughly confirmed when we turn to its specifically religious dimension, as expressed in the divinatory self, to which we now turn.

Artemidorus and the Divinatory Self

Given as much interest as Artemidorus has justifiably generated for under-standing the lives of individuals in the second century c.e., it is strange that his usefulness for understanding the particularly religious dimension of the self has hardly been noticed. He is, after all, doing nothing other than explicating at length a phenomenon that both he and most of his audience would have considered religious. Perhaps we have been blinded to this aspect of the work by the colorful spectrum of data it presents for understanding any number of other cultural phenomena and attitudes. But without doubt the self that is presented in Artemidorus' dream book is a religious self; and more specifically, it is a divinatory one. If we allow ourselves to substitute the Greek idea of "the soul" *(psychē)*, Artemidorus makes "the self" the very instrument of communi-cation between humans and the large forces that move the world around them. A few immediate observations suggest that *psychē* and soul are plausible ana-logs. What we likely mean when we say "self" and what Artemidorus and his contemporaries likely meant by *psychē* each contain some reference to an entity at the core of each human being's identity: everybody is thought to have one, and each one is unique. Both self and *psychē* are thought to endure through change, and both are tied up with the idea of agency; Greek philosophers were rather consistent in assigning volition specifically to the soul. The self and the *psychē* are also granted an equally broad range of additional functions having to do with intellection and emotion.

Artemidorus gives us his most explicit account of the divinatory self in his explanation of how divination through dreams comes about. At the very begin-ning of his first book, he divides visions that appear to people in sleep due to overeating or overwhelming desires, and fears *(enhypnia)* from dreams that are predictive of the future. The latter class he calls *oneiroi*.

> An *oneiros*, which can take many forms, is a movement [*kinēsis*] or shaping [*plasis*] of the soul. The movement or shaping signifies good or bad things that will occur in the future. This being the case, whatever is going to happen, whether the lapse of time until the event is great or small, all these things the soul predicts [*proagoreuei*] through images, [*dia eikonōn*] called "elements," [*stoicheiōn*] which are personal to it [*idiōn*], a part of its nature [*physikōn*]. The soul does this because it considers that we, in the intervening time, can learn what is going to happen, since we are trained by our reasoning power. But whatever takes place with no lapse of time before the event (that is, it delays nothing, whoever it is that guides us in regard to the introduction of images) the soul, since it considers a prediction no help to us, unless we grasp things before we learn them by experience, reveals things through themselves, and waits for nothing outside of what is indicated for a revelation. (1.2)

Several aspects of this theory repay close attention. Artemidorus appears less than precise about the origin of dreams. He first claims that the dream is a movement or shaping of the soul. This is rather straightforward, given traditional Greek psychology. The soul, according to many different Greek thinkers, was a breathy entity (whether material or immaterial) that was subject to being manipulated by outside influences, a capacity that most often comes up in connection with the perceptions. That a dream should arise this way from some outside agency manipulating the soul is also a traditional view in Greek thinking and is in line with Aristotle's theory of dreams as expressed in his short treatises *On Dreams* and *On Divination through Dreams,* not to mention with a long tradition of viewing some divine agency as the source of the dream. But beginning in the third sentence of the translation above, he implies a slightly different scenario: that the soul itself is the active agent in the dream. The soul "predicts," but not merely as the passive recipient of a perception. It also takes an active role in deciding what images will be produced for any given dream, based on its preunderstanding of whether the events are imminent, in which case direct images will reveal the future, or not imminent, in which case indirect ones will. This grants the soul an agency that exists independent of the sleeping body, which operates while we are asleep, making judgments about how to communicate to "us." So the soul has a volition independent from the individual person. This suggests that the soul is simultaneously part of the self (since it is the entity that receives the dream, as an organ that belongs to us) but also has a mind of its own, which is manifested in the dreaming process.

If we go back to considering the soul as a passive player in the dream, we find another entity granted agency in dreaming, the one that "guides us" in the introduction of dream images. This entity ("whoever it is") seems also to be the controlling agent behind the events to which the dreams images correspond, since it is said to be responsible for delaying or not delaying the events the dream images portend. The reason Artemidorus resists naming this entity can be found in his discussion of the role of the divine in dreaming. He tells us that he will follow convention and call dreams "god-sent," but he does not want to commit himself on the question of exactly where they come from:

> I do not, like Aristotle, inquire as to whether the cause of our dreaming is outside of us and comes from the gods or whether there is some internal cause, which disposes our soul in a certain way and causes a natural event to happen to it. Rather, I use the word in the same way that we customarily call all unforeseen things god-sent. (1.6)

Tellingly, this statement equates the idea of an external cause and a divine one, and it does not leave much wiggle room as to the identity of that unnamed "whoever it is" mentioned at 1.2. If there is an external cause that guides the introduction of dream images, as the text at 1.2 suggests, the text at 1.6 implies that it is divine. At this point Artemidorus' theory may seem merely inconsistent and perhaps a bit coy. He resists labeling as "god" an entity that at another point he assumes can only be "god." This seems to suggest that his agnosticism is strategic rather than heartfelt. But there is actually a little more to it than that.

Artemidorus articulates his position one last time at the beginning of book 4, in a rephrasing that casts a new light on his views. Book 4 was written, he tells us, to answer critics who had read the first installments. He repeats his broadest theoretical positions with justifications that are sometimes more elaborate or slightly tweaked. When he comes to the issue of the "whoever it is," he tells us: "The god—or whatever it is that causes a person to dream—presents to the dreamer's soul, which is, by its very nature, prophetic, dreams that correspond to future events" (4.2). Artemidorus reiterates his reluctance to take a firm position on the true force behind the dream but also adds something new. The notion that the soul might be "by its very nature prophetic" is actually a crucial formulation that prompts a second look at the earlier evidence. In each earlier statement of theory, we now notice, Artemidorus goes out of his way to mention a "natural" dimension to the dreaming process. We recall that the soul produces images "that are personal to it [*idiōn*]," and "a part of its nature [*physikon*]" (1.2).[9] Again later, the shaping the soul undergoes (whether at the hands of the divine or from some internal cause) is characterized as an event that belongs to the soul's "nature" (1.6). So when "nature" comes up for the third time, in book 4, we are right to pay close attention.

Artemidorus' broad and fascinating claim that the soul "in its nature" is prophetic reconfigures an idea that can be traced to Aristotle, to the section of his *On Divination through Dreams* that Artemidorus references in his discussion of the term "god-sent": "On the whole, since certain of the other lower animals dream, dreams should not be considered to be 'god-sent,' and they are not from this source. They do, however, have a divine aspect [they are *daimonia*], for nature itself has a divine aspect, but is not divine" (463b12–15). This remarkable claim is not repeated elsewhere in Aristotle's surviving corpus. What precisely he means is difficult to determine,[10] but the general picture that the statement paints is in keeping with Artemidorus' statement about souls. Dreams belong to the natural order of things, which itself carries a trace of the divine (which Aristotle states outright and Artemidorus implies but avoids saying). Artemidorus adds a layer of specificity, making the soul the specific site where nature (tinctured with the divine) makes dreaming happen. We can gain a greater purchase on Artemidorus' thoughts here if we turn to a philosophical school whose views are proximate to those of his own.

Artemidorus' Divinatory "Soul" in the Currents of Stoicism

The Stoics remake many traditional Greek views quite radically, and their thinking on the gods is not an exception. They reinterpret the traditional anthropomorphic divinities as allegorical expressions of different aspects of a single divine principle. Like all features of the Stoic cosmos, this divine principle is material in nature, a highly rarified and diffuse mist they call *pneuma*. Like an aerosol, it suffuses everything in the cosmos. It penetrates even dense matter and shapes it into the discrete entities we see around us, maintaining them in a particular state. The *pneuma* that holds together a human body is *pneuma* in its purest form, which is also called soul *(psychē)*. The soul formulates perceptions, via the senses, by accepting all manner of physical impressions from without. In a Stoic cosmos, selves are what they are because the divine *pneuma* makes them so, by maintaining a physical presence inside of them. The soul (now indistinguishable from the divine) is to be understood as part of a synthetic whole that permeates the entire cosmos. The self is in its very nature, then, in direct communication with the divine, and through that with every other entity in the cosmos.

Exotic as they might sound, these general views would have been rather elementary for those familiar with Stoic ideas (in other words for any educated person in the second century c.e.). This background opens up some interesting vistas on Artemidorus' religious self. First of all, his apparent sloppiness in distinguishing the precise cause of dreams—that is, whether it be the divine or the soul—is almost unnoticeable in a world shaped by Stoic common sense. Since the soul is the divine, attributing agency to one or the other is a matter over which one needn't be overly scrupulous. Second, Artemidorus' discussion of the "whoever it is" who seems to regulate both our dream images and the future events they indicate is a bit more comprehensible, since the *pneuma* is the great regulating force of the everything in the universe. All events and states of affairs in the world are attributable to it, so it makes sense to talk about a single guiding principle for the whole system (in the form of both events and the signs that presage them).

Finally, in a Stoic scheme an entirely new prominence is possible for the idea of a personal religious identity at the core of the human being (that is, a "religious self"). One can surely have a personal relationship with the divine, since humans are literally permeated by it. In keeping with this, the Stoics also remove public cult from its position of unquestioned supremacy among the hierarchy of acts of worship. It begins to be replaced by a more inwardly directed meditative spirituality, based on learning rather than action (see, for example, Cicero, *Nat. d.* 2.72, Persius 5.120–23; and Cornutus, *Nat. d.* 35). Specifically, one is to learn about the ways of the *pneuma* and to act in accordance with it (see, e.g. Seneca, *Ep.* 124.13–14). A focus on divination, that is, on personal communication with the divine, fits in perfectly with the Stoics more personal understanding of religious expression. Of course, one needs to nuance this view in at least a small way. The notion of the self is complicated a bit by the idea that the inner core of one's being is in some sense alien to oneself because it is a part of a large collective. This aspect of Stoicism explains Artemidorus' notion that our souls have a volition of their own, separate from "us," in the dreaming process. If we are right to conclude that Artemidorus' soul is written in the broad context of Stoic views of the soul (and I believe we are), then this alien presence is the divine itself. It hardly presents an issue to the notion of a *religious* self, but it does provoke the question of what kind of religious *self* we have.

The Greek Religious Self Reconsidered

We mentioned above the reasons why the Greek soul seemed to be a plausible analog to the modern notion of the self: core identity lay in both places; both admit of change but are thought to endure as a coherent entity over time; and both are loci of volition. The matter has been complicated at a couple of points in the discussion above, which suggests that Artemidorus' self/soul has a few distinct contours worth highlighting. Artemidorus' dreaming soul is a self that is deeply embedded in larger structures, marked out most concisely in the six "elements": nature, custom, law, *technē*, language, and time. This poses no serious problem for "selfhood," since we are used to thinking of selves as being the sums of their externally determined identities. (So was Homer, for that matter.) But Artemidorus pushes the idea of embeddedness beyond the familiar in his description of the dreaming soul as standing apart from the dreaming person. He most clearly shows this alienation in his discussion of the soul calculating which language to use to speak to "us" in the dream. Artemidorus' self is to some extent alien to itself. This reminds us that the distances between Artemidorus and Freud, which Price was right to point out, ought not to blind us to certain similarities.

Perhaps the very act of dreaming, at once supremely personal and yet totally out of our own control, uniquely provokes the self into a dialectic of selfhood and alterity. If this dialectic is indeed part and parcel of dreaming, this fact may also go some way to explaining Artemidorus' easy agnosticism. Dreaming requires some other with whom the self comes into intimate contact. Call this the divine if you wish, call it the divine pneuma inside the self (which is probably closest to Artemidorus' own view), or even call it an unconscious, locked away and banished from our waking minds. In any case, the dream brings the self into contact with an other within. Interestingly enough, this schematization is equally at home both in Artemidorus' pre-Cartesian notion of the self and in Ricoeur's struggles with reconstructing a post-Cartesian self. Neither self answers to the autonomous, fully sovereign *cogito* of Descartes, but both must contend, at some fundamental level, with being alien to itself.

NOTES

1. Greek puts *autos* in one position (predicate position) when it means self and another (attributive) when it means same.

2. The position that marks it as meaning self (predicate position) is usually used in an entirely different way, to make whole statements about things by making adjectives and nouns into predicates. It admits only a very few lexical items that do not work this way. *Autos* meaning "self" is one of them, but most prominent by far in this class are the demonstrative pronouns like "this" and "that." This suggests an affiliation between the

Greek *autos* and words with a deictic function, a capacity to show or to point out something unique, in other words, a particular thing-A against a background of what is not thing-A.

3. The bibliography on Artemidorus is expanding, and deservedly so. To the early studies by Roger Pack, whose most accessible treatment is "Artemidorus and His Waking World," *TAPA* 86 (1955): 280–90, one must now add Simon Price, "The Future of Dreams: From Freud to Artemidorus," *Past and Present* 113 (November 1986): 3–37; Michel Foucault, "Dreaming of One's Pleasures," in *The Care of the Self* (vol. 3 of *The History of Sexuality;* trans. Robert Hurley; New York: Pantheon Books, 1986), 4–36; John Winkler, "Unnatural Acts: Erotic Protocols in Artemidorus' *Dream Analysis*," in *The Constraints of Desire: The Anthropology of Sex and Gender in Ancient Greece* (New York: Routledge, 1990), 17–44; Luther Martin, "Artemidorus: Dream Theory in Latin Antiquity," *The Second Century* 8 (1991): 97–108; Patricia Cox Miller, "Artemidorus and the Classification of Dreams," in *Dreams in Late Antiquity: Studies in the Imagination of a Culture* (Princeton, N.J.: Princeton University Press, 1994), 77–91.

4. Glen Bowersock's concerns on this point seem a bit overblown ("The Reality of Dreams," in *Fiction as History: Nero to Julian* [Sather Classical Lectures 58; Berkeley: University of California Press, 1994], 77–98). He characterizes Artemidorus' evidence as being hopelessly skewed toward an idle elite who have leisure to dabble in the *arcana mundi*, but the sheer size of Artemidorus' data set inclines one in the direction of taking his claim to have talked to all sorts of people at face value. It is also true that divination in the ancient world (unlike in contemporary analogs) had a demonstrably democratic appeal.

5. Translations are based on Artemidorus, *The Interpretation of Dreams* (trans. Robert J. White; Noyes Classical Studies; Park Ridge, N.J.: Noyes Press, 1975).

6. "Nature" is invoked explicitly with a certain regularity in the text. Things declared to be natural *(kata physin)* include having one's internal organs in the normal places (1.44), and the color a swallow normally has (2.66). Things declared to be unnatural include having a head that is larger or smaller than the norm (1.17), having two noses (1.27), holding a head in one's hands as opposed to having it in the "natural" place (1.38), and having more than ten fingers (1.42). One further place in the text shows Artemidorus' attentiveness to culture, even within and through the idea of the "natural." He declares drinking warm water to be unnatural *(ou kata physin)*, but he makes an exception for those for whom it is customary *(chōris tōn ethos echontōn)* (1.66). A single example can not be asked to bear a great deal of weight, but the notion of culture is here on the ascendancy, interrupting the usual axis between the "natural" and the universal in Greek thinking. Winkler's work shows that Artemidorus' line between nature and culture, specifically in the case of sexual behaviors (where nature is the central category), is hardly a matter of simple observation but depends critically on cultural assumptions (1.79–80). One might find other such instances in the dream book, and it would be well worth doing so.

7. On this topic, see Brent Shaw, "Judicial Nightmares and Christian Memory," *JECS* 11 (2003): 533–63.

8. Greeks, like Romans, indicated number by means of alphabetic characters.

9. Artemidorus adds the idea of nature in an explanatory asyndeton, a rather rare construction for Greek, which really draws attention to it

10. A useful discussion of this passage is to be found in Philip J. van der Eijk, *De insomniis. De divinatione per somnum* (Werke in deutscher Übersetzung/Aristoteles 14.3; Berlin: Akademie-Verlag, 1994).

Part II

SENSING RELIGIOUS SELVES

——7——

Sensory Reform in Deuteronomy

STEVEN WEITZMAN

In the sixth century B.C.E., some in the ancient world became aware that their senses were not revealing the whole truth. "Bad witness are the eyes and ears for men," declared the pre-Socratic philosopher Heraclitus, apparently meaning to impugn sensory experience as a way of knowing reality (ca. 540–480 B.C.E.). While disagreeing with him about the nature of that reality, Parmenides (ca. 515 B.C.E.) seems equally distrustful of sensory experience, telling of how a goddess had warned him not to rely on "an aimless eye or ear and a tongue full of meaningless sound." Distrust of the senses emerges even more clearly in later Greek thinkers like Plato. For him the senses, especially sight, could lead to understanding, but only when governed by a questioning of appearance. Aristotle too acknowledged that the senses did not tell all. People love their senses because they allow us to know, he tells us, but there are truths the senses cannot penetrate, such as the causes of things. These are precisely Aristotle's focus in his *Metaphysics,* an investigation of those universals which lie "farthest from the senses" (1.2).[1]

By the first century C.E., some Jews believed they had a solution to the problems of sense perception. Philo of Alexandria was keenly aware of these problems, remarking frequently on the eyes' inability to penetrate beyond superficial appearance and on the sluggishness of hearing and taste (*Virt.* 12; *Decal.* 35, 147; *Spec.* 1.174). The sense's failings rendered Israel vulnerable to idolatry, a bewitching of the senses in Philo's understanding of this sin. Fortunately for the Jews, Mosaic law offered a remedy, a way to retrain the senses. Some laws kept bodily experience in check—the Sabbath, for instance, was a festival devoted not to the delight of the eye and belly but to wisdom (*Mos.*

2.211–12). Others, like the ban on worshipping heavenly beings, enabled Israel to overcome the limits of its senses, carrying its thoughts "beyond all the realm of visible existence" (*Spec.* 1.20).

This reading of biblical law is obviously anachronistic, projecting onto the Bible ideas borrowed from Greek philosophers like Plato. And yet there is one biblical text, predating Plato and even perhaps the pre-Socratics, that can be plausibly read as an attempt to retrain the senses—the book of Deuteronomy. Near the end of this book, in a speech addressed to Israel just as it is able to enter the land of Canaan, Moses claims that the people have not understood the sensory experiences it has had—a problem, I wish to propose, that preoccupies the first eleven chapters of Deuteronomy: "You have seen all that the Lord did before your eyes in the land of Egypt to Pharaoh and to all his servants and to all his land, the great trials that your eyes saw, the signs, and those great wonders. *But the Lord did not give you a mind to understand, eyes to see and ears to hear until this very day*" (29:1–4). Despite having seen God's miracles with its own eyes and hearing God's words with its own ears, Israel has remained obtuse, failing to comprehend what God has been communicating to it through its senses. One of Deuteronomy's main goals, at least in chapters 1–11, is to teach Israel how to properly understand the testimony of the eyes and the ears, a process that requires retraining and refocusing its use of its senses.

Tracing this process as it unfolds over the course of Deuteronomy 1–11 enhances our understanding of this book. It also contributes, I would venture, to what we know about the history of the self. Historians of this subject often go back to the ancient Greeks to begin their narrative. Foucault discovered the first hermeneutics of the self in Greek philosophy, and that is where the philosopher Charles Taylor also looks to begin his history of the self.[2] Does the Hebrew Bible have anything to contribute to our understanding of the early history of the self, of how it was perceived in the ancient world? According to Stephen Geller, it does, especially in Deuteronomy, which as Geller reads it, marks the emergence of a more integrated self than that reflected in earlier biblical and ancient Near Eastern sources.[3] Building on Geller's insights, I argue that Deuteronomy reflects not just a new conception of the self but an unprecedented attempt to reform it through what Georgia Frank refers to elsewhere in the present volume as a "regimen of perception"—a set of practices by which to discipline, train, and refocus Israel's senses.

To discern such an effort in a biblical text composed in the seventh or sixth century B.C.E. may at first seem anachronistic since what Foucault and Frank are describing emerged long after the biblical period, but what I argue here can be read as a kind of prehistory to what they are describing, raising the possibility that the conception of the self as something that can be retrained through ritual, diet, and other forms of disciplined practice has pre-Hellenistic—indeed, pre-Hellenic antecedents—in the ancient Near East. If I am correct in this proposal, Deuteronomy may qualify as one of the earliest extant efforts at *self*-reform on record, one that seeks to reshape how the self relates to the world by teaching the senses that mediate between them—the eyes, the ears, and the tongue—to act in new ways.

A Supernatural History of the Senses

What I am proposing here takes Deuteronomy in a different direction than where it has been in mainstream biblical scholarship. For many scholars what is revolutionary about Deuteronomy is its effort to reform Israelite cultic worship, to centralize and confine it to a single locale.[4] As compelling as this reading might be, it is based chiefly on the law code in Deuteronomy 12–26 and says little about the rhetorical frame now introducing this code, chapters 1–11, which do not address centralization in any explicit or direct way that I can detect. What these chapters do address—and often—is Israel's senses. The Deuteronomic Moses makes frequent appeals to the senses, instructing Israel to remember what its eyes have seen (4:9; 7:19; 10:21), calling repeatedly for Israel to hear (5:1; 6:3, 4); warning it about forgetting God after it has eaten its fill (8:12). The senses even make an appearance in the threats Moses makes: if Israel makes an idol, he warns, it will find itself scattered among the nations, serving gods "that do not see, hear, eat, nor smell" (4:25–28).[5]

Read in a glancing, superficial way, Deuteronomy's various references to the senses can be seen as reflecting the sort of conventional rhetoric one finds in biblical wisdom texts, especially Proverbs. They begin to take on added significance only when one notices that they often appear in stories in which sensory experience plays some role in Israel's relationship with God: Israel's attempt to see the land (1:22–40); its encounter with God at Horeb/Sinai where Israel "hears the sound of words but sees no form" (4:12); and the famine and feasting of the wilderness, when God humbles Israel with hunger, then feeds it with manna (8:2–3, 16). The references to the senses in Deuteronomy 1–11, though in all likelihood drawing on established didactic motifs, are deeply woven into the fabric of these chapters.

There is, in fact, a recognizable pattern governing these references, following the same order that appears in 4:28: seeing, hearing, eating. Material related to the eyes—the spying episode, God's unseeability at Mount Horeb, the commandment forbidding the worship of idols—cluster in chapters 1–4. In the midst of the latter chapter, the narrative switches its attention to hearing. It is here that one finds the famous exhortation "Hear O Israel," among other appeals to auditory experience. Another transition occurs in chapter 6 when the text turns from hearing to eating. Here, for the first time in Deuteronomy, Canaan is described as a "land oozing milk and honey" (6:3)—a phrase found earlier in the Pentateuch but appearing in Deuteronomy only now.[6] It is also in this section that the text reports how God fed Israel with manna (3, 16) and how Moses went without bread and water (9:9, 18). Sensory experience is not just a central concern in chapters 1–11; it is a key structuring device that earlier studies of Deuteronomy's redactional design have missed.[7]

Many of Deuteronomy's references to the senses have specific parallels in, and are very likely drawn from, earlier Pentateuchal texts or the traditions they draw on. Deuteronomy's creativity, I thus want to stress, lies not in the invention of this language but in how it adapts and organizes it for its own purposes, a view in line with recent scholarship that has argued for Deuteronomy as an innovative reuse/reinterpretation of earlier textual material.[8] Most of that scholarship, however, has focused on the legal corpus in Deuteronomy 12–26 and the way it serves the goal of cult centralization. A different agenda motivates the revisionary efforts I focus on here. As in Deuteronomy 12–26, these revisions also include a reinterpretation of Israelite ritual tradition, but their effect is not to relocate Israelite worship but to re-purpose it, to invest it with a new role as a way of retraining the senses.

Following the order of things in Deuteronomy 1–11, it is possible to read these chapters as a sustained history of the senses in Israel's religious life, the ways in which its eyes, ears, and mouth threatened its covenant with God, and the solutions that Moses contrives to counter this threat.

Wandering Eyes

The theme we are tracing first emerges through a revision of the spy episode that is first told in Numbers 13–14. Deuteronomy's version parallels Numbers and may even borrow from the JE strand within it. It also contains many differences, however, including several references to seeing whose resonance is amplified by being clustered within a smaller textual space.[9] Beyond heightening the role of the visual, these changes affect the meaning of the story as a whole, transforming it into a cautionary tale of what happens when Israel fails to absorb what its eyes have seen.

Thus, for example, Deuteronomy revises the story to suggest a disconnect between what the spies actually see in the land and Israel's later interpretation of that experience. In Numbers, the report that the spies bring back is mixed, telling of the land's prosperity but also of its dangers: "We came to the land to which you sent us; it flows with milk and honey, and this is its fruit. However, strong are the people who live in the land, and the towns are fortified and very large, and we saw the children of Anak (a giant people) there" (13:27–28). Hearing such a report, the people have solid grounds for hesitating to enter the land. By contrast, Deuteronomy's version of the report is entirely positive, "It is a good land that the Lord your God is giving to us" (1:25). The people complain about the land, as if the spies had also reported negative things (1:27–28), but nothing in the report itself as described by Deuteronomy substantiates this anxiety. In Numbers, in other words, the problem is what the spies say, a "bad report" that overstates the dangers of entering the land; this is why God singles out the report-givers for punishment (14:36–37). In Deuteronomy, the problem is how Israel responds to the report, its dismissal of what its "eyes," the spies, tell it. The effect of this change is to shift responsibility for the delayed entry into the land from the spies to a skeptical Israel that discounts empirical evidence that should have encouraged it to trust God, a point made explicitly by Moses in the speech that follows.

That speech, without parallel in Numbers, explicitly accuses Israel of ignoring what its eyes have seen:

> I said to you, "Have no dread and do not be afraid of them. The Lord your God, who goes before you—he is the one who will fight for you just as he did for you in Egypt *before your eyes*, and in the wilderness, where *you saw* that the Lord your God carried you, as a man carries his son, all the way that you have traveled until you came to this place. But in this matter you (still) do not believe in the Lord your God, who goes before you on the way to seek out a place for you to camp, in fire by night and in the cloud by day, *to show you* the route you should take." (1:29–33)

Moses reminds Israel that its own eyes have seen evidence of God's protective power—the defeat of the Egyptians at the Red Sea and the other miracles performed in the wilderness. Even now God's presence is visually manifest, showing Israel the way. Yet even having seen these things, Israel is still distrustful. For this sin, he continues, the Israelites will be deprived of the visual experience for which they long: "Not one of these . . . shall see the good land that I swore to give to your ancestors" (1:34). This element is also paralleled in Numbers (14:22–23), but the visual connection between sin and punishment is easier to recognize in Deuteronomy that elides an intervening and lengthy episode falling between them in Numbers' version (14:10–22).

Thus reconfigured, the spy episode becomes an illustration of the misperception that Moses complains about in chapter 29: "You have seen all that the Lord did before your eyes. . . . But the Lord did not give you . . . eyes to see." In intervening chapters, Moses will urge his audience to remember its visual experiences of God: "Watch yourself lest you forget the things that your eyes have seen" (4:9; 11:2–7). The spy story as retold by Deuteronomy illustrates the peril of ignoring this advice; the Israel of the wilderness generation was prevented from seeing what it longed to see (the land) because it failed to understand what its eyes had seen of God's power and protective presence.

In Deuteronomy 4, Moses recounts another episode where the Israelites are confronted with something they *cannot* see: "You approached and stood at the foot of the mountain and the mountain was burning to the heart of heaven, darkened by heavy clouds. The Lord spoke to you from the midst of a fire. The sound of words you were hearing *but a form you did not see—only a voice*" (4:11–12). The text is not necessarily suggesting that God is invisible. Dwelling in heaven, he may simply have been too far away for humans on earth to see (cf.

4:36). Regardless of the reason, Israel was unable to see God at Horeb, experiencing his presence directly but only aurally, through the medium of a divine voice speaking from the midst of a fire.

For this reason, Moses warns, Israel is to make no attempt to try to see God, whether by making an image of him or by turning its eyes upwards to what it can see in heaven: "Since you did not see a form on the day God spoke with you at Horeb from the midst of the fire, watch yourselves lest you act corruptly by making for yourselves an idol in the image of any figure" (4:15). Here too, Deuteronomy is not inventing out of whole cloth but drawing on preexisting traditions also preserved in Exodus 19–20.[10] The way Deuteronomy ties these elements together goes beyond Exodus, however. Exodus juxtaposes the story of how God refused to be seen (Exodus 19) with the ban of idols (Exodus 20), but it does not draw a specific connection between God's unseeability and the ban as Deuteronomy does. Also going beyond Exodus, Deuteronomy expands the ban to include the worship of another kind of visible deity: "Watch yourselves . . . lest you *raise your eyes* to heaven *and see* the sun and moon and stars, all the host of heaven, and you go astray and worship them" (4:19). The ban against idols in Deuteronomy's retelling is an attempt, not simply to prevent Israel from worshipping other gods as in Exodus, but to preserve the sensory character of the Horeb theophany, an experience devoid of anything visible to focus the eyes on.

Read as a unit, Deuteronomy 1–4 establishes two optical problems that threaten Israel's relationship with God. Deuteronomy 1 illustrates the danger of discounting what the eyes reveal; Deuteronomy 4, the danger of trying to see a god that only wants to be heard. It also cleverly attaches sensory consequences to both kinds of problem. For the sin of not believing its eyes, the Israelites are prevented from seeing the land; for the sin of trying to see God, Israel will be forced to worship deities who sense nothing. The solution to both of these problems is introduced in Deuteronomy 4: future generations of Israel must act to avoid the extremes of misperception, remembering what its eyes have seen of God's power (4:9) without trying to see more of God than its ancestors were able to see at Mount Horeb (15–31).

Deuteronomy may seek to model the kind of posture it is advocating through its representation of Moses, poised in this section between seeing and not seeing. Just prior to chapter 4, in 3:23–29, the prophet recounts how after seeing some of God's greatness, he hoped to see more: "O Lord God, you have only begun to *show* your servant your greatness . . . let me cross over to *see* the good land" (3:24–25). God refuses, but he does allow the prophet an attenuated visual experience, instructing him to ascend Mount Pisgah and view the land from a distance. Moses is thus able to see what his ancestors have yearned to see, and yet his desire to see is stopped short at a boundary beyond which it is forbidden to go. Embodied in Moses, I would argue, is the intermediate optical posture that 1–4 as a whole seeks to instill in Israel, a posture between the desire to see more than God shows to humans and seeing nothing at all. What allows Israel to avoid either extreme is a regime of sensory practice that combines the cultivation of memory (remembering what one has seen) with self-discipline (turning away from falsely visible gods) to form a self connected to God by what it has seen of his power but habituated not to want to see God directly.

Attuning the Ears

Although the God of Deuteronomy cannot be seen, he can be heard: "The Lord spoke to you from the midst of a fire. The sound of words you were hearing . . . only a voice" (4:12). This experience of God's voice is not available to other peoples; it is revealed to Israel alone: "Has anything so great as this ever happened, or has its like ever been heard of? Has a people *heard* the voice of God speaking out of a fire, as you *have heard* and lived?" (4:32) While God has allowed Israel unprecedented sensory access to him, hearing his voice poses dangers of its own, Moses marveling that Israel has survived the experience: "Has a people heard the voice of God . . . and lived?" Deuteronomy 4–6 seeks to mitigate the danger of hearing God by instituting a kind of virtual hearing, an indirect way to hear his voice.

Deuteronomy makes its transition to hearing subtly, moving away from the visual motifs it has been employing (though not abandoning them) in favor of aural motifs: "they hear all these statues" (4:6); "I will cause them to hear my words" (4:10). The switch is even apparent in small rhetorical gestures such as Moses prefacing his speech in this section with the command "Hear" in contrast to the previous section where his addresses begin with "See!" (1:21; 2:31). All this occurs in tandem with the text's increasing emphasis on hearing as a conduit between God and Israel, an emphasis detectable in how it reworks material known from Exodus.

A famous example is Deuteronomy's reworking of the Ten Commandments in chapter 5, words given a special status in Deuteronomy because God is thought to have spoken them directly to Israel, as opposed to the rest of his commandments, which were revealed through Moses' mediation. Deuteronomy's version of the commandments themselves is more or less parallel with Exodus 20, but it offers a slightly different account of what it was like to receive them. In Exodus 20:18–19, in a passage that appears just after the commandments, the people are said to have been frightened by a mixture of sounds and sights that follow God's speech: "All the people, seeing the thunder and lightning, the sound of the trumpet, and the mountain smoking, were afraid and trembled and stood at a distance, and they said to Moses, 'You speak with us, and we will listen, but do not let God speak with us lest we die.'" Deuteronomy 5:22–27 also notes the fire and smoke, but its version focuses much more attention on the terror of *hearing* God:

These words the Lord spoke *with a loud voice* to all your assembly at the mountain, from the midst of the fire, the cloud and thick darkness, a *great voice*, and he added no more. He wrote them on two stone tablets and gave them to me. *When you heard the voice from the midst of the darkness,* the mountain burning with fire, you approached me, all the heads of your tribes and your elders; and you said, "Look, the Lord our God has shown us his glory and greatness, *and his voice we heard out of the midst of the fire.* Today, we have seen *that God may speak to someone* and he may live. Now, why should we die? For this great fire will consume us; *if we continue to hear the voice of the Lord our God any longer,* we shall die. For who is there of all flesh *that has heard the voice of the living God speaking out of the midst the fire* like us and lived. You go near and *hear all the Lord our God will say* and then tell us everything that the Lord our God tells you, *and we will listen* and do it."

Whereas Israel saw nothing of God's form, this passage makes it very clear that it did enjoy a direct experience of God's voice, an experience so intense, in fact, that Israel wonders that it survived the experience and turns to Moses to mediate God's words. All this may be implicit in the Exodus account, from which Deuteronomy seems to draw its building blocks, but as in its retelling of the spy episode, Deuteronomy has reshaped its source material, drawing explicit connections between episodes that are merely juxtaposed in Exodus and increasing the references to hearing in order to emphasize the role of sense-perception as the foundation of Israel's relationship with God and as a threat to that relationship.

Deuteronomy's change from seeing to hearing in this passage has been recognized by Geller in an illuminating analysis of Deuteronomy 4 to which I am indebted.[11] Geller reads Deuteronomy 4 as a reaction against wisdom texts like Job that privilege seeing over hearing as a more authoritative source of knowledge about God (cf. Job 42:5–6). Casting itself as a new form of wisdom, Deuteronomy 4 seems at first to embrace this view, urging Israel to remember what its eyes have seen, but as the chapter continues, that experience is eclipsed by the experience of hearing God's voice. We are now in a position to recognize how Deuteronomy 4 fits into a larger argument about the senses that begins in chapter 1 and continues beyond chapter 4. Deuteronomy 1–4 had established the advantages and disadvantages of seeing as a medium of connection with God, making it possible to detect his protective presence at work but also threatening to alienate Israel from God. Chapters 4–5 do the same for hearing, establishing it as another way to learn about God, the sense through which Israel directly encounters God, in fact, but one also fraught with risk.

To avoid this risk, Israel asks Moses to serve as an intermediary, hearing God's voice and then reporting back: "Tell us everything that the Lord our God tells you, and we will listen and do it." Deuteronomy 5:5 inconsistently reports that even the Ten Commandments were mediated in this way ("I was standing between the Lord and you to declare the word of the Lord, for you were afraid because of the fire") despite the impression given elsewhere in Deuteronomy that these words were heard directly by Israel.[12] Moses' role, it turns out, is to buffer God's voice, to mediate it through the filter of his voice. Deuteronomy did not invent this role for the prophet any more than it invented the ban against images (Cf. Exod 20:19); its contribution is to reframe this tradition in ways that make it a significant turning point in the history of the senses we have been tracing. Departing from the version in Exodus, the Deuteronomic Moses tells Israel that God himself approved its proposal:

> The Lord *heard* your words when you spoke to me, and the Lord said to me: "I *heard* the voice of the words of this people, which they have spoken to you. They have done well in what they have spoken. . . . You, stand here by me, and I will tell you all the commandments, the statutes and the ordinances so that you may teach them." (5:25–28)

This is the first time in Deuteronomy that God is said to have *heard* Israel in an approving way. In earlier passages, Israel tries to make its voice heard by God but is not successful. In the spy story, after hearing Israel's words about him, God grows angry with Israel and punishes it (1:34). Israel petitions God for forgiveness, but God still does not "hear" its voice or "give ear" to it (1:45). Now at last, God attends to its voice—and just as Israel begins hearing his voice. What seems to make this breakthrough possible is Moses' role as a go-between, hearing God's words on Israel's behalf and conveying Israel's words to God.

Since so much of Deuteronomy is a citation of Moses speaking God's words, one is tempted to read this section as a kind of etiology for the book as a whole. The sensory material in Deuteronomy 1–5 rules out the direct perception of God: seeing God is impossible because he does not reveal himself in a visible form; hearing God is possible but it is too overwhelming to bear for long. What is sustainable is precisely the kind of mediated audition that Deuteronomy purports to record—*the indirect* audition of God's voice through the filter of Moses. The sensory history that we have been tracing, in other words, may be an attempt to cast Deuteronomy itself as an alternative to direct sensory experience, a kind of auditory compromise like the visual compromise achieved by Moses in Deuteronomy 3 that balances between too much raw sensation and no sensation at all.

There is one difference between Mosaic speech and Deuteronomy, however: the former is delivered orally, whereas the latter is written down in a text. As the text moves from chapter 5 to 6, however, it begins to suggest a role for writing as a way of extending the experience of God's voice to those who did not experience things for themselves, future generations of Israel not present to see God's miracles or hear his voice at Horeb. Deuteronomy 1–11 seems especially concerned with those generations, defining them in 11:2 as those "who have not known or seen the discipline of the Lord our God" ("to know" here connoting empirical experience). In a famous passage, Deuteronomy 6 establishes a series of techniques to help insure the transmission of God's Mosaically mediated voice to those future generations:

> These words that I am commanding you today will be in your heart. Recite them to your sons and talk about them when you are sitting at home and when you are on the road, when you lie down and when you rise. Bind them as a sign on your hand, fix them as an emblem between your eyes, and write them on the doorpost of your house and on your gates. (6:7–9)

This passage reflects the same pattern of creative re-use we have observed in earlier chapters, recycling language that appears in Exodus 13 in reference to Passover and the rite of the firstborn, but it introduces several telling changes consistent with what I am arguing here. In Exodus, the memory that is being preserved is Israel's redemption from slavery, whereas here it is God's words as transmitted through Moses ("these words that I am commanding you today"). To insure their transmission, Deuteronomy relies on conventional pedagogical mnemonic techniques known from Proverbs—continuous recitation, stringing reminders to one's body, and writing things down. Deuteronomy itself may fall into the latter category of practice, preserving Moses' speech in written form so that the experience that it mediates—the sound of God's voice speaking through Moses—is remembered by future generations.

The section devoted to hearing (chapters 4–6) ends in much the way that the section devoted to seeing does, finding its solution to the sensory problem that it has introduced in preexisting mnemonic and ritual practice. In Deuteronomy 4, it had developed its remedy from the ban of divine images attested in (the presumably earlier) Exodus 20. In Deuteronomy 6, the solution is constructed in a similar way, with elements drawn from the ritual legislation in Exodus 13 to construct a regimen of remembered auditory experience. Deuteronomy's goal in all this is to retrain Israel's eyes and ears to accept indirect sensory experience in lieu of raw religious sensation—the visual experience of God as mediated through the memory of what its ancestors have seen, the auditory experience of God as filtered through Mosaic speech.

Eating Disorders

Deuteronomy looks to Israel's memory to transmit the sensory experience of seeing God's power and hearing his voice over time, but another sensory experience threatens that transmission, that of the mouth. Biblical wisdom tradition recognizes eating as a potentially perilous activity, the satiated appetite forgetting what it owes to God: "Feed me (only) with the food that I need, or I shall be full, and deny you and say, 'Who is the Lord?'" (Prov 30:8–9). Deuteronomy registers this danger as well. In Canaan, a land of milk and honey, Israel will find more than enough food to satisfy its appetite—so much, Moses worries, that it may forget its dependency on God. The speech in which Moses articulates this anxiety is precisely the moment in Deuteronomy 1–11 at which the text transitions from the language of hearing so prevalent in chapters 4–5 to the eating motifs that take center stage in chapters 6–9:

> Hear, Israel and watch that you do what is good for you and so that you will multiply greatly, as the Lord the God of your fathers spoke to you *in the land flowing with milk and honey* [at this point follows the Shema, "Hear O Israel," and the instructions for how to keep God's words in one's heart]. . . . It will be that when the Lord your God brings you to the land he swore to your fathers Abraham, Isaac and Jacob to give to you—with great and good cities that you did not build, houses full with every good thing that you did not fill, hewn cisterns that you did not hew, vineyards and olives that you did not plant— and *you eat and are sated, watch yourself lest you forget the Lord.* (6:3–12)

Moses returns to this worry again in chapter 8:

> The Lord your God is bringing you to a good land, a land with streams of water and springs and fountains issuing in valley and hill, a land of wheat, barley, vines, figs and pomegranates, a land of olives and honey, a land where you may eat bread without scarcity, where nothing is lacking. . . . When you have eaten and are sated, bless the Lord your God for the good land he has given you. Watch yourself lest you forget the Lord your God by not keeping his commandments, statutes, and laws that I am commanding you today, lest when you eat and are satisfied . . . your heart grows lofty and your forget the Lord your God. (8:7–14)

Establishing a way to hear God is not enough to sustain Israel's relationship with him. Israel must also find a way to overcome the memory degradation caused by a full stomach, a danger to which it is especially susceptible in a land of milk and honey, where it is easy to eat and be satisfied.

Although the appetite can distort understanding in this way, it can also serve to focus it. During Israel's wandering through the wilderness, God had afflicted it with hunger and then fed it with manna, a food miraculously delivered to it, to make Israel "understand that a man does not live by bread alone, but lives by all that comes out from the mouth of the Lord" (8:3). Through a wonderful play on words, Moses connects the act of eating to the act of hearing featured in Deuteronomy 4–6, warning Israel not to allow the food that enters its mouth to eclipse what comes out of God's mouth. Diet thus serves as a kind of educational discipline; God uses the withholding and supply of food to make sure that Israel's appetite does not distract it from God's words.

In Deuteronomy 4 and 6, we saw attempts to establish specific techniques, a regimen of ritual behaviors through which Israel might train itself to perceive in the right way—to sense God without over-exposure. These techniques seek to shape Israel's subjective experience from the outside in, creating new patterns of behavior through which it might screen out certain perceptions (visually manifest gods); sharpen the memory of other perceptions (the sight of God's miracles, the sound of his voice), and even generate a kind of virtual sensory experience to be shared with those not present to see and hear for themselves. Deuteronomy makes a similar effort to influence eating and its effects on the understanding. In 8:10, Moses tells Israel: "When you have eaten and are sated, bless the Lord your God for the good land he has given you," the verse that inspired the Jewish practice of blessing God after a meal.[13] To compensate for its effects on the memory, eating is to be accompanied by a ritual performance, a scripted recitation of gratitude, to remind Israel that it does not live by bread alone.

Although our analysis here is confined to chapters 1–11, it is worth noting that later chapters return to the subject of eating, seeking to restrain or reshape it through ritual experience, especially in Deuteronomy 26, which establishes the following ritual practices. First, after the Israelites settle in the land, they are to bring an offering of the first-fruit harvest to the sanctuary and make a declaration there that acknowledges what God has done for them by freeing them from Egypt and bringing them to this land "flowing with milk and honey" (vv. 1–11). The text then commands a second recitation, to be uttered when the Israelite has set aside a tenth of his agricultural yield so that the Levite, the stranger, the orphan and the widow "might eat in your gates and be satisfied." In this speech, the Israelite vows that he has followed God's commandments ("I have not transgressed or forgotten any of your commandments") and petitions God to bless the land he has given Israel, again described as a land "flowing with milk and honey" (vv. 13–15). Some of the language in these declarations harks back to chapters 6–9: "a land flowing with milk and honey" (26:9, 15; cf. 6:3); "eat . . . and be satisfied" (26:12; cf. 8:10); "I have not forgotten" (Cf. 8:11, 14).[14] Were it not for the intervening material in chapters 12–25, it would be easy to read chapter 26 as the solution to the sensory problem introduced in chapters 6–10, its recitations an effort to counter the mnemonic damage inflicted by unrestrained eating. In fact, given that Deuteronomy appears to have been expanded over time, with much of the material in 12–26 originating independently of 1–11, it is possible that chapter 26 did follow directly upon chapter 11 in as earlier form of the book as yet another step in its effort to retrain the senses.

Even confining ourselves to chapters 6–10, however, we find that it follows the pattern established for seeing and hearing in 1–4 and 4–6 respectively. The section begins with Moses warning Israel about a sensory problem, the text recycling already existing material known from earlier Pentateuch sources (the story of Israel's hunger in the wilderness; the description of Canaan as a "land of milk and honey") to make its point. Once again, Moses' personal story is reshaped to mirror the sensory focus of the section, in this case the prophet recalling how he went without bread and water on Mount Horeb (9:9, 18). And once again, the text finds a solution in memory and ritual, the prophet appealing to Israel's past dietary experiences as a model for how to eat, then imposing a ritual practice, the blessing after the meal, to prevent it from forgetting God after it is full.

Whether we think of Deuteronomy 1–11 as a single speech or as a series of speeches as some scholars do, there is an overarching logic that draws much of its material into a single sustained oration about sensory experience. Each sense reveals something about God: his protective power (which Israel has seen with its eyes), his discipline (transmitted through the sound of God's voice), the fulfillment of his promise to the Patriarchs (symbolized by Israel's satiety in the land of Canaan). Each also threatens Israel's relationship with God, however. In its desire to see a god it cannot see, Israel may go astray in worshipping false gods that it can see. Without mediation, God's voice inspires terror, but in its absence, Israel may soon abandon God. Eating one's fill is a sign of a divine promised fulfilled, but it can also lead to forgetfulness and complacency. Deuteronomy is not a treatise on the senses, systematically investigating how the senses work, but it does constitute a sustained attempt to work through the problems that sensory experience poses to Israel's religious life. The novelty of its reformative project is obscured by its traditional cast, the way it couches itself in the guise of preexisting stories and rituals, but what it develops out of this material is a radically new interpretation of Israelite memory and ritual practice, a program of sensory reform.

This is not to suggest that all of Deuteronomy is to be read as an effort at sensory reform. Deuteronomy 11 rehearses many of the sensory motifs that tie this argument together (albeit in a different order), urging the Israelites to remember what God did before their very eyes (11:1–7), revisiting its description of the teeming land where Israel will eat its fill (8–17), and repeating its command in chapter 6 to carefully transmit Moses' words to future generations (18–21), but after that, Deuteronomy all but abandons the sensory theme until the final chapters. Scholars have long suspected that material in between, the law code in chapters 12–26, may have originated independently of the frame in the surrounding chapters, at least some of it to be identified with the text discovered (or composed) during the reign of Josiah and launching his effort to centralize Israelite worship. What we have argued here does not speak to the genesis or purpose of that material, only to the way in which Deuteronomy 1–11 now frames it.

Although chapters 12–26 may have been written for very different purposes, the fact is that in their present form their meaning is now conditioned by the introductory material that precedes them in Deuteronomy 1–11. If what I have argued here is correct, that frame casts the book of Deuteronomy itself as a solution to the sensory problems it identifies, an alternative to direct sensation that seeks to compensate for the absence of visual experience in divine theophany, to buffer Israel from the overwhelming intensity of God's voice, and to transmit that voice to future generations unable to experience it directly. While what we have seen here does not speak to the original intent of the laws recorded in 12–26, it does suggest how these laws were understood by the redactor who placed them in their present redactional setting. Reading Deuteronomy in light of this later understanding, I would argue that its reformative project is much more innovative than scholars have realized, seeking not merely to resituate religious experience in a new setting but to intervene in the nature of religious experience itself by reorienting the sensory self through which it is filtered.

Deuteronomy as Sensory Counter-Reformation

Scholars think they can place Deuteronomy's project of cultic centralization within the reign of King Josiah and infer its motivation based on that assumption. We cannot contextualize Deuteronomy's engagement with the senses so precisely, but it is tempting to connect it with the emergence of a similar engagement with the senses in the Greek world in the sixth century B.C.E.—by happenstance, the century in which many scholars would place Deuteronomy 1–11. Reading it within this context may require us to nuance our understanding of Deuteronomy as a program of sensory reform.

As we noted in the introduction, one of the first Greek thinkers to express doubts about the senses was Parmenides of Elea, author of a poem in which a goddess warns against relying on "an aimless eye or an ear and a tongue full of meaningless sound." This statement has been construed in different ways,[15] but the standard interpretation reads it as using the authority of a divine voice to urge distrust of the senses. All this makes for an intriguing parallel with Deuteronomy, where another divinely inspired sage, Moses, is imagined warning Israel about how not to use its eyes and ears. Direct influence one way or the other is impossible to prove, but some kind of connection is not implausible. Cultural exchange between the Greek and Near Eastern worlds can be documented for as early as the age of Hesiod, influence usually moving from the Near East to the Greek world.[16] The Greek empirical sciences—especially medicine and astronomy—built on insights and methods received from Babylon and Egypt; and some Greek philosophers, such as the first philosopher, Thales, reputedly of Phoenician origin, may themselves have been a bridge to the Near East.[17] What we have learned about Deuteronomy raises the intriguing possibility that Greek sensitivity to the limits of the senses also had ancient Near Eastern antecedents.[18]

Even as we register the plausibility of a connection, however, we must also note that Deuteronomy's engagement with these limits differs in key respects from the directions this interest took among the Greeks. In their efforts to understand and transcend the limits of sensory experience, some Greeks ventured beyond the framework of myth into the realm of philosophy and science—

optics, harmonics, physiology, physics, or metaphysics. Deuteronomy, though revising earlier tradition in innovative ways, does not break from the paradigm of earlier mythical thinking in so radical a way, seeking its solutions within inherited stories of divine intervention and ritual traditions. The historian of Greek science G. E. R. Lloyd argued for a fundamental distinction between the mythical orientation of ancient Near Eastern "science," which in its explanation for reality never went beyond supernatural causality, and the rationalist, non-mythical orientation of Greek thought.[19] Despite certain intriguing parallels with Greek thought, Deuteronomy's treatment of sensation leaves this distinction intact.

Why ancient Israelite sages, keen to acquire wisdom, did not make the conceptual leap that Greek sages did is a question that is easier to complicate than to answer. All that we can say at present is that the author of Deuteronomy seems to want to discourage his audience from being too curious about the world, from looking for wisdom beyond the realm of the perceptible and the already known:

> This commandment that I am commanding you today is not too astonishing for you nor is it too far away. It is not in heaven that you should say, "Who will go up to heaven for us, and take it for us so that we may hear it and observe it?" Nor is it beyond the sea that you should say, "Who will cross to the other side of the sea and take it for us, so that we may hear and observe it?" The word is very near to you, in your mouth and in your heart. (30:11–14)

According to the author of this text, what Israel needs to understand is not hidden or far away; it is already readily available to it through the medium of Moses' voice. The pursuit of wisdom as framed in this way requires, not the searching out of matters undetectable by the senses, but a turning back to the past, to the memory of God's voice as mediated through Deuteronomic speech. Deuteronomy thus comes to the very border of an epistemological revolution akin to that in ancient Greece, but in the end, like Moses stopped short on the border of Canaan, it does not cross over into the radically new way of understanding the self and its relationship with reality that the ancient Greeks developed.

NOTES

1. On the senses in early Greek philosophy, see Dimitri Andriopoulos, *Sense and Perception in Greek Philosophy* (Athens: Library of Philosophy, Psychology and Education, 1975); André Laks, "Soul, Sensation and Thought," in *The Cambridge Companion to Early Greek Philosophy* (ed. A. A. Long; Cambridge: Cambridge University Press, 1999), 250–70.

2. Michel Foucault, "Technologies of the Self," in *Technologies of the Self: A Seminar*

With Michel Foucault (ed. Luther H. Martin, Huck Gutman, and Patrick H Hutton; Amherst: University of Massachusetts Press), 16–49; Charles Taylor, *Sources of the Self: The Making of Modern Identity* (Cambridge, Mass.: Harvard University Press, 1989), 111–26.

3. Stephen A. Geller, "The God of the Covenant," in *One God or Many? Concepts of Divinity in the Ancient World* (ed. Barbara Porter; Transactions of the Casco Bay Assyriological Institute 1; Chebeague, Maine: Casco Bay Assyriological Institute, 2000), 273–319, esp. 295–302.

4. Among recent studies focused on this aspect of Deuteronomy's religious program, see Norbert Lohfink, "Zur deuteronomischen Zentralisationsformel," *Bib* 65 (1984): 297–328; Eleonore Reuter, *Kultzentralisation: Entstehung und Theologie von Dtn 12* (Frankfurt: Anton Hain, 1993); Bernard M. Levinson, *Deuteronomy and the Hermeneutics of Legal Innovation* (New York: Oxford University Press, 1997).

5. The "senselessness" of cult statues is a common motif in biblical polemic against idolatry (e.g., Ps 115:5–7; 135:16–17). It also has parallels in Greek sources. See Deborah Steiner, *Images in Mind: Statues in Archaic and Classical Greek Literature and Thought* (Princeton, N.J.: Princeton University Press, 2001), 136–45.

6. For the meanings of this phrase and its distribution in the biblical corpus, see Hans Ausloos, "'A Land Flowing with Milk and Honey' Indicative of a Deuteronomistic Redaction?" *ETL* 75 (1999): 297–314.

7. Finding such a pattern in Deuteronomy 1–11 is at odds with the widely accepted view that it is not the work of a single author but developed over time through supplementation and revision. One influential theory holds that Deut 4:44–28:68 constitutes the original core of the book, with the material on the book's edges added later, perhaps when the book was integrated into the so-called Deuteronomistic History that spans Deuteronomy through 2 Kings. Even individual chapters have been broken down into multiple sources or redactional layers. See, for example, Siegfried Mittmann, *Deuteronomium 1:1–6:3 literarkritisch und traditionsgeschichtlich untersucht* (Berlin: de Gruyter, 1975), 115–28; and for response, Georg Braulik, "Literarkritik und archäologische Stratigraphie. Zu S. Mittmanns Analyse von Deuteronomium 4, 1–40," *Bib* 59 (1978): 351–78. What I argue here does not exclude the possibility that Deuteronomy 1–11 is a composite or redacted work—there is much material within these chapters that does not fit into the sensory theme that I trace here—but it does suggest a principle of organization, a plan, integrating much of its content into a single, unfolding discourse focused on the senses of seeing, hearing, and eating.

8. Levinson, *Deuteronomy and the Hermeneutics of Legal Innovation*. Some would contest this characterization of Deuteronomy's relationship to the rest of the Pentateuch, denying any relationship of dependence between it and other Pentateuchal sources, or reversing the direction of this influence. See, for instance, John Van Seters, "Comparing Scripture with Scripture: Some Observations on the Sinai Pericope of Exodus 19–24," in *Canon, Theology and Old Testament Interpretation: Essays in Honor of Brevard S. Childs* (ed. Gene M. Tucker, David L. Petersen, and Robert R. Wilson; Philadelphia: Fortress, 1988), 111–30.

9. In Deut 1:21–39, there are 8 instances of words like "see," "show," or "in your eyes," admittedly less than the 10 times that "see" appears in Numbers 13–14. However, the cases in Deuteronomy appear within 16 verses, whereas the instances in Numbers 13–14 are scattered over 78 verses. For analysis of this incident and others as recounted in Deuteronomy 1–3, see Norbert Lohfink, "Narrative Analyse von Dtn 1,6–3,29," in *Mincha: Festgabe für Rolf Rendtorf zum 75 Geburtstag* (ed. Erhard Blum; Neukirchen: Neukirchener Verlag, 2000), 121–76; Patrick D. Miller, "The Wilderness Journey in Deuteronomy: Style, Structure and Theology in Deuteronomy 1–3," in *Israelite Religion and Biblical Theology: Collected Essays* (JSOTSup 267; Sheffield: Sheffield Academic Press, 2000), 572–92.

10. Although some argue that the ban on idols is largely a Deuteronomic innovation. See, for example, Christoph Dohmen, *Das Bilderverbot: Seine Entstehung und seine Entwicklung im Alten Testament* (BBB 62; Frankfurt: Athenäum, 1985).

11. Stephen A. Geller, "Fiery Wisdom: Logos and Lexis in Deuteronomy 4," *Prooftexts* 14 (1994): 103–39.

12. In 5:25, Israel says, "If we hear the voice of the Lord our God any longer, we will die," as if it had been hearing God's voice directly up until that point.

13. On the development of the Jewish tradition of "grace after meals" initiated by this verse, see Moshe Weinfeld, *Deuteronomy 1–11: A New Translation with Introduction and Commentary* (AB 5; New York: Doubleday, 1991), 392–94.

14. For evidence that 26:5–9 is a Deuteronomic composition, or at least a Deuteronomic adaptation of a preexisting speech, see Norbert Lohfink, *Theology of the Pentateuch: Themes of the Priestly Narrative and Deuteronomy* (trans. L. Maloney; Minneapolis: Fortress Press, 1994), 265–89.

15. For a challenge to the conventional reading of this passage, see Jaap Mansfeld, "Parménide et Héraclite avaient-ils une théorie de la perception?" *Phronesis* 44 (1999): 326–46.

16. Among numerous studies of Near Eastern influence on Greek myth, thought, and practice, see Walter Burkert, *The Orientalizing Revolution: Near Eastern Influence on Greek Culture in the Early Archaic Age* (Revealing Antiquity 5; Cambridge, Mass.: Harvard University Press, 1992); R. Rollinger, "The Ancient Greeks and the Impact of the Ancient Near East: Textual Evidence and Historical Perspective (ca. 750–650 BC)," in *Mythology and Mythologies: Methodological Approaches to Intercultural Influences: Proceedings of the Second Annual Symposium of the Assyrian and Babylonian Intellectual Heritage Project* (ed. R. M. Whiting; Malammu Symposia 2; Helsinki: The Neo-Assyrian Text Corpus Project, 2001), 233–64.

17. See M. L. West, *Early Greek Philosophy and the Orient* (Oxford: Clarendon, 1971); G. E. R. Lloyd, "The Debt of Greek Philosophy and Science to the Near East," *Methods and Problems in Greek Science* (Cambridge, Mass.: Cambridge University Press, 1991): 278–98.

18. Since Deuteronomy seems indebted in other respects to intellectual currents reflected in Neo-Assyrian and Neo-Babylonian literature, I would not be surprised if its engagement with sense-experience had parallels there. Indeed, I have stumbled across a Neo-Assyrian source from the seventh century B.C.E. that acknowledges the senses' limits, an inscription from the reign of Esarhaddon: "This task of refurbishing (the statues) which you have constantly been allotting to me (by oracle) is difficult. *Is it the right of deaf and blind human beings who are ignorant of themselves and remain in ignorance all their lives?*" So impaired are the senses of "deaf and blind humans," this text claims, that they cannot know themselves, much less the gods. Whether Mesopotamian literature truly evinces an engagement with sense-perception and its limits merits more sustained investigation by Assyriologists. The translation is drawn from Christopher Walker and Michael B. Dick, "The Mesopotamian mīs pî, Ritual," in *Born in Heaven, Made in Earth: The Making of the Cult Image in the Ancient Near East* (ed. Michael B. Dick; Winona Lake, Ind.: Eisenbrauns, 1999), 55–121, esp. 64–65.

19. See G. E. R. Lloyd, *Magic, Reason and Experience: Studies in the Origin and Development of Greek Science* (Cambridge: Cambridge University Press, 1979), 229–34.

—8—

Locating the Sensing Body:
Perception and Religious Identity in Late Antiquity

Susan Ashbrook Harvey

Around the year 155 C.E., the elderly bishop Polycarp was martyred in the city of Smyrna (now Izmir on the southwestern coast of Turkey) on charges of refusal to sacrifice to the Roman gods. Christian witnesses to Polycarp's execution wrote a letter reporting the event to their neighboring church in the city of Philomelium in Phrygia. The letter described Polycarp's arrest, trial, and execution in the public stadium of the city in the presence of the gathered populace. The execution was by burning at the stake, but when the fire was slow to do its work, Polycarp had been stabbed to death by an attending official.

A striking feature of the letter was the Smyrneans' use of familiar sensory experience to articulate and interpret what had taken place. The witnesses describe their own experience of Polycarp's martyrdom as follows:

> The men in charge of the fire started to light it. A great flame blazed up and those of us to whom it was given to see beheld a miracle. And we have been preserved to recount the story to others. For the flames, bellying out like a ship's sail in the wind, formed into the shape of a vault and thus surrounded the martyr's body as with a wall. And he was within it not as burning flesh but rather as bread being baked, or like gold and silver being purified in a smelting furnace. And from it we perceived such a delightful fragrance as though it were smoking incense or some other costly perfume.
>
> At last when these vicious men realized that his body could not be consumed by the fire they ordered a *confector* to go up and plunge a dagger into the body. When he did this there came out such a quantity of blood that the flames were extinguished.[1]

The experience these Christian witnesses claimed was one in which their senses redefined the event. The fire they saw enshrined rather than destroyed their bishop. The air they breathed billowed with the aroma of baking bread—for Christians, the comfort of food and fellowship in the name of Christ. Moreover, the fire seemed not to destroy Polycarp's body, but rather to purify it as in a crucible until the air no longer carried the stench of burning flesh but instead a fragrance as sweet as frankincense, the precious savor of sacrifice pleasing to God. The dove recalled the presence of the Holy Spirit at Christ's baptism (Mark 1:10, Matt 3:16; Luke 3:22), and blood pouring from the martyr's side recalled Christ's own crucifixion (John 19:34). Visuality framed this scene, starting with fire and ending with blood. But olfactory experience marked its meaning, as the smells of bread and frankincense evoked the Eucharist as the moment of Christian sacrifice ("This is my body . . . broken for you"). With a few deft sensory images—a glimpse, a fragrance, a texture—Polycarp's followers turned a traumatic political event into a theological teaching that would become foundational for the emerging Christian identity. Their bishop's death was neither meaningless nor a defeat. Rather, it had been a pure and holy sacrifice acceptable to God. Like the death of Jesus Christ to which it conformed in style and manner, it heralded the promise of salvation, eternal life, for all believers.

What, indeed, was the role of bodily experience for ancient Christianity? In this essay I will argue that late antique Christians chose to engage the body deliberately, through actions and through sensory awareness, in order to seek religious knowledge—knowledge of the divine and of the human person in relation to the divine. Religious epistemology in these terms established a specific religious identity, sustained and enhanced continuously through attunement to sensory experience. Insofar as the ancient concept of self denoted identity within a given community, Christianity can be seen to have cultivated an understanding of the human person (and hence, the self) as a religious person: a self existing in relation to the divine and as part of a larger religious community, in a manner that established order, connection, and meaning. That relation could be rightly or wrongly realized or enacted, or even ambiguously fulfilled with elements of both. But to the ancient Christian mind, rightly enacted it was a relation that revealed God's truth and expressed Christian teaching. Moreover, it was a relation affirmed repeatedly by the basic encounters of the senses.

For the early Christians, the model Christ had offered was the use of the body as an instrument through which to seek eternal life. To them, this world was an alien place, governed by heathens and filled with a human race that lived in ignorance of—or in active opposition to—God's truth. One second-century commentator described Christians as strangers in a strange land: "They exist in the flesh, but they live not after the flesh. They spend their existence upon earth, but their citizenship is in heaven" (*Diogn.* 5.8–10). Within this view, the instructions churches gave to their members called them to live as simply as possible, attending to care for the sick and needy as they waited quietly for a future life in God's own kingdom.

Such a life, early Christians were taught, should also be austere in its sensory experiences. As Clement of Alexandria argued,[2] physical pleasures known through the bodily senses fixed one's attention to the physical world, distracting the soul from its appropriate focus on the unchanging and eternal realm of God. As God's creation the world was not evil, Clement wrote, but a strict regulation of sights, sounds, smells, tastes, and textures was nonetheless in order. The body was important, not for what the senses perceived, but rather for how one lived in it, for the actions by which one expressed one's faith: with fasting, chastity, voluntary poverty, and service to others. One might be mindful of sensory experiences insofar as they brought to mind creation's Maker.[3] But for the most part, pre-Constantinian Christian writers focused on bodily activity and not bodily experience or perception.

Hence, Tertullian urged the recognition that among one's most treasured possessions, one should "count also the distinctive religious observances of your daily life."[4] Indeed, he argued that daily life was the reason that marriage between Christians and pagans should not take place. Constituted of numerous religious practices, daily life was a continual exercise of religious identity. One could not be a Christian wife to a pagan husband and fulfill either the duties of household management or the obligations of marital service without serious harm to one's faith. The feasts of paganism would clash with the fasting observances of Christianity; prayer requirements would have the wife at vigil when her husband expects to have her in bed; the Christian duty of visitation to the poor and sick would have her in neighborhoods offensive to her husband's moral code. Her every move would betray the deity to whom her life is dedicated: fasting before communion, making the sign of the cross over her bed or body, exsufflation to cast away demons (and since the pagan gods were held to be demons by Christians, such warding off of evil would be constant). In turn, her every sensory experience would implicate her in pagan practices. Tastes, sounds, and sights would not be extricable from their religious contexts. Most difficult to avoid would be the olfactory assaults. Incense offerings would burn in the house on the first of every month and at the new year; laurel wreaths and scented lamps would adorn the front door to celebrate the imperial cult.

Mixed marriage, then, was a series of sensory hazards wherein the delectable odors (and sights, sounds, textures, and tastes) of false religion would tempt or deceive or taint the Christian partner at every turn. A Christian marriage, however, depends upon two spouses working together as partners in the common tasks of a life of faith. Together they pray, worship, fast, visit the sick and the poor, suffer persecution, instruct one another, exhort one another, and sing the praise of God. They are "one in the way of life they follow, one in the religion they practice."[5] Tertullian makes no reference to the sensory aspects that would attend such a marriage. Thus he characterizes them: one type by sensory experience, and the other by works. By their actions and way of life, Christians could define themselves within the non-Christian world around them.

But the situation did not stand still. Around 313 c.e., in the aftermath of a devastating final effort of persecution, Christianity was declared a legal religion in the Roman Empire. It was also an imperially favored one, for the emperor Constantine himself became a devotee of the new religion, showering it with gifts and benefits. By the 380s Christianity was declared the state religion of the Roman Empire, and the public worship of all other religions save Judaism alone was declared forbidden by law. No secular state this, but a Christian empire in which the emperor was seen to reign as Christ's own image, in triumph in this world, now seeking to conform the empire to the image of the heavenly kingdom itself, God's kingdom on earth. A new understanding of earthly citizenship took hold with the view that history now fulfilled God's purpose through the rightful ascendancy of Christ's faithful.

At the same time that this huge political shift took place, a changed sensibility came to dominate Christian expression in its various forms. As Christianity laid increasing claim to social and political power, Christians also showed increasing interest in claiming the physical world as a realm of positive spiritual encounter through the engagement of physical experience. As a legal religion, Christianity had the right to be publicly practiced and publicly displayed. The sensory qualities of Christian piety bloomed in this changed situation. The Christian's religious experience in ritual, art, and devotional piety, previously austere in their sensory aspects, became in the post-Constantinian era a feast for the physical senses.

The fourth century brought the emergence of pilgrimage, relics, and the cult of saints; the flowering of church art and architecture on a monumental scale; the enrichment of liturgy in which the grandeur of imperial court ceremony and biblical temple imagery were transposed into the ecclesial setting and liturgical celebration spilled beyond church walls into civic streets. The fourth century also brought the emergence of monasticism, with a growing intensity in the severity of ascetic discipline. At every turn, Christianity encouraged and engaged a tangible, palpable, physically experienced and expressed piety.

This turn in sensory appreciation was not a change in Christian belief about the created order or the nature of the physical world.[6] In part it accompanied Christianity's rise to power and concomitant investment in the world in which it operated. But it also stemmed from the penetrating influence of theological discussions. Earlier apologists and theologians had stressed the physical reality of Christ's crucifixion and resurrection in opposition to docetic views that denied it; and they proclaimed the goodness of God's creation in opposition to dualist teachings that disallowed positive value or salvific worth to the body or the physical domain. In the changed political context of the post-

Constantinian era, the Trinitarian and Christological controversies of the fourth and fifth centuries continued the trajectory with the teaching that at the incarnation the divine itself had entered into matter, sanctifying and renewing the whole of material existence. The elaboration of Christian piety in sensory terms was both a response to and a further expression of this view. Within a century of Constantine's death, these changes in sensibility were everywhere evident. Christians lived in the world as in a new place.

To note one instance as exemplary: the liturgy of the church over the course of the fourth century came to full expression, offering a feast for the physical senses. Huge and magnificent church buildings were built, adorned with dazzling frescoes and mosaics, decked in shining draperies. Exquisitely crafted silver and gold communion plates and chalices gleamed from the altars, jeweled chandeliers filled the sanctuaries with light from glimmering candles of scented wax and glistening lamps that burned with perfumed oil. The elaborate pageantry of the ceremony carried visual and tactile richness in the embroidered vestments, brocaded banners, and large, intricately carved crosses that accompanied the celebrants in procession. The faithful participated, making the sign of the cross repeatedly and performing prostrations accompanied by the glorious sounds of choirs, the sweet taste of the Eucharist, and the perfumed delight of holy chrism (for the holy oil with which the baptized were anointed was now scented with sweet spices). Drenching the air itself—as the witnesses to Polycarp's execution had once sensed faintly—the abundant fragrance of incense now filled Christian sanctuaries, the very enactment of prayer ascending to God: "Let my prayer arise in thy sight as incense, and let the lifting up of my hands be an evening sacrifice" (Ps 141:2).[7]

These features were changes to most liturgical practices of the pre-Constantinian era; their impact was notable and was noted by contemporaries. When late antique Christians described the liturgical celebrations in which they participated, they did so with wonder and appreciation for more than the spectacle they witnessed. Liturgy, in their telling, was a thickly textured sensory weaving.[8] Worship declared the splendor of God's majesty, and participants perceived, felt, and experienced that splendor with all of their senses.

But this enrichment also obscured the distinction in ritual activity that Christians had earlier used to maintain an identity separate from other religions around them. Jerome had to defend the elaboration of Christian piety from those who charged it was nothing other than pagan idolatry. He upheld the veneration of relics by kiss and touch, the beautifully worked reliquaries in which they were kept, the use of scented candles, the celebrations at martyrs' shrines, all as devotional practices that served the faithful and did not detract from the distinctiveness of their Christian identity. Christ had not refused the perfumed ointment of the sinful woman, Jerome admonished, nor did the martyrs require candlelight; but through these the faithful could express their devotion. "In the one case [paganism] respect was paid to the idols and therefore the ceremony is to be abhorred; in the other [Christianity] the martyrs are venerated, and the same ceremony is therefore to be allowed."[9]

Paulinus of Nola extolled the beauty of Christian celebrations at the shrine of St. Felix. The saint's holy bones lay in a "fragrant tomb," its threshold hung with shining linens, its altar "crowned with crowds . . . of fragrant lamps"; the crowds of devotees sounded forth their hymns of praise while strewing the roads with flower blossoms and adorning the shrine with garlands as the countryside, too, lay ripe with blooming promise.[10] Paulinus poems are an eloquent example of the continuity between ancient local custom and the fashioning of Christian practice.[11] For while Paulinus was careful to distinguish Christian celebrations from those of native religious occasions in the Italian province, the accoutrements and gestures of ritual celebration were recognizably the same—including the lavish olfactory ornamentation in the use of flowers, scented oils, and ritual fragrances so often praised by him when describing Christian devotions.[12] Prudentius, too, applauded the generous gifts of flowers and perfumes with which the crowds bedecked the shrines and tombs of saints and martyrs.[13] Such practices might be termed "ritual habits"; these were the actions by which peoples of the ancient Mediterranean world expressed identity, need, and order.

The practices of Christian worship and piety did not differ in ritual form or instrument from their non-Christian neighbors or predecessors: processions, incense, holy perfumes, vestments, lights, candles, music, sacred spaces, buildings, and objects all characterized the religious observances of ancient Mediterranean religions.[14] What Christian leaders, homilists, and theologians sought, however, was the use of these ritual elements to articulate a distinctly Christian identity—an identity that would be expressed and experienced by participants and observers alike. Bodily engagement and sensory awareness could be highlighted (in homilies, hymns, or didactic writings) with the intention of reinforcing the religious identity thus declared.[15]

Recall the letter about Polycarp's martyrdom. There the witnesses wrote that their sensory experiences of the event directed their attention *away* from this world and the suffering and injustice enacted before them. Instead, their senses turned them toward their relationship with the divine, a relationship recalled and confirmed in the sacrificial scents of bread and frankincense. In late antiquity, in the midst of political and social triumph, Christians increasingly used their senses to direct their attention to *this* world as God's world. The world from which Christians had been alienated in bearing witness to their God, now became the world that expressed that witness.

It is important to emphasize when and how this change in sensibility took place. Christian triumph in the Roman Empire brought with it an intensified significance for all things physical. That intensity had both negative and positive articulations, but its cause was the same: a heightened importance of the physical realm. Christianity had inherited an ancient discourse, familiar across the Mediterranean world as a whole, in which the senses were derided as sources of moral danger and identified with sexual licentiousness—"wanton sensuality." It was a discourse known in biblical literature as well as in Greek and Roman philosophy. Christianity continued the tradition and in late antiquity increased its tenor. Discussion of sexuality, of celibacy, of bodily discipline, of ascetic training—all took on an indisputably shrill tone in late antique Christian texts (whether by Augustine, Jerome, John Chrysostom, or the Egyptian desert fathers). Recent scholarship has focused on this discourse about the body with little attention to the fundamental ritual context in which bodily practices were in fact being defined.[16] For the negative discourse became more shrill at the very moment that the deliberate engagement of sensory experience became prominent in Christian worship; devotional piety; and domestic, civic, and monastic practices.

These were competing discourses, serving different agendas within the late antique world but responding to the same stimuli. The discourse of celibacy and self-mortification that utilized a rhetoric of sensory danger served a Christian identity and community defined against the prevailing political order. It undermined the possibility of complacency even in a triumphant era. By contrast, the discourse of a sensorily engaged piety—the sensorium, as we will see, trained through the ritual practices of late antique Christianity in its daily activities—supported a public and imperial order that saw the Empire as God's earthly kingdom, albeit not without ambiguity and nuance. Political triumph did not alter the cosmic condition in which humanity lived, as Christianity defined it: a fallen condition, tragically impoverished from God's intention. But a discourse that imbued physical experience with positive religious valuation allowed a powerful reorientation to humanity's physicality.

Increased attention to the importance of sensory experience prompted a fresh rhetoric of the body in which the sensory body contextualized the sexual body. Much scholarly attention has been paid to the rhetoric of sexuality and gender that emerged in late antiquity.[17] My intention here is to offer a reminder of the larger discourse on the body in which sexual discussion was set. That larger discourse presented the body as a sensing body, one for which its sensory experiences mattered profoundly as vehicles for religious knowledge (knowledge of God). The religious knowledge Christians described and interpreted, in turn, served to establish a particular religious identity (Christian), maintained through individual and collective practices that reinforced the epistemological significance of sensory perception.

Ancient Christian writers presented the sensing body as a fundamental source of religious identity. The body, in their view, was the unique site of human relation to God, a relation known in three ways. First, the body was fundamental existentially, through experience: at the most basic level the body is where we are and who we are as human beings. It is in the body—literally through the body's senses—that the human person receives divine revelation and experiences divine truth. Second, the body is the instrument through which religious identity is expressed. What one does matters. By actions, one declares one's relationship with God and demonstrates its meaning. Third, the body shapes human expectation. It is the human location, and in early Christian teaching, it is the human location now and in eternal life—for the resurrected life was also taught to be a bodily life. For ancient Christians, then, the sensing body provides the context for how and what the human person can and will know about God, now and in the life to come. As John of Damascus said, the mind could seek understanding, but by itself it was limited (*Apol.* 1.11). Rationality was insufficient for comprehending divine truth. More was needed. In experience, expression, and expectation, the sensing body offered knowledge that could not be obtained in any other way, forming a religious self that located Christian identity in this world as God's world.

Experiencing God

Christian apologists had stressed the importance of affirming God as the Creator whose creation was manifestly good. This position was essential to their claim that the Christian God was to be identified with the God of Genesis, who had declared the goodness of his creation at the moment of its making. Occasionally, early Christian writers would comment further that as God's creation, the physical world in its beauty pointed to its Maker—a sentiment often celebrated in the Psalms and voiced in early Christian hymns.

In the fourth century, Christian writers seized upon this theme with delight. In hymns and homilies they extolled God as one whose every divine action revealed him and made him known. Ontologically, Creator and creation were separated by a vast unbreachable gap. Yet as God's handiwork, the created universe had an endless capacity to reveal its Maker. Through that revelation, one could learn something of the divine nature itself. "The world," wrote Basil of Caesarea, "is a work of art. . . . Let us glorify the Master Craftsman for all that has been done wisely and skillfully; and from the beauty of the visible things let us form an idea of Him who is more than beautiful, and from the greatness of [what is perceptible and circumscribed] let us conceive of Him who is infinite and immense and who surpasses all understanding in the plenitude of His power."[18] Indeed, Basil's brother, Gregory of Nyssa, wrote that this was the reason why Adam was created at the end of the six days of creation, that "by the beauty and majesty of the things he saw [he] might trace out that power of the Maker which is beyond language and speech."[19]

But creation was not simply God's workmanship. Ephrem the Syrian pointed out that as God's work it was also marked, engraved indelibly with his touch: "In every place, if you look, [God's] symbol is there / . . . For by Him were created all creatures, / and He engraved his symbols upon His possessions."[20] Even a bird cannot fly if its wings are not outstretched in the sign of the cross.[21]

Still, it was not enough that nature should reveal. Humanity must receive this revelation, reading nature as it read Scripture. In Ephrem's understanding, humanity's alienation resulting from the fall had led to a weariness in nature, an exhaustion born of the discouraging effort to make known a revelation obscured by humanity's sinful state (*Virg.* 29). Christ's incarnation renewed the sanctification of the natural world even as it redeemed the human body. Prudentius wrote a hymn for Christmas Day that offered a similar sense, linking the nativity celebration with winter's turn toward spring.[22]

For Ephrem, this sanctification specifically included the capacity to reflect and encounter the divine within the physical world. Through baptism, the believer entered into the renewed condition of the created order, acquiring "new senses" by which to experience it (*De fide* 81.9).[23] The sanctified human body could then receive knowledge of God through its own sensory experiences, could know something of God through its own physicality. In turn, the natural world revealed knowledge of God to those capable of perceiving it through bodily awareness. Thus, Ephrem wrote that it was the whole person of the believer, body as well as soul, in which God delighted to dwell: "Your bride is the soul, the body Your bridal chamber / Your guests are the senses with the thoughts" (*Fide* 14.5).[24] Moreover, it pleased God to provide a world for the believer to experience that would celebrate the grandeur of God's physical creation, as fitting complement—and as foretaste—to the celestial glory:

> Let us see those things [God] does for us every day!
> How many tastes for the mouth! How many beauties for the eye!
> How many melodies for the ear! How many scents for the nostrils!
> Who is sufficient in comparison to the goodness of these little things?
>   (*Virg.* 31.16)[25]

Cyril of Jerusalem contributed to this picture in his *Catechetical Homilies*, when he stressed the marvel of the human body as God's workmanship.[26] "Let no one tell you that this body of ours is a stranger to God," he exhorted, lambasting those ("heretics") who would insist that the body either could not be saved or was itself the obstacle to salvation.[27] Consider, he urged, how each of the senses was perfectly formed to receive its appropriate experience and enact its proper task, how skillfully the organs and body parts were woven together, how intricate their design, how fittingly they performed their work. By stressing the unique worth of each of the five senses, Cyril reminded his listeners that God's actions were always purposeful. The care with which the human sensorium was designed was not gratuitous.

Within this view, the incarnation set in motion a sanctifying process that the Christian, once baptized, could experience at every moment of every day. The process was ongoing, reinforced and sustained through the church's liturgical celebration of the Eucharist. Just as Christ entered the created order at his birth, so too, Ephrem wrote, he entered into every person who consumed his holy bread: "The priests of the churches grasp You in their hands / the Bread of Life that came down and was mingled with the senses" (*Virg.* 35:12). Sanctified, the body received revelation from within and without: as the divine was "mingled with the senses," the senses could then perceive the divine in the world they experienced. Through this process of sanctification, the liturgy taught not only *how* to experience God with the body, but *what* to experience. Again, Ephrem exhorted his congregation,

> [Christ's] body was newly mixed with our bodies,
> and His pure blood has been poured out into our veins,
> and His voice into our ears, and His brightness into our eyes.
> All of Him has been mixed with all of us by His compassion. (*Virg.* 37.2.)[28]

As Ephrem here recalled, the faithful consumed body and blood, bread and wine; received the Word through the Scripture readings, beheld divine glory in the worship service. Christ filled the faithful, their bodies, their senses. Just as baptism caused the body to acquire new senses in its rebirth, so too the liturgy ritually transformed human condition and location, bringing the faithful to stand, redeemed, in the presence of God. With every sense, they encountered God's presence and God's work. With every sense, they knew themselves to be Christians.

Bodily Expression

All this was very grand. But it was not the whole story. For if the body was the way to experience and know one's Maker in every right sense, it was also the way to experience and know every wrong element of the human condition. The true Christian devoted the whole self, body and soul, to God. Yet the consistent human experience was that of a divided self: the soul was willing, the flesh was weak. Even when the soul was steadfast, the body sickened and died. Mortality was the punishment for Adam and Eve's disobedience against God, and therefore it was a moral condition more than a physical trait. But the physical consequences of mortality—sickness, bodily decay, and disintegration—were the direct results of that sin and therefore always the indication of sin's presence. To be mortal was to reek of sin; rottenness and putrefaction were mortality's nature, revolting stink its unmistakable mark. Wherever such physical sensations were encountered, they announced Satan's continuing presence.

The oneness of the believer had been God's intention, as ancient Christian writers consistently repeated.[29] Ephrem the Syrian addressed God from the midst of this tragic division: "You had joined [body and soul] together in love, but they parted and separated in pain. / . . . Body and soul go to court to see which caused the other to sin; / but the wrong belongs to both, for free will belongs to both" (*De Nisibe* 69.3, 5).[30] Thus the body was at fault but was not in itself the cause of humanity's fallen condition. Rather, its state revealed (or expressed) the soul or the inward disposition of the heart. What the sacraments of baptism and communion accomplished, then, was the restoration of oneness of being. With that restoration came the appropriate sensory experience, one that validated self-perception in Christian terms.

Still there was more to be done. The fallen order, death's dominion, was known because of bodily suffering—at the level of the individual (who suffers sickness, hunger, weariness, despair) and at the level of society (which suffers poverty, injustice, tyranny, and war). Just as Christ defeated Satan in and by his body at the temptation in the wilderness and then on the cross, so too must the victory be rendered in the whole body of Christ: the body of the believer, the body of the church. The pervasive imagery of Christ as the Good Physician or Treasury of Healing and of the Eucharist as the Medicine of Life poignantly evokes the early Christian identification of salvation with healing. And what was eternal life if not the healing of human mortality? But fallenness was not a personal state; it was one's human, and therefore one's social, condition.

Herein lies the context for the emphasis on ascetic behavior that pervades early Christian teaching, an emphasis that is always ethical in its consequences. For the Christian ascetic did not renounce the world as evil, but renounced a world—and a body—gone awry. The body of the ascetic, the body of the saint, was a body rescued from the fallen order—like Christ, triumphant over hunger or thirst (fasting), over weariness (vigils), over lust (chastity). It was a body healed of mortal suffering, a body made holy in the oneness, body and soul, of the saint's devotion to God. The saint displayed what redemption would be. In turn, the condition of the saint's body must mirror the condition of the community as the whole body of Christ. Caring for others, feeding the hungry, tending the sick, comforting the sorrowful—these actions did not simply fulfill the commandment to love one another. They also forged a community whose life was healed and thereby consecrated, a community (the church) literally reflecting paradise regained, where suffering and sorrow would pass away.

For the ancient Christian, then, the body is both the place in which salvation happens and the instrument by which it is done.[31] The body is more than the physicality of human existence. It provides the activity, or the external expression, by which the salvific process takes place. Bodily acts express the believer's interior condition even as they display the living image of the body, individual and collective, redeemed. Ephrem the Syrian called for the life of faith to be one in which the believer would manifest the very image of God by literally enacting God's healing, saving activity:

> Let charity be portrayed in your eyes, and in your ears the sound of truth.
> Imprint your tongue with the word of life and upon your hands [imprint] all alms.
> Stamp your footsteps with visiting the sick,
> and let the image of your Lord be portrayed in your heart.

Tablets are honored because of the images of Kings.

How much [more will] one [be honored] who portrayed his Lord in all his senses.
(*Virg.* 2.15)[32]

The intensification of ascetic piety—as a pervasive Christian ideal but also in the exploding monastic movement of late antiquity—involved a complicated array of issues. The remaking of the human body, as guided through liturgical piety, was one primary theme, and arguably the framing theme for all ascetic activity.[33] Its social counterpart in ethical works was another. A further issue was raised earlier, that of negotiating a discourse of moral danger through a rhetoric that problematized bodily experience and the impact of sensory encounter. An important aspect of ascetical and monastic writing in late antiquity was the redirection of that rhetoric of sensory danger. As liturgical splendor flourished, so too did an ecclesiastical discourse of sensory austerity in which ascetic piety was encouraged among laity as much as among monastics. In the pre-Constantinian world, such a discourse served to differentiate Christian identity from a non-Christian world (as Clement and Tertullian had done). In the post-Constantinian era, it was a summons to pay heed to where and how Christian prosperity should be realized.

Thus Ambrose of Milan, in his catechetical homilies, urged his catechumens to attend closely to the sensory richness of the liturgy and sacraments and to be instructed thereby.[34] But elsewhere he presents the senses as the Christian's most vulnerable point. In his sermon "Flight from the World," he asks how, with so many bodily passions and so many worldly enticements, a Christian can remain virtuous:

> The eye looks back and leads the mind's perception astray, the ear hears and turns one's attention away, a whiff of fragrance hinders thought, a kiss of the mouth introduces guilt, a touch kindles the fire of passion. . . . Indeed, Adam would not have come down from paradise unless he had been beguiled by pleasure.[35]

The Christian must discipline the body to take notice of sensory experience within the confines of an ecclesiastically defined situation. In this way, Christian anti-sensory rhetoric sets the location of "worldly" sensory pleasures outside the ritual context of devotional or liturgical practices, while heightening the importance of sensory awareness within those ecclesiastically controlled spaces. When authors like Basil or Ephrem draw attention to the instructive qualities of nature, they are doing so by associating (and eliding) the sensory experience of nature with its counterparts in liturgical and devotional rituals. At the same time, where pre-Constantinian Christian asceticism often served to demarcate the Christian community within its larger social context, in late antiquity the need was to locate ascetic practices (increasingly severe as they were) within the liturgical life of the church and within the liturgical body of the Christian.

Amidst the diversity of asceticism in late antiquity, two primary impulses guided the practices of Christian ascetics. One was the desire to use the body in a constructive sense—to remake the body, and with it the human person, into the image of its redeemed state. The second, often guiding the expression of the first, was the Bible itself. Ancient Christians read Scripture as an epic story culminating in—and encapsulated in—the specific narrative of the Gospels. The narrative purpose of Scripture was summarized in the church's creeds, represented and re-enacted in every Christian liturgy and therefore able to be represented in any Christian body. Sensory images were a primary means for linking biblical texts with liturgical actions and with ascetic practices; they enabled the entire scheme to be held together in a coherent whole. For example, when Ambrose of Milan cites often from the Song of Songs in his address *Concerning Virgins,* and indeed in his letters to virgins, he can link the bridal imagery from the Song to the wedding parables of the Gospels, and both into the imagery of baptism and resurrection. Such a form of exegesis allows the ascetic practice of celibacy to be located squarely within the sacramental, but specifically, the liturgical life of the larger church. The intensity of incense piety associated with the practices as well as veneration of the stylite saints would be another example: the stylite on the pillar is seen to be the incense rising heavenward from the altar, among other transfigurative biblical images that guided the devotional and hagiographical practices accompanying stylitism.[36]

There was, however, another domain to be considered from an ascetic view. Ancient Christians found numerous biblical models for experiencing a domain beyond the physical senses but to which the senses gave entry. In the narratives of Moses on Mt. Sinai, of Ezekiel's visions of the chariot or Isaiah's of the celestial altar, of the disciples at the transfiguration of Christ on Mt. Tabor, and of the Apostle Paul "caught up into Paradise" (2 Cor 12:2–4), Christians saw the examples of holy men whose prayers had culminated in a direct encounter with the divine. These encounters were shown in Scripture to have exceeded the confines of the natural, finite world and of the physical body within it, yet to have been bodily experienced and known by their recipients. The biblical accounts gave these narratives vivid sensory characteristics: the cloud and the pillar of fire, rustling wings, sapphire blue, burning tongs and sweet-tasting scroll, dazzling white, sights "that cannot be told." The Songs of Songs was a favorite example among both Christian and Jewish commentators, who seem not to have doubted that the Song's content was explicitly, or even solely, about human-divine relation—with God or Christ as the bridegroom, and Israel or the Church or the individual believer as the bride. Through the Song, sumptuous scents and fragrances appeared to mark every human encounter with the divine. In the Bible, divine revelation was made known to the faithful in experiences of a sensory nature, even as their content defied the contours of natural, physical experience.

The language of the Bible thus contrasted with that of Greek and Roman philosophical tradition, which from the time of Plato had fostered a notion of the contemplative life as one that necessarily separated the experience of soul from body. The philosophical models for contemplative perfection were "out of body" experiences, literally *ekstasis* (standing outside oneself): Socrates in silent, unseeing rapture on the battlefield at Plateia; Plotinus lifted out of his body in unitive encounter with the One. Ancient Christians found a way to reconcile these contrasting languages of human-divine encounter in the notion of the "spiritual senses." These were envisioned as a set of senses parallel to the five physical senses but operating within the interior self and open to the perception of the divine realm at the exclusion of the physical one. Within Christian contemplative writings both east and west, the spiritual senses have had a long and rich history.[37] Scholars have sometimes presented this development as one that presumed an anti-sensory, anti-physical focus: prayer in which the soul was "freed" from the body. Indeed, Origen, Gregory of Nyssa, Ambrose of Milan, and Augustine all exhort that the spiritual senses can only be brought into use by a careful training of the self that requires the extinguishing, or even the destruction, of the "carnal" senses; each of them would insist that ultimately even the "spiritual senses" must be abandoned in the quest for God.[38]

But the very term "spiritual *senses*" should be a clue that ancient Christian teachings on contemplative prayer recognized the critical role of sensory experience in any human form of knowledge, including the understanding of God. There were two problems in this recognition: how to rightly interpret the figural language of the Bible, and how to reconcile the finite quality of sensory experience in the physical world with the infinite nature of the divine. The spiritual senses provided a way to answer both puzzles. In some writers, like Evagrius Ponticus and those who followed the system of noetic prayer he developed late in the fourth century, the spiritual senses receive scant attention, functioning at best only at an early stage of the contemplative's progress.[39] For others, discussion of the spiritual senses attended the effort to capture some hint of the intense experience of the divine that prayer might yield.[40] Pseudo-Macarius had urged his fellow monks, "We ought to pray, not according to any bodily habit nor with a habit of loud noise nor out of a custom of silence or on bended knees. But we ought soberly to have an attentive mind, waiting expectantly on God until he comes and visits the soul by means of all its openings and its paths and senses."[41]

What was meant by the term "spiritual senses" in its practical use? How did the rhetoric of these senses function within the presentation of devotional activity, of prayer, and of human-divine relations? Did these interior "senses" perform an altogether different task from that of their physical counterparts? What was conveyed by the spiritual sense of smell? In different authors and different writings, these questions find various responses. But in broad strokes, the prevailing themes indicate that the rhetoric of the spiritual senses was one that recast the bodily experience of the contemplative, shifting it away from a location in the physical world in its finite existence and placing it within the domain of divine presence. The actual content of spiritual sensory experience—how these senses functioned, what they perceived, and how the contemplative should process that knowledge—seems in fact to rely closely on a deep appreciation for physical sensory experience. Instead of separate sets of senses, the goal was the transformation of the physical senses into vehicles through which bodily sensation conveyed experience and knowledge of the divine. One did not, in fact, seek to separate the physical and spiritual realms as if mutually exclusive—a Cartesian model that distorts ancient cosmology. Rather, one sought to perceive the divine through and beyond the limits of the physical world. Spiritual senses were senses open to that infinitely larger sensory field.

Bodily Expectation

Christian experience of the divine (in nature, in worship) and Christian expression of faith (in actions, in ethical activity, in ascetic practice) had as their ultimate focus the understanding that the true believer lives in expectation of what will come. Whatever healing, beauty, or goodness might be experienced in this world, it offered the barest glimpse of what the redeemed life would be. Ancient Christian writers shared the Pauline understanding that in the final resurrection "we shall all be changed" (1 Cor 15:51), and the belief that the resurrected body will not be the same as the body now inhabited. Yet they were also certain it would be a body nonetheless, one in which the oneness of the believer, body and soul, would find its true meaning. For the body changed in the life to come will remain the body in which and through which the human person knows God—and in the resurrected life, so these writers said, knowing God will be the sum total of human existence. Freed of the earthly uses and weaknesses of the body, redeemed humanity will find the continuity from mortal to immortal life through the body's continuation as the human instrument of knowledge. Indeed, the body will continue its existential role: it will be the location in which one receives God's revelation. It will continue its expressive role: it will enact and manifest one's relationship with one's Creator. And it will at last fulfill its epistemological role: if, in this life, the body provides limited knowledge of God, in the world to come, the body will be unlimited in what it can convey of the divine.

At the end of the day, ancient Christian writers had to confess, without the body the soul would not, could not stand wholly in the presence of God. Though baffled at the thought, Augustine pointed out that Adam and Eve before the fall had inhabited "a paradise both material and spiritual."[42] As Ephrem put it, God did not place Adam in paradise until he was fully made, body and soul. Together body and soul entered paradise, together they left after the fall, together they would enter again in the resurrection.[43] For both Augustine and Ephrem (and they come from widely divergent cultural traditions), knowledge requires a sensory, noncognitive base. Gaining access to knowledge requires the body's active receptivity to what lies outside it. Sensory experience is not the whole content of what can be known, but without its contribution nothing can be fully encountered or comprehended. Furthermore, the soul itself has no real existence without the body to render it present and active. Sense perception is an essential method of knowing, particularly crucial to that which defies the limitations of human rationality—God.

Augustine and Ephrem wrote from opposite edges of the late antique Christian world, representing different poles of Christian culture. Both gave unusually sustained attention to the question of sense perception in the resurrected body as they struggled to provide definitive understandings of what the resurrected life would be. It is worth completing our explorations with their respective presentations: Augustine in Book 22 of the *City of God*, and Ephrem in his *Hymns on Paradise*. For both writers, the entire reason for human existence is knowledge of God. That knowledge, in their view, defined them as Christians. But how in the life to come would the human person know? And what would be known?

In the *City of God*, Augustine addressed the senses when he turned to the question of the resurrection. In painstaking detail he considered the form and constitution of the resurrected body. His primary concern was to ensure a continuity of the self as an individual person with an individual history.[44] Hence, he insisted on the continuation of gender; and he insisted that martyrs would still have their scars, although their wounds would no longer be able to hurt them—for humanity must never be allowed to forget the particular history that it forged while inhabiting its fallen state (*Civ.* 22.17, 20).

Bodily integrity ensured, there remained to ask what modes of knowledge the body would have in its redeemed life of glory. In Book 22, Augustine envisions paradise as above all else a place of rest, where knowledge of God will fill our being because of the new kind of body we shall inhabit. Yes, we shall be there bodily, but in bodies that have "a new beauty," "a beauty *in* the body, and yet not of the body" (*Civ.* 22.17, 19). In this body,

> How complete, how lovely, how certain will be the knowledge of all things, a knowledge without error, entailing no toil! For there we shall drink of God's Wisdom at its very source, with supreme felicity and without any difficulty. How wonderful will be that body which will be completely subdued to the spirit, will receive from the spirit all that it needs for its life, and will need no other nourishment! (*Civ.* 22.24)

Augustine admitted that the philosophers raised a serious problem in delimiting the perceptions available to the bodily senses as opposed to those of the mind. But in the resurrected body, he argued, such a distinction could no longer be sustained. Bodily and spiritual perception would be one and the same: perfection was that condition in which all things would be held still, in utter unity. There too, sight would be the highest sense (Augustine's Platonism is at its fullest expression here), its operation fulfilling the requirements of true knowledge. Redemption would be that "rest" which would accompany perfect contemplation of God. For Augustine, in paradise, seeing will be the consummation of the human experience of God.

> [W]e shall then see the physical bodies of the new heaven and the new earth in such a fashion as to observe God in utter clarity and distinctness, seeing him present everywhere and governing the whole material scheme of things by means of the bodies we shall then inhabit . . . in the future life, wherever we turn the spiritual eyes of our bodies we shall discern, by means of our bodies, the incorporeal God directing the whole universe. (*Civ.* 22.29)

There, at last, Augustine says, we will find our rest and behold our Lord:

> There that precept will find fulfillment: "Be still, and know that I am God," (Ps 46:11). . . . There we shall have leisure to be still, and we shall see that He is God. . . . [R]estored by Him and perfected by His greater grace we shall be still and at leisure for eternity, seeing that he is God, and being filled by Him when he will be all in all (1 Cor 15:28). . . . This we shall then know perfectly, when we are perfectly at rest, and in stillness see that he is God. . . . There we shall be still and see; we shall see and shall love; we shall love and we shall praise. (*Civ.* 22.30)

Although Augustine concedes a final paradise that is material and embodied, his highest reflection is founded on the vision of the heavenly city in Revelation 21–22. Remembrance of Eden's garden, that place of God's first creation, is not present in his discussions here, but rather is considered earlier, in Book 14 when he discusses the prelapsarian existence of Adam and Eve. The choice of biblical texts is important, for Augustine's use of Revelation 21–22 allows him to present the resurrected sensorium in essentially mono-sensory terms: it is the vision of Revelation 21–22, the sight of heavenly city, that is the canvas for his depiction of the resurrected life. It is a vision requiring only sight for its realization, a privileging of visuality that carries to its culmination Augustine's Neoplatonic training.

For Ephrem, however, paradise will be all that Eden was and more. The nature of the resurrected body, then, must be such as to enable full awareness of its home. Ephrem's biblical base is both the Garden of the Genesis creation account and its poetic echo in the Song of Songs. Hence, Ephrem's *Hymns on Paradise* are a dazzling tour de force for the senses, reminiscent of the Song of Songs in their lush sensuality.[45] Paradise in these hymns is a place of breathtaking, sumptuous beauty—shimmering in resplendent light, billowing with myriad exquisite scents, its colors gleaming, its tastes and sounds a marvel. Flowers, fountains, perfumes, blossoms, trees laden with fruits abound "in endless variety." To be in this place requires the means to experience it. Thus, Ephrem explains, in paradise the body, healed and glorified in its resurrected state, will be robed in "garments of glory" that replace its former "garments of shame."[46] In this condition the body, no longer hindered, will receive utterly the sensory feast that paradise pours forth on every side. "Being unburdened, / the senses stand in awe and delight / before the divine Majesty" (*De parad.* 9.17). In paradise one's entire being will be permeated by the encounter with the divine. Living there will be the absolute experience of God's presence.

In Ephrem's view, soul and body require each other for existence even in the world to come. In *Hymns on Paradise* 8, he makes his point: without the body, the soul would not be able to perceive or be conscious of paradise. What Ephrem describes is an encounter between subject and object in which the person will be saturated at every level of awareness and being by the object sought, swallowed up by the immensity of presence in the midst of what is divine. The resurrected life would be that condition in which nothing separates us from God. Bathed in divinity from without, we will radiate divinity from within, aglow from our inmost heart to our outermost limbs. Those who enter paradise will be astonished at what they become:

> People behold themselves
>   in glory
> and wonder at themselves,
>   discovering where they are.
> The nature of their bodies,
>   once troubled and troublesome,
> is now tranquil and quiet,
>   resplendent
> from without in beauty,
>   and from within with purity,
> the body in evident ways,
>   the soul in hidden ways. (*Parad.* 7.12)

For Ephrem, God's constant activity is revelation; the means by which human persons know that revelation are the sensory experiences of the body by which they encounter it. In the incarnation God poured himself into the body, the instrument of human knowing. In the sacrament, Christ enters into each person's body, so that nothing separates the believer's body from his. "Ears even heard Him, eyes saw Him, / hands even touched Him, the mouth ate Him. / Limbs and senses gave thanks to/the One Who came and revived all that is corporeal" (*De nativitate* 4.144–45). Ephrem insists that sense perception is the foundational experience of the human-divine encounter, while at the same time he repeatedly admonishes that the senses are insufficient for the task. Inadequate at best, the senses are a feeble medium through which to receive knowledge of God. Nonetheless, in Ephrem's view it is precisely their inadequacy that renders them crucial. When open to God, the senses receive God's revelation at every turn; they take it in, they convey it, they mediate, they actively encounter and transmit. What the senses do *not* do, in Ephrem's view, is intentionally, willfully, or consciously manipulate what they receive; they do not function as does the rational mind. For Ephrem, rationality alone is the seeking of *disembodied* knowledge: therein it fails. God cannot be known except when allowed to permeate the whole of one's being. This will be true in the resurrected body as it is now.

Ancient Christianity defined God as ineffable and inconceivable. It thereby heightened the significance of sense perception specifically as a noncognitive process of knowing. In more basic terms, attention to sense perception allowed Christians to perceive even the most mundane of daily activities as religiously significant. To the faithful late antique Christian, properly trained through liturgical and sacramental participation as well as by didactic instruction, sensory experience articulated religious identity. The valuation of sense perception as a mode of religious knowing yielded a vivid sense of the religious self as an embodied and sensing self in a world God had created for just that purpose. The religious self was a sensing self: what it sensed was God.

NOTES

This essay consists of some of the main points of discussion in my book *Scenting Salvation: Ancient Christianity and the Olfactory Imagination,* forthcoming from University of California Press. The book deals specifically with smell, its cultural meanings and religious significations for the first seven Christian centuries (but also drawing on earlier and later material). However, its arguments depend on a larger orientation toward the senses as a whole: this essay seeks to identify that larger orientation. One of the crucial aspects omitted here for reasons of space is the necessary foundation in ancient medicine, physiology, and science that provided the understandings by which religious practices and writings intersected with cultural patterns of sensory orientation.

Helpful studies on the senses for purposes of ancient religion are, e.g., David Chidester, *Word and Light: Seeing, Hearing and Religious Discourse* (Urbana: University of Illinois Press, 1992); Georgia Frank, *The Memory of the Eyes: Pilgrims to Living Saints in Christian Late Antiquity* (The Transformation of the Classical Heritage 30; Berkeley: University of California Press, 2000); Sarah Coakley, ed., *Religion and the Body* (Cambridge Studies in Religious Traditions 8; Cambridge: Cambridge University Press, 1997); David Howes, ed., *The Varieties of Sensory Experience: A Sourcebook in the Anthropology of the Senses* (Anthropological Horizons; Toronto: University of Toronto Press, 1991); Constance Classen, *The Color of Angels: Cosmology, Gender, and the Aesthetic Imagination* (New York: Routledge, 1998); C. Classen, D. Howes, and Anthony Synnott, *Aroma: The Cultural History of Smell* (New York: Routledge, 1994).

1. *Mart. Pol.* 15.1–16.1 (*The Acts of the Christian Martyrs* [trans. Herbert Mursurillo; OECT; New York: Oxford University Press, 1972], 14–15).

2. Clement of Alexandria, *Paedagogus* (*Christ the Educator* [trans. Simon P. Wood; FC 23; New York: Fathers of the Church, 1954]); see especially Books 2 and 3.

3. Tertullian is very close to Clement on these matters, agreeing only grudgingly and in passing that the senses can guide the believer to focus on God: for example, the beautiful scents and colors of flowers ought to remind the faithful believer of the beauty of the One who made them. See esp. Tertullian, *De Corona* in *Tertullian: Disciplinary, Moral and Ascetical Works* (trans. R. Arbesmann, E. J. Daly, and E. A. Quain; FC 40; New York: Fathers of the Church, Inc., 1959); Clement, *Paed.* 2.8.70–6. Origen, by contrast, stays for the most part in the realm of ethical behavior, and has little positive to say about sensory experience as significant in and of itself. See for example his *Hom. Gen.* and *Hom. Exod.* (*Homilies on Genesis and Exodus* [trans. R. Heine; FC 71; Washington, D.C.: Catholic University of America Press, 1981]).

4. Tertullian, *Ux.* 2.5 (*Tertullian: Treatises on Marriage and Remarriage* [trans. William P. Le Saint; ACW 13; Westminster, Md.: Newman Press, 1951], 30). On the adornment of entrances with lamps and wreaths to honor the imperial cult, see also Tertullian, *Idol.* 15 (*De Idololatria* [trans. and ed. J. H. Waszink and J. C. M. van Winden; Supplements to *VC* 1; Leiden: E. J. Brill, 1987]).

5. Tertullian, *Ux.* 2.8 (ACW 13:35).

6. Consider Theophilus of Antioch's treatise, *Ad Autolycum*, written ca. 168 C.E. (*The Three Books of Theophilus of Antioch to Autolycus* [ANF 3: 49–133]).

7. On these and other developments of fourth-century worship see, e.g., Paul F. Bradshaw, *Daily Prayer in the Early Church: A Study of the Origin and Early Development of the Divine Office* (New York: Oxford University Press, 1981); Robert F. Taft, *The Great Entrance: A History of the Transfer of Gifts and Other Pre-Anaphoral Rites* (vol. 2 of *The History of the Liturgy of St. John Chrysostom;* OrChrAn 200; Rome: Pontificium Institutum Studiorum Orientalium, 1978); and idem, *The Liturgy of the Hours in East and West: The Origins of the Divine Office and Its Meanings for Today* (Collegeville, Minn.: Liturgical Press, 1986).

8. For a sense of how the dictates of imperial ceremony influences liturgical developments, see Eusebius of Caesarea on the consecration of the church at Tyre in 312: *Eccl. Hist.* 10.3–4. Sensorily rich descriptions of Christian worship from the late fourth, early fifth centuries: Egeria, *Itinerarium* 24–5, on liturgical customs in Jerusalem; the Spanish poet Prudentius, *Cathemerinon* 5, "Hymnus ad incensum lucernae"; Paulinus of Nola on the piety and practices at the shrine of St. Felix of Nola, *Poem.* 14, 18, 21, 25, 33. Like other Christian writers of the period, Paulinus goes to some lengths to distinguish Christian ritual practices from those of traditional, pre-Christian religions.

9. Jerome, *Vigil.* 4–7 (NPNF² 6:418–20).

10. Paulinus of Nola, *Poem.* 14 (*The Poems of Paulinus of Nola* [trans. P. G. Walsh; ACW 40; New York: Newman, 1975], 77–81).

11. See especially Dennis Trout, "Christianizing the Nolan Countryside: Animal Sacrifice at the Tomb of St. Felix," *JECS* 3 (1995): 281–98. For further discussion, idem, *Paulinus of Nola: Life, Letters, and Poems* (The Transformation of the Classical Heritage 27; Berkeley: University of California Press, 1999) 160–97.

12. Paulinus of Nola, *Poem.* 14, 18, 21, 25, 33.

13. Prudentius, *Cath.* 10, "Hymnus circa exsequias defuncti"; and *Peristephanon* passim (*The Poems of Prudentius* [trans. M. Clement Eagan; FC 43; Washington, D.C.: Catholic University of America Press], 1962).

14. Especially helpful for working with the sensory aspects of ancient Mediterranean religion: Marcel Detienne, *The Gardens of Adonis: Spices in Greek Mythology* (new ed.; Mythos; Princeton: Princeton University Press, 1994); M. Detienne and Jean-Pierre Vernant, *The Cuisine of Sacrifice among the Greeks* (trans. Paula Wissing; Chicago: University of Chicago Press, 1989); Saara Lilja, *The Treatment of Odours in the Poetry of Antiquity* (Commentationes humanarum litterarum 49; Helsinki: Societas Scientariarum Fennica, 1972); Mary Beard, John North, and Simon Price, *A Sourcebook* (vol. 2 of *Religions of Rome;* Cambridge: Cambridge University Press, 1998). Helpful for seeing the use of traditional practices in the competition for religious "supremacy" during the

fourth century: Thomas Mathews, *The Clash of the Gods: A Reinterpretation of Early Christian Art* (rev. ed.; Princeton, N.J.: Princeton University Press, 1999); Sabine Mac-Cormack, *Art and Ceremony in Late Antiquity* (The Transformation of the Classical Heritage 1; Berkeley: University of California Press, 1981); John F. Baldovin, *The Urban Character of Christian Worship: The Origins, Development, and Meaning of the Stational Liturgy* (OrChrAn 229; Rome: Pontificium Institutum Studiorum Orientalium, 1987).

15. I am much influenced by Catherine Bell, *Ritual Theory, Ritual Practice* (New York: Oxford University Press, 1992) and draw particularly on her notion of the "ritual body" (94–117).

16. The influence of Michel Foucault's magisterial work *The History of Sexuality* has been especially powerful in this regard.

17. The literature is vast. Among the most important on sexuality and asceticism are Peter Brown, *The Body and Society: Men, Women, and Sexual Renunciation in Early Christianity* (Lectures on the History of Religions, new ser. 13; New York: Columbia University Press, 1988); Dale Martin, *The Corinthian Body* (New Haven, Conn.: Yale University Press, 1995); Teresa Shaw, *The Burden of the Flesh: Fasting and Sexuality in Early Christianity* (Minneapolis: Augsburg Fortress, 1998). Ross Shepherd Kraemer, Elizabeth Clark, Averil Cameron, and Virginia Burrus have provided crucial work on the rhetoric of gender and sexuality in late antique culture.

18. Basil, *Hex.* 1 (*Saint Basil: Exegetical Homilies* [trans. Agnes Clare Way; FC 46 Washington, D.C.: Catholic University of America Press, 1963] 12, 19).

19. Gregory of Nyssa, *De humani corporis fabrica* 2.1 (*NPNF*[2] 5:390).

20. Ephrem, *Virg.* 20.12 (*Ephrem the Syrian: Hymns* [trans. Kathleen McVey; Mahwah, N.J.: Paulist Press, 1989]). All translations from *Hymns on Virginity* and *Hymns on Nativity* are by McVey.

21. *De fide* 18 is a particularly well-known example. See P. Yousif, "St. Ephrem on Symbols in Nature: Faith, the Trinity, and the Cross (Hymns on Faith, No. 18)," *ECR* 10 (1978) 52–60; idem, "Le Symbolisme de la croix dans la nature chez Saint Éphrem de Nisibe," in *Symposium Syriacum 1976* (ed. René Lavenant; OrChrAn 205; Rome: Pontificium Institutum Studiorum Orientalium, 1978), 207–27.

22. Prudentius, *Cath.* 11.61–76. Compare Maximus of Turin in his *Sermones* 56, "On Pentecost": "Indeed, as the result of Christ's resurrection the air is healthier, the sun warmer, and the earth more fertile. As a result of it the young branch comes into leaf, the green stalks grow into fruit, and the vine ripens into vine sprouts. If all things, then, are clothed in flowers when the flesh of Christ blossoms anew, then it must be the case that when it bears fruit, everything else must bear fruit as well" (*The Sermons of Saint Maximus of Turin* [trans. Boniface Ramsey; ACW 50; New York: Newman Press, 1989], 234–37).

23. See now Edward G. Mathews Jr., "St. Ephrem, Madrashe on Faith, 81–5: Hymns on the Pearl, 1–V," *SVTQ* 38 (1994): 45–72.

24. Ephrem, *Des heiligen Ephraem des Syrers Hymnen de Fide* (ed. Edmund Beck; CSCO 154–5/ Scriptores Syri 74–5; Louvain: L. Durbecq, 1955), my trans.

25. For Ephrem's presentation of the senses and theory of their modes of perception, see now Ute Possekel, *Evidence of Greek Philosophical Concepts in the Writings of Ephrem the Syrian* (CSCO 580/ Subsidia 102; Louvain: Peeters, 1999), 186–229. Possekel focuses most closely on Ephrem's treatment of sight and hearing, as being his dominant concern in terms of the senses; however, she also primarily draws on his *Prose Refutations*, which in this matter would appear to differ from the full sensory imagination employed in his hymns.

26. Cyril of Jerusalem, *The Works of Saint Cyril of Jerusalem* (trans. Leo P. McCauley and Anthony Stephenson; 2 vols.; FC 61, 64; Washington, D.C.: Catholic University of America Press, 1969–70).

27. Cyril of Jerusalem, *Cat.* 4.22 (FC 61:130).

28. Cf. Gregory of Nyssa on the digestion of the sacramental bread and wine in his *Oratio Catechetica* 37 (*The Catechetical Oration of St. Gregory of Nyssa* [trans. J. H. Strawley; Early Church Classics; London: Society for the Promotion of Christian Knowledge, 1917], 107–12).

29. The *Confessions* of Augustine are in fact an extended exposition on this very theme. Another striking example is Cyril of Jerusalem's *Catecheses*.

30. Ephrem, *The Harp of the Spirit: Eighteen Poems of St. Ephrem* (trans. Sebastian P. Brock, 2nd ed.; Studies Supplementary to Sobornost 4; London: Fellowship of St. Alban and St. Sergius, 1983), 77.

31. Jason BeDuhn, *The Manichaean Body: In Discipline and Ritual* (Baltimore, Md.: Johns Hopkins University Press, 2000) argues similarly for the significance of the body in Manichaean religion, but by wholly other means and on wholly other grounds.

32. Ephrem has a number of similar passages. Interestingly in relation to Manichaeism, however, is his *Discourse to Hypatius III, Against the Teachings of Mani*. Stating that the human body can in fact be pure and holy, Ephrem writes, "For the eyes of the glorious body clothe themselves with chastity, its ears with purity, its limbs with glory, its senses with holiness, in its mouth is praise and on its tongue is thanksgiving and in its lips is blessing, in its feet is the habit of visiting the sick, in its hands alms for the needy, in its heart is true faith" (*The Discourses Addressed to Hypatius* [vol. 1 of *S. Ephraem's Prose Refutations of Mani, Marcion, and Bardaisan;* ed. A. A. Bevan and F. Crawford Burkitt; trans. W. Mitchell; Text and Translation; London: Williams & Norgate, 1912], lxxi).

33. Bell, *Ritual Theory, Ritual Practice,* is again crucial.

34. Ambrose, *De sacramentis* in *Saint Ambrose, Theological and Dogmatic Works* (trans. R. J. Deferrari; FC 44; Washington, D.C.: Catholic University of America Press, 1963), 269–328.

35. Ambrose, *Fug.* 1.3 (*Saint Ambrose, Seven Exegetical Works* [trans. Michael McHugh; FC 65; Washington, D.C.: Catholic University of America Press, 1972], 282).

36. Discussed at length in S. A. Harvey, "The Stylite's Liturgy: Ritual and Religious Identity in Late Antiquity," *JECS* 6 (1998): 523–39; idem, "Olfactory Knowing: Signs of Smell in the *Lives* of Simeon Stylites," in *After Bardaisan: Studies on Continuity and Change in Syriac Christianity in Honour of Professor Han J. W. Drijvers* (ed. G. J. Reinink and A. C. Klugkist; OLA 89; Leuven: Peeters, 1999), 23–34.

37. To sense the breadth of this tradition, especially in eastern monasticism, see, e.g., B. Fraigneau-Julien, *Les Sens Spirituels et la Vision de Dieu selon Syméon le Nouveau Théologien* (Théologie Historique 67; Paris: Beauchesne, 1985); Harry Austryn Wolfson, "The Internal Senses in Latin, Arabic, and Hebrew Philosophic Texts," *HTR* 28 (1935): 69–133.

38. E.g., Origen, *Cels.* 1.48, 7. 38; idem, *Hom. Lev.* 3.2; idem, *Comm. Cant.* prologue, 2, 1.4; Gregory of Nyssa, *Comm. Cant.,* Hom. 1, Hom. 11, Hom. 15; Ambrose, *Spir.* 2.7 (67); Augustine, *Lib.* 2.3.27–37; idem, *Trin.* 9.6–7, 11, 15. 12.

39. Evagrius has very few references to the senses in his *Praktikos.* The *Kephalaia Gnostica* contains more extensive discussion of sense perception both physical and spiritual, and several references to spiritual (or sacramental) anointment (1.33, 34, 36; 2.35; 3.29, 43, 76, 85; 4. 18, 21, 22, 25, 29, 68; 5. 53, 58, 59, 78). The work is extant in Syriac in *Les Six Centuries des "Kephalaia Gnostica" d'Évagre le Pontique* (trans. and ed. Antoine Guillaumont; PO 28; Paris: Firmin-Didot, 1958), 5–264. In his *Sentences to Virgins,* Evagrius includes an epithalamium closely modeled on the Song of Songs, including the image of the bridegroom's sweet-smelling perfume: Susanna Elm, "Evagrius Ponticus' *Sententiae ad Virginem,*" *DOP* 45 (1991): 97–120, at 106. For an especially illuminating treatment of Evagrius on the senses and imageless prayer, see Columba Stewart, "Imageless Prayer and the Theological Vision of Evagrius Ponticus," *JECS* 9 (2001): 151–71. In this article Stewart also emphasizes the critical problem of how the ascetic could make use of key biblical texts that present human encounter with the divine as a sensory one.

40. Columba Stewart has an insightful discussion contrasting Evagrius and pseudo-Macarius on just this point in *"Working the Earth of the Heart": The Messalian Controversy in History, Texts, and Language to AD 431* (Oxford Theological Monographs; Oxford: Clarendon, 1991), 116–38.

41. Pseudo-Macarius, *Hom.* 33.1 (*Pseudo-Macarius, The Fifty Spiritual Homilies and the "Great Letter"* [trans. George Maloney; CWS; New York: Paulist Press, 1992], 201).

42. Augustine, *Civ.* 14.11 (*St. Augustine, Concerning the City of God, against the Pagans* [trans. Henry Bettenson; New York: Penguin Books, 1984], 569). All translations from *City of God* are by Bettenson.

43. Ephrem, *De paradiso* 8.9 (*St. Ephrem the Syrian, Hymns on Paradise* [trans. Sebastian P. Brock; Crestwood, N.Y.: St. Vladimir's Seminary Press, 1990]). All translations from *Hymns on Paradise* are by Brock.

44. See Caroline Walker Bynum, *The Resurrection of the Body in Western Christianity, 200–1336* (Lectures on the History of Religion, new series 15; New York: Columbia University Press, 1995), 94–104; idem, "Material Continuity, Personal Survival and the Resurrection of the Body: A Scholastic Discussion in its Medieval and Modern Contexts," in her *Fragmentation and Redemption: Essays on Gender and the Human Body in Medieval Religion* (New York: Zone Books: 1992), 239–98.

45. Jean Daniélou, "Terre et Paradis chez les Pères de l'église," *ErJb* 22 (1953): 433–72, has a fine discussion of Ephrem's *Hymns on Paradise* in this study on the physicality of the early Christian conception of the afterlife. See also N. Sed, "Les Hymnes sur le Paradis de Saint Ephrem et les traditions Juives," *Mus* 81 (1968): 455–501.

46. Here as elsewhere, Gary A. Anderson, *The Genesis of Perfection: Adam and Eve in Jewish and Christian Imagination* (Louisville, Ky.: Westminster John Knox Press, 2001), esp. 117–34, is particularly insightful.

—9—

Dialogue and Deliberation: The Sensory Self in the Hymns of Romanos the Melodist

GEORGIA FRANK

The quest for a Christian self might typically begin and end in the realm of biographical works. Jesus of the gospels provided a paradigm that would be refracted through martyrs' accounts, legends of the apostles, and, eventually, saints' lives, including those of ascetics.[1] Beyond biography, however, there was another apparatus by which to construct a Christian self: the retelling of stories from the Bible. New versions of old stories could tie up Scripture's "loose ends" or fill nagging "gaps."[2] Yet biblical expansions also had the potential to develop characters that might, in the words of philosopher Charles Taylor, "bring to the fore a kind of presence to oneself."[3]

An important figure in this development was the poet Romanos the Melodist (ca. 485–ca. 560), best known for his versified homilies focused on individual episodes or characters from the Bible. With centrifugal license, Romanos retold familiar biblical episodes, weaving garlands of biblical types.[4] Another technique of biblical expansion was to give obscure or silent characters new voice by paying scrupulous attention to their sense perceptions. That sensory interiority does not necessarily mean a superhuman sensory acuity. Romanos is more interested in sensory awareness than in visionary powers or clairvoyance. Romanos's characters demonstrate their ability to scrutinize their perceptions, question what they perceive, and ask what it means, often through dialogue with themselves or with others.

How a self emerges from Romanos's rhetoric of sense perception is the central concern of this essay. To illustrate this interplay between sensory perceptions and the interior deliberations they elicited, I focus on five characters: Adam and Eve, the sinful woman who washes Jesus' feet with her tears and anoints them, and Hades and Satan. As I shall argue, the formation of self emerges from the transformation of perception these characters undergo.

More precisely, that transformation requires a "reeducation of the senses," a phrase taken from Leigh Schmidt's study of hearing in the Enlightenment. In *Hearing Things,* Schmidt demonstrates how natural philosophy, politics, medicine, science, and theology all shared a "learned fascination with acoustics."[5] To take but one example, the invention of the stethoscope not only augmented hearing but also refined it. The enhancement of hearing, however, also coincided with greater suspicion of other voices, namely the miraculous, marvelous, and revelatory.[6] As Schmidt put it, "The Enlightenment changed the senses"; it "dulled and sharpened simultaneously."[7] It was more a matter of reeducating perception than of privileging any single sense.

What Schmidt calls "reeducating perception"[8] is not necessarily dependent on devices, however. The ritualized dialogue of Romanos's metrical sermons provided a patterned and habitual process of calling subjects into existence through right use of the senses. As I shall argue, his chanted sermons, or *kontakia,* served as devices with which to augment and refine perception. Specifically, the dialogue, that clash and exchange of views, sharpened the imagined senses of the characters and thereby those of the audience. Before we turn to those characters, however, it is important to recall the liturgical setting for these chanted sermons.

The Kontakia *of Romanos the Melodist*

Romanos the Melodist was born around 485 C.E. in the Syrian city of Emesa.[9] After serving as deacon in Beirut, he moved to Constantinople during the reign of Anastasius I (491–518), where he established himself as a significant composer of versified homilies. He remained active there until about 551. *Kontakion,* from the Greek word *kontos,* the rod that held parchment scrolls read aloud during the liturgy, refers to a biblical tale typically retold in metrical verse.[10] It is unlikely that *kontakia* were staged dramas, since all the voices were performed by a single soloist, who typically sang a short prelude, followed by nearly two dozen stanzas of identical meter. Additional voices would have come from the congregation, who probably joined the soloist in singing the same one-line refrain that punctuated every stanza.[11]

By the sixth century, the stories and characters of the Bible were settled. It remained the homilist's task to interpret them for the public.[12] Romanos achieved dramatic results by "do[ing] the Gospels in different voices."[13] His hymns retell the major events of Christ's life and that of the Virgin Mary, as well as stories of Old Testament characters encountered in lectionary readings. Some sixty *kontakia* composed by Romanos survive, although far more are ascribed to him.[14] In them, congregants encountered a variety of biblical characters, including Jesus, his mother, the Leper, Peter, Judas, and Doubting

Thomas. He also developed characters who were silent in the gospels, such as nameless women Jesus encountered in his ministry or the mother of Jesus at the crucifixion.

Dialogue is a key element in many *kontakia*. Two or more characters might enter a dialogue, as in the underworld exchange between the serpent and Hell personified (discussed below). Or, a single character might embark on an interior monologue, as does the woman with the hemorrhage. Although Romanos did not pioneer the invented dialogue or the genre, many scholars count his hymns as some of the genre's finest examples.[15]

It is important to recall that the setting for these hymns was paraliturgical, that is to say, separate from the eucharistic service. They were performed on the outskirts of the city, at the church of the Theotokos in the Kyrou district in the north of the capital, where Christians gathered for nocturnal vigils during festivals of the church calendar.[16] As Romanos describes the scene in one *kontakion*,

> The people of Christ, loyal in their love, have gathered to keep a night-long vigil with psalms and songs. / The congregation can never sing too many hymns to God. / So now that the Psalms of David have been sung and we are blessed by the clear reading of Scripture / let us raise an anthem to Christ and an anathema to Satan. [. . .] He is the master of All.[17]

This passage illustrates nicely the sequence of blessings, readings, and hymns that prepare the worshipers for the sung sermon. The sermon, however, promises a qualitatively different engagement with the scriptural story. As Romanos continues, "It is wonderful to sing psalms and hymns to God, and to wound [*titrōskein*] the demons with reproaches: they are our eternal enemies. / By 'wounding' them we mean the ridicule enacted every time we rehearse the drama of their fall."[18] The terms "wounding," "reproach," and "ridicule" convey the participatory drama and raw emotions unleashed by these hymns.[19] That these vigils were connected to the liturgy of the Word, apart from eucharistic rites is significant, for the paraliturgical setting allowed Romanos to probe biblical stories but also to wander beyond them.

With so many voices in play, the sensory worlds proliferate. Through dialogue and deliberation, Romanos evokes a wide range of sense experiences. For instance, the sinful woman is saved by smell, whereas John the Baptist is transformed by sight. Adam recognizes paradise through hearing, while the hemorrhaging woman speaks by her hand. Peter still tastes the last supper in his mouth, while Doubting Thomas's touch composes the book of life.[20] To say that his work is multisensory states the obvious. More interesting, however, is how Romanos articulates the complexity of sensory experience without imposing any hierarchy of the senses.

One is struck by his characters' ability to *reflect on* their senses with imagined deliberation, occasional confusion, and steadfast trust in the evidence of those senses. Rather than discuss the senses *seriatum*, a more effective plan is to focus on the interaction of senses, or how attention to one sense results in the refinement of another. As the senses clash and interact, none prevails or claims primacy. Rather, Romanos keeps several in play as a way to enhance all sensory knowing for the Byzantine worshiper. Taken in their liturgical context, these hymns can suggest how lay Byzantine Christians were instructed to sharpen and even to dull the senses for clearer perception of the divine. To illustrate what I mean by this sensory self, I turn to one of Romanos's many stories about Eden, specifically, the primordial couple's final hours in paradise.

Five Characters, Five Senses

ADAM AND EVE

"On the Epiphany"[21] includes a detailed discussion of the consequences of Adam and Eve's eating the fruit in Eden. According to Genesis, its effects were swift. Immediately after they consumed the fruit, the couple's "eyes . . . were opened, and they knew that they were naked" (Gen 3:7 NRSV). Romanos, however, described a different ocular effect. Adam consumed "the fruit which produces blindness," and found himself "naked and maimed and groping; he tried to seize the one who had disrobed him; but the latter, seeing him, laughed at / How he stretched out his hands everywhere and demanded His cloak, even after having been made naked" (17.2).[22] God's ridicule eventually leads to his restoration of Adam's sight. Yet that "healing" is postponed. Why?

To remake Adam, the poet plots redemption along a trajectory of knowing blindness, then unknowing vision. God takes pity on the blind Adam and approaches him. The singer of this hymn urges Adam to "fall down before Him who comes to you / For He has appeared for you as you come forward to see Him, to grope after Him, and to greet Him" (17.3). Flailing and groping about is indeed comic, but it is also salvific, as Adam eventually draws closer to God.[23] Yet it is not only his touch that becomes refined through blindness. Romanos also imagines how blind Adam learned to feel his world. At the birth of Jesus, Adam felt the sun on his skin. As we are told, "to Adam, blinded in Eden, appeared a sun from Bethlehem" (17.1). Eventually, the Jordan's waters, like a healing salve, opened Adam's eyes at the moment of Jesus' baptism (17.2).

Once restored, Adam's vision must hold up to scrutiny. Thus, Romanos introduces a catena of biblical exemplars: Abraham saw God, but he could not recognize him as God (17.4); Jacob saw God, but in a dream and with God disguised as a man (17.5); Moses saw God, but only the backside (17.6); Isaiah saw God, but "in the 'slumber of the spirit,' not with physical eyes" (17.7; cf. Rom 11.8); and Daniel is remembered as one who "wished to gaze at the One who beholds us" (17.8). None of these patriarchs or prophets experienced blindness, but they never saw God completely either. The fullness of vision belongs to Adam and, by extension, to those who sing the hymn, who may boast, "But we behold with the eyes of our bodies" (17.7). The congregation's confidence in their own restored sight also appears in the final strophes: "Let us all raise our eyes to God in the Heavens, / Crying . . . Our God is the One seen on earth" (17.5).[24] Romanos reinterprets the opening of the eyes in Genesis 3:7 as an epic sweep from blind groping to partial or unwitting sight, to fullness of an unabashedly physical vision shared by Adam and ultimately by a redeemed humanity. As in Genesis, eating the fruit opens the eyes. For Romanos, however, the blindness must precede any true opening of the eyes. To some extent, Adam's blindness is a punishment.[25] Yet his adaptation is also a path to salvation: without blindness, the rest of his body would not have known its creator. Blindness, then, allows the body to know by groping, feeling, and listening.

By blinding Adam, then, Romanos can take the Genesis account in two separate directions. There is a turn inward, made possible by isolating the fruit's effects on Adam, not Eve. In addition, there is a turn forward in space and time to Jesus' baptism. Forward in space, as the extended hands of the blind man suggest, first aimless then directed toward God. But also forward in time, through a series of biblical visionaries, toward Jesus' baptism, and, by the end of the hymn, toward the congregation's open eyes. Why such attention to the disability and rehabilitation of vision? Why do Romanos's hymns so deeply bind the formation of the self to the impairment of physical senses?

What Romanos captured in Adam's gesticulations he develops further in hymns that focus on Adam and Eve's interrogations. This connection between self and senses is even more pronounced in Romanos's hymns on the nativity, specifically, the second hymn in the series.[26] Whereas the first hymn, sung on December 25,[27] opens with the proclamation "Bethlehem has opened Eden, come, let us see" (10.1), the actual opening of Eden is commemorated on the following Sunday.[28] The intervening days provided Romanos with an interval in which to forge a dialogue between the first parents, Adam and Eve.

The chanted sermon opens with Mary's lullaby to the infant Jesus, a hymn praising his divinity. As Mary sings and caresses the baby, Eve listens to the lullaby and shares her delight with Adam. Says Eve: "Who has caused this hoped-for news to ring out in my ears? / Her voice alone has released me from my torment" (11.4). Adam is listening, but not necessarily to Mary. Apparently oblivious to Eve's words, he is roused instead by the sound of the bird, "the swallow which sings at dawn." Still, Eve persists and recounts the fall as a drama of the senses. "Hear me," she commands. "The serpent hitherto saw me and leaped for joy; But now seeing those who are descended from us, he flees." Jolted awake, Adam "opening the ears which he had blocked through disobedience" (11.5), ponders what he hears. He admits the sound is sweet, yet he still mistrusts its source, the voice of a woman. To convince Adam of the truth of her words, Eve summons other senses: "Catch the scent of this fresh smell, and at once burst into new life. . . . Jesus Christ breathes forth a fresh breeze" (11.6). Strangely, Adam announces not what he smells but what he sees: "Indeed, I see a new, another paradise, bearing in her arms the tree of life itself, which once the cherubim kept sacred, kept me from touching" (11.7). Vision, the sense by which Adam recognizes what he and Eve once lost, signals Adam's full awakening. This "breath-bringing life," he proclaims, "mak[es] me come alive. And now, strengthened by this fragrance, I advance to her [Mary]" (11.7). As Romanos choreographs the senses in this episode, hearing launches sight, which triggers smell. Here Adam suffers no impairment of the senses, only their misdirection. Eventually, the properly trained ear knows what to see; the sharpened eye learns how to smell.

Adam's supplication engages Mary's senses. He calls upon her to see his misery and listen to his words: "Seeing my tears, have mercy on me, / And lend a favoring ear to my lamentations, / Beholding the rags which I wear, which the serpent has woven for me" (11.8). It is striking that Mary, celebrated in patristic tradition for her "receptive ear,"[29] should be presented by Romanos as a viewer. Her response to Adam's plea is deeply visual: "The eyes [*ophthalmoi*] of Mary as she beheld [*theōrēsantes*] Eve and as she looked on [*katidontes*] Adam, quickly filled with tears" (11.10). Moved by this gaze, Mary then approaches Jesus' cradle and pleads to her son on their behalf. Again, the baby's response is presented visually, as a prophetic word-picture, or *ekphrasis,* of his death: "You will see me, the babe whom you carry in your hands, with his hands nailed to the cross in a short while" (11.16). Seeing dominates these predictions ("you will see," "you have to see," and "I will be seen by you").[30] By these images Mary returns to assure Adam and Eve of their eventual deliverance.

The reeducation of perception begins early in this *kontakion.* That Eve is attentive to Mary's lullaby and not asleep is significant in a homiletic tradition that otherwise blames Eve's senses for precipitating the expulsion from paradise.[31] In Romanos's rendition, the senses draw the couple *closer* to God. They may falter at first, yet each of Adam's senses prepares the next. First he must shake off sleep, then he hears, but the hearing is misdirected. When he hears Eve, he still cannot decide where to put his trust. Finally, he chooses to listen to his wife. And only then can he recognize and approach Mary. As the sensory awakening slowly unfolds, we also witness a new creation of the first man: lifeless, slumbering, aware of other creatures, then of woman, animated by divine breath. Yet whereas God in Genesis animated the first human when he "breathed into his nostrils the breath of life" (Gen 2:7 NRSV), this Adam draws in the "breath-bringing life" whose "fragrance" fortifies him. For Romanos, the reeducation of the senses is none other than the re-creation of the first human, patterned on the account in Genesis 2.

Adam and Eve pioneer humanity's redemption through the reeducation of their senses. The senses may have precipitated the couple's expulsion, yet they also directed the couple back to God. To be sure, there were obstacles. Adam needed to discern Eve's words from the swallow's songs, not to mention to trust those words. And his return from blindness would have to overcome the limited perceptions or partial visions of the patriarchs and prophets. Whether the senses of hearing or sight are misdirected, maimed, or misunderstood, Romanos shows the steps toward their full knowing of the incarnate Christ. By this combination of restoration, reeducation, and coordination, Romanos attends to several senses without privileging one.[32] Even hymns focused on one sense will articulate its relation to the others. To illustrate this interactive dimension, we turn to Romanos's hymn on the "Sinful Woman."

THE SINFUL WOMAN

The nameless woman who washed Christ's feet with her tears, dried them with her hair, and anointed them with perfume was a popular figure in Syriac and Greek homilies.[33] It is not surprising that she should become the subject of one of the Melodist's *kontakia,* performed on the Wednesday before Easter.[34] Although she is utterly silent in the gospel account (Luke 7:36–50), Romanos seizes the opportunity to make her speak. He follows the basic structure of the gospel account: the woman's intrusion, then the host's dialogue with Christ over the proper response to her actions. Yet he also develops her actions beyond the house as he devotes more than half the *kontakion* to her preparations and deliberations prior to her arrival at the dinner party.

Like Adam's story, her tale is marked by a series of sensory tensions. There is a tension between sense perceptions that redeem and those that spell ruin. She asks Christ, "How may I, who have trapped all with my glance, gaze on you?" (21. prol. 2) She also encounters olfactory confusion. Because she saw "Christ's words like sweet drops of fragrance raining down everywhere," she came to "hate the foul stench of her actions" (21.1). Still, "the fragrance of Christ's table breathed gently on her" (21.3). These paradoxes (fragrance/stench, seductive/adoring gaze) shape her reflections and engage the audience.[35] Her ability to recognize the inner conflict of competing sense perceptions sets an important foundation for her subsequent actions within the house.

In addition to generating sensory tensions, the Melodist experiments with various types of invented speech. He could have amplified or elaborated on the dialogue between the Pharisee and Jesus. Instead, he endows the woman with several speech types. She engages in interior monologues addressed to her soul: "Come then," she bids it, "see the moment you are seeking" (21.4). She anticipates each step of her transformation: how she will "blow" on her tainted past, transform the Pharisee's house into a "place of enlightenment" *(phōtistērion)* (21.5), "mix the font with weeping, oil and sweet myrrh," and "wash away [her] sins" (21.6).[36] Few in the audience would have missed the references to baptismal rites: a reminder of the exorcisms in which priests blow on the candidate's face; the *phōtistērion,* another name for the baptistery; and the scenting of the baptismal waters. Romanos also employs hypothetical dialogue as she imagines Christ's response: "He does not say to me, 'Until just now you were in darkness and have you come to see me, the sun?' " (21.6)

Her most extensive interior monologue involves a series of comparisons to biblical women: the anonymous Canaanite woman from the gospels, the prostitute Rahab who protected Israelite spies, and Hannah, the once-barren mother of the prophet Samuel.[37] The sinful woman recalls the Canaanite woman's hunger, Rahab's hospitality, and Hannah's tears. Still, taken as a group, what do these three women have in common with the sinful woman? After all, only Rahab was a prostitute.[38]

One implicit commonality is their ability to speak up. Rahab vowed to protect the Israelite spies. Hannah sang her thanksgiving in 1 Samuel 2 (cf. Luke 1:46–55). And the Canaanite woman's famous come-back—"Even the dogs eat the crumbs that fall from their Lord's table" (Matt 15:27)—convinced Jesus to heal a sick child. Such outspoken women may seem misplaced in a narrative about the actions of a silent woman who never addresses Christ after the prologue. Beyond that, we witness her "crying out in silence" (21.8). The narrator also draws the contrast: whereas the Canaanite woman was "redeemed by a cry," the sinful woman was "saved by silence" (21.3). Perhaps these vocal women are invoked to contrast to her silence. It is also possible that the memory of their external speeches enhance our appreciation for her *internal* eloquence. None of these effects can be ruled out. Yet all these explanations overlook what happens next.

These apparent *contrasts* to the harlot's silence actually prove to be *catalysts* to speech. For only after invoking these women does the sinful woman find herself capable of shattering the very silence that saves her. As if emboldened by these vociferous women, she hastens to her perfume seller, to whom she "comes crying out [*boōsa*]" (21.9). Now the dialogue begins. Fearing the loss of a good customer, an incredulous merchant questions her motives. In reply to his disbelief, she "cried out with boldness" *(boai sun parrēsiai)* (21.10). Her outburst marks the transition from inaudible to audible speech, from interior thoughts to external demands. The sinful woman is indeed capable of crying out to the perfume merchant—and ultimately to Romanos's audience—even if she does not breach her silence in the house of the Pharisee. Yet her outburst is as forceful as it is brief. No sooner had she confronted the merchant than, as Romanos describes the scene, "she cut off the flow of words with silence, and the holy woman took her fair sweet myrrh and entered the chamber of the Pharisee" (21.12). Silence descends, propelled by the memory of her outcry.[39] I need not rehearse Jesus' subsequent exchange with the host, since it follows the gospel account quite closely.

In this *kontakion*, olfactory experience is, according to Susan Ashbrook Harvey, the "primary frame of reference."[40] Indeed, olfaction intersects in novel ways with hearing. As this woman deliberates on good and bad odors, the audience learns to hear the innermost movements of the heart. In addition, as long as Christ remains unseen, her olfactory and aural perceptions are most acute. It is also significant that her most detailed anticipation of baptism's fragrances occur during these contemplative moments. One sense sharpens the other.

Sensory suppression also enhances the evidence of hearing. Her final words, "I have not seen him, but I heard and was wounded" (21.11), capture that honing of perception. Likewise, the audience's hearing is sharpened through the silencing of her voice. Witnessing her movement from silence to speech, the audience also bears silent witness. In this hymn, then, the complex relationships between hearing and olfaction, as well as between the heard and the unheard/unseen are carefully worked out by engaging the audience's imagined senses. From interior monologue, we turn to external dialogue.

HADES AND DEATH

My final example focuses on a full-fledged dialogue between Hades and Death in the hymn known as "The Victory of the Cross."[41] Here, Romanos explores how Jesus' death affected Hell (in this instance, personified) and Satan. Many Christians were familiar with stories about Christ's descent to hell during the days after his death and before his resurrection. Apocryphal gospels vividly recounted horrified disputes between Satan and Hades, the shattering of hell's chains and gates, and Jesus' eventual liberation of souls, including those of Adam and Eve as well as righteous patriarchs and prophets.[42] These legends were told as part of the Good Friday observances in Edessa, Antioch, and Constantinople in the fourth and fifth centuries. By the sixth century they became fixed as part of the resurrection celebrations throughout the empire.[43]

"On the Victory of the Cross" takes place on Good Friday and tracks Hell's reaction to the events above ground. This subterranean plunge occurs in the first strophe. To appreciate how Romanos establishes these vertical, or "stacked" narrative planes, it is worth quoting the strophe at length:

> Three crosses Pilate fixed on Golgotha,
> two for the thieves and one for the Giver of life,
> whom Hell saw and said to those below,
> "My ministers and powers, who has fixed a nail in my heart?
> A wooden lance has suddenly pierced me and I am being torn apart.
> My insides are in pain, my belly in agony,
> my senses make my spirit tremble,
> and I am compelled to disgorge Adam and Adam's race. Given me by a Tree,
> a Tree is bringing them again to Paradise." (38.1)

By these words Romanos aligns the familiar site of three crosses during the dialogue between Jesus and the thief with the underworld dialogue between Hell and Satan. What joins these two realms is a piercing wound, first Christ pierced *on* the cross, at the same time that Hell is pierced *by* that cross.

Having set up this parallax view, Romanos then launches the dialogue between Hell and Satan (in the form of the serpent), who rushes to his wounded ally's side. At first the serpent tries to convince Hell that there is no problem. Like a craftsman who stands by his product, the serpent vouches for the Tree *he himself* carpentered into a cross on which they nailed the second Adam (38.2). With Job-like indignation, Hell rebuffs these empty assurances: "Away with you, come to your senses. . . . Run, open your eyes, and see the root of the Tree inside my soul" (38.2). Still the devil sees no danger, no damage. Once again, Hell chides him,

> Lift up your eyes and see that you have fallen into the pit which you created.
> Behold that Tree, which you call dry and barren,
> bears fruit; a thief tasted it
> and has become heir to the good things of Eden. (38.5)

So continues this dialogue between the "eyeless [and] the sightless, the blind [and] the blind," reminiscent of the miscommunication between the agonized Cyclops and his unwitting countrymen. All are blind in their refusal to acknowledge the *present* events.[44] Indeed, darkness is blindness as Hell cautions Satan to "feel around [*psēlapha*] lest you fall" (38.7). Here, *psēlapha* is the same verb Romanos used to describe blind Adam groping about Eden discussed above. Satan, however, replies with mockery, accusing Hell of being frightened by a mere tree (38.8). Vision has failed.

Aware that his words fall on deaf ears, Hell next urges Satan to listen: "Now is the moment for you to open your ears," he insists, "Jesus is nailed and hears the thief crying to him." Hell reports the dialogue from the Gospel of Luke: "Lord, remember me in your kingdom," the thief beseeches Jesus, to which he is assured that he will go with him to Paradise (38.9; cf. Luke 23:42–43). At the mention of these words, Satan, the "all-resourceful dragon," "began to wilt, and what he heard he saw" (38.10). He sputters in disbelief and finally cries out, "Receive me, Hell. My recourse is to you; I submit to your views, I who did not believe them. I saw the Tree at which you shuddered, crimsoned with blood and water" (38.11). Hell's warnings fell on deaf ears, but Christ's words open those same ears.

The sight of the cross could have provided tidy closure to this dialogue of misperception, had it not been interrupted by Satan's call to silence:

> "Wait, wretched Hell," said the demon with a groan,
> "Quiet, be patient, lay hand on mouth,
> for I hear a voice revealing joy.
> A sound has reached me bringing good tidings,
> a rustle of words like the leaves of the Cross.
> For Christ at the point of death cried out, 'Father, forgive them.'"
>   (38.14; cf. Luke 23:34)

Christ's words, not Satan's or Hell's, arrest the conversation and signal the tale's dramatic turns.[45] Whereas Luke's Jesus says, "Father, forgive them; for they do not know what they are doing" (23:34 NRSV),[46] Romanos punctuates the utterance differently, inserting Satan's affective commentary: "But he grieved me when he then said / 'the lawless do not know what they are doing.' "[47] As Jesus catches his breath, it is clear that Satan and Hell (not to mention the congregation) are listening. Like aftershocks, each phrase from the cross drives the drama below. Mired in an infernal impasse, the heated exchange between Satan and Hell comes to an end with Christ's promises to the thief. Only then do Satan's eyes open.

As Jesus' words, "Father, forgive them," put a stop to the evil duo's bickering and elicit harmonized lamentation, Satan invites Hell to join him in song: "Now therefore, Hell, groan and I will harmonize with your wails. / Let us lament as we see the tree which we planted / transformed into a holy trunk" (38.16). Together the pair vows to stop tormenting the race of Adam. The final song, however, belongs to the narrator, who sings on behalf of redeemed humanity, "[We] sing to you, the Lord of all, from the songs of Sion" (38.18).

From the agonized words at Golgotha, Romanos has generated a sensory operetta for four voices, Jesus and the thieves, with Hell and Satan's *basso continuo* below. Like a musical score, the gospels have the upper register, while the infernal parallel tale grounds the drama. Unlike the drama of the sinful woman, whose tale combines dialogue and monologue, the "Victory" is a double dialogue between Jesus and the thief above and Satan and hell below. The latter pair's dispute moves the audience along a path of witnessing, wounding, groping blindness, and finally reverent listening. Hearing Christ's words, seeing the cross, tasting the fruit, all these perceptions conspire to awaken and redirect each sense. Finally, silence draws Satan upward from the pit of Hades to the precipice of truth. The sheer verticality of the narrative provides a sensory path along which Satan moves from blindness to sight, hearing to listening, lamentation to silence. As this *kontakion* closes, Hell and Satan remain silently attentive to the songs of the faithful, the redeemed voices that may prevail and fill the void left by the departed Christ's words.

Hell's agony introduces another important sense: pain. Pain is not only a catalyst to perception, as in Hell calling Satan to see, to hear, and so on. It is also a mode of perception in its own right insofar as it prompts dialogue, hones other senses, and has the power to transform both protagonist and congregation. From the drama on Golgotha, Christ's pain moves to the depths of Hell's organs. As Christ is punctured, so is Hell, a transfer that allows the congregation to see, taste, and hear Christ's final hours on more than one plane.[48] Hell's gaping wound is the space from which this drama unfolds and a sensing self emerges. Even as his agonized words fall on Satan's deaf ears, Hell draws the congregation's senses into the passion account. Thus, another's pain awakens the senses among those who relish "wounding the enemy."[49] To hear Christ's words read from the lectionary is an invitation to hear the refrains of Hell's bitter agony. To speak of Christ's wounds is an invitation to recall Hell's gaping wound.[50] In the end, the sounds that linger will not be Hell's or Satan's laments, but the chorus of praise resonating in the enemy's silence.

As these examples demonstrate, the dialogue was the device by which Romanos both dulled and sharpened the senses to form a newfound interiority within the audience. Not only did voices collide, but sensory impressions also conflicted. Hands spoke, seductive glances turned into devoted gazes. The dialogue drew attention to the physical senses and their power to reveal divine truths. In the context of the evening liturgy, Romanos formed the inner self. The real drama emerged in the dialectical relation between physical senses and the internal deliberations that query what one heard, saw, smelled, tasted, and touched. And as the final example illustrates so keenly, those who claim to see must be *made to* see, made to listen, and even demand silence so that truth may prevail.

It is important to remember that for Romanos the interior life is deliberative yet guided by the physical senses. His *kontakia* represent an ongoing project of training the Christian sensory body through liturgy. I am not speaking here of the interior or spiritual senses. Romanos does not invoke a separate set of senses capable of sensing divine realities that are imperceptible to the physical senses of the body.[51] Instead, he builds the interior life from external senses.

In Romanos's retellings, deliberation becomes a mode of catechesis,[52] but not in the strict sense of explaining sacraments and doctrine. The term *catechesis* often calls to mind the instructions to new Christians by the likes of Cyril of Jerusalem, Ambrose of Milan, or John Chrysostom.[53] By the sixth century, adult baptism had declined as more Christians were born into the faith.[54] Despite declining need for the instruction *on* the liturgy, the liturgy itself could serve as a form of instruction. Romanos reflects this shift in his use of dialogue to draw attention to the physical senses, those conduits to the interior life.

Romanos's trust in the capacities of physical sense perception marks a departure from earlier preaching on the senses. In his pre-baptismal instruction, John Chrysostom invoked "the eyes of the soul" *(hoi tēs psychēs ophthalmoi)*, as well as "spiritual eyes" *(pneumatikoi ophthalmoi)*, or "eyes of faith" *(ophthalmoi tēs pisteōs)*.[55] All these terms stand for a suprasensory mode of seeing beyond the eyes of the body that "make the unseen visible from the seen."[56]

Compared to earlier appeals to the spiritual senses, Romanos's use of the idiom is rare. In "On the Nativity I," Jesus "invisibly touched" his mother's mind and told her to greet the magi, who were guided by what appeared to be a star "to the eyes of the flesh," but was in fact a power "to the eyes of the spirit."[57] In the "Adoration of the Cross," the criminal on the cross opened the eyes of his heart *(diēnoichthē tēs kardias autou to omma)* to see Eden.[58] Thus, Romanos employs language of the spiritual senses to connote suprasensory realities, but without debasing the physical senses.

One should not confuse Romanos's rare references to the spiritual senses with his protagonists' intense deliberations over the physical senses. No character speaks of his or her own spiritual senses in the first person. Moreover, Romanos provides no basis for a fully developed internal set of senses beyond vision, as John Chrysostom did. That Romanos's most deliberative moments focus on physical perceptions suggests a trust in his characters to learn from their *physical* senses. Even so, the education of the senses does not stop there. As Romanos's characters remind us, the need was still there for Christians to reeducate the physical senses to discern God. Romanos achieved this education, not through liturgical commentary,[59] but rather through liturgical allusions in the course of biblical retelling. Through these stories, the inner self was dramatized and thereby called into a subjectivity formed by the sensory deliberations of his characters. He endowed silent figures with unseen voices, capable of instructing the senses in what to see, hear, and touch. The stories were familiar, but the body that sensed them would be transformed.

Romanos's hymns suggest a new direction for liturgical instruction, away from explicit liturgical explanation toward the use of biblical characters as embodied, deliberative agents. When the church gathered as a body at these nighttime vigils, the reeducation of perception valorized physical senses. The internal dialogue provided the vehicle by which to reexamine and even alter a given character's sensory experiences. Interior voices took the place of interior senses to express greater confidence in the senses and their augmentation through ritual.

NOTES

I thank Derek Krueger and Susan Ashbrook Harvey for their valuable essays and stimulating conversations regarding Romanos. The Greek text of Romanos used here is *Hymnes* (ed. and trans. José Grosdidier de Maton; 5 vols.; SC 99, 110, 114, 128, 283; Paris: Cerf, 1964–81). Another fine edition, *Sancti Romani Melodi Cantica: Cantica Genuina* (ed. Paul Maas and C. A. Trypanis; Oxford: Clarendon, 1963) numbers the hymns differently. I follow the SC edition hymn and strophe number, with the Oxford [Oxf.] hymn number supplied in brackets in the first citation of any given hymn. References to the SC volume and page number appear in parentheses. For consistency, I have used the hymn titles provided in the Oxford edition. Grosdidier de Matons provides a useful concordance of various editions' numbering of the hymns in *Romanos le Mélode et les origines de la poésie religieuse à Byzance* (Beauchesne Religions; Paris: Éditions Beauchesne, 1977), 329–32. Wherever possible, I have used the fine translation in St. Romanos the Melodist, *Kontakia: On the Life of Christ* (trans. Ephrem Lash; The Sacred Literature Series; San Francisco: HarperSanFrancisco, 1995). Additional translations available include *Kontakia of Romanos, Byzantine Melodist* (trans. Marjorie Carpenter; 2 vols.; Columbia: University of Missouri Press, 1970, 1973), hereafter MC; and Robert Schork, *Sacred Song from the Byzantine Pulpit: Romanos the Melodist* (Gainesville: University of Florida Press, 1995).

1. What Averil Cameron calls "the construction of a specifically Christian self"

(*Christianity and the Rhetoric of Empire: The Development of Christian Discourse* [Sather Classical Lectures 55; Berkeley: University of California Press, 1991], 57).

2. Ibid., 113.

3. On Augustine's "radical reflexivity," see Charles Taylor, *Sources of the Self: The Making of Modern Identity* (Cambridge, Mass.: Harvard University Press, 1989), 127–42, esp. 131.

4. For instance, in a single strophe (38.8), the wood of Christ's cross elicits the memory of the tree on which Haman hung (Esth 7:10), the wood Jael used to stab Sisera (Judg 4:21–22), and the trees on which the slain Amorite kings were displayed (Josh 10:26–27). In the same *kontakion*, Romanos completes the sequence by linking the cross to the salvific wood of Noah's ark and Moses' staff (38.13; cf. Gen 6:9–8:22; Exod 9:23). Additional examples are discussed in Schork, *Sacred Song*, 14–16; Grosdidier de Matons, *Romanos le Mélode et les origines*, 255–63.

5. Leigh Eric Schmidt, *Hearing Things: Religion, Illusion, and the American Enlightenment* (Cambridge, Mass.: Harvard University Press, 2000), 3–9.

6. Schmidt, *Hearing Things*, 4–5, emphasis his.

7. Ibid., 3.

8. Ibid., 6.

9. Grosdidier de Matons, *Romanos le Mélode et les origines*, 159–98, esp. 163. What follows draws extensively from Derek Krueger, "Writing and Redemption in the Hymns of Romanos the Melodist," *Byzantine and Modern Greek Studies* 27 (2003): 2–44, esp. 12–18.

10. Lash, "Introduction," in *St. Romanos, Kontakia*, xxviii. Romanos himself titled his works in acrostics, such that the first initial in each strophe might spell out a "hymn / chant / praise / poem / ode / psalm by / of humble Romanos" (Krueger, "Writing and Redemption," 18–26).

11. Grosdidier de Matons, "Liturgie et Hymnographie: Kontakion et Canon," *DOP* 34–35 (1980–81): 40–41. The fact that the same refrain might be on the lips of a different character each time effectively rendered the congregation more "understudy" than chorus to a broad cast of biblical characters. One *kontakion* that is missing such a refrain is "On Baptism," (52 = Oxf. 53), a hymn delivered to new (forced?) converts (Grosdidier de Matons, *Hymnes*, SC 283:329).

12. Averil Cameron, "Disputations, Polemical Literature and the Formation of Opinion in the Early Byzantine Period," in *Dispute Poems and Dialogues in the Ancient and Mediaeval Near East: Forms and Types of Literary Debates in Semitic and Related Literatures* (ed. G. J. Reinink and H. L. J. Vanstiphout; OLA 42; Leuven: Peeters, 1991), 97.

13. Krueger, "Writing and Redemption," 16.

14. Grosdidier de Matons estimates that 1000 *kontakia* are attributed to Romanos, although only 89 are extant, either in their entirety or fragments. Of these, he deems some 58 to be authentic (*Romanos le Mélode et les origines*, 199–202).

15. Averil Cameron, "Disputations," 91–108, esp. 94; Mary Cunningham, "Dramatic Device or Didactic Tool? The Function of Dialogue in Byzantine Preaching," in *Rhetoric in Byzantium: Papers from the Thirty-Fifth Spring Symposium of Byzantine Studies, University of Oxford, March 2001* (ed. Elizabeth Jeffreys; Society for the Promotion of Byzantine Studies, Publications 11; Burlington, Vt.: Ashgate, 2003), 101–13. Romanos's debt to Syriac forms and themes is the subject of a lively debate, but one that falls outside the scope of this essay. For a helpful overview of the debate regarding Syriac prototypes, see Cameron, "Disputations," 93–97; Lucas Van Rompay, "Romanos le Mélode, un poète syrien à Constantinople," in *Early Christian Poetry: A Collection of Essays* (ed. J. den Boeft and A. Hilhorst; Supplement to *VC*, 22; Leiden: Brill, 1993), 283–96, esp. 284–88. On earlier Christian uses of the inner thoughts, see Philip Sellew, "Interior Monologue as Narrative Device in the Parables of Luke," *JBL* 111 (1992): 239–53.

16. Grosdidier de Matons, "Liturgie et Hymnographie," 31–44, esp. 37–39.

17. "On the Man Possessed with Devils" 22.2 [Oxf. 11] (SC 114:54–56); trans. Schork, 87–88 (modified).

18. 22.2 (SC114:58; Schork, 88 [modified]).

19. It is important to bear in mind that their dramatic content and language notwithstanding, the *kontakia* were not dramas. On this distinction, see Krueger, "Writing and Redemption."

20. Smell: "On the Sinful Woman," 21.1, 3, 7–12 [Oxf. 10]; Susan Ashbrook Harvey provides a rich analysis of these episodes in "Why the Perfume Mattered: The Sinful Woman in Syriac Exegetical Tradition," in *In Dominico Eloquio/In Lordly Eloquence: Essays on Patristic Exegesis in Honor of Robert Louis Wilken* (ed. Paul M. Blowers et al. [Grand Rapids, Mich.: Eerdmans, 2002], 69–89, esp. 81–84). Sight: "On the Baptism of Christ" 16.16 [Oxf. 5], cf. 16.10, 14, 17. Hearing: "On the Nativity II" 11 [Oxf. 2] discussed below. Taste: "On Peter's Denial" 34.5 [Oxf. 18]. Touch: "On Doubting Thomas," 46.3, 13, 17 [Oxf. 30]; cf. "The Woman with an Issue of Blood" 23.13 [Oxf. 12].

21. [Oxf. 6]; trans. Carpenter 1:57–65.

22. To grope *(psēlaphaō)* is also used to describe the blind Isaac in "Isaac and Jacob," 4.9 [Oxf. 41] (SC 99:182).

23. An apt comparison to the groping as advancement is found in Jacques Derrida's description of two drawings of blind men by Antoine Coypel (1661–1722): "Like all blind men, they must *advance,* advance or commit themselves, that is, expose themselves, run through space as if running a risk. They are apprehensive about space, they apprehend it with their groping, wandering hands" (*Memoirs of the Blind: The Self-Portrait and Other Ruins* [trans. Pascale-Anne Brault and Michael Naas; Chicago: University of Chicago Press, 1993], 5, emphasis his).

24. Cf. Bar 3:35–38.

25. Here I am inclined to follow Gary A. Anderson's remarks regarding patristic interpretations of Gen 3:7 as a transformation of the body, thereby recasting the "punishments" of Gen 3:14–19 as the effects of that changed body ("The Garments of Skin in Apocryphal Narrative," in *Studies in Ancient Midrash* [ed. James L. Kugel; Cambridge, Mass.: Harvard University Center for Jewish Studies, Harvard University Press, 2001], 101–43, esp. 135).

26. "On the Nativity I" 10 [Oxf. 1]; "On the Nativity II" 11 [Oxf. 2]; trans. Carpenter 1:13–21; "On the Nativity III" 12 [Oxf. 37= "On the Annunciation II"]; cf. Grosdidier de Matons calls "Adam and Eve" no. 1 (= Oxf. 51 ["On Fasting"]).

27. Grosdidier de Matons, *Hymnes* (SC 110:49).

28. Ibid, 79.

29. On *conceptio per aurem,* see Gary A. Anderson, *The Genesis of Perfection: Adam and Eve in Jewish and Christian Imagination* (Louisville, Ky.: Westminster John Knox Press, 2001), 92–93.

30. lines 6, 9: *opsei . . . echeis idein;* 11.18 line 3: *soi orōmai.*

31. On Eve's culpability in patristic writings, see Anderson, *Genesis of Perfection,* 99–116.

32. In this regard, Romanos is not promoting a synaesthetic experience so much as he is advancing the fullness of each discrete sense. On synaesthesia, see David Chidester, *Word and Light: Seeing, Hearing, and Religious Discourse* (Urbana: University of Illinois Press, 1992).

33. "On the Sinful Woman" 21 [Oxf. 10], trans. Lash, 77–84; cf. Mk 14:2–9; Matt 26:6–13. On this theme in biblical expansions, see Susan Ashbrook Harvey, "Spoken Words, Voiced Silence: Biblical Women in Syriac Tradition," *JECS* 9 (2001): 105–31, esp. 120–24; idem, "Why the Perfume Mattered," esp. 81–84; Sebastian Brock, "The Sinful Woman and Satan: Two Syriac Dialogue Poems," *OrChr* 72 (1988): 21–62.

34. Grosdidier de Matons, *Hymnes* (SC 110:13–14).

35. Harvey ("Why the Perfume Mattered," 83) remarks: "By attending to the variant

qualities of olfactory experiences as the homilist draws upon them, the audience is led to a richer understanding of Christ . . . a process involving change both in one's inner person and in one's external behavior."

36. Or, "I shall mix the font with weeping, oil and sweet myrrh. I shall bathe and wash myself" (21.6; Lash, *Kontakia*, 80).

37. Canaanite Woman: 21.3; cf. Matt 15:21–28; Mark 7:24–30, where she is called the Syro-Phoenician woman; Rahab: 21.7; cf. Josh 2:1–24; Hannah: 21.8; cf. 1 Sam 1:13–15.

38. In this regard, Rahab is similar to Romanos's woman (prol. 1–2), but not to Luke's prototype, whose occupation is unmentioned.

39. She cries out once to Christ. It is significant, I think, that her only direct appeal to Christ should appear in the prologue (21. prol. 2), rather than in the narrative strophes. For the strophes, Romanos reserves external dialogue for the woman and the merchant, then for Simon the Pharisee and Christ.

40. Harvey, "Why the Perfume Mattered," 81.

41. [Oxf. 22]; Lash, *Kontakia*, 155–63.

42. On the theme of the Harrowing of Hell, see *Gospel of Nicodemus* and *Questions of Bartholomew*, in *The Apocryphal New Testament: A Collection of Apocryphal Christian Literature in an English Translation* (ed. J. K. Elliott; Oxford: Clarendon, 1993), 164–204, 652–68, respectively. A helpful discussion of the theme appears in Alan E. Bernstein, *The Formation of Hell: Death and Retribution in the Ancient and Early Christian Worlds* (Ithaca, N.Y.: Cornell University Press, 1993), 272–82. More detailed analysis of the textual evidence is to be found in the excellent study by Rémi Gounelle, *La descente du Christ aux enfers: Institutionnalisation d'une croyance* (Paris: Institut d'études augusti-niennes, 2000). Also useful, J. A. MacCulloch *The Harrowing of Hell: A Comparative Study of an Early Christian Doctrine* (Edinburgh: T. & T. Clark, 1930) and Robert F. Taft, "In the Bridegroom's Absence: The Paschal Triduum in the Byzantine Church," in *La celebrazione del Triduo pasquale: Anamnesis e mimesis: Atti del II Congresso Internazio-nale di Liturgia, Roma, Pontificio Istituto Liturgico, 9–13 maggio 1988* (ed. Ildebrando Scicolone; Analecta Liturgica 14 = Studia Anselmiana 102; Rome: Pontificio Istituto Liturgico, 1990), 71–97; repr. in idem, *Liturgy in Byzantium and Beyond* (Collected Studies Series 494; Brookfield, Vt.: Ashgate, 1995). On Romanos's appropriation of the theme, see Schork, *Sacred Song*, 25–27.

43. Gounelle, *La descente du Christ aux enfers,* 161–63, 213–15.

44. Like Homer's Cyclops, Hell is portrayed as a pierced and wailing monster, whose agonized pleas are comically dismissed by countrymen (*Od.* 9. 371–412, esp. 401–12). Middle Byzantine iconography captures the visual parallels in an ivory carving of the crucifixion, see Helen C. Evans and William D. Wixom, eds., *The Glory of Byzantium: Art and Culture of the Middle Byzantine Era, A.D. 843–1261* (New York: Metropolitan Museum of Art, Harry N. Abrams, 1997), 151–52.

45. A fuller discussion on the dramatic function of silence in Greek tragedy appears in Silvia Montiglio, *Silence in the Land of Logos* (Princeton, N.J.: Princeton University Press, 2000), see esp. 158–60.

46. Luke 23:34: *pater, aphes autois, ou gar oidasin ti poiousin.*

47. *Ouk oidasin ti poiousin* (38.14 [modified]).

48. For a thought-provoking treatment of the affective and sensory response to ritualized poetry, see A. Whitney Sanford, "Painting Words, Tasting Sound: Visions of Krishna in Paramānand's Sixteenth-Century Devotional Poetry," *JAAR* 70 (2002): 55–81.

49. Cf. wounding the enemy in "On the Man Possessed with Devils" 22.2 [Oxf. 11] and the Sinful Woman's claim, "I have not seen him, but I heard and was wounded [*etrōthēn*]" (21.11). Hell is repeatedly wounded in the *kontakia*. He also suffers viscerally in "On the Raising of Lazarus I" (26.9–12 [Oxf. 14]; cf. 27.10; cf. Jer 4:19), as he bewails his indigestion that causes him to vomit the dead Lazarus.

50. On pain as stimulus and path to memory in the Christian West, see Mary

Carruthers's fascinating discussion of puncture wounds as rhetorical trope in *The Craft of Thought: Meditation, Rhetoric, and the Making of Images, 400–1200* (Cambridge Studies in Medieval Literature 34; Cambridge: Cambridge University Press, 1998), 96–97, 100–103.

51. On the concept of spiritual senses, see K. Rahner, "Le début d'une doctrine des cinq sens spirituels chez Origène," *Revue d'ascétique et de mystique* 13 (1932): 113–45; John M. Dillon, "*Aisthêsis Noêtê*: A Doctrine of Spiritual Senses in Origen and Plotinus," in *Hellenica et Judaica: Hommage à Valentin Nikiprowetzky* (ed. A. Caquot, M. Hadas-Lebel and J. Riaud; Leuven: Peeters, 1986), 443–55. Canévet, "Sens spirituel," *Dictionnaire de spiritualité* 14:599–617; Pierre Adnès, "Gout Spirituel," *Dictionnaire de spiritualité* 6: 626–44; B. Fraigneau-Julien, *Les sens spirituels et la vision de Dieu selon Syméon, le Nouveau Théologien* (Théologie historique 67; Paris: Beauchesne, 1985), 27–43.

52. On the catechetical needs of Romanos's lay audience, see Grosdidier de Matons, "Liturgie et hymnographie," 40. Romanos's hymn to the newly baptized (52 [Oxf. 51] "On Fasting") offers little explicit catechetical instructionto an audience that may have included forced converts (see Grosdidier de Matons, *Hymnes*, SC 283: 330–32).

53. A concise introduction to these works appears in E. J. Yarnold, "Baptismal Catechesis," in *The Study of Liturgy* (ed. Cheslyn Jones et al.; New York: Oxford University Press, 1992), 91–95. On the sensory dimensions of these catechetical instructions, see my " 'Taste and See': The Eucharist and the Eyes of Faith in the Fourth Century," *CH* 70 (2001): 619–43.

54. E. J. Yarnold, "The Fourth and Fifth Centuries," in *The Study of Liturgy*, 129–44, esp. 142.

55. John Chrysostom, *Catech. ult.*, in *Huit catéchèses baptismales* (ed. Antoine Wenger; SC 50; Paris: Cerf, 1957) includes the Stavronikita series (hereafter Stav.); additional homilies are known as the Papadopopulos-Kerameus series, included in *Trois catéchèses baptismales* (ed. Auguste Piédagnel; SC 366; Paris: Cerf, 1990). *Catech. ult.* (Stav.) 2.9–10 (SC 50:138), cf. 2.17, 28 (SC 50:143, 149); cf. 4.20 (SC 50:93) *to omma tês dianoias*. See also, Adam's and David's "prophetic eyes" (*Catech. ult.* [Stav.] 1.13; 3.2.25 [P-K]; SC 366:216).

56. Chrysostom's most extensive treatment appears in *Catech. ult.* (Stav.) 2.9 (SC 50: 138; *Baptismal Instructions* [trans. Paul W. Harkins; ACW 31; New York: Paulist Press, 1963], 46): "God has made for us two kinds of eyes: those of the flesh and those of faith. When you come to the sacred initiation, the eyes of the flesh see water; the eyes of faith behold the Spirit. Those eyes see the body being baptized; these see the old man being buried. The eyes of the flesh see the flesh being washed; the eyes of the spirit see the soul being cleansed. The eyes of the body see the body emerging from the water; the eyes of faith see the new man come forth brightly shining from that sacred purification. Our bodily eyes see the priest as, from above, he lays his right hand on the head and touches [him who is being baptized]; our spiritual eyes see the great High Priest as He stretches forth His invisible Hand to touch his head." Cf. *Catech. ult.* 3.3.9–22 [P-K] (SC 366:220–22; ACW 31: 164 [= Hom. 11.11–12]).

57. (SC 110:58) *astēr men estin pros to phainomenon, dynamis de tis pros to nooumenon.*

58. (SC 128:326; MC I:241–42). Cf. SC 114:24.1 (visible bread); man born blind receives eyes of senses and of soul, SC 114:140 25.1; eyes of mud, SC 114:25.2; opened the eye of his heart, SC 128:36 39.2; SC 283:49 (divine nature beyond senses). The term appears in a hymn falsely attributed to Romanos, "The Man Born Blind," in which the soloist confesses that his own "eyes of the soul" are maimed *(tēs psychēs ta ommata peptērōmenos)*. Cf. *ophthalmous men aisthētous apolambanei kai tous tēs psychēs* 25. prol. [Oxf. 88] (SC 114:138), see Grosdidier de Matons, *Hymnes* (SC 114: 134–35).

59. René Bornert, *Les commentaires byzantins de la divine liturgie, du VIIe au XVe siècle* (Archives de l'Orient chrétien; Paris: Institut français d'études byzantines, 1966).

Part III

TEACHING RELIGIOUS SELVES

—10—

From Master of Wisdom to
Spiritual Master in Late Antiquity

GUY G. STROUMSA

In his last set of lectures at the Collège de France, delivered shortly before his death, Michel Foucault defined it as his goal to describe and to explain the transmission of Hellenistic and Roman conceptions of the self to Christianity. Foucault rightly estimated that the process of this transmission was of prime importance for the future history of Europe. Although he was able to discern some major points of similarity and difference between "pagan" and Christian views of the self, he did not live to develop his intuitions into a sustained comparative study. The recent publication of these lectures, *L'herméneutique du sujet*, allows us to make a more precise assessment of both his achievements and his shortcomings.[1]

Foucault realized the importance of Christian anthropological conceptions and understood them correctly as rooted in a religious worldview. He disregarded, however, the Jewish origin and the essentially Jewish nature of this worldview, thus depriving himself of the means to offer a correct analysis of the new view of the self. The crystallization of a new anthropology in late antiquity cannot be understood solely as an internal development within Greco-Roman culture and society. In what follows, I will focus on the figure of the intellectual and spiritual teacher in late antiquity as a case study exemplifying the passage from pagan to Christian conceptions of the self and its implications.

*   *   *

When the great rhetorician Libanius was asked on his deathbed which one of his disciples should be considered as his successor, he answered: "John would have been my successor, had the Christians not snatched him." This vignette

alludes to the conversion of John of Antioch, "the most holy John," as Theodoretus calls him, a disciple of Libanius who had also studied with the philosopher Andragathius. Stemming from a noble family, John had planned to
become a lawyer. After his conversion, however, he abandoned his previous
plans and persuaded his disciples Theodore of Mopsuestia and Maximus of
Seleucia to renounce the life of affluent merchants and to choose a life of
simplicity. The story of this conversion, as summarized by Sozomenus, shows
to what extent, toward the end of the fourth century, the passage from pagan
wisdom to Christian spirituality was both possible and easy.[2]

I have juxtaposed, too schematically, pagan wisdom to Christian spirituality on purpose. The life of thought and spirit is of course infinitely more
complex. One can certainly also speak of pagan spirituality and of Christian
wisdom; however, my intention here is to underline mainly the vectors, the
main trends. The issue at hand is a rather understudied aspect of the Christianization of the elites in the Roman Empire and of its anthropological
consequences.

Identity, which in the Hellenistic world had been defined, first of all, in
cultural and linguistic terms, became essentially religious in the Roman Empire. This change amounted to nothing less than a revolution in the criteria of
identity. This revolution was also reflected in the educational patterns of elites,
in the modes of transmission of knowledge and of intellectual and spiritual
power. The Christian elites knew, perhaps better than others, how to adapt to
the cultural frameworks of the Roman Empire, and they adapted these frameworks to their spiritual demands and needs, in particular to their own educational traditions. In the Christianized empire, the education of the traditional
elites (both the cultural and the social elites) would remain more or less identical to what it had been in the pagan empire. The clearer and most drastic
change occurred within the new, purely Christian monastic movement, which
radically broke from the traditional forms of elite education. A complete picture of the new forms of spiritual formation in early Christianity remains
beyond the scope of this essay, which will be limited to some expressions of the
monastic movement and will not deal with the Christian *didaskalia* or with
theological schools such as the one in Alexandria.

Although "spiritual direction" is a modern concept invented by post-
Tridentine Catholicism,[3] it is legitimately used to describe a phenomenon already present in the formative period of Christianity in the Roman Empire. The
term may be modern, but not the phenomenon. Spiritual direction represents a
central aspect of religious practice in late antiquity, from Roman and Con-
stantinopolitan aristocratic society to the monks of the Egyptian desert. No less
important than the existence of the phenomenon itself, however, is the fact that
this spiritual direction was expressed rather differently in the various cultural
and religious milieus: among cultural elites and in humbler social strata, in
cities and in the desert, among pagans and Christians. We thus find a series of

different attitudes, which express various aspects of spiritual direction in late antiquity.[4] Conversion, the passage from philosophy to monasticism (which was defined by its early theoreticians as "true philosophy"[5]), entails some significant transformations of the person. These transformations reflect the radical character of the Christian revolution.

Without denying the evident elements of continuity between Greco-Roman and Early Christian thought, we must recognize a major discontinuity in the very concept of person that is closely related to some fundamental traits of Christian theology. I have sought elsewhere to analyze these traits. They are linked to the implications, direct and indirect, of the relationship of body/soul in a religion that insisted, like Judaism, on the unity of man, created by God as the conjunction of soul and body, and expecting the resurrection of the body. The incarnation of Jesus Christ, however, adds power and urgency to this anthropology. Manifestly, such an anthropology went against various current or acceptable Greek conceptions (in particular the Platonic ones), according to which the human being was first of all the human soul or mind.[6]

Here I shall approach this transformation from the particular angle of spiritual direction. My intention is to examine the conditions under which spiritual direction was possible, and what it meant. I shall try, in particular, to identify the differences in the relationship between master and disciple among pagans and Christians. Oddly enough, such a comparison does not seem to have been attempted until now.

Arnaldo Momigliano once noted that "the type of priest who is also a spiritual director and a confessor remains almost unknown in Greece and in Rome until the oriental religions come to replace the old cults." "A part-time priest," he added, "is not likely to become an effective spiritual guide."[7] Momigliano's remark is only half true, and it puts us on the wrong track, it seems to me, by suggesting we look for the origins of spiritual direction in a "full-time priesthood." Spiritual direction in the ancient world is not related to priesthood. The spiritual master is by nature opposed to the priest. For as a religious functionary in charge of daily cult, the priest does not care for restless souls and does not help them, intensely and individually, in their search for salvation.

Because there was no such thing as a "pagan spiritual leadership" in antiquity, it is probably in the direction of prophecy that one should look for the origin of spiritual direction. In ancient Israel, it was the prophet (and the apocalyptic writer under the second temple) who appealed to the individual and insisted on the demands of personal responsibility, ethical as well as religious. A Talmudic passage seems to corroborate this view (*b. B. Bat.* 12a). The rabbis discuss the respective merits of the prophet and the sage. The prophet is the hero of a time-hallowed tradition, as reflected in the biblical books. For the rabbis, however, the gates of prophecy have been closed for a long time. The sage, on the other hand, represents the urgent intellectual and spiritual needs of the present. The rabbis thus conclude that the sage is superior to the prophet (*ḥakam ʿadip mi-navi):* this represents a victory of the moderns over the ancients, too rare in Judaism as elsewhere. Note that the priest is not seriously considered in this context, for his role has become merely symbolic. After the destruction of the temple, indeed, the priest had no function. But even prior to that destruction, his role remained limited to temple cult. The sages, successors of the prophets, became the *exempla* of elitism.[8]

Scholars of spiritual direction (or what the Germans call *Seelenführung*) in the ancient world, and in particular in the Roman world, have sought to compare philosophical and patristic or monastic texts.[9] Oddly enough, the role of the Talmudic sage and his relationship with his best students (the *talmidê ḥakamim*) has not been compared either to that of the abbot, or *gerōn*, or to that of the philosopher.[10] One wonders at this strange absence of the Talmudic sage in the comparative history of the formation of elites in the Roman world.[11] It is, after all, in synagogues and not in philosophical schools that Jesus and Paul preached, and it is around the *bêt ha-midrash* that they had received their education.[12] To be sure, the Talmudic sage is not the exact equivalent of the monastic spiritual guide. Nevertheless, even a superficial analysis of the sage's status would easily detect numerous and significant parallels with the role and ways of both the philosopher and the hegumen.

Side by side with his properly didactic role, the Talmudic sage is also a spiritual master. Or rather, for the rabbi (the Talmudic sage), just as for the philosopher (the Hellenic sage), the path of wisdom is also a spiritual path. In the frame of rabbinic education, way of life and patterns of teaching are as intertwined as in the philosophical schools. Indeed, Elias Bickerman once suggested that we see the Talmudic schools of thought as an imitation of the various Greek philosophical schools.[13] In a sense, the rabbi's role appears to be a combination of the didactics of the pagan teacher and the spiritual guidance of the Christian teacher. Like the latter, the rabbi sees it as his role to care for the formation of those whom Max Weber called "religious virtuosi." One should note, however, the complexity of the picture in Israel in the first century of our era. From Qumran to the Pharisees, through priests, scribes, and magicians, solutions to the relationship between master and disciple varied greatly.

The following pages, however, have a different task: that of outlining, at least roughly, a comparative phenomenological analysis of the master-disciple relationship among pagan philosophers and the Christian "new philosophers," the monks.[14] In other words, I shall seek to describe the transformation of one kind of personal authority and elite formation into another. Phenomenological analysis, which emphasizes the major trends, must avoid simplistic taxonomies; thus, the various intellectual and charismatic elements are probably to be found among the different groups. What distinguishes elite formation among Jews, pagans, and Christians is mainly the relative weight of intellectual and soteriological tendencies within the internal equilibrium of the system.

One should underline the element of rupture with the past, rather than that of continuity in early Christianity. This is true regarding the transmission of both cultural traditions and religious ideals. The paramount importance of charisma and the weakening of intellectual tradition among the disciples of Jesus represent notable landmarks here. So are the Pauline epistles, which preach a revolt against ideas of knowledge and wisdom as they were understood by both in the Pharisaic teaching of his youth and in contemporary Greco-Roman philosophical *koinē*. It is within such a perspective that one can first discern the roots of subsequent Christian spiritual direction. Only at the end of the second century would the idea of a school of thought similar to the Greek philosophical schools, at least in its fundamental structures, appear among some Christian intellectuals (in particular Clement of Alexandria and Origen). This would bring, in the third and fourth centuries, the rise of two competing models of religious virtuosity. On the one hand, the gnostic model, with its ideal of contemplation, of *theiois;* on the other hand, the holy man, the ideal of *askēsis,* of *imitatio Christi.* To be sure, these two models do not oppose one another in a radical fashion. The patristic authors even often tell us that one leads to the other, that one can reach saving knowledge *(gnōsis)* only through faith *(pistis).* Nonetheless, we can clearly identify here two distinct intentions, two different vectors.

Spiritual direction, as it is found among the desert monks from the fourth century on, bears only a vague resemblance to the role of the theologian-teacher in third century Alexandria or Caesarea. The whole didactic and intellectual element, which was so central in the Christian "schools," seems to have disappeared from early monastic literature. Following the Jews, the Christians had picked up the Greek idea of *paideia*—and had transformed it.[15] Among the monks, wisdom is only found in a metaphorical, weak sense. It is not even identical with the new Christian wisdom, which the church fathers call "true gnosis" (in contradistinction to the false *gnōsis* of the heretics) and whose strong soteriological character differentiates it at once from Jewish and from Greek wisdom.

It is tempting to see the growth of the spiritual element in the teacher-disciple relationship among the Christians as related to the shrinking of the intellectual dimension. It is perhaps more helpful, however, to stress the new direction in which the formation of the new Christian elites evolves. Spiritual direction appears most clearly where personal charisma is most important and where the intellectual element remains limited. The idea of spiritual direction grows precisely with the weakening of the intellectual dimension in teaching and as the power of the individual (at least the elite individual) to find within himself and by himself the way to his personal salvation diminishes. One sees, then, how much spiritual direction reflects a deep mutation of ancient culture.

In order to better understand the Christian novelty, let us first observe some aspects of the teaching of Greek wisdom, common to the various philosophical schools. The philosopher (the "pagan" sage) may not be a real spiritual master in the Christian sense of the word. Nevertheless, the "master of wisdom" is a traditional and well-established figure in the Roman world, a sage standing in front of a few disciples, to whom he offers an oral teaching based on a series of texts.

The search for the origins of the idea of spiritual direction in the Greek philosophical tradition should go back to the great formative period from the seventh to the fourth centuries B.C.E. Socrates is of course the main figure of reference. He is the first to have established dialogue, and hence personal and privileged relations between master and disciple, as the foundation of any teaching of wisdom. But the master's authority would grow mainly in the leading Hellenistic philosophical schools. Consider, for instance, Epicurus, who is referred to explicitly as *hēgemōn,* guide, in the writings emanating from his teaching, such as in his third letter, the *Letter to Menoeceus.* The complex transformation of philosophy under the Roman Empire deeply modifies teaching in the various schools. Doctrines and methods mix, in particular among the Stoics and the Platonists, who establish themselves as the two leading schools. This transformation dramatically emphasizes the soteriological dimension of philosophy. To become the disciple of a philosopher means, more and more (and, from the third century on, under growing Christian influence), to confide in him in order to find the way of personal salvation.

As A. D. Nock showed in his seminal study on conversion, one speaks in antiquity about conversion to philosophy as one speaks of religious conversion. This conversion entails not only the acceptance of new doctrines but also that of a strictly structured way of life, including alimentary and clothing rules, and the submission to a master.[16] The transformation of philosophy will be finally accomplished with Proclus, for whom the *Chaldaean Oracles,* that strange mixture of cavernous verbosity, became the staple of philosophical diet, together with Plato. Epictetus and Marcus Aurelius represent key moments in this history, but I have chosen Seneca to illustrate our theme. Seneca is contemporaneous with Paul—we even possess an interesting apocryphal correspondence between them.[17] Christian writers would call him "Seneca, saepe noster," thus revealing a certain "family resemblance" between the tone of his writing and that of their own, at least regarding anthropology and ethics.

The Stoic sage, as he appears in Seneca's writings (especially in his admirable *Letters to Lucilius*), does not shun ordinary people, from whom he differs drastically. On the contrary, he agrees to appear in public, although he does not make an exhibition of himself: "Act so as your retreat may be seen, though without attracting looks. [*Id age, ut otium tuum non emineat, sed appareat*]" (*Lucil.* 2.19.2). As Paul Veyne writes in his brilliant introduction to Seneca's prose writings, the Stoic sage is a "man-doctrine." It is with formulas from religious language that Seneca describes the sage: he shows the way toward *securitas,* toward wisdom. This permits him to neutralize troubling passions (*apatheia*) and to reach total peace of the soul in face of the passions and storms of the world (*hēsychia*, which will become one of the main goals of the Christian monk).[18] The true Stoic sage transforms himself in a radical way, enacting a real transfiguration, rather than accomplishing some moral or intellectual progress: "*Intellego, Lucili, non emendari me tantum sed transfigurari*" (*Lucil.* 6.1). He thus reaches a real divinization: "You must recognize that the sage has in himself something divine, celestial, splendid. [*Des opportet illi divinum aliquid, caeleste, magnificum*]" (*Lucil.* 9.87.19). He becomes, as it were, a heavenly figure similar, *mutatis mutandis*, to the Confucian sage, as pointed out by Veyne.[19] One may perhaps detect here the trace of the strong influence exerted by Neo-Pythagoreanism upon Seneca (hence his vegetarianism). In the Pythagorean tradition, Pythagoras, the very *exemplum* of the sage, was in intimate contact with the divinity.[20]

Such a sage is in no need of any kind of spiritual guidance. What he does need is the presence of another sage with whom he may discuss and reflect (*Lucil.* 18.109). Practically, meeting such a sage is very rare, as Seneca knows well.[21] Lucilius, Seneca himself, and all of us can only hope, in our weakness, to reach the status of disciples of wisdom. We thus need to put our trust in a master of wisdom, who will show us the way to follow, through his teaching, but also through his example.[22] "Meantime, the man who is still imperfect, but is doing progress, needs to be shown the way in order to behave in life" (*Lucil.* 15.50). "He needs to be directed, as long as he only begins to be able to govern himself. In order to educate children, we put them in front of a model" (*Lucil.* 15.51). Pierre Hadot insists that the real question here is not *what* one talks about, but *who* talks. The Stoic master of wisdom thus appears to his closest disciples as a true model, a living *exemplum*, with the power of this term in the Christian intellectual tradition.[23] One can observe the same phenomenon among the Neo-Pythagoreans as reflected, for instance, in Porphyry's *Life of Pythagoras,* and even more in the one written by Iamblichus.[24]

But who are the disciples of the philosopher? What is this elite that he is supposed to educate and form? Up to late Neoplatonism, the philosophical schools do not really have fixed structures. It is less a matter of buildings and institutions than of persons. If the master disappears, everything collapses. It is the relationship between master and student that creates the school, through teaching and learning, model and following.[25] But this teaching, the observation of this example, is not free of charge. The students of wisdom are hence those whose parents can afford such an education. Intellectual and spiritual elites are being recruited in the privileged socioeconomic classes—only, that is, within the urban elites. The observation of this sociological phenomenon points to one of the essential differences with regard to education between the Hellenic tradition and that of both Jews and Christians.

In the ancient world, spiritual direction was thus inscribed in a preexisting social link: urban elites.[26] While Christian intellectuals and teachers from the second century on do not scorn to proselytize among these elites in Alexandria,

Rome, or elsewhere, these elites are in no way the single or privileged field of their efforts. Christian propaganda reflects the tension, noted long ago by Troeltsch, between two opposite tendencies, between the desire for cultural continuity and that for religious novelty. It is this desire of religious novelty that permits the Christians to make good use of new forms of expression, such as the codex, rather than the traditional scroll.[27] Those among the Christian thinkers whom we can identify as radicals seek to abolish traditional social links. The society they want to build is an ideal one, an anti-city, whose model they will establish in the desert in the fourth century. The teaching of these new masters of wisdom is, first of all, free of charge. Thus Justin Martyr, in the first chapters of his *Dialogue with Trypho,* written before 150, describing his quest for a real school of wisdom and truth, rejects the Aristotelian philosopher because he will teach only for a fee. The teaching of true wisdom should be free of charge and offered to all equally. In this school of a new kind, instead of tuition fees, a total commitment is demanded of the student, entailing a radical break with the realm of the city, that of ideas as well as of passions.

This is not to say that there was no existential commitment in philosophical schools. There too, it is a way of life that one was asked to choose. But for the philosophers, this way of life permitted them to devote themselves to a life of ideas, to epistemological reflection. For the first Christian thinkers and for the desert fathers after them in the fourth century, philosophy is already, much before the medieval scholastics, *ancilla theologiae.* Even more powerfully, Theodoretus will be able to say in the fifth century—in Marxist fashion, as it were—that while the Greek philosophers have offered explanations of the world, the monks, philosophers of a new kind, propose to transform it.

It is thus a new kind of wisdom that Christian thinkers from Paul on offer, a paradoxical wisdom, madness for the wise of this world (1 Cor 1:18–25). The first Christian teachers are often martyrs, like Justin Martyr, Pionios (who is called *didaskalos*), or Origen; hence, the importance of Socrates in patristic literature, a figure well studied, long ago, by Harnack.

It has often been said that the Christian school of Alexandria claims to be a philosophical school.[28] At least it appears to be one, since Christian thinkers want to present a legitimate alternative to Hellenic intellectuals. But the wisdom they seek is of quite a different nature, and so are the ways to seek it. *Sōtēria* is the goal much more than *epistēmē.* To be sure, one comments on the texts (the biblical texts rather than those of Plato or Aristotle), but the aim is to put them into practice in order to be saved. The new wisdom is less dialectical than apodictic in nature. This transformation goes a long way in explaining the development of the literary genre of apophthegms among the monks.

"Tell me a word, that I might be saved." This phrase of the *Apophthegmata Patrum* encapsulates the role of the Christian teacher: he is the one who permits his disciple, the monk, enrolled in the new school and totally involved in it, to achieve his goal of personal salvation. The nature of the teacher's word is no longer explanatory, putting the disciple on the track of intellectual autonomy. This word has acquired quite a different authority and power. The role of the Christian teacher is thus quite different from that of the philosopher, the master of wisdom. He does not guide his disciple only in order to let him follow his way, but he accompanies his disciple in his quest for salvation until he reaches his goal. His role is no longer contingent. He is no longer someone simply more advanced in the path whose teaching helps the disciple. The coinage "spiritual master" refers not to a vague spirituality but rather to the different mode of his activity.

The new wisdom is anti-intellectual by nature, as shown by the transformation of the concept of *logismos*. In the literature stemming from the monastic milieus, even with an intellectual like Evagrius Ponticus, *logismoi* have become evil thoughts (all thoughts are evil!) that invade the monk's mind, preventing him from reaching salvation. The goal of the spiritual master, then, is to chase these thoughts away, to prevent the disciple from thinking for himself. On the other hand, one must insist on the central role of the conflict with demons in ascetic life. In monastic literature, this conflict is a real metaphor of ascetic life.[29] We should note the radical transformation effected since the time of the Greco-Roman master of wisdom. The power of the spiritual master over his disciple now seems to be total. One can follow the emergence and development of the new form of authority being thus developed among the monks.[30] This new pattern of authority is parallel to that of the bishop, with which it sometimes conflicts.

Prima facie, this transformation of spiritual authority may look surprising in a religion established on evangelical *logoi* such as "Do not give anyone the name of Father!" (Matt 23:9). And yet the desert fathers, heirs to the Pharisaic fathers, have an authority that the Pharisians, like the philosophers, never had. This authority stems from the fact that there is almost no knowledge to communicate, or methods of thinking to teach. Even the sacred texts are not necessarily perceived as texts to be mastered. Athanasius' *Life of Antony*, for instance, perhaps the most influential Christian text after the New Testament, reflects an attitude of deep ambiguity toward the study of Scripture. In his discussion of what monks must know about Scripture, Abba Isaiah of Gaza praises ignorance (*agnoia*), which draws the monk near God (*Ascetic Discourses* 6). Antony becomes in the desert "a father for the monks in the surroundings."[31] Utterances of the Christian fathers have received a quasi-magical power, ensuring salvation on the spot. The spiritual director is less a sage than a saint.[32] In this sense, he is the image of divine perfection. The evangelical injunction: "Be perfect, as your heavenly Father is perfect!" (Matt 5:46) can be followed through the imitation of the saint, the intermediary model.

Perhaps the clearest example of the spiritual master's new function is that of Barsanuphius, in the desert of Gaza. His letters constitute the richest corpus of the literary genre of spiritual direction. I shall only allude to this corpus here, as it is at the present being seriously studied from various viewpoints. Lorenzo Perrone, for instance, has recently called attention to the suppression of will and the importance of the master's advice as they are reflected in the correspondence between Barsanuphius and John of Gaza. Perrone notes that in the ancient monastic system of spiritual direction, pedagogical experience informs the whole life of the teacher as well as that of the disciple.[33]

This paradox, namely, the relative weakness of knowledge in the new teaching, is not easily explained. And yet I cannot but ask myself if the new power of Christian speech does not originate in the religious structures of Christianity. For these structures, almost unknown elsewhere in the ancient world, there is no salvation except through an intermediary, a *mesitēs*, a teacher at once human and divine. Another evangelical logos justifies the great power of the master, a disciple of Jesus: "Who listens to you listens to me!" (Luke 10:16). As is well shown, for instance, in the texts of Dorotheus of Gaza, the desert master relays the divine master, as exemplified by Moses (see Gregory of Nyssa's *Life of Moses*). For the latter, the spiritual master must destroy self-confidence in his disciple: "He lived in the monastery for five years, without having ever done, in any way, his own will, or having been moved by passion."[34]

Obedience to the spiritual father does not simply mean submission to authority, however, but is established upon faith, confidence, and love.[35] The pagan master of wisdom has absolutely no need of a disciple; he can return at any time to his personal reflection and abandon humanity to its fate. The Christian spiritual master, on the other hand, is closely tied to his disciples from an existential point of view. He is worth as much or as little as they are, and his own salvation depends on theirs. Abba Isaiah explains to his disciples that if they practice his precepts, he will ask God on their behalf. If they do not, however, God will not only ask them to account for their negligence but will also accuse Isaiah of being useless.[36] John Cassian, who carried to the West the methods and the goals of Eastern monasticism, tells us similar things: "It is your diligence, my children, which brought me to such long speeches, and I feel that a mysterious fire gives my teaching more soul and more warmth, to the very measure of your desire." Or else: "The more I detect in you demanding zeal for your belief, the more I must exert myself in accomplishing my duty."[37]

The phenomenological analysis of the relationship between master and disciple has dealt here only with some of its aspects. But it exemplifies the true transformation of the status of the self in late antiquity. This transformation, which came with the victory of Christianity, upset the relationship between master and disciple as it was known among Jewish and pagan sages alike. The recognition of such a transformation means that we do not see in Evagrius simply "a philosopher in the desert," as Antoine Guillaumont has called him.[38] For Evagrius, the gnostic has only one goal in his teaching (a goal ignored by the philosopher): he must teach salvation.[39] Even as deep a thinker and independent a mind as Evagrius, then, remains first of all a spiritual master. Only metaphorically can one still speak of a master of wisdom. With the conversion of the empire to Christianity, we witness a real mutation of the relationship between master and disciple, at least in monastic milieus, where the element of parting of the ways of cultural traditions prevails over that of continuity. The historical paradox, then, is perhaps that it was precisely the monastic movement that would be the main carrier of the ancient intellectual heritage into the Middle Ages.

NOTES

1. Michel Foucault, *L'herméneutique du sujet: Cours au Collège de France (1981–1982)* (Hautes études; Paris: Gallimard, 2001). A former version was presented to the Research Group "From Hellenistic Judaism to Christian Hellenism" at the Institute of Advanced Studies of the Hebrew University of Jerusalem in May 2001. A French version, "Du maître de sagesse au maître de spiritualité," was published in *Maestro e discepolo: Temi e problemi della direzione spirituale tra VI secolo a.C. e VII secolo d.C* (ed. Giovanni Filoramo; Le scienze umane 2.1; Brescia: Morcelliana, 2002), 13–24.

2. Sozomenus, *Hist. eccl.* 8.2 (PG 67:1513b-1519b); Theodoretus, *Hist. eccl.* 5.40 (*Kirchengeschicte* [ed. Léon Parmentier; 3rd ed.; GCS, NF 5; Berlin: Akademie-Verlag, 1998] 347); Socrates, *Hist. eccl.* 6.3 (PG 67:665a-668a). These texts are analyzed by André Jean Festugière, *Antioche païenne et chrétienne: Libanius, Chrysostome et les moines de Syrie* (Bibliothèque des Écoles françaises d'Athènes et de Rome 194; Paris: E. de Boccard, 1959), 181. I should like to thank Brouria Bitton-Ashkelony for reminding me of Festugière's book and for her remarks on a previous version of this text.

3. See, for instance, J.-P. Schaller, "Direction spirituelle," in *Dictionnaire critique de théologie* (ed. Jean-Yves Lacoste and Paul Beauchamp; Paris: Presses Universitaires de France, 1998), 336–38.

4. See J. Hevelone Harper, "Spiritual Direction," in *Late Antiquity: A Guide to the Post Classical World* (ed. G. W. Bowersock, Peter Brown, and Oleg Grabar; Harvard University Press Reference Library; Cambridge, Mass.: Belknap, 1999), 704–5.

5. See Anne-Marie Malingrey, *'Philosophia': Étude d'un groupe de mots dans la littétature grecque, des Présocratiques au IVe siècle après J.-C.* (Études et commentaires 40; Paris: C. Klincksieck, 1961).

6. See G. G. Stroumsa, *Barbarian Philosophy: the Religious Revolution of Early Christianity* (WUNT 112; Tübingen: Mohr Siebeck, 1999), 132–56. The transformation of ethics represents another aspect of what I have called the religious revolution of early Christianity. On this topic, see Paul Veyne, "Païens et chrétiens devant la gladiature," *Mélanges de l'École française de Rome: Antiquité* 111 (1999): 883–917. Veyne insists on the decisive newness of the Christian ethics of interiority.

7. Arnaldo Momigliano, "Seneca Between Political and Contemplative Life," in *Quarto contributo alla storia degli studi classici e del mondo antico* (Storia e letteratura 115; Rome: Edizioni di storia e letteratura, 1969), 239–65 (written in 1950). Cf. G. G. Stroumsa, "Arnaldo Momigliano and the History of Religions," in P. N. Miller, ed., *A. Momigliano and the Antiquarian Foundations of Modern Cultural History* (Toronto: University of Toronto Press, forthcoming).

8. See Efraim E. Urbach, "The People of Israel and Its Sages," in *The Sages: Their Concepts and Beliefs* (trans. Israel Abrahams; Cambridge, Mass.: Harvard University Press, 1987), 525–648; cf. idem, *Class-Status and Leadership in the World of the Palestin-*

ian Sages (Proceedings of the Israel Academy of Sciences and Humanities 2.4; Jerusalem: The Israel Academy of Sciences and Humanities, 1966) (Hebrew). On rabbinic attitudes toward prophecy, see idem, "When Did Prophecy End?" *Tarbiz* 17 (1946): 1–11 (Hebrew).

9. See in particular Pierre Hadot, "Exercices spirituels antiques et 'philosophie chrétienne,'" in *Exercices spirituels et philosophie antique* (Paris: Études augustiennes, 1981), 59–74. Hadot points out that what was for the philosophers an exercise of ethical nature becomes with the Christians a spiritual exercise (60), adding that the ideas of penance and obedience totally transform the philosophical practice of spiritual direction (73–74). See further idem, "The Spiritual Guide," in *Classical Mediterranean Spirituality: Egyptian, Greek, Roman* (ed. A. H. Armstrong; New York: Crossroad, 1988), 436–59, which treats the problem in the *longue durée*, throughout antiquity. For the philosophical tradition, see mainly Ilsetraut Hadot, *Seneca und die griechisch-römische Tradition der Seelenleitung* (Quellen und Studien zur Geschichte der Philosophie 13; Berlin: de Gruyter, 1969); and before her, Paul Rabbow, *Seelenführung: Methodik der Exerzitien in der Antike* (Munich: Kösel-Verlag, 1954) [*non vidi*].

10. See Elias Bickerman, "The Historical Foundations of Post-Biblical Judaism," in *The Jews, Their History* (ed. Louis Finkelstein; 4th ed.; New York: Schocken Books, 1970), 111: "Post-Maccabean Judaism adopted the most important idea of Hellenism, that of *paideia*, of perfection through liberal education."

11. See, for instance, the entries on "Direction spirituelle" in *Dictionnaire de spiritualité* 3:1002–214, where much attention is given to the phenomenon in Greece and in Rome, but where Judaism is wholly absent.

12. On this topic, see the remarks of K. H. Rengstorf, "*Didaskô, ktl,*" *TDNT* 2:135–65, on the Hellenistic origins of the concept of *rav* in that of *didaskalos.*

13. See n. 10 above. One may consider the relationship between master and disciple in Judaism as reflecting the direct influence of Greek models. See for instance K. H. Rengstorf, "*Manthanō, ktl,*" *TDNT* 4:390–461, esp. 439.

14. For a comparative study of spiritual direction among pagans and Christians in the third century, see Richard Valantasis, *Spiritual Guides of the Third Century: A Semiotic Study of the Guide-Disciple Relationship in Christianity, Neoplatonism, Hermetism, and Gnosticism* (HDR 27; Minneapolis: Fortress, 1991). Valantasis mainly studies four texts, the *Speech of Thanks to Origen* by Gregory the Wonderworker, Porphyry's *Life of Plotinus,* and two texts from Nag Hammadi, *On the Eighth and the Ninth,* and *Allogenes.*

15. See Henri Irénée Marrou, "Le christianisme et l'éducation classique," in *Histoire de l'éducation dans l'antiquité* (Collections esprit; Paris: Éditions de Seuil, 1948), 416–34. See further, Werner William Jaeger, *Early Christianity and Greek Paideia* (Cambridge, Mass.: Belknap, 1961).

16. Arthur Darby Nock, *Conversion: The Old and the New in Religion from Alexander the Great to Augustine of Hippo* (London: Oxford University Press, 1933).

17. See Laura Bocciolini Palagi, *Epistolario apocrifo di Seneca e San Paolo* (Biblioteca Patristica 5; Florence: Nardini, 1985).

18. Seneca, *Lucil.* 5.52.3: "Some, says Epicurus, have reached virtue without anybody's help; they found their way themselves [*fecisse sibi ipsos viam*]" (Epicurus, *Frag.* 192). For *securitas,* see Veyne, introduction to *Entretiens; Lettres à Lucilius* (Paris: R. Laffont, 1993), xlv.

19. Cf. Hubert Cancik and Hildegard Cancik-Lindemaier, "Senecas Konstruktion des Sapiens: Zur Sakralisierung der Rolle des Weisen im 1. Jh. n. Chr.," in *Weisheit* (ed. Aleida Assmann; Archäologie der literarischen Kommunikation 3; Munich: W. Fink Verlag, 1991), 205–22.

20. So does Iamblichus in particular, represent him in his *Vita Pythagorae.* See

Iamblichus, *On the Pythagorean Way of Life* (ed. and trans. John Dillon and Jackson Hershbell; Atlanta, Ga.: Scholars Press, 1991), 2.

21. Similarly, Porphyry will note in his *Vita Plotini* (ch. 23) that his teacher had reached the mystical experience of unification with the divine only four times in his lifetime.

22. *Lucil.* 94. 50: the sage is helpful to those who lack self-confidence. "The very meeting of a sage does good. Some inner progress can result even from the silent presence of a great soul" (Ibid., 40).

23. See Peter Brown, "The Saint as Exemplar in Late Antiquity," *Representations* 1 (1983): 1–25.

24. Rather than a life of Pythagoras, this last text presents in effect a model of Pythagorean lifestyle. See, for instance, Dillon and Hershbell, *On the Pythagorean Way of Life*. Cf. Iamblichus, *Vie de Pythagore* (ed. and trans. L. Brisson and A. Ph. Segonds; Roue à livres; Paris: Les belles lettres, 1996).

25. Garth Fowden, "The Platonist Philosopher and His Circle in Late Antiquity," *Philosophia* 7 (1977): 359–83, who points out that the disciples tended not to maintain the group identity after the master's death; cf. Joseph Bidez, "Le philosophe Jamblique et son école," *REG* 32 (1919): 29–40.

26. See Veyne in *Entretiens, Lettres à Lucilius,* 596. When Origen is expelled from Alexandria by bishop Demetrios, his whole "School of Advanced Religious Studies," as Marrou calls it, collapses (Marrou, *Histoire de l'éducation,* 2.145).

27. See G. G. Stroumsa, "Early Christianity: A Religion of the Book?" in *Homer, the Bible and Beyond: Literary and Religious Canons in Ancient Societies* (ed. Margalit Finkelberg and G. G. Stroumsa; Jerusalem Studies in Religion and Culture 2; Leiden: Brill, 2002), 153–74.

28. See Robert L. Wilken, "Alexandria: A School for Training in Virtue," in *Schools of Thought in the Christian Tradition* (ed. Patrick Henry; Philadelphia: Fortress, 1984), 15–30.

29. See David Brakke, "The Making of Monastic Demonology: Three Ascetic Teachers on Withdrawal and Resistance," *CH* 70 (2001): 19–48.

30. See Philip Rousseau, *Ascetics, Authority, and the Church in the Age of Jerome and Cassian* (Oxford: Oxford University Press, 1978), 21–32. See further, Graham Gould, *The Desert Fathers on Monastic Community* (Oxford Early Christian Studies; Oxford: Clarendon, 1993), 26–87.

31. Athanasius, *Vit. Ant.* 15–16 (*Vie d'Antoine* [ed. and trans. G. J. M. Bartelink; SC 400; Paris: Cerf, 1994], 176–81).

32. See, for instance, Douglas Burton-Christie, *The Word in the Desert: Scripture and the Quest for Holiness in Early Christian Monasticism* (Oxford: Oxford University Press, 1993).

33. L. Perrone, "The Necessity of Advice: Spiritual Direction as a School of Christianity in the Correspondence of Barsanuphius and John of Gaza," in *Christian Gaza in Late Antiquity* (ed. B. Bitton-Ashkelony and A. Kofsky; Jerusalem Studies in Religion and Culture, 3; Leiden: Brill, 2004).

34. Dorotheus of Gaza, *Vita Dosithei* 9 (*Ouevres spirituelles* [ed. and trans. L. Regnault and J. de Preville; SC 92; Paris: Cerf, 1963], 136–37).

35. As pointed out by Jean-Claude Larchet, *Thérapeutique des maladies spirituelles: Une introduction à la tradition ascétique de l'Eglise orthodoxe* (Collection l'arbre de Jesse; Suresnes: Les éditions de l'ancre, 1993), 548. Larchet insists on the therapeutic role of the spiritual father (523–51).

36. Isaiah, *Ascetic Discourses* 1 (*Ascetikón: Vida y doctrina de los padres desierto* [trans. Manuel A. Arrojo; Madrid: Caparrós Editores, 1994], 21).

37. John Cassian, *Conferences* 1.22; 2.1 in *Conférences* (ed. and trans. E. Pichery; SC 42; Paris: Cerf, 1955), 107, 111.

38. See A. Guillaumont, "Evagre le Pontique: Un philosophe au désert," in *Aux origines du monachisme chrétien* (Spiritualité orientale 30; Bégrolles en Mauges: Abbaye de Bellefontaine, 1979), 185–212. On spiritual direction in Evagrius, see Gabriel Bunge, *Paternité spirituelle: La gnose chrétienne chez Evagre* (Spiritualité orientale 60; Bégrolles en Mauges: Abbaye de Bellefontaine, 1994).

39. Evagrius Ponticus, *Gnostikos* (*Le gnostique* [ed. and trans. Antione Guillaumont and Claire Guillaumont; SC 356; Paris: Cerf], 30).

—11—

The Beastly Body in Rabbinic Self-Formation

Jonathan Schofer

We may not have access to late ancient rabbinic selves, but we do have many sources for studying how they would have been made. Rabbinic texts have numerous accounts characterizing human beings, and specifically men: the nature and significance of the body, the dynamics of the emotions and desires, the features of the breath or soul that inspires life. These representations of the self occur in the midst of a largely prescriptive literature that includes extensive instructions for what an aspiring sage should do and strive to become. The discourse was performed in a context of teaching and learning—spoken, heard, read, and ultimately written—where its internalization and creative appropriation could be a key element in the transformation of a student into a cultivated member of the rabbinic movement.[1]

Among the numerous motifs in rabbinic pedagogical discourse, in this essay I examine the beastly body—the human body as an entity that consumes, excretes, has intercourse and reproduces, and dies and decays. The category is my own formulation, developed from a term that most specifically means cattle and that can denote domestic animals more broadly. In the passages I address, it is placed in contrast with plants and inanimate materials on one hand, and humans on the other.[2] I will attend to ways that rabbis characterize, invoke, care for, and exalt the animal features of their bodies amidst their instructions for the formation of ideal selves.

The Body

There is a rabbinic term for the body *(gûp)*, though several of the passages I examine name specific parts or functions rather than the body as such, and other cases discuss the person but then focus upon physical, tangible aspects of the self. My use of the term "the body" emerges at the intersection of native categories and contemporary scholarly formulations that understand the body to be a site or spatial location—not a location in an abstract or objective conception of space, but a position in space as lived and experienced by humans who, at least as living in this world, are embodied. In such an account, bodies are a starting point for human existence in the world from which both inner space and larger social and cosmic spaces are perceived, delineated, and experienced.[3] As physical, sensual, and tangible, the body can function as a baseline for the analysis of more abstract processes and dynamics, including punishment, gender relations, ritual law and practice, and in this case, ethics and self-formation. The body as a spatial location is implicated in any action. Every aspect of self-formation, for example, is embodied in some sense, and one could inquire into the embodied aspects of rabbinic study (which often involves sitting), teaching, dining, and so on. My focus in this paper, though, is on ways that the body, its parts, and its functions are directly addressed, classified, and invoked in rabbinic discourse.

This formulation draws upon David Harvey's theoretical work in *Justice, Nature, and the Geography of Difference* and *Spaces of Hope*. In addition to his general focus on the spatiality of the body, Harvey sets out two valuable observations. First, "the body is an unfinished product, historically and geographically malleable in certain ways." It is not infinitely malleable, but it evolves and changes based on both internal and external processes. Second, "the body is not a closed and sealed entity but a relational 'thing' that is created, bounded, sustained, and ultimately dissolved in a spatiotemporal flux of multiple processes." The body is, in an apt metaphor, "porous"—internalizing elements from the social as well as natural world.[4]

I would like to specify Harvey's observations in certain directions that are significant for the rabbinic sources. The texts I will examine presume a body that is *discursively* malleable in the sense that it can be configured and understood in a tremendous variety of ways, and *physically* malleable in that it can be conditioned by how people manage their diet, sleep, sexual activity, and so on. Rabbinic discourse also presents the human body in highly relational terms in the sense that it is regularly compared and juxtaposed with other things, including God, angels, demons, statues, or parts of the world. Finally, rabbis are highly concerned with the body as porous, with what their bodies consume, excrete, cry, ejaculate, and sweat. They both reflect on the symbolic significance of these functions as such and give attention to specific foods and to other matter that goes in and out of their bodies.

The Sources

My study centers on a cluster of texts entitled *The Fathers According to Rabbi Nathan*,[5] which is a large collection of rabbinic ethical literature having a significant concentration of teachings related to the ways that study of tradition and observance of divine commandments affect a person's desires and emotions. *R. Nathan* consists of maxims or short sayings—the base text is a version of *'Abot,* or *The Fathers,* that has significant differences from the collection canonized in the Mishnah—along with often extensive commentary that includes midrash, narratives, lists, and further maxims. All of these genres have significant pedagogical features, instructing the listener or reader through techniques such as direct address and portrayals of exemplary figures. *R. Nathan* has also been characterized as scholastic, having a particular concern with the workings of rabbinic disciple circles: the orientation one is to maintain in the course of study and teaching, the relations that students are to have with their teachers and peers, and the responsibilities that teachers have in relation to students. The intersection of the scholastic and ethical concerns means that *R. Nathan* frames the rabbinic disciple circle as a place where an aspiring student forms himself in relation to the sage and the community, the tradition of Torah, and service of his God.[6]

R. Nathan exists in two major recensions, commonly labeled versions A and B, though each has multiple manuscripts with numerous variants. I will focus upon *R. Nathan A,* though in some cases I will study both versions, highlighting differences between them, and I will also discuss other rabbinic sources. The texts are seen as being of Palestinian origin, though *R. Nathan A* appears to have been significantly shaped at some point by Babylonian editors. *R. Nathan* probably developed over a long period of time, and scholars since Solomon Schechter have agreed that *R. Nathan* as it exists now cannot be assigned a single date, but rather that any given passage or line has to be assessed individually. Some have attempted to recover Tannaitic (late first and second centuries c.e.) or even earlier viewpoints from the text, though recent scholarship by Menahem Kister has emphasized the extent and significance of the "post-talmudic" editing (approximately sixth to eighth centuries c.e.).[7] Most of the passages that I focus on should probably be considered this late, at least when I address them as parts of larger edited units.

The text contains no single sustained treatment of the body, though certain edited units are fairly long. Even though *R. Nathan* is a relatively rich source of material on the topic, part of my work will be to gather fragments throughout the text and to delineate patterns among them. The texts were not compiled by individual people with consistent viewpoints, though certain tendencies can be identified in the selection, editing, and arrangement of the materials. In some respects, *R. Nathan* gathers together motifs that appear dispersed in other sources in rabbinic literature. To the extent possible, I aim to use these ethical collections as lenses into the broader web of rabbinic texts, giving us insight into aspects of rabbinic culture broadly conceived (in Palestine and Babylonia, from roughly 70–600 c.e.). In other respects, this collection contains unique materials and distinctive shaping of sources that show the particular interests of those that developed it. I will address these points on a case-by-case basis, comparing the material in *R. Nathan* with parallel teachings and related sources in other anthologies.

The Argument

My work draws from and contributes to the existing scholarly examination of the body in rabbinic sources. In breadth and scope, perhaps the greatest work is Julius Preuss's *Biblical and Talmudic Medicine,* which predates the current surge of interest in the topic, as does research on rabbinic anthropology by Ephraim Urbach, Emero Steigman, and Nissan Rubin. More recently, Howard Eilberg Schwartz published an edited volume entitled *People of the Body,* and in his Introduction he wrote that he aimed to disrupt the "excessively disembodied image of the Jews." He and others interested in Jewish bodies have largely been successful in that project, at least in academic circles. Since that time, articles and book-length studies centered on the body have addressed issues such as gender, sexuality, menstruation, asceticism, and nakedness.[8]

My argument is that the passages in *R. Nathan* and their resonances in other sources reveal a rabbinic concern with the body and its role in self-formation that has not been fully addressed in the scholarship. Specifically, the passages tend to present an embodied self that is monistic yet characterized through comparison with elements in binary opposition (beasts and angels, angels and demons) and also with the cosmos and God. Such comparisons result in portraits of the self as at the same time both animal/beastly/porous and divine/angelic/cosmic. The question of whether rabbis had a positive or negative view of the body is much less relevant than how they invoke the body for homiletical purposes: they tend to cite the beastly aspects in order to inspire humility before God, and the divine aspects in order to exalt humans or inspire care of the self. The care of the body, moreover, tends to focus on the management and appropriate use of the porous, animal elements—matters such as what one eats, how one excretes, when one has sexual activity, and how long one sleeps. These discussions appear to be distinct from those concerning the animating force of the breath/spirit/soul and also from accounts of desire and transgression, for such concepts are not in this material.

Configuring Bodily Processes

One way that rabbis describe the body and give it symbolic significance is to focus on its functions. Such discursive configuration appears in chapter 37 of *R. Nathan A,* which is a collection of lists organized by the numbers six, seven, and eight. The first compares seven creations or entities, humans being the sixth. It plays on a phrase that can mean both "above" and "superior," starting out by implying that the concern is with what is physically above another, and then shifting, mid-list, to a notion of superiority:

Seven creations, one above the other.

He created the firmament above (everything).[9]

Above the firmament He created the stars, which give light to the world.

Superior to the stars, He created trees, for trees produce fruit and stars do not produce fruit.

Superior to the trees, he made bad spirits,[10] for bad spirits go here and there, and trees do not move from their places.

Superior to the bad spirits, He created beasts, for beasts work and eat, and the bad spirits neither work nor eat.

Superior to the beasts, he created humans, for in humans there is knowledge, and in beasts there is no knowledge.

Superior to humans He created the ministering angels, for ministering angels go from one end of the world to the other, and humans are not like that (*'Abot R. Nat. A*, ch. 37).[11]

A striking aspect of this passage is that the criteria for what is above or superior keep shifting. Each of these stages is inclusive of that immediately previous but not earlier ones, adding something more. Stars are high above the earth like the firmament but also produce light. Trees create something as well, and their produce may become a living being. The next step to bad spirits is not fully clear, but it seems to presume that they reproduce in some way and also move about. From there, beasts or cattle are mobile like spirits, but they also work and eat. Humans work and eat, but also have knowledge. Angels have knowledge and also move across the world.[12]

The last four elements in the first list are bad spirits, beasts, humans, and angels. People are characterized as working, eating, and having knowledge. The next set of passages takes up the comparisons between these four elements in much more detail ("bad spirits" is replaced by "demons"), with much more extensive treatments of humans and especially corporeality:

Six things are said of human beings, three like a beast and three like the ministering angels.

Three like a beast—they eat and drink like a beast, reproduce and multiply like a beast, and excrete feces like a beast.

Three like the ministering angels—they have understanding like the ministering angels, and they go about upright like the ministering angels, and they converse in the holy language (Hebrew) like the ministering angels.

Six things are said of demons, three like human beings and three like the ministering angels.

Three like human beings—they eat and drink like human being, reproduce and multiply like human beings, and die like human beings.

Three like the ministering angels—they have wings like the ministering angels, know what will be in the future like the ministering angels, and go from one end of the world to the other like the ministering angels. And some

> say that they change their faces to any likeness that they want, so they see
> and are not seen. ('*Abot R. Nat. A,* chap. 37).

These lists have parallels in relatively early Palestinian exegetical midrashic collection (*Genesis Rabbah*), the Babylonian Talmud, and later sources.[13] They juxtapose humans with angels and demons and give particular attention to both the body's movement and what goes in and out of it. The beastly functions of the self concern bodily processes (consumption, excretion, reproduction), and the demonic includes the first two as well as death. The angelic are varied: a mental/intellectual process (understanding), the ability to communicate (language), and a bodily orientation (posture). This account of the human self plays on the edge of what today's scholars may call dualism. The human is said to have angelic and beastly/demonic characteristics, yet these are expressed as similes, not as competing parts of the self. The person is monistic, not divided between spirit and flesh, but the figurative predications are dual and emphasize both earthly and divine qualities.[14]

These passages contain certain themes that resonate throughout the texts I will examine: (a) the idea that certain processes of the self are lowly or beastly, particularly those having to do with the body being porous (consuming, excreting, procreating, and decaying), and (b) the idea that in other respects the self is divine/angelic/cosmic, and that these qualities should be embraced. In the next sections, I will turn to passages in which these themes are developed in more detail and with greater pedagogical force.

Invoking the Beastly Body: Cultivating Humility

Rabbis not only describe the body, but they appeal to parts and functions of the body in symbolically charged ways in order to inspire particular states or actions. We will consider two cases in which sages exhort humility through focus on the mortal or beastly parts of human existence. The first is a famous maxim attributed to the first-century Akabya ben Mahalalel. Though I quote and analyze the version in *R. Nathan A,* the basic points I emphasize hold also for parallels in *R. Nathan B* and *The Fathers* as well as in *Ecclesiastes Rabbah, Leviticus Rabbah, Derek 'Eres Rabbah,* and *Kallah Rabbati.*

One aspect of rabbinic self-transformation is the practice of various exercises of attention, ways of focusing one's thoughts throughout one's daily life.[15] Akabya ben Mahalalel's exercise contrasts the finitude of humans with God's power as king and judge:

> Akabya ben Mahalalel says, Anyone who gives four things to his heart will sin
> no more: from where he comes, to where he goes, what in the future he will
> be, and who is his judge.
> From where he comes—from a place of darkness.
> To where he goes—to a place of darkness and gloom.

What in the future he will be—dust and worm and maggot.

Who is his judge—the King of the Kings of Kings, the Holy One, blessed be He

(*'Abot R. Nat. A,* ch. 19).[16]

The focus on finitude is made most concrete by imagery that appears throughout *R. Nathan*—that the end of humans is "dust, worm, and maggot." This phrase likely has exegetical roots that combine passages in Genesis and Ecclesiastes that center on dust (Gen 2:7, 3:19; Eccl 12:7), with those in Isaiah and Job that center on "worm and maggot" (Isa 14:11; Job 25:6).[17] The specific imagery varies somewhat in other sources, and the commentary in *R. Nathan* adds more possibilities—perhaps most common is characterizing the origins of human beings as being a "putrid drop" (of semen). In all these cases, a key issue is the contrast between human mortality and divine power that appears, not as a general proposition, but with a distinct ethical ideal. Attending to these images diminishes the human in relation to God and leads a person to "sin no more."[18]

In the commentary to this teaching in *R. Nathan A* (and also in *Derek Eres Rabbah*), a parable takes up the theme of humility more explicitly, focusing on the point that human bodies excrete feces:

> Rabbi Simeon ben Elazar says, I will tell you a parable. To what can this matter be compared? To a king who built a great palace and lived in it.[19] A tannery pipe passes through its midst and empties upon the opening. Every passerby says, How beautiful and praiseworthy would this palace be, were a tannery pipe not to pass through it. So too, a human is similar. While now, a filthy stream issues from his bowels, and he exalts himself over the other creatures— if a stream of fine oil, balsam, and ointment did so, how much the more that he would exalt himself over the other creatures! (*'Abot R. Nat. A,* ch. 19)[20]

As in the teaching of Akabya ben Mahalalel, distinct features of the body are called upon for pedagogical purposes. The large intestines function as a constant reminder that humans are not fully divine—in the imagery discussed above, humans are like beasts but not like either angels or demons. No matter how much people may try to beautify themselves, excrement is the filthy stream that reminds them that they are not gods.

While excrement is dirty, it is not necessarily impure; rather, it has an odd and interesting place in schemes of cleanliness. On the one hand, the Bible indicates that cow dung was used for cooking (2 Kings 6:25; Ezek 4), and rabbinic sources state that dog excrement was gathered for some purpose, perhaps in relation to tanning. At the same time, in Deuteronomy 23:13–15 excretion in a military camp is forbidden and called indecent. In the Dead Sea Scrolls, a vision of a new temple emphasizes that excrement should be far away and not seen (11Q19 XLVI, 13–18). In rabbinic sources, the occupation of gathering excrement is one for which a wife has grounds to divorce (*m. Ket.* 7:10 and *b. Ket.* 77a). And in the discussion of "blessings," the Babylonian Talmud gives a fair amount of attention to questions concerning prayer in the proximity of excrement. The issue, then, is not purity in a legal sense, yet there seems to be an agreement that in at least some places and times excrement is at least not divine. Having a body that excretes is at the least a reason not to exalt oneself.

The creators of this edited unit, then, value humility and uphold God's grandeur. Through emphasizing the body's excretions and ultimate decay, they exhort people to take on their values. We now turn to a very different kind of pedagogy in which sages uphold the body as divine, including its beastly elements, in order to inspire respect and care for oneself and for other persons.

Invoking the Body as the Divine Image

A teaching attributed in *R. Nathan A* to R. Meir begins, "Beloved is the human that is created in the image of God, as it is written, 'In the image of God He made the human' (Gen. 9:6)" (*'Abot R. Nat. A,* ch. 39).[21] This passage is part of a larger rabbinic preoccupation with the idea that people are in some sense or in some part divine, and with the exegesis of Genesis 1:26–27 and 9:6, both of which assert that humans are created in "the image" of the deity. These materials and related themes have received extensive scholarly examination, and here I will simply note a few key methodological points and highlight relevant themes.[22]

The assertion that humans embody the image of God is powerful but lacks specificity, creating a discursive space of immense significance for interpreters to fill with their understandings of what people are and should do. It can carry a political charge—in a cultural context where a king claims to have a distinct connection to the divine, these verses present a challenge to that authority, asserting that all people are in the image of the deity.[23] There is, then, no fixed or set meaning to this claim, but rather a key scholarly problem is to examine what a given person or group does with it. Three questions may be salient. First, since the verses turn on the word *'ādām,* does an exegete treat the verse as applicable to all humans, to specific humans (such as men, Jews, or rabbis), or specifically to the first human named Adam? Passages that focus on Adam, for example, often emphasize that humans lack godly features: Adam originally had divine qualities that have since been lost to the rest of humanity.[24] Second, what aspects of *'ādām* constitute the image of God? What parts of the self are upheld as divine? A given interpreter may highlight material elements such as the body or a specific part of it, or immaterial ones such as the soul or mind. In *R. Nathan A,* for example, one passage focuses on the human penis, citing Genesis 1:27 to argue that Adam was among a number of figures who were born circumcised (*'Abot R. Nat. A,* ch. 2).[25] Third, especially when the verse is understood as referring to human beings, what does the writer or speaker want people to do, given that they are created in the divine image?

The homiletic or pedagogical role is present even in the biblical text itself:

in Genesis 1:26–28, being in the image of God means that humans have dominion over the creatures of the earth, while in Genesis 9:6–7, the claim supports
the prohibition of manslaughter and the relevant legal retribution. Several cases
of rabbinic exegesis build on these claims. For example, one passage in the
Mekilta de Rabbi Ishmael strengthens the emphasis on killing by linking Genesis
9:6 with the Decalogue prohibition on murder. In the Tosefta, one sage cites
Genesis 9:6 to argue that bloodshed diminishes the likeness of God, while
others emphasize the end of the verse that calls for procreation to say that
reproduction is the central responsibility for those who are created in the image
of God.[26]

Another interpretation of Genesis 9:6—found in *R. Nathan B* (though not
in version A) as well as the midrashic collection *Leviticus Rabbah*—centers on
the body and calls for its care. In *R. Nathan B* the exegetical context is a teaching
attributed to the first century R. Yose, "Let all your actions be for the sake of
heaven."[27] The commentators assert that one should do so "like Hillel," and
they present two stories to illustrate and justify this point:

> When Hillel would leave to go some place, they would say to him, Where are you
>   going?
> I am going to fulfill a commandment.
> Which commandment, Hillel?
> I am going to the toilet.
> Is that a commandment?
> Hillel said to them, Yes, so that one would not degrade the body.

> Where are you going Hillel?
> I am going to fulfill a commandment.
> Which commandment, Hillel?
> I am going to the bath house.
> Is that a commandment?
> He said to them, Yes, to clean the body.

> Know for yourself that this is so. If it is the case that, for statues standing in the
> palaces of kings, the government gives an allowance every year to the one appointed
> to polish and shine them, and not only that, but he is raised up among the
> important people in the kingdom—then for us, who are created in the image and
> likeness, as it is written, "For in the image of God He made the human" (Gen 9:6),
> how much the more! (*'Abot R. Nat. B*, ch. 30)[28]

Hillel focuses here on the body as an entity that excretes and that gets dirty.
As we have seen above, other passages characterize excretion as beastly and
reason for humility; and to the extent that the need to bathe is a result of sweat
and other skin emissions, then the second story may address this animal body
as well. This set of teachings, however, characterizes all of these functions as
part of the image and likeness of God.[29] They predicate the animal features of

humans as being similar to the divine rather than in contrast, and this comparison has a distinct pedagogical purpose: a person should care for the body, and toilets as well as baths are central to this care.[30] This point is made in a manner that also makes a political statement, juxtaposing a statue of a king with the human body, and implicitly, the king himself with God. Upholding the human body over the statue also asserts that God is greater and more important than a human ruler (even or especially if the ruler claims divine status or favor for himself).[31]

Care of the Body

The care of the body extends beyond bathing and toilets. Attention to oneself was a widespread and well-developed concern in the ancient and late ancient Mediterranean. In their very different studies of self-formation, both Michel Foucault and Maude Gleason have highlighted the importance of regimen as described in the Hippocratic corpus, Galen's writings, and other medical texts—the balancing of diet, sleep, exercise, sexual activity, and other activities to bring health and strength.[32] Rabbinic literature has no equivalent to these treatises, though guidelines regarding diet and blessings over food are central to their practice.[33] Certain ideals that are similar to those of Greco-Roman regimen, moreover, are conveyed through lists that appear in both versions of R. Nathan as well as in Palestinian and Babylonian sources.

In R. Nathan A, a number of such lists appear near the end of the corpus. One of them, located in the same chapter as the lists of "six things" discussed above,[34] presents eight things that are healthy or beneficial in moderation and harmful in excess: "Eight things, much of them is harmful and a little of them is beneficial: wine, business, sleep, wealth, derek 'ereṣ, hot water, copulation and blood letting" ('Abot R. Nat. A, ch. 37).[35] The list presents several realms of bodily action—work and wealth, consumption, sexual activity, rest, bathing, and medical treatment—presenting them as good in moderation but harmful in excess. The rabbinic list echoes an influential catalogue in the Hippocratic corpus of things that are valuable in moderation: exercise, food, drink, sleep, and sexual activity.[36] However, R. Nathan makes no mention of physical exercise and includes other elements, one of which—derek 'ereṣ (depending on how this is understood)—may be distinctive to rabbinic culture.

Some of the activities listed here are at the center of polemics and debates in other rabbinic sources. In this list, though, the issue at stake is the effect on the body. Whether bathing is upheld through the exemplary model of Hillel, or baths exemplify the corrupting influence of Roman culture upon the Jews, this list states that a moderate amount of hot bathing is beneficial but that too much is harmful. The inclusion of sex is particularly interesting on this point. Often rabbinic thinking concerning this topic mediates a tension between the divine command to procreate, and the conviction that desire, beyond the minimal required for procreation within marriage, is problematic. Here we see another factor: a moderate amount of sexual activity is simply healthy, just as wine, sleep, and so on. Sexuality appears in the larger context of bodily well-being and is not evaluated in terms of law or ascetic impulses.[37]

In the last chapter of *R. Nathan A*, we find a series of other lists concerning what is beneficial and harmful to the body, starting with sweat and tears:

> Three kinds of sweat are beneficial for the body: sweat of the sick person, sweat of the bath, sweat of work. Sweat of sickness is healing. Sweat of the bath—there is nothing like it.[38]
>
> There are six kinds of tears, three are beneficial and three are bad. Those of weeping, smoke, and the toilet are bad. Those of drugs, laughter, and fruit are beneficial. (*'Abot R. Nat. A*, ch. 41)[39]

These are followed by two lists that address, not the body, but vessels of clay and glass. Then we find a list concerning sexual activity after trying or strenuous circumstances, which presents a challenge in translation that is intertwined with the overall understanding of the relation between sex and health for the rabbis: it may concern cases in which sexual activity is "harmful," but another possibility is that the situations are ones when it is "difficult." The latter would imply a more positive rabbinic evaluation of sex. The ambiguities are heightened by the fact that there are two different recensions of the opening words. In either case, the four examples are the following: "One who comes from the road. One who returns from the surgeon. One who recovers from sickness. One who returns from prison" (*'Abot R. Nat. A*, ch. 41).[40] The underlying issue is the condition of the body: after great stress or exertion, sexual activity is not recommended. The broader point, though, is that again sex is treated as part of the management of bodily functions. Issues concerning sexual excretions appear along with those of the skin and the eyes without a significant distinction.

Such concerns extend beyond *R. Nathan A*. More of these lists appear in *R. Nathan B*:

> Three tears are harmful for the eyes . . .
> Three tears are beneficial for the eyes . . .
> Three things make the body grow . . .
> Three things increase sperm . . .
> Three things decrease sperm . . .
> Three things increase excrement . . .
> Three things enter the body as they are . . . (*'Abot R. Nat. B*, ch. 48)

In addition, several sections of the Babylonian Talmud collect lists of foods and bodily processes, and one Palestinian midrashic collection includes a list of "six kinds of tears."[41]

Many of these lists concern the very functions of the body that elsewhere are characterized as beastly, particularly sexual activity and the consumption of food followed by excretion of waste. Others relate to very different kinds of excretions (those of the eyes and skin) as well as bathing (a concern that appears in the narrative of Hillel). While we have no systematic presentation of rabbinic regimen, numerical catalogues such as these reveal that rabbis in different regions and at different times collected and transmitted information on how to take care of their porous animal bodies through managing their diet and expenditures of energy.

Celebrating the Microcosmic Body

In the passages I have examined so far, we have seen various ways that rabbis compare the body with other entities: animals, angels, demons, a palace, and God. The next set of passages set out relationships between human beings and the world or cosmos. The material centers on creation imagery and sets out three juxtapositions: one human is as important or valuable as the entire world; Adam encountered all the future generations that would come into the world; and the human body is a microcosm in such detail that individual parts of the body can be correlated with elements or processes in the natural and social world. In the third the body is discussed with great elaboration, and the bulk of my analysis will concern this section.

The literary context is a numerical list: "With ten utterances the world was created."[42] The commentators presume that this detail must have pedagogical significance:

> What need do those who enter the world have for this?[43] To teach you that anyone who carries out one commandment, anyone who observes one Sabbath, and everyone who sustains one life, Scripture accounts it to him as if he sustained the entire world, which was created with ten utterances. ('Abot R. Nat. A, ch. 31)[44]

The phrase "Scripture accounts it to him as if . . . " often appears in R. Nathan to convey that an apparently small act will generate large consequences. Here, one good act is said to bring the same reward as if one preserved the entire world, and of the three acts listed, the key one for the larger sequence is sustaining one life. The next passages turn to the question of transgression—a negative act destroying the world—and center on the figure of Cain. These two discussions, positive and negative, culminate in the statement: "Thus you learn that one person is weighed in correspondence to the entire work of creation."[45]

How do the commentators justify this point midrashically? They draw upon two verses in Genesis:

> Rabbi Nehemiah says, From where do we derive that one person is weighed in correspondence to the entire work of creation? For it is said, "This is the book

of the generations of Adam. On the day that God created Adam, in the likeness of God He made him" (Gen 5:1). And there it says, "These are the generations of the heavens and the earth when they were created, on the day that the Lord God made earth and heavens . . . " (Gen 2:4). Just as in the other case there was creation and making, so too here there is creation and making. (*'Abot R. Nat. A*, ch. 31)[46]

The exegesis centers on the words "create" and "make." Both terms appear in describing the creation of Adam and the creation of the world, and the interpretation is that this similarity means that both are equal in the divine accounting. The ensuing discussion, though, shifts attention to the word "generations" *(tōlĕdōt)*, which is also used both for the world and for Adam, to state that Adam saw all of the generations that would come upon the earth. This motif appears in *Genesis Rabbah* to Genesis 5:1, and the later midrashic collection *Exodus Rabbah* includes the specification that the future generations emerge from Adam's body.[47]

The final passage in the unit presents the homologies between the human body and the cosmos. The term *'ādām* is ambiguous here, for it can refer to humans in general (as in the first teaching) or Adam (as in the second). Because of the focus on cosmogony and anthropogony in the literary unit as a whole, I see the text as concerning "Adam," but here with the qualities of the first human representing those of all people. The opening is a parable that puns on the words for "form" *(yṣr)* and "draw" *(ṣwr)*:

A parable: to what can this matter be compared? To one who takes some wood and wants to draw many forms, but does not have room to draw—he is frustrated. But one who draws on the earth can go ahead and spread them out. Yet, the Holy One, blessed be He, may His great name be blessed for ever and ever, in His wisdom and understanding created the entire world, all of it, and created the heavens and the earth, the beings on high and the those below, and He formed in Adam everything that He created in his world. (*'Abot R. Nat. A*, ch. 31)[48]

Then we find a long list specifying this formation, each time asserting the close relation between humans/Adam and the world or cosmos:

He created bushes in the world and He created bushes in Adam: this is Adam's hair.

He created evil animals in the world and He created evil animals in Adam: this is Adam's vermin.

He created channels in the world and he created channels in Adam: these are Adam's ears.[49]

He created wind in the world and He created wind in Adam: this is Adam's nose.[50]

Sun in the world and sun in Adam: this is Adam's forehead.

Filthy water in the world and filthy water in Adam: this is Adam's nasal mucus.

Salty water in the world and salty water in Adam: this is Adam's urine.[51]

Rivers in the world and rivers in Adam: these are [Adam's] tears.

Walls in the world and walls in Adam: these are Adam's lips.

Doors in the world and doors in Adam: these are Adam's teeth.

Firmaments in the world and firmaments in Adam: this is Adam's tongue.

Sweet water in the world and sweet water in Adam: this is Adam's saliva.

Stars in the world and stars in Adam: these are Adam's cheeks.[52]

Towers in the world and towers in Adam: this is Adam's neck.

Masts in the world and masts in Adam: these are Adam's forearms.

Pegs in the world and pegs in Adam: these are Adam's fingers.

A king in the world and a king in Adam: his head.[53]

Clusters in the world and clusters in Adam: these are Adam's breasts.

Advisers in the world and advisers in Adam: his kidneys.

Smells in the world and smells in Adam: this is Adam's stomach.

Mills in the world and mills in Adam: this is Adam's spleen.

Cisterns in the world and cisterns in Adam: this is Adam's navel.[54]

Living water in the world and living water in Adam: this is Adam's blood.

Trees in the world and trees in Adam: these are Adam's bones.

Hills in the world and hills in Adam: these are Adam's buttocks.

Pestles and mortars in the world and pestles and mortars in Adam: these are Adam's knees.

Horses in the world and horses in Adam: these are Adam's ankles.

The Angel of Death in the world and the Angel of Death in Adam: these are Adam's heels.

Mountains and valleys in the world and mountains and valleys in Adam: when he stands he resembles a mountain, and when he falls he resembles a valley.

Thus you learn that all that the Holy One, blessed be He created in His world, he created in Adam. (*'Abot R. Nat. A,* ch. 31)[55]

This list is very difficult to pin down in terms of both its relation to other notions of correlation and homology, and its pedagogical or rhetorical force. I will start with the features of the list itself, then turn to resonances in other rabbinic sources, and finally consider similar materials in other cultural contexts.

The general structure appears to move from the upper part of the body to the lower, starting with hair and ending with heels, but this order is not strictly followed.[56] The list is quite long. There are a strong proportion of items focused on the head (ears, nose, forehead, lips, teeth, tongue, cheeks, neck, head, perhaps hair) and a strong attention to fluids (mucus, urine, tears, saliva, blood). This body, though, is not fully elaborated, and the list omits a number of items that figure prominently in other rabbinic discussions. The human portrayed here is not gendered, having no penis, scrotum, or semen, and no vagina, uterus, or menstrual blood.[57] Only a couple of internal organs are named (kidneys, stomach, and spleen), and it is particularly striking that there is no mention of the heart.[58] There is also no reference to excrement despite the attention to several liquid excretions. Of the beastly functions discussed above, perhaps the most prominent is eating (lips, teeth, tongue, saliva, and stomach). If we turn to the depiction of the "world," perhaps most prominent are natural elements and forces, including several kinds of water (filthy, salty, sweet, living water, and also rivers). We also see certain social positions (a king and advisers), instruments in labor and production (mills, cistern, pestles and mortars, horses, pegs, and masts), and human ways of defining space (doors, walls, towers).

In large part, the passage can be seen as collecting themes that appear in the Bible and in rabbinic literature. Some items are straight forwardly exegetical, as the associations of tower/neck and clusters/breasts are from lists of the body in the Song of Songs 4:4 and 7:8.[59] Other images are developed elsewhere in rabbinic material with more complex exegetical bases. Perhaps the most prominent of these is the link between the kidneys and advice or counsel, which appears in *R. Nathan* as well as in other texts.[60] The image of the tongue being surrounded by walls appears amidst a discussion of malicious speech in one Babylonian passage.[61] Also, in both Palestinian and Babylonian sources, a midrash on Ecclesiastes 12:2, which calls upon the reader to appreciate youth "before the sun, light, stars, and moon grow dark," presents correspondences that include the sun and the brightness of the face, light and the forehead (those two are combined in sun/forehead of *R. Nathan*), the stars and the cheeks, and also the moon and the nose (this fourth one is not in *R. Nathan*). The exegesis of Ecclesiastes 12 continues with numerous other comments about body parts, most of which are different than in *R. Nathan,* though an association between the stomach and milling is close to the correlation of mills/spleen above.[62]

In terms of larger themes and literary structure, we find in the list of *R. Nathan* three intertwined motifs that appear individually in other rabbinic sources. The first is that Adam is in some way a cosmic being. As I discussed, this passage appears in an exegetical unit that explores various correlations between Adam and the larger world, and other versions of this link appear elsewhere in rabbinic sources. Perhaps most notable is the image that, at creation, Adam's size matched that of the cosmos, stretching from one end of the universe to another, and that he lost his great stature through transgression; often this image is derived from a midrashic interpretation of Deuteronomy 4:32.[63] The second motif is that the human body, or part of it, is a microcosm of the larger world. Such thinking appears, for example, in the late extracanonical tractate *Derek 'Ereṣ Zuṭa,* in which the eye appears as having elements corresponding to the ocean, the world, Jerusalem, and a vision of the future temple.[64]

The third trope or motif, which here is the organizing principle for the other two, is the listing of body parts. The key scriptural inspiration for this practice is likely three passages in the Song of Songs, one listing the man's body and two listing the woman's. These were the source of much exegetical activity, and at some point a mystical tradition developed through which the male figure became the center of speculation and perhaps contemplative practice.[65] Rabbis also developed their own lists with different foci. The closest parallel to the list in *R. Nathan*, in terms of form, may be one in *Ecclesiastes Rabbah* that also sets out a correspondence between what God created in the world and in humans/Adam. Rather than linking parts and functions of the body with objects, however, biblical verses are cited that contain the same juxtaposition.[66] A very different list in the Mishnah enumerates the number of parts in each region of the body; and yet another, naming internal organs of the body that are central to thought, emotion (anger, laughter) speech, digestion, and sleep, appears in the Babylonian Talmud *Berakot*.[67]

The microcosmic list in *R. Nathan* has a number of similarities to sources from cultures that, in different ways and different times, may have been contiguous with rabbis. The correspondence of heel/death may be associated with the figure of Achilles.[68] At a larger thematic level, the list of Adam as a microcosm of the world is developed in Christian sources; perhaps most relevant is the Slavonic *2 Enoch*, which states that God made Adam out of seven elements: flesh from earth, blood from dew and sun, eyes from the sea, bones from stone, reason from angels and clouds, veins and hair from grass, and spirit from God's spirit and the wind.[69] While there is a superficial resemblance to the passage in *R. Nathan*, few of the items are similar: blood/dew (= water), hair/grass. Perhaps more importantly, the relation between body and cosmos differs. The Christian accounts of the microcosmic Adam present Adam as being made from the earthly elements, whereas the rabbinic account presents juxtaposition without directionality or transformation: the first human is neither made from the elements of the earth, nor is the earth created from a human body. While most "Indo-European" accounts set out some form of directionality, two key examples do not: the Zoroastrian *Greater Bundahišn* and the pseudo-Hippocratic *Peri Hebdomadōn*. There is similarity between the rabbinic list and these accounts regarding as many as four items—hair/plants, blood/water, sun/eye, and breath/wind.[70]

If we shift from the features of the list to its purpose, the most striking feature is its lack of integration with the rest of rabbinic thought and its minimal role in practice. In many cultures of the world, including but not only regions now known as Europe, South Asia, and China, homologies between the body and the cosmos were part of broad webs of correlations between the human, the social order, and the world. The specific ways of framing these relations have varied tremendously within and across cultures, and they have been employed for, or implicit in, many practices, including but not only sacrifice, diet, medicine, divination, law, legitimating political and social order, music, historiography, broad explanation of change and transformation, and restoring lost hair.[71] The rabbinic list, however, appears outside of such contexts. While there are various rabbinic sources that employ correlations, they appear sporadically and are not consistent from one to the other. Each appears for a specific occasion, often the significance is not developed at length, and there is little instrumental function.

The rabbinic list of the cosmic Adam, then, is best understood as an extremely detailed elaboration of the ideal that establishing or sustaining a person's life is weighed equally with sustaining all of creation: each part of every person correlates with a distinct part of the created world. In the broader literary context of *R. Nathan,* this passage can be seen as strengthening the view of the self that exalts the entire body, including its animal elements. While linking the body with the cosmos is not as strong a claim as saying that it is in God's image, the sheer length and repetition that characterizes this list makes the overall impact quite significant. I see this passage, then, as among the strands of rabbinic culture that celebrate the body as such, and this celebration reinforces both a concern for others (particularly the prohibition against murder) and a care for oneself. Such a discursive framing of corporeality counters or balances others, both within rabbinic culture and in surrounding ones, that invoke the body as a reason for lowliness or humility.

This essay has examined ways that rabbis describe, invoke, care for, and uphold their bodies. The materials I have addressed touch on the topics of sexuality, gender, asceticism, and relations between body and soul, but their central foci differ in significant ways. Sexual activity appears in lists along with other bodily functions characterized as beastly, or along with other activities that are beneficial in moderation. The material likely presumes a male body, but distinctions between men and women are not highlighted. Several sources counsel humility and moderation, but they do not call for self-denial. Binary thinking appears in a number of passages—human/beast, human/angel, human/demon, human/God, human/world—yet the self is characterized as monistic and unified, comparable to or negotiating the various oppositions but not divided by them. Distinctions between body and soul are not explored.

While each of the passages I have analyzed sets out a distinct anthropology, certain patterns are present. The list of "Six things are said of human beings, three like a beast and three like the ministering angels" expresses, I believe, a tendency that runs through the sources. People have features that are beastly, mortal, and porous—consumption, excretion, reproduction, decay—and those that are comparable to God, angels, and the cosmos. Sages may draw upon one or both of these aspects for various purposes: humbling the self by emphasizing mortality, exhorting care of the self by describing all of the body (including excretion) as in the image of God, or elevating the self by showing the entire body (including urine and mucus) to have close correspondence with the natural and social world. The care of the self generally focuses on beastly features—what one consumes, how consumption affects health as well as what comes out of the body (excrement, sweat), how often and when one should have sexual activity, and more.

While these accounts of the self may appear familiar to those who have studied grotesque traditions, they do not quite fit the influential dichotomy set out by Mikhail Bakhtin in his famous study of Rabelais. Bakhtin identifies a "grotesque" characterization of the body as employing exaggeration and hyperbole, emphasizing the nose, mouth, phallus, and anus, as well as processes of eating, drinking, defecation, and elimination. This body is linked with the cosmos and the universal, and it is celebrated as such, even if this celebration comes with ambivalence. By contrast, "classic" accounts of the body focus on closed, smooth, and impenetrable features, with all orifices closed or ignored. These categories have been productively employed in relation to certain rabbinic passages to illuminate moments when sages embrace the grotesque,[72] but the binary of grotesque/classic is too sharp for the material I have examined here.

The rabbinic sources emphasize eating, drinking, excretion, sexual activity, and decay with a frankness that is unlike the classic accounts. At the same time, the rabbinic discourse of the beastly body is not like that of the grotesque in that vivid depictions of semen, decay, and excretion are employed in teachings calling for humility. Other passages uphold the entire body as being in the divine image, but they do so in order to exemplify its care through cleaning and going out to a distinct location when excreting, and this concern with managing the beastly body appears in more detail through the lists delineating regimen. The list of homologies may be the closest to the grotesque in its attention to minute details and extensive linking of the human and the cosmos, yet here the body is not celebrated for its intrinsic fecundity but rather as created by God.

While I have examined several genres (including maxims, parables, and narratives), the most prominent has been the list or catalogue. Each has a distinct way of selecting and arranging its items, and often we see notable pedagogical features. The list of "seven creations" sets out a hierarchy based on shifting characteristics, culminating in bad spirits, beasts, humans, and angels with brief characterizations of each. Immediately following are two lists of "six things" that not only cluster but also juxtapose these four classes of beings. The result is a complex trope that predicates humans as like animals, angels, and demons, each in distinct ways. The care of the body is conveyed through lists that advise certain behaviors and the consumption of certain foods through saying that they are beneficial, and that counsel against others by characterizing them as harmful. A list of ten utterances in God's creation becomes the focal point of exegetical activity whose interpretation has explicit pedagogical concern, and this commentary culminates in an extended list of homologies exalting the human body as a cosmic analog. These varied persuasive styles are perhaps all the more effective because of the apparent impersonal and objective features of the genre, in contrast with, for example, epigrams of instruction centered on imperatives and attributed to specific sages. Such maxims also may employ lists, however, as we could see in the teaching of Akabya ben Mahalalel, who calls for constant attention to four (or in some accounts three) aspects of human existence in relation to God.[73]

How widespread is the concern with the beastly body in rabbinic literature and culture?[74] The answer varies from case to case: the list of "six things" also appears in both Palestinian midrash and the Babylonian Talmud; the maxim of Akabya ben Mahalalel in the Mishnah, midrashic collections, and extracanonical tractates; the story of Hillel in a midrashic collection; and lists of diet and related matters primarily in the Babylonian Talmud. The list of the cosmic Adam has no distinct parallels, yet the various themes implicit in this teaching are conveyed in many other sources. Study of *R. Nathan*, then, reveals a widespread set of rabbinic concerns both with the description of the body and with ideals for what one should do as an embodied student aspiring to be a sage.[75]

NOTES

1. This account summarizes a broader argument made in my book, *The Making of a Sage: A Study in Rabbinic Ethics* (Madison: University of Wisconsin Press, 2005).

2. The specific passages discussing "beasts" focus on consumption, excretion, and reproduction. I will treat death and decay as part of the same cluster of concerns, justified in part by certain juxtapositions of teachings that I will discuss.

3. Even in cultural systems that devalue the significance of embodied existence or that see embodied reality as fundamentally illusory, one's behavior and comportment while inhabiting a body tends to have a significant role in conditioning other states of being.

4. David Harvey, *Spaces of Hope* (California Studies in Critical Human Geography 7; Berkeley: University of California Press, 2000), 98–99 and also 117–21; idem, *Justice, Nature, and the Geography of Difference* (Oxford: Blackwell Publishers, 1996), esp. 48–57, 79–87.

5. The current critical edition of the text is Solomon Schechter, *Aboth de Rabbi Nathan, Edited from Manuscripts with an Introduction, Notes, and Appendices* (1887; repr. New York: Jewish Theological Seminary of America, 1997) (Hebrew). Major textual studies include Louis Finkelstein, *Introduction to the Treatises Abot and Abot of Rabbi Nathan* (Texts and Studies of the Jewish Theological Seminary of America 16; New York: Jewish Theological Seminary of America, 1950) (Hebrew with an English summary); and in English, idem, "Introductory Study to *Pirke Abot*," *JBL* 57 (1938): 13–50. A recent and crucial study is Menahem Kister, *Studies in Abot de-Rabbi Nathan: Text, Redaction, and Interpretation* (Jerusalem: Hebrew University Department of Talmud, 1998) (Hebrew). All translations of Hebrew and Aramaic texts in this essay are my own.

Both versions A and B of *R. Nathan* appear in reliable English translations that have excellent notes and scholarly commentary: Judah Goldin, *The Fathers According to Rabbi Nathan* (Yale Judaica Studies 10; New Haven, Conn.: Yale University Press, 1983); Anthony Saldarini, *The Fathers According to Rabbi Nathan (Abot de Rabbi Nathan) Version B* (Leiden: E. J. Brill, 1975). Very important studies include Goldin, *Studies in Midrash and Related Literature* (ed. Barry Eichler and Jeffrey Tigay; SJLA 11; Philadelphia: Jewish Publication Society, 1988), 3–117; Anthony Saldarini, *Scholastic Rabbinism: A Literary Study of the Fathers According to Rabbi Nathan* (BJS 14; Chico, Calif.: Scholars Press, 1982).

6. The emphasis on the scholastic features of R. Nathan appears most strongly in Saldarini, *Scholastic Rabbinism,* and the focus on ethics and pedagogy is my own and argued at length in *The Making of a Sage.*

7. This point runs throughout Kister, *Studies in Abot de-Rabbi Nathan.*

8. See Julius Preuss, *Biblical and Talmudic Medicine* (trans. Fred Rosner; Northvale, N.J.: Jason Aronsen, 1978); Ephraim Urbach, *The Sages: Their Concepts and Beliefs* (trans. Israel Abrams; Cambridge, Mass.: Harvard University Press, 1979), 214–54; Emero Steigman, "Rabbinic Anthropology," *ANRW* 19.2: 487–579; Nissan Rubin, "The Sages Conception of the Body and Soul," in *Essays in the Social Scientific Study of Judaism and Jewish Society* (ed. Simcha Fishbane, Jack N. Lightstone, and Victor Levin; Montreal: Department of Religion, Concordia University, 1990), 47–103; Howard Eilberg-Schwartz, ed., *People of the Body: Jews and Judaism from an Embodied Perspective* (SUNY series, The Body in Culture, History, and Religion; Albany: SUNY Press, 1992); Daniel Boyarin, *Carnal Israel: Reading Sex in Talmudic Culture* (The New Historicism 25; Berkeley: University of California Press, 1993); Michael Satlow, *Tasting the Dish: Rabbinic Rhetorics of Sexuality* (BJS 303; Atlanta, Ga.: Scholars Press, 1995); idem, "Jewish Constructions of Nakedness in Late Antiquity," *JBL* 116 (1997): 429–54; idem, "'And on the Earth You Shall Sleep': Talmud Torah and Rabbinic Asceticism," *JR* 83 (2003): 204–24; Aharon Agus, "The Flesh, the Person, and the Other in Rabbinic Anthropology," in *Self, Soul, and Body in Religious Experience* (ed. A. I. Baumgarten, J. Assman, and G. Stroumsa; SHR 78; Leiden: Brill, 1998), 148–70; Charlotte Fonrobert, *Menstrual Purity: Rabbinic and Christian Reconstructions of Biblical Gender* (Contraversions; Stanford, Calif.: Stanford University Press, 2000); Eliezer Diamond, *Holy Men and Hunger Artists: Fasting and Asceticism in Rabbinic Culture* (New York: Oxford University Press, 2004).

9. Goldin suggests omitting "everything" and writes, "a copyist may have misunderstood the word 'superior' to mean 'higher'" (*R. Nathan,* 213 n.2; also see Schechter's comments in *R. Nathan,* 109 n.1). Goldin may be correct, though as stated above, I hold that the play between height and superiority is part of the opening lines.

10. These could be simply "bad winds," but I choose to translate as spirits in part to make sense of their superiority to the trees and because I see them as similar to the "demons" that appear in the next unit, as I discuss.

11. See Schechter, *R. Nathan,* 107, and also the parallel in *'Abot R. Nat. B,* ch. 43 (Schechter, *R. Nathan,* 120).

12. In *'Abot R. Nat. B,* the parallel concludes differently: "Superior to humans are the ministering angels, for humans eat, drink, reproduce and multiply, sleep, and die; but ministering angels do not eat, drink, reproduce and multiply, sleep, or die" (ch. 43; Schechter, *R. Nathan,* 20). This is a negative rather than positive claim, but it seems to focus on angelic immortality. Angels do not have qualities that are distinctive of earthly embodiment. In *R. Nathan A,* this point is developed in subsequent passages that are not in *R. Nathan B,* which I will address next. It is possible that this line in B is a summary of what appears in more expanded form in A or that the material in A is an expansion of what is in B.

13. See Schechter, *R. Nathan,* 107; *Gen. Rab.* 8:11; J. Theodor and Ch. Albeck, eds., *Midrash Bereshit Rabba: Critical Edition with Notes and Commentary* (3 vols.; 2nd printing with additional corrections; Jerusalem: Shalem Books, 1996), 64–65; *b. Ḥag.* 16a, but note the difference in order; also *Seder Eliyahu Zuṭa* 12; Meir Friedmann, ed., *Seder*

Eliahu Rabba and Seder Eliahu Zuṭa and *Pseudo-Seder Eliahu Zuṭa* (3rd printing; Jerusalem: Wahrmann Books, 1969), 193; *b. Yomaʾ* 75b; Michael Swartz, *Scholastic Magic* (Princeton, N.J.: Princeton University Press, 1996), 167.

14. Urbach, in analyzing the parallel to this passage in *b. Ḥag.* 16a, writes, "Stress is laid on the difference between man's spiritual attributes and his bodily needs" (*Sages,* 221). I differ here with his use of "spiritual," which implies a division between body and spirit that is not warranted by the passage. One of the angelic features is posture, which is a bodily orientation; and language is deeply linked with the body in *b. Ber.* 59a–b (see the list of the body quoted above and Preuss, *Talmudic Medicine,* 87).

15. I argue this point at length, with examination of this passage among others, in "Spiritual Exercises in Rabbinic Literature," *Association for Jewish Studies Review* 27/2 (2003): 203-25.

16. See also *ʾAbot R. Nat. B,* ch. 32 (both appear on Schechter, *R. Nathan,* 69–70); *M. ʾAbot* 3:1. The claim that people go "to a place of darkness and gloom" does not appear in *ʾAbot.* Finkelstein claims that this change reflects an attempt to bring the maxim in accord with rabbinic belief in future life; see Finkelstein, *Introduction,* 53–55 and 64–67 on this point and generally on the textual variants. Saldarini summarizes the issues in English with references (*R. Nathan B,* 189 n. 15). A parallel also appears in *Der. ʾEr. Rab.* 3:1, though the maxim is in the name of Ben Azzai; Michael Higger, *The Treatises Derek Erez* (New York: Debe Rabanan, 1935), 155–58 (Hebrew section). In *Kallah Rab.* 6, all the material in *Der. ʾEr. Rab.* 3 is presented as a "mishnah," to which there is a commentary. The teaching is also quoted and expanded upon in *Lev. Rab.* 18:1; Mordecai Margulies, *Midrash Wayyikra Rabbah* (New York: Jewish Theological Seminary, 1993), 389–90; and *Eccl. Rab.* 12:1.

17. The image of moving into "darkness" appears in Eccl 6:4 with reference to a stillbirth. On these tropes, also see Swartz, *Scholastic Magic,* 69, 166–70.

18. While Urbach often overemphasizes a distinction between body and spirit/soul in rabbinic sources, here he does not. He writes concerning the version of this passage in *Fathers* 3:1 that "the tanna does not mention body and soul, but addresses himself to the whole man." Urbach also points out the pedagogical force of the passage, writing that the sage "wishes to emphasize the responsibility and status of man" (*Sages,* 224; see also Rubin, "Sages' Conception of Body and Soul," 94 n. 15).

19. The text is difficult, and the manuscripts show some significant differences. See the discussions in Goldin, *R. Nathan,* 195 n. 5 and Schechter's appendix B in *R. Nathan,* 158.

20. See Schechter, *R. Nathan,* 70; also *Der. Z. ʾEr. Rab.* 3:3 (Higger, *Derek Erez,* 159–61).

21. See Schechter, *R. Nathan,* 118; a slightly longer version of this maxim is attributed to Rabbi Akiva in *ʾAbot* 3:14.

22. See especially the recent essay with extensive references by Alon Goshen Gottstein, who emphasizes the bodily connotations of "image" and "likeness" in rabbinic sources: "The Body as Image of God in Rabbinic Literature," *HTR* 87 (1994): 171–95; see also Urbach, *Sages,* 217.

23. Samuel E. Loewenstamm argues, with reference to ancient Near Eastern materials, that this significance was present in ancient Israel. See "Man as Image and Son of God," *Tarbiz* 21/1 (1957): 1–2 (Hebrew).

24. See Goshen Gottstein, "The Body as Image of God," 183–86; I thank Elaine Pagels for her comments on an earlier version of this section.

25. See Schechter, *R. Nathan,* 12; also Urbach, *Sages,* 230, 788 n. 50; Goshen Gottstein, "The Body as Image of God," 175.

26. See the analysis in Michael Fishbane, *Biblical Interpretation in Ancient Israel* (Oxford: Clarendon, 1985), 318–21; *Mekilta de-Rabbi Ishmael, Ba-Ḥodesh* 8; H. S. Horovitz and I. A. Rabin, eds., *Mechilta d'Rabbi Ishmael* (Jerusalem: Shalem Books, 1997), 233;

t. Yebam. 8:7; *b. Yebam.* 63b; and Boyarin, *Carnal Israel,* 134–36; Goshen Gottstein, "The Body as Image of God," 190–92.

27. See ʾ*Abot R. Nat. B,* ch. 30; ʾ*Abot R. Nat. A,* ch. 17; Schechter, *R. Nathan,* 65–66; *Fathers* 2:12.

28. See Schechter, *R. Nathan,* 66; also *Lev. Rab.* 34:3 (Margulies, *Wayyikra Rabbah,* 775–77).

29. Note that this way of comparing the body with the divine is similar to, but not the same as, prayers that thank God for the proper function of orifices; on the latter, see the discussion in Boyarin, *Carnal Israel,* 34–35.

30. On the character and importance of bath houses for Jews in late antiquity, see Yaron Eliav, "Did the Jews at First Abstain from Using the Roman Bath House?" *Cathedra* 7 (1995): 3–35 (Hebrew); he discusses the parallel to this story in *Lev. Rab.* 34:3 on pp. 30–31; idem, "The Roman Bath as a Jewish Institution: Another Look at the Encounter Between Judaism and the Greco-Roman Culture," *JSJ* 31 (2000): 416–54. Urbach cites the version of this story in *Leviticus Rabbah,* juxtaposing it with Philo's anthropology in *Sages,* 226–27; and Rubin cites the same version to argue that "in the Tannaitic generations before the destruction of the Temple, we do not hear of any opposition between the body and the soul" ("Sages' Conception of Body and Soul," 56). See also Goshen Gottstein, "The Body as Image of God," 174–75.

31. I thank Azzan Yadin for his help with this entire section. The current version is in many ways working out ideas he suggested in response to an earlier presentation of this paper. Parts of this section have appeared in J. Schofer, "In the Image of God," *Sh'ma* 34 (2003): 5.

32. Michel Foucault, *The Use of Pleasure* (trans. Robert Hurley; New York: Vintage Books, 1985), 95–139; idem, *The Care of the Self* (trans. Robert Hurley; New York: Vintage Books, 1986), 99–144; Maud Gleason, *Making Men: Sophists and Self-Presentation in Ancient Rome* (Princeton, N.J.: Princeton University Press, 1995), esp. 82–102.

33. A maxim in ʾ*Abot R. Nat. A,* ch. 26 concerning food has a very complex set of variants with various emphases, including health and appropriate blessings. See Schechter, *R. Nathan,* 83 n. 17; Goldin, *R. Nathan,* 112; Finkelstein, *Introduction,* 161; Kister, *Studies,* 47.

34. After the material discussed above, the very next passage in the chapter is a list of seven or eight (depending on the witness) different types of Pharisees. It is a list that appears in many different sources, and scholars have had great difficulty understanding it, but it does not appear to have specific references to the body. Kister calls it one of the most enigmatic passages in rabbinic literature (*Studies,* 54). Following this list is the one I examine here.

35. Schechter, *R. Nathan,* 109. The phrase *derek* ʾ*ereṣ* is multivocal: literally "way of the world," it can indicate a number of activities including business, supererogatory action, or sex. This ambiguity may be related to the textual problem that not all witnesses mention "copulation" as a distinct item. See the overview in Marcus van Loopik, *The Ways of the Sages and the Way of the World* (Tübingen: J. C. B. Mohr, 1991), 2–6.

36. Hippocrates, *Epidemiae* 6.6.2; Foucault, *Use of Pleasure,* 101–2.

37. In his introduction to *Carnal Israel,* Daniel Boyarin emphasizes that the body is a site of human significance and should not be devalued in relation to a spiritual reality and that sexuality is central to this significance. He then writes, "Sexuality is accordingly not just a subheading under ethics but situated at the cores of alternate individual and collective self-understandings" (6). I agree with his basic point here, but I see sexuality and ethics as independent discourses with points of overlap. In this passage as well as others that I examine below, the concern with sexual activity is one element in a broader concern for care of the body: sexuality here is a subset of ethics, though a very different sense of ethics than I think Boyarin had in mind at the time.

38. Goldin amends: "Sweat of the bathhouse [makes one strong. As for the sweat of labor] there is nothing like it" (*R. Nathan*, 171 and 219 n. 12).

39. See Schechter, *R. Nathan*, 131–32. Regarding "fruit," some manuscripts and parallels have "mustard," and probably for that reason Goldin translates "herbs" (Schechter, *R. Nathan*, 132 n.14 and Goldin, *R. Nathan*, 171 and 219 n. 14).

40. See Schechter, *R. Nathan*, 132 and especially n. 17; Goldin translates, "On four occasions cohabitation is harmful . . . " (*R. Nathan*, 171). For "surgeon," I follow Goldin, who interprets the line as referring to bloodletting (*R. Nathan*, 171 and 219 n. 15).

41. See Schechter, *R. Nathan*, 132; *b. Ber.* 57b; *b. Pesaḥ*, 42a-b, and *b. Yoma* 18a–b; *Lam. Rab.* 2:15 to Lam 2:11; also *b. Šabb.* 151b–152a.

42. See ʾ*Abot R. Nat. A*, ch. 31; ʾ*Abot R. Nat. B*, ch. 39; Schechter, *R. Nathan*, 90; *M. ʾAbot* 5:1. This statement is likely derived from the observation that the phrase "and God said" appears nine times in Genesis 1 and once in Genesis 2.

43. On this question, see Kister, *Studies*, 42 and ʾ*Abot R. Nat. A*, ch. 32; Schechter, *R. Nathan*, 92–93.

44. See Schechter, *R. Nathan*, 90; contrast *m. ʾAbot* 5:1.

45. I discuss "Scripture accounts it to him as if . . . " in *Making of a Sage*, chapter 3. The discussion of negative acts is probably a development of material in *m. Sanh.* 4:5; see also ʾ*Abot R. Nat. A*, ch. 3; Schechter, *R. Nathan*, 17; Kister, *Studies*, 138. The rhetorical move of comparing a person to the cosmos as a way of upholding individual lives and condemning killing is similar to citing biblical verses stating that humans are in the image of God to support the prohibition against murder (see my discussion above).

46. See Schechter, *R. Nathan*, 91.

47. See *Gen. Rab.* 24:2 (Theodor-Albeck, *Bereshit Rabba*, 230–31); *Exod. Rab.* 40:3; Goshen Gottstein, "The Body as Image of God," 192–93.

48. See Schechter, *R. Nathan*, 91. In the Oxford manuscript of *R. Nathan A*, the unit is attributed to R. Yose ha-Gelili, and Schechter includes this in his text. The opening here is: "R. Yose Ha-Gelili says, Everything that the Holy One, blessed be He created in the Earth He created in Adam" (Schechter, *R. Nathan*, 91 n. 8). Somewhat similar puns appear in the *Mekilta of R. Ishmael, Beshallaḥ* 8 (Horovitz-Rabin, *Mechilta d'Rabbi Ishmael*, 144).

49. This is following Goldin's interpretation in *R. Nathan*, 127, 204 nn. 15, 16. Another is "He created destructive insects in the world and He created destructive insects in Adam: these are Adam's intestinal worms." See also Schechter, *R. Nathan*, 92 n. 12; Marcus Jastrow, *A Dictionary of the Targumim, The Talmud Babli and Yerushalmi, and the Midrashic Literature* (New York: Judaica Press, 1992), 1343–44.

50. Goldin translates "breath" for "nose" in *R. Nathan*, 127 and 204 n. 17.

51. Goldin reverses this item and the next one; see *R. Nathan*, 127 and 204 nn. 19, 20; also Schechter's comments in *R. Nathan*, 92 n. 16.

52. The text in *R. Nathan A* literally says, "cheeks in the world and cheeks in Adam: these are Adam's cheeks." I follow Goldin, *R. Nathan*, 127 and 204 n. 24; also see Schechter's comments in *R. Nathan*, 31, 92 n. 21 and *Lev. Rab.* 18:1 (Margulies, *Wayyikra Rabbah*, 391).

53. Schechter suggests substituting "heart," which would reinforce an order from top to bottom (*R. Nathan*, Appendix A, 147). The heart is associated with a king in ʾ*Abot R. Nat. B*, ch. 13; Schechter, *R. Nathan*, 30; I discuss this passage as well as the understandings of the heart in rabbinic literature more broadly in chapter 2 of *The Making of a Sage*.

54. Preuss interprets this line to indicate that "one considered the deep-lying type of navel to be the most common one" (*Talmudic Medicine*, 59).

55. See Schechter, *R. Nathan*, 91–92.

56. There are significant difficulties in sorting out the order of the items among the

manuscript variants. Schechter suggests an order from above to below and presents a reconstruction in *R. Nathan*, Appendix A, 147.

57. This omission contrasts with the passages discussed in Boyarin, *Carnal Israel*, esp. 197–225; Satlow, "Jewish Constructions of Nakedness"; and Fonrobert, *Menstrual Purity*, esp. 40–67, 103–27.

58. However, as noted above, Schechter suggests that it should be present instead of "head."

59. The connection between "living waters" and blood may be based on the statement in Jer 2:13 and 17:13 that God is the source of "living waters" (linking this image with God being the source of human life).

60. See Preuss, *Talmudic Medicine*, 102–08; *'Abot R. Nat. A*, ch. 31, 33; Schechter, *R. Nathan*, 91–92 n. 27, 94; Goldin, *R. Nathan*, 131; and *Gen. Rab.* 61:1; Theodor-Albeck, *Bereshit Rabba*, 657–58 including their listing of sources. In biblical literature, the heart and the kidneys are often paired. See Jer 11:20; 17:10; 20:12; Ps 7:10.

61. See *b. 'Arakin* 15b.

62. I am summarizing *Lev. Rab.* 18:1 (Margulies, *Vayyikra Rabbah*, 389–93); there are small differences in *Eccl. Rab.* 12:2 and *b. Šabb.* 151b.

63. This image appears *'Abot R. Nat. B*, ch. 8 (Schechter, *R. Nathan*, 22–23) and in both Palestinian and Babylonian sources: *Gen. Rab.* 8, 21, and 24 (Theodor-Albeck, *Bereshit Rabba*, 55–56, 199, 230); *Lev. Rab.* 14, 18 (Margulies, *Wayyikra Rabbah*, 297, 400–401); *b. Ḥag.* 12a; *b. Sanh.* 38b. A key verse that generates this motif is Deut 4:32, which interestingly also inspires a very different idea: one should not speculate concerning what is above, below, before, and after; see *Gen. Rab.* 1 (Theodore-Albeck, *Bereshit Rabba*, 8–9); *t. Ḥag.* 2:7; *b. Ḥag.* 11b. Note that for both *Genesis Rabbah* and *b. Ḥag.*, both interpretations appear in the same collection. Another way rabbis describe Adam in massive terms is to compare the radiance of his heel to the sun; see, for example, *Pesiq. Rab. Kah.* 12:1; Bernard Mandelbaum, ed., *Pesikta de Rav Kahana* (2nd ed.; New York: Jewish Theological Seminary of America, 1987), 203; *Lev. Rab.* 20:2 (Margulies, *Wayyikra Rabbah*, 456); and more generally Goshen Gottstein, "The Body as Image of God"; Urbach, *Sages*, 228, 230.

64. The passage is, "Abba Isi ben Yohanan in the name of Samuel the Small says: This world is similar to the eyeball of a human. The white that is in it is the ocean that surrounds the entire world. The black [i.e., the iris] that is in it, this is the world. The pupil that is in the black, this is Jerusalem. The image that is in the pupil, this is the Temple that will be built quickly, in our days, and in the days of all Israel, Amen"; *Der. 'Er. Zut*. 9:13; Higger, *Derekh Eretz*, 150–51; Preuss, *Talmudic Medicine*, 68; Urbach, *Sages*, 233.

65. See Song 4:1–8, 5:9–6:3, and 7:1–10. The list of the male body in 5:8–6:3 is the most crucial for mystical speculation. See Saul Lieberman, "The Teaching of the Song of Songs," in *Jewish Gnosticism, Merkabah Mysticism, and Talmudic Tradition* (ed. Gershom Scholem; New York: Jewish Theological Seminary, 1960), 123, and 118–26 generally (Hebrew).

66. See *Eccl. Rab.* 1:4; Isaak Heinemann, *The Ways of the Aggadah* (Jerusalem: Magnes Press, 1970), 19 (Hebrew).

67. See *m. 'Ohal.* 1:8; *b. Ber.* 61a–b. The exegetical context of the Talmudic list is a law concerning giving blessing over evil. The commentary leads into a discussion of bad and good impulses, God's creation of human beings, and then this map of the body: "Our sages taught, The kidneys advise. The heart understands. The tongue cuts. The mouth completes. The esophagus brings [food] in and sends [it] out. The trachea sends out the voice. The lungs absorb all sorts of liquids. The liver becomes angry, and if a drop of bile sprinkles into it, it assuages it. The spleen laughs. The stomach grinds. The stomach sleeps. The nose awakens." A number of these lines are discussed in Preuss, *Talmudic Medicine*, including the kidneys (107–8; also *Lev. Rab.* 61:1), the mouth (87),

the trachea (101), the liver and gall bladder (74, 98), the spleen (99), and the two listings for the stomach (92–93, 94–95, 135). On the image of the tongue cutting, the trachea sending forth, and the mouth completing, he writes that these are "the characteristics of the popular physiology of speech" (87). The material is presented with no distinct hierarchy and no homiletical interpretation, and there is no attention to sexual activity or excretion.

68. Goldin suggests this in *R. Nathan*, 204 n. 30.

69. See 2 Enoch 30:8; James Charlesworth, ed., *The Old Testament Pseudepigrapha* (2 vols.; Garden City, N.Y.: Doubleday, 1983), 1:150; J. M. Evans, "Microcosmic Adam," *Medium Aevum* 35 (1966): 38–42.

70. On Indo-European creation imagery and the issue of directionality, I draw on the work of Bruce Lincoln, who argues that there are nine central homologies in Indo-European cosmogonies: flesh/earth, bone/stone, hair/plants, blood/water, eyes/sun, mind/moon, brain/cloud, head/heaven, breath/wind. Of these, four are present in the rabbinic account, if we allow the nose to be the breath and the forehead to be the eyes: hair/bushes, forehead/sun, blood/water, and nose/wind. There are also clear differences, such as the rabbinic link of bones with trees rather than stone. Few of the non-core items in the various cosmogonies fit as well. See Bruce Lincoln, *Myth, Cosmos, and Society: Indo-European Themes of Creation and Destruction* (Cambridge, Mass.: Harvard University Press, 1986), 1–40; Alex Wayman, "The Human Body as Microcosm in India, Greek Cosmology, and Sixteenth Century Europe," *HR* 22 (1982): 172–90; M. L. West, "The Cosmology of 'Hippocrates,' *De Hebdomadibus*," *CQ* 21 (1971): 365–88. Urbach discusses the possible significance of the *Greater Bundahišn* in rabbinic thought, but in treating the issue of microcosmic imagery, he focuses on Philo's study of plants (*Sages*, 230, 233).

71. The literature on these topics is tremendous. Works that I have found particularly helpful are Lincoln, *Myth, Cosmos, and Society*; Aihe Wang, *Cosmology and Political Culture in Early China* (Cambridge Studies in Chinese History, Literature, and Institutions; New York: Cambridge University Press, 2000); John Henderson, *The Development and Decline of Chinese Cosmology* (Neo-Confucian Studies; New York: Columbia University Press, 1984), 1–58; David Gordon White, *The Alchemical Body: Sidtha Traditions in Medieval India* (Chicago: University of Chicago Press, 1996), esp. 184–262.

72. See Mikhail Bakhtin, *Rabelais and His World* (trans. Helene Iswolsky; Cambridge, Mass.: MIT Press, 1968), esp. 303–22; Boyarin, *Carnal Israel*, 197–225.

73. On lists in *R. Nathan*, see Finkelstein, *Introduction*, 81–114; Saldarini, *Scholastic*, 109–19; and more broadly in rabbinic literature, W. Sibley Towner, *The Rabbinic "Enumeration of Scriptural Examples"* (StPB 22; Leiden: E. J. Brill, 1971). I have learned much from the highly sophisticated theoretical and comparative study of lists by Valentina Izmirlieva, *The Christian Art of Listing: Naming God in Slavia Orthodoxa* (Ann Arbor: University of Michigan Dissertation Services, 1999).

74. I have focused on teachings that are collected in *R. Nathan A*, with secondary attention to *R. Nathan B*. While there are differences between the texts regarding specific passages, I do not see a significant contrast in the overall presentation of the body. In terms of comparisons that elevate the self, the list of the cosmic Adam appears only in version A, but version B has the story of Hillel tending to his body and also more extensive lists concerning regimen. Both versions have the maxim of Akabya ben Mahalalel, though in version B the commentary is more expansive. On the whole, though, my summary holds for the material in both recensions that directly addresses the body and its processes.

75. Another relevant theme, which I have addressed elsewhere, is concern with the control of the body by either the good or bad impulse (*yeṣer*). See Schofer, *The Making of a Sage*, chapter 2, and idem, "The Redaction of Desire: Structure and Editing of Rabbinic Teachings Concerning *Yeṣer* ('Inclination')," *Journal of Jewish Thought and Philosophy* 12 (2003): 31–33, 45.

Making Public the Monastic Life:
Reading the Self in Evagrius Ponticus' Talking Back

DAVID BRAKKE

In his unfinished genealogy of the subject, Michel Foucault identified *exo-mologēsis*, the public acknowledgment of oneself as a sinner, and *exagoreusis*, the verbalization of one's thoughts and desires to a spiritual master, as two distinctively early Christian contributions to the development of the self. "Throughout Christianity," he wrote, "there is a correlation between disclosure of the self, dramatic or verbalized, and the renunciation of the self."[1] He considered the second form of self-disclosure, verbalization of one's thoughts, to be the more important of the two since it developed into the institution of penance and, although this is usually left implicit, into the practice of psychoanalytic therapy. Foucault located *exagoreusis* primarily in the monastic life: the monk was expected to disclose all of his thoughts to a more advanced monk for the elder's scrutiny. Thus, the monastic subject represents an ancient ancestor of the modern subject, who discloses his or her self by speaking to the therapist or the talk show host. This model appears to assume that the self is interior or hidden and so requires or permits "disclosure," and here Foucault's work may dovetail with Charles Taylor's claim that Augustine, an ancient Christian monk, bequeathed to the modern self a "radical reflexivity" predicated on the notion of the self as being an *inner* space (presumably disclosed in Foucault's *exagoreusis*).[2]

For his understanding of monastic confession, Foucault relied primarily on the *Conferences* of John Cassian, who composed his work in Gaul in the 420s but presented his teachings as those of monks whom he had known during a sojourn in Egypt in the 380s and 390s. If we are to look for the origins of the verbalized and renounced self that Foucault attributed to monastic Christianity and perhaps also for the interior self that it appears to require, we must turn to the Egyptian desert of the late fourth century.

There Cassian's principal teacher in the monastic life was Evagrius of Pontus, who settled in the Egyptian desert in 383 after a brief but tumultuous career in ecclesiastical politics in Constantinople. Although Evagrius' teachings profoundly influenced his work, Cassian never mentions him because, shortly after Evagrius' death in 399, a controversy broke out over the orthodoxy of monastic teachings like his. Bishop Theophilus of Alexandria ordered the forced eviction of "Origenist" monks from the monastic settlements of Nitria and Scetis in Lower Egypt, and most likely John Cassian was among the ascetics who departed Egypt at this time.[3] Despite these unfortunate events, Evagrius' writings remained highly influential, especially in eastern Christian monasticism, and they provide precious evidence for the spirituality of the monks of Lower Egypt during the fourth century. Unlike the much better known *Apophthegmata patrum,* the earliest surviving collections of which originated in Palestine during the latter half of the fifth century, Evagrius' works were actually composed in fourth-century Egypt and directly reflect the guide-disciple relationship that formed Cassian's spirituality and that so interested Foucault.

Among the several writings of Evagrius that survive, *Antirrheticus,* or *Talking Back,* provides some of the most intriguing material for the historian investigating the ancient religious self. Extant today completely only in Syriac and not at all in the original Greek, *Talking Back* lists some 498 thoughts, situations, or conditions that may trouble or characterize the monk, along with verses from the Bible. Most of the items are thoughts suggested by demons, and thus the monk should use the biblical verse to "talk back" to the demon or thought, just as Jesus responded to the temptations of Satan with biblical quotations (Matt 4:1–11; Luke 4:1–13). For example: "Against the thought of love of money that calls blessed our corporeal brothers and our kinfolk in the world because they possess visible wealth: 'For what can be seen is temporary, but what cannot be seen is eternal' (2 Cor 4:18)."[4] Other biblical verses are to be addressed to a monk suffering from a certain condition (e.g., "For the soul that is stingy with money . . . ") or to God in a situation of distress or thanksgiving.

Evagrius organized the 498 chapters by the eight primary demons that he believed afflict the practicing monk: gluttony, fornication, love of money, sadness, anger, listlessness, vainglory, and pride. The book, then, is a kind of manual for the monk and his spiritual director, designed to give practical aid in times of real difficulty. Evagrius admits that the book might be an embarrassing disclosure of personal experience: "I have struggled 'to open my mouth' (Ps 118:131 LXX) and to speak to God, to his holy angels, and to my own afflicted soul. I have made public the entire struggle of the monastic life, which the Holy Spirit taught David through the Psalms and the blessed fathers handed over to us" (Pref.). Here, it seems, in the collected thoughts and problems of the ancient monk, the modern reader might gain entrance to the monk's most intimate self.

The form of *Talking Back,* a short preface followed by eight lists of thoughts or situations paired with biblical verses, may strike the modern person as odd, but the ancient reader probably saw affinities to several literary genres. Evagrius nearly always wrote in short *kephalaia* or "chapters," which could range in length from a single sentence to a paragraph or two.[5] His central work is a trilogy, consisting of the *Praktikos* of 100 chapters, the *Gnostikos* of 50 chapters, and the *Kephalaia Gnostica* of 540 chapters.[6] The roots of the *kephalaia* genre are biblical (Proverbs and other wisdom books) and philosophical (the *Manual* of Epictetus and the *Meditations* of Marcus Aurelius), and these literary precedents, like Evagrius' works, arose from actual practice—for instance, the teacher giving the student a short maxim to learn and contemplate, or the person in pursuit of virtue memorizing aphorisms to aid him in his discernment of good and bad thoughts and actions. *Talking Back* represents a variation on this genre: it provides a handbook of scriptural sayings to be deployed in varied circumstances.

Because Evagrius intended the majority of the sayings to be addressed to what we would call supernatural beings—demons, God, and angels—*Talking Back* invites comparison as well with the magician's spell manual, which likewise listed various words or actions under brief headings: "For one who is swollen"; "For your enemies, that they (may) not prevail over you."[7] Although each of the eight books of *Talking Back* presents its passages in canonical order, the overall effect is to atomize the scriptural text into a series of powerful sayings appropriate for various circumstances of need. Like Athanasius of Alexandria's *Epistle to Marcellinus,*[8] *Talking Back* may have contributed to the efforts of Christian leaders to differentiate the Christian monk from the "magician" by scripturalizing the way in which religious adepts addressed demonic and other supramundane beings.[9]

Just as the magician's handbook sought to meet the actual needs of his clients, so too Evagrius' handbook must have addressed actual thoughts and situations that confronted himself and the monks that he knew. If the use of the first person singular is any indication, then some of the thoughts were Evagrius' own: "Against the thought that prophesies to me concerning the scourge that comes from demons" (4.39). Or more certainly: "Against the demon that threatens me with curses and says, 'I will make you an object of laughter and reproach among all the monks because you have investigated and made known all the kinds of all unclean thoughts'" (4.25). But most of the thoughts must have come from other monks. The monks in Evagrius' community at Kellia spent the week living in their own cells, following their own ascetic regimes, but they gathered on Saturdays and Sundays for common worship. According to the Coptic version of Palladius' *Life of Evagrius,* Evagrius would lead all-night discussion groups on Saturday evening in which monks would reveal their thoughts and share methods of coping with them. If a monk expressed trouble over a particularly severe or embarrassing thought, Evagrius would invite him to stay after the others left for a private session.[10] Meetings such as these, as well as numerous visits and informal consultation, may have been a primary source for the thoughts that Evagrius gathered in *Talking Back*.

Still, it is not the case that we have in this work direct access to the monastic self or to the "average" monk's thoughts and anxieties. For one thing, *Talking Back* gathers mostly the monk's negative thoughts, his fears and worries, to which he must respond in a defensive or aggressive manner; there are only intimations of the positive experiences of prayer, stillness of soul, fellowship with other monks, and the like, which also characterized the monastic life. One may question also whether the monks who consulted with Evagrius were typical either in their particular concerns or in their willingness to share them with others. Recently scholars have begun to free themselves from a tendency to marginalize Evagrius and his circle as idiosyncratic or out of touch with the majority of monks, whom scholars understood to be simpler and less philosophically inclined; yet this salutary development should not lead us to the other extreme of taking the Evagrian monk as the norm. The diversity of monastic literature should caution against speaking of "the typical Egyptian monk" without qualification: in *Talking Back* we meet not *the* monastic self, but one representation of the monastic self. That representation was Evagrius'.

Although most if not all of the thoughts that he presents doubtless came from actual monks, Evagrius still has packaged them according to his own vision of the monastic life.[11] The monk who told Evagrius that he was considering doing less manual labor and relying more on the support of others may not have understood his inclination to have been a temptation or demonic suggestion, much less specifically a thought of gluttony, until Evagrius identified it as such (and even then, for all we know, he may not have accepted the diagnosis) (1.63). Evagrius also assumed progression in his arrangement of the eight thoughts. While few monks would ever free themselves completely from the thoughts gathered under his first two demons, gluttony and fornication, Evagrius did expect that the advanced monk would be troubled more by those that came from the final two, vainglory and pride. As Evagrius saw it, the monk toiled through ascetic discipline in a stage called *praktikē* to reach a state of *apatheia* and could then approach a condition that he called being a Gnostic. *Talking Back* belongs primarily to the stage of *praktikē*, but the thoughts gathered under vainglory and pride suggest a monk who, if he was not yet a Gnostic, was nonetheless approaching that stage. Finally, by pairing each thought or condition with a biblical verse, Evagrius invited the monk to understand his experience in light of the Bible. He sought to shape the self into a self that speaks to its temptations and fears in biblical language. With these caveats in mind, let us explore aspects of the self that emerges in *Talking Back*.

It was, first of all, an embattled and vulnerable self, as Evagrius described it in the preface to the work:

> In the case of rational nature that is "beneath heaven" (Eccl 1:13), part of it
> fights; part assists the one who fights; and part contends with the one who
> fights, strenuously rising up and making war against him. The fighters are
> human beings; those assisting them are God's angels; and their opponents are
> the foul demons. It is not because of the severity of the enemies' power, nor
> because of negligence on the part of the assistants, but because of slackening
> on the part of the fighters that knowledge of God disappears and perishes
> from them. (Pref.)

The monastic self was a self at war, not only besieged by the demons but also
attempting to "drive them out . . . as warriors and soldiers of our victorious
King, Jesus Christ." As much as Evagrius tried in his preface to rally the monk
with his martial imagery, struggle and vulnerability characterized the monastic
self: the monk was fighting for his life.

This embattled self was also embodied, anxious about the body's condition
and sensitive to its pleasures and pains. Monks worried that their ascetic regime
harmed the body and could even hasten their death, and the body's weakness or
illness suggested to them that they should relax their fasting, eat more, and get
more sleep.[12] The Church's feast days (e.g., Epiphany, Easter) provided especially tempting occasions to give the body a break, perhaps an indication also of
a desire to participate in the wider life of the Church.[13] Evagrius condemned as
"bound by gluttony" the monk who held that a robust body is a good thing
("the road of life") and reminded him that "the road is hard that leads to life"
(1.48, citing Matt 7:14). Monks feared that they would get sick, and when they
did get sick, the temptation to abandon the monastic life grew especially
acute.[14] They worried about growing old and the corresponding decline in the
body's health (1.57; 6.32). It is not surprising that monks attributed arousal of
the body's "members" and of the area "between the thighs" to demons, but they
reported to Evagrius (and he claimed to have seen) also a range of bodily
injuries—burned eyes and skin, punched noses, branding marks in the skin—
which demons inflicted on them and which caused them discouragement.[15] If
the monastic self was a self in battle, that warfare was not simply mental or
spiritual but engaged the body as well.

The material needs of the embodied self gave rise to another set of anxieties. Although some early monks were reported to have wandered the desert
relying on God's providence for support, Evagrius supported an emerging
expectation that the monk would stay in his cell, earn enough through manual
labor to provide himself and any guests with the basic necessities, and then give
any excess to the poor.[16] But this principle did not free the monk from engagement with practical matters. Rather, it could raise the question of when the
monk had moved beyond an efficient and laudable industriousness either to an
avaricious desire for more wealth or to a simple pleasure in the process of
acquisition itself. To accumulate supplies of even necessary items could suggest

a problem, but monks who did not store up bread, oil, and other staples worried that they would not have enough and so fall into a poverty greater than that which they had chosen.[17] What if Egypt suffered some great famine or affliction (1.21)?

Monks could perform too much manual labor or require such from their disciples, taking them away from their primary duties of prayer, biblical study, and care for the sick; on the other hand, an aversion to manual labor could indicate sloth or listlessness.[18] Because a monk could get sick and be unable to work and because his labor was vulnerable to general economic and meteorological conditions, receiving help from others loomed as a problematic possibility: dependence on non-monastic persons, whether one's family or (especially as monks gained prestige) lay admirers, could be a "disgrace," a source of shame (1.61–63). Material possessions, necessary to life in the body, confronted the self not only with the issue of its own industry and attitude to labor but also with ambiguous connections to other people: guests, the poor, one's family.

Others in need, particularly guests and poor people, made demands on the monk, challenging his desire for independence and solitude with the requirement of openness and generosity. He was obliged to offer hospitality to a visiting monk: there are only a few indications of reluctance to offer such (3.14), perhaps because one was not expected to be lavish in entertaining fellow ascetics. Instead, this hospitality could become a pretext for acquiring more than one should.[19] Poor people, whether fellow monks or impoverished lay persons, were a different matter, however: here the monk confronted the problem of the potential limit to one's obligation. Was one required just to give and give, even at the risk of endangering one's own livelihood? There are frequent references to a general reluctance to give to the poor,[20] but Evagrius mentions specific objections as well: the poor person has other sources of financial help, while I do not; I do not have enough for both me and the poor person; the person really is not very poor or at least not as poor as others; I would just make myself poor; the poor person is my enemy.[21] Here we see a self that calculates the threat to its own security and the worthiness of the needy other, manifesting a defensive and judgmental posture that Evagrius sought to undermine with biblical exhortations to trust in God and to be open to others. But even the act of giving could send the monk into regret and donor fatigue: maybe I am spending my money too freely; the recipients of my aid do not show sufficient gratitude; those monks to whom I lend show no interest in repaying; these burdens always seem to fall on me.[22] The vulnerability and insecurity required by the needy other placed stress on the monk, whose ascetic regime already positioned him as living on the edge of poverty, perilously close to the "disgrace" of dependence on others.

Scholars sometimes contrast the ancient person's group orientation—the assumption that he or she was embedded in a network of relations defined by kinship and other ties—with the individualism of the modern self, which (whether accurately or not) considers itself essentially autonomous and so connected to others by choice.[23] Especially for elite persons in Roman imperial society, "selfhood was . . . understood through identification with family honor."[24] Indeed, while the essentially social nature of the ancient self understandably presented problems for the monk (the *monachos* or "solitary one"), the family in particular appears to have been a persistent reference point for the monastic self, even long after the monk had abandoned household life for the desert. Pleasant memories of family life reminded the monk of the warmth, security, and comfort that come with sex, financial stability, and good food shared with loved ones.[25] Monks continued to love their families, desiring to see them and be with them, if only temporarily, a longing that Evagrius labeled a temptation from listlessness *(akēdia)*, a restless dissatisfaction with the ascetic life.[26] Such familial love also fostered guilt over not being present to minister to aging or ill parents (4.42). Money was an important aspect of family ties: while some monks at times felt resentment, disappointment, or regret at having given up their share of their families' wealth, other monks might worry about receiving financial aid from their relatives.[27] Sibling rivalry could continue for the withdrawn monk when he heard (perhaps like the modern academic who studies him), "Look, your brothers in the world are honored by everyone because of their wealth"; the monk himself could be tempted to judge the financial success of his relatives as indications of their being "blessed" (3.18, 46). The family provided a focus for lingering desires for companionship, financial security, prestige, and approval.

Among the self's desires was, of course, erotic desire: the monks in *Talking Back* desired beautiful bodies, specifically, female bodies. Interactions with actual women, few as they must have been, were charged with erotic possibilities: the visit of a Christian matron in search of spiritual guidance or a trip to the village market, crowded with shopping women, posed dangers to the monk's self-control (2.35, 58). But mostly the monk, alone in his cell, saw images of women that ran across his mind like figures on a movie screen. Married women and prostitutes, pious women and dancing women, beautiful women, naked women, women who were beautiful *and* naked—these were the images that flooded the monk's intellect, sometimes at such a great speed that the monk could barely keep up.[28] Sometimes only a sudden appearance of "the angel of the Lord" in the monk's intellect could stop these sexual pictures (2.14). The monk not only saw individual women but also witnessed "unspeakable acts," things so shocking that Evagrius dared not put them in writing lest he scandalize non-monastic readers and scare away novice monks (2.65). The persistence of such images, despite their best efforts at renouncing them, discouraged monks, leading them to think that the monastic life was too difficult or that they would succumb to sexual temptation and so suffer shame.[29] Some monks, however, took pleasure in this mental pornography and, perhaps reasoning that it was less culpable than actual sexual activity, did not want to get rid of such thoughts and images.[30] The self's erotic energy was strong, even virulent, and expressed itself visually. Rare is the reference to sexual temptation as merely the desire for the warmth of marriage and family (2.49): remembered meals appear to have been the preferred images for lingering attraction to family.

On the other hand, not all thoughts of the family were happy or attractive ones: some monks suffered from their parents' or relatives' opposition to their monastic vocation (5.34, 56). Family members could say that the monk had chosen the ascetic life because he was such a bad sinner or because he was unsuccessful in normal life (6.46). Evagrius argued that the monk's understandable desire to persuade such family members that the monastic life was the right path was in fact the temptation of vainglory: he should give up to trying to get the approval of other people (7.39, citing Gal 1:10). For some monks at least, the family did not recede completely as a horizon for the self: it could represent a persistent and attractive alternative to his difficult life or a continuing reference for the monk's estimation of himself as a success or a failure.

Fellow monks, however, provided the more immediate context for the monk's evaluation of himself. Anger toward their monastic brothers, often prompted by slander or gossip, troubled the monks.[31] Differing social backgrounds provided another source of tension: a monk could experience taunting from others because he had been a slave, or he could feel superior to his colleagues because he came from a prestigious family (5.44; 8.37). Conflicts such as these are expected in human communities, but the monks had devoted themselves to a program of self-transformation, one that promised to make them more virtuous than other people, and thus they tended to compare themselves to their monastic brothers and even to compete with them. While monks could envy or find annoying colleagues who appeared to have advanced farther than they, the reader finds more frequently a sense of superiority over one's fellows, who are in turn characterized as negligent or even sinful.[32] The struggling monk, on the other hand, might focus his discouragement on senior monks, those guiding him in the ascetic life, by complaining that they are too harsh or uncaring or by scorning them as in fact not as virtuous as himself.[33] Alternatively, the improving monk could mistakenly consider himself to be so advanced on the monastic path that he should instruct others.[34] Charged with the task of eliminating the passions and acquiring the virtues, the monk understandably sought means by which to measure his progress and evaluate his shortcomings, and fellow monks provided one such means. But comparison to others created its own set of problems: jealousy, anger, resentment, discouragement, and the like.

Ultimately, the greatest danger to the monastic self was pride, an excessive self-esteem that blasphemously assessed the self against God—and found that it measured up. At its basic level, the proud monk simply held an overly positive estimate of himself: "I am the Lord's holy one"; "I am pure and no longer receive healthy thoughts"; and so on.[35] Along with this positive estimation of self went a negative judgment on the qualities of others: "Look, they are neglecting the service of the commandments" (8.31). The proud monk might find fault with the brother who had taken on a more stringent discipline of fasting—"He is not able to stand in the battle when eating, and so he has devoted himself to fasting"—as well as with the one who had not done so—"It is because he cannot control himself" (8.53–54). But the self could become so inflated in its self-estimation that it no longer compared itself to mere human beings, but to the angels and even to God.

A monk could imagine that he had achieved virtue without the help of the angels or the grace of God: he did it all on his own.[36] Here the monk might fall prey to "blasphemous thoughts" that even the otherwise frank Evagrius could not bring himself to describe in writing, but that seem to have blurred the distinctions among one's self, Satan, and God.[37] And thus the proud monk lost the necessary "frankness in prayer": what need did he have of prayer, of praising and petitioning a higher being?[38] Instead, he might ask himself whether or not God was present within himself (8.12). Satan and the demons appeared to him as divine beings or wise teachers.[39] The ideal monastic self recognized its subordinate place in a hierarchy of rational beings and did not attempt to elevate itself above its station or fellows: that is, it was humble. Yet the ideal Evagrian monk sought to transform himself in an effort to return to a higher state of passion-free contemplation of God akin to that of the angels. The danger was that the monk might overestimate his progress in that effort and so lose all sense of himself as a limited, created self.

The ancient or modern reader of the monastic self in *Talking Back* follows this progress as the monk struggles with his embodied condition, finds his place in a network of others, and confronts the dangers of the inflated self. Through the arrangement of thoughts from gluttony to pride, the work carries one on an upward trajectory in which the stakes for the self become ever greater. In *Talking Back,* one modern interpreter has said, Evagrius "leads his reader to an increasingly acute introspection."[40] This characterization conforms the work to the modern understanding of the self as an interior space that can be ever more deeply probed or, as Foucault might have it, ever verbalized and revealed to the master. From our perspective, the thoughts that Evagrius enumerated appear to be artifacts of that introspection, discoveries brought forth in words from an increasingly acute examination of one's self. And in fact, Evagrius' student Cassian, Foucault's primary source for his understanding of the monastic subject, worked with something like this model: he could speak of "hidden places of our heart" and "hidden depths of the soul," the contents of which the monk must disclose to his elder.[41] The persistence of such hiding places within the self (and of the thoughts lodged secretly therein) provided legitimation for the cenobitic monastery and its hierarchical structure of leaders and subordinates, the context in which Cassian—but not Evagrius—wrote.[42] Also unlike Evagrius, Cassian had read Augustine.

It is not clear, however, that Evagrius' self was an inner space like that of Cassian or Augustine. In an introductory treatise on the monastic life, *To Eulogios,* Evagrius spoke of the monk having "inner places" *(hoi entos),* but he called the thoughts "raindrops" that the monk should "shake off" from his "inner places" rather than seeing them as originating in those places.[43] In *Talking Back,* Evagrius, in contrast to Cassian's and Foucault's model of the self-revealing monastic subject, claimed that the thoughts that the monk shared were not in fact his thoughts at all: they were the suggestions of demons, "arrows" that the demons hurled at the monk as they made war against him (Pref.).

Although at the center of the monastic self as Evagrius conceived of it lay a core intellect ("inner places") capable of knowing and loving God, the actual characteristics of the self as I have read them in this work—the self's anxieties, concerns, attractions, estimations of self and others—took place at the surface of the self, at the battle line between the self and its demonic enemies. The monk's goal was to ward off these adversaries, to shake off their thoughts as so many raindrops that obscure the self's vision, and ultimately to contemplate God in a state beyond thoughts or images.[44] By using *Talking Back,* the "I" or "we" that spoke of its hunger, its fears, and its family memories had to learn that the thoughts it spoke were not "I" or "we." And in turn, it had to learn to speak instead the words of Scripture, which would direct it to the Trinity that Scripture revealed. What the monastic self in *Talking Back* verbalized to its director was not its self but the haunting possibility of losing its self and falling short of its transcendent goal.

NOTES

1. Michel Foucault, "Technologies of the Self," in *Technologies of the Self: A Seminar with Michel Foucault* (ed. Luther H. Martin et al.; Amherst: University of Massachusetts Press, 1988), 16–49, at 48. Many of the fragments of Foucault's unfinished work on early Christian sources are gathered in Michel Foucault, *Religion and Culture* (ed. Jeremy R. Carrette; New York: Routledge, 1999).

2. Charles Taylor, *Sources of the Self: The Making of the Modern Identity* (Cambridge, Mass.: Harvard University Press, 1989), 127–42.

3. Columba Stewart, *Cassian the Monk* (Oxford Studies in Historical Theology; New York: Oxford University Press, 1998); Elizabeth A. Clark, *The Origenist Controversy: The Cultural Construction of an Early Christian Debate* (Princeton, N.J.: Princeton University Press, 1992).

4. Evagrius, *Antirrheticus (Ant.)* 3.46. I have used the critical edition of the Syriac text by Wilhelm Frankenberg, *Euagrios Ponticus* (Abhandlungen der königlichen Gesell-

schaft der Wissenschaften zu Göttingen, Philologisch-historische Klasse, Neue Folge 13.2; Berlin: Weidmannsche Buchhandlung, 1912), 472–544. All translations are my own. Brief references to this work will be made parenthetically in the text by book and chapter number; lengthy references will appear in the notes. Among the few scholarly treatments of this work are two pioneering and perceptive essays: Michael O'Laughlin, "The Bible, the Demons and the Desert: Evaluating the *Antirrheticus* of Evagrius Ponticus," *Studia Monastica* 34 (1992): 201–15; and Gabriel Bunge, "Evagrios Pontikos: Der Prolog des *Antirrhetikos*," *Studia Monastica* 29 (1997): 77–105.

5. On Evagrius' use of this genre and for a general introduction to his life and approach to monasticism, see Columba Stewart, "Evagrius Ponticus on Monastic Pedagogy," in *Abba: The Tradition of Orthodoxy in the West: Festschrift for Bishop Kallistos (Ware) of Diokleia* (ed. John Behr et al.; Crestwood, N.Y.: St. Vladimir's Seminary Press, 2003), 241–71.

6. For a recent translation of Evagrius' ascetic works that survive in Greek (which do not include the *Kephalaia Gnostica*), see Evagrius Ponticus, *The Greek Ascetic Corpus* (ed. and trans. Robert E. Sinkewicz; Oxford Early Christian Studies; Oxford: Oxford University Press, 2003).

7. Marvin Meyer and Richard Smith, eds., *Ancient Christian Magic: Coptic Texts of Ritual Power* (San Francisco: HarperSanFrancisco, 1994), 271–72, 305–7, 339–41 (nos. 128, 133, 135).

8. Athanasius, *Epistula ad Marcellinum* 33 (PG 27:11–46).

9. For elaboration on this point, see David Brakke, "Monks, Priests, and Magicians: Demons and Monastic Self-Differentiation in Late Ancient Egypt," in *Living for Eternity: Monasticism in Egypt* (ed. Sheila McNally and Philip Sellew; Louvain: Peeters, forthcoming).

10. E. Amélineau, ed., *Histoire des monastères de la Basse-Égypte* (Annales du Musée Guimet 25; Paris: Leroux, 1894), 114–15.

11. O'Laughlin calls *Antirrheticus* "an aggressive, programmatic work" ("The Bible, the Demons, and the Desert," 214).

12. Harm: *Ant.* 1.14, 15, 19, 22, 26, 59, 65. Relax: *Ant.* 1.3, 20, 33, 43, 44, 47, 52.

13. *Ant.* 1.3, 25, 29, 32, 40, 60.

14. Fear: *Ant.* 1.56; 4.76; 6.32. Abandon: *Ant.* 6.6, 36.

15. Arousal: *Ant.* 2.11, 23, 25, 45, 55, 63; 4.22. Injuries: *Ant.* 4.15, 33, 36, 41, 49, 52, 53, 56, 65.

16. On this issue in early Egyptian monasticism, see Daniel Caner, *Wandering, Begging Monks: Spiritual Authority and the Promotion of Monasticism in Late Antiquity* (The Transformation of the Classical Heritage 33; Berkeley: University of California Press, 2002), 19–49.

17. *Ant.* 1.8, 10, 16, 62; 3.2, 26, 28, 56.

18. *Ant.* 3.4, 6, 8, 29, 56; 6.1, 28, 37.

19. *Ant.* 1.10, 12, 47; 3.25, 35, 54.

20. *Ant.* 3.5, 7, 9, 10, 27, 31, 37, 38, 40, 43, 44, 47, 48, 58.

21. *Ant.* 1.28, 49; 3.28, 57; 5.28.

22. *Ant.* 1.58; 3.12, 30, 33, 45; 5.48, 51, 57.

23. This contrast is emphasized by Dale Martin, *The Corinthian Body* (New Haven, Conn.: Yale University Press, 1995), but contested by Troels Engberg-Pedersen, *Paul and the Stoics* (Louisville, Ky.: Westminster John Knox Press, 2000), 13–14.

24. Kate Cooper, *The Virgin and the Bride: Idealized Womanhood in Late Antiquity* (Cambridge, Mass.: Harvard University Press, 1996), 4.

25. Food: *Ant.* 1.30, 36, 38, 39. Sex: *Ant.* 2.40. Financial stability: *Ant.* 3.22, 34.

26. *Ant.* 6.7, 39, 43–45, 53, 57.

27. *Ant.* 3.3, 16, 17, 20, 22. Receiving aid: *Ant.* 3.1.

28. *Ant.* 2.1, 6, 9, 15, 19, 21, 23, 24, 31, 32, 36, 54, 56, 60. On the speed of such images, see Evagrius, *Praktikos* 51.

29. *Ant.* 2.2, 4, 5, 8, 18, 28, 29, 43. Shame: *Ant.* 2.33, 42.

30. *Ant.* 2.7, 13, 16, 41.

31. *Ant.* 5.5, 17, 20, 29, 31, 35, 39, 62–64; 6.9. Slander/gossip: *Ant.* 5.4, 6, 11, 13.

32. More advanced: *Ant.* 6.23; 7.2. Negligent/sinful: *Ant.* 5.14, 47, 49; 6.5; 8.31, 33, 38, 42.

33. *Ant.* 6.2, 30, 50, 55; 8.8.

34. *Ant.* 7.1, 9, 10, 13, 29, 41.

35. *Ant.* 8.1, 2, 6, 14, 15, 30, 35, 39, 43, 45, 48, 50, 55, 58.

36. *Ant.* 8.3, 5, 7, 13, 18, 25, 34.

37. *Ant.* 8.21, 23, 29, 41, 44, 49.

38. *Ant.* 8.10, 20, 28.

39. *Ant.* 8.24, 47, 56.

40. Irénée Hausherr, *Spiritual Direction in the Early Christian East* (trans. Anthony P. Gythiel; Cistercian Studies 116; Kalamazoo, Mich.: Cistercian Publications, 1990), 224.

41. John Cassian, *Institutiones* 6.9, 11 (*The Institutes* [trans. Boniface Ramsey; New York: Newman, 2000] 157; *Institutions cénobitiques* [ed. and trans. Jean-Claude Guy; SC 109; Paris: Cerf, 1965], 271–74).

42. David Brakke, "The Problematization of Nocturnal Emissions in Early Christian Syria and Gaul," *JECS* 3 (1995): 419–60, at 448–51. For a contrasting interpretation of Cassian on this subject, see Conrad Leyser, "Masculinity in Flux: Nocturnal Emission and the Limits of Celibacy in the Early Middle Ages," in *Masculinity in Medieval Europe* (ed. D. M. Hadley; Women and Men in History; London: Longman, 1999), 103–20.

43. Confronted with the devil's suggestions that he can pursue the ascetic life in the household, the monk should "shake off the raindrops of these thoughts from his inner places"; "Shake off the praise of people from your inner places"; the demons sometimes try to deceive the monk by "hiding impure thoughts from his inner places" (*Ad Eulogium* 2.2; 4.4; 31.33 [Sinkewicz, *Ascetic Corpus*, 30, 32, 58 (Eng. trans. alt.); 311, 312, 332 (Greek text)]).

44. Columba Stewart, "Imageless Prayer and the Theological Vision of Evagrius Ponticus," *JECS* 9 (2001): 173–204. O'Laughlin is somewhat close to my view: "Evagrius does not allow the inner conflicts and doubts of the monks to ferment within an introspective and private enclosure; they are held up for analysis, classified, and remedied with sound counsel from the Scriptures" ("The Bible, the Demons and the Desert," 214). Compare Pierre Hadot on writing as a spiritual exercise among the Stoics and the Epicureans: "The point is not to forge oneself a spiritual identity by writing, but rather to liberate oneself from one's individuality, in order to raise oneself up to universality. . . . Writing, like the other spiritual exercises, *changes the level of the self,* and universalizes it" (*Philosophy as a Way of Life* [ed. Arnold I. Davidson; trans. Michael Chase; Oxford: Blackwell, 1995], 210–11, emphasis in original).

—13—

The Student Self in Late Antiquity

EDWARD WATTS

Ammonius (Saccas) was a Christian who was brought up in Christianity by his parents. However, when he began to think and study philosophy, he immediately changed [*metebaleto*] to a way of life that conformed with the laws.
—Porphyry quoted in Eusebius, *Hist. eccl.* 6.19.6–7

[The Alexandrian intellectuals Epiphanius and Eu-prepius] were not born into the traditional way of life [i.e., paganism] but they encountered and spent time with those who had been and, having benefited from their company, they became [*egenonto*] for their as-sociates the source of many blessings and, among other things, the great voiced messengers of ancient stories.
—Damascius, *Isid.* frg. 100 = Athanassiadi frg. 41

Each of these passages describes the religious experiences of Christian students who were studying at a major intellectual center in the later Roman Empire. As such, they provide an interesting and somewhat unique look into late Roman classrooms. But the specific language used in these passages reveals something that is equally important to a discussion of the religious self in antiquity. In each passage, a verb of changing or becoming is used to describe the transition of an individual from one religious category to another. So Ammonius Saccas began to study philosophy and then "changed" from a Christian to a pagan way of life. Epiphanius and Euprepius began to associate with philosophers and they "be-came" an important part of a pagan religious community. Admittedly, the categories of pagan and Christian are imprecise ones that are subject to the endless interpretation of both ancient and modern authors.[1] Nevertheless, our inability to comprehensively and conclusively define these categories need not render them meaningless. As these two passages make clear, in their own minds,

Ammonius, Epiphanius, and Euprepius seem to have once identified themselves as Christians. Following their experiences as students, they no longer did so. On a personal level, then, it seems clear that individual students in the ancient world understood their identification as a Christian or a pagan to be a significant one. They were also aware that a change in this identification was notable.

In the same way that students' understandings of their religious identity were individually determined, so too were the approaches Christian students took to the basic challenge of rectifying their Christianity with grammatical, rhetorical, and philosophical curricula that contained much explicitly pagan material.[2] Ammonius Saccas, for example, apparently became so disenchanted with Christianity as he progressed in his study of philosophy that he converted to paganism. Others, like Choricius of Gaza or Basil of Caesarea, focused on the utility of their education and disregarded any inconvenient pagan elements. Choricius was said to have "culled from poetry whatever was useful while smiling at the myths,"[3] while Basil urged young Christians to be aware that they do not "take the poisons along with the honey."[4]

The doctrinal difficulties faced by Christians who were studying in a traditional educational curriculum were well understood by their contemporaries.[5] These difficulties were real, and as the chronological range of the examples cited above suggests, Christian student conversion to paganism was a persistent problem that represented as much a danger in the sixth century as it did in the third. While this provides modern scholars of ancient education with an interesting topic for study, ancient observers probably would have had a ready explanation for the phenomenon. To them, Christian students were intellectuals in training, and as such, they were interested in intellectual discussion but not yet able to judge good arguments from bad. The conversion of a student, then, arose because the individual student had been swayed, rightly or wrongly, by a learned argument. Indeed, no text illustrates this belief better than the sixth-century dialogue, the *Ammonius* of Zacharias Scholasticus.[6] This text, which purports to record a series of conversations between Zacharias and the philosopher Ammonius Hermeiou, presents refutations of philosophical doctrines that conflict with Christian teaching. At the beginning of the text, Zacharias makes clear that Ammonius had used these doctrines to induce Christian students to turn away from Christian teachings (*Ammon.*, lines 19–32). The subsequent discussions then refute these doctrines systematically. After one such exchange, for example, Zacharias states, "Many of those present in the class at that time . . . were placed among us and leaned towards our arguments, or more correctly, they leaned towards Christianity out of faith and love of truth" (*Ammon.*, lines 357–60). To make this even more clear, the final exchange ends with Ammonius so forcefully discredited that the students applaud while Ammonius blushes from embarrassment. The dialogue then concludes with a prayer, as if to illustrate how the dangers of pagan teaching could be eliminated by effective argumentation.

Although the setting of this dialogue is unique, the dramatic progression of the piece is not exceptional. Conversion through argumentation was something of a trope in Christian literature of the later Roman period. Dramatic dialogues like the *Ammonius* worked from the common premise that effective argumentation could change the religious direction of both the inexperienced student and the seasoned intellectual. Nevertheless, as modern studies of conversion have shown, actual conversions seldom result solely from doctrinal or ideological discussions.[7] While doctrinal elements may play a secondary role in conversion, these studies have found that the true catalysts of religious change are more often social or personal factors.

With these findings noted, this essay will turn away from the doctrinal issues and dialectic discussions that ancient authors so emphasize. Instead, it will explore how the nature of Roman student life and the personal experiences of Roman students shaped their identities while they were at school. It will be shown that the later Roman educational environment encouraged students to develop a distinct personal identity that was shaped by the rituals and rhythms of both the specific teaching circle to which they belonged and the larger intellectual community in which they functioned. For most students, both Christian and pagan, this process was rather benign, and the inherent contradictions between the values of the classroom and the set of values they previously held were insignificant. In some cases, however, the student experience caused a very real crisis in personal identity in which the attitudes of the "student self" could not be effectively assimilated with those in which the student was raised. This was a traumatic event, and in a small number of such cases our sources enable us to see how this irreconcilable conflict resulted in religious conversion.

Establishing the Student Self-Identity

It is well acknowledged that education in the Roman world was attractive to students and parents as a social marker that distinguished those who possessed it from those who did not.[8] The importance of education went beyond simply its prestige value. The late Roman educational curriculum was designed to shape a student's basic way of functioning in the world.[9] This was true throughout the different levels of education, but as a student progressed, this element became an increasing focus of the curriculum. The stages of education that had potentially the greatest impact on students were the higher-level disciplines of rhetoric and philosophy. This sort of training was rare. Only a small minority of people in the Roman world had the means to afford such training, and only large cities appear to have had the resources to support teachers of rhetoric and especially of philosophy.[10] This meant that students who sought such training often had to travel to a major center of learning for instruction.[11] When such a trip was made, the curricular elements that shaped student behaviors were reinforced by the physical introduction to a foreign environment. Students who arrived at a school in Athens, Alexandria, or one of the other elite teaching centers of the Roman Empire literally entered into a new life, complete with a new family (the teacher and his fellow students), a new appearance (the gowns required of students), and a new set of acceptable behaviors. In the years that they remained at school, students were expected to function fully as a part of this new world and uphold the values inherent in it.[12]

Although student life at an elite teaching center represented a real change from the world in which students grew up, it seems that few students arrived in, say, Athens without a basic awareness that student life differed from what they had previously known. Libanius, for example, speaks of his days as a young student in Antioch and recalls how Iasion, a fellow student, "would describe the things which he had heard from older men about Athens and the doings there" (*Or.* 1.11). As a respectable intellectual himself, Libanius could claim that the eloquence of the professors and their rhetorical competitions were the elements of Athenian intellectual life that attracted him. At the same time, Libanius also left for Athens aware of some of the extra-curricular activities in which Athenian students were expected to participate. "From my boyhood," he begins, "I had heard tales of the fighting between the schools . . . and all of the deeds of daring that students perform to raise the prestige of their teachers. I thought them noble for going forth in such dangers and [thought this] no less honorable than taking up arms for one's nation, and I used to pray to the gods that I too would distinguish myself in such actions" (*Or.* 1.19). Among the other activities Libanius had heard about and longed to take part in were "the kidnapping of arriving students, being taken to Corinth for trial on kidnapping charges, giving many feasts, blowing all [his] money, and looking for someone to give a loan" (*Or.* 1.19).

Libanius' words reveal that students arrived in Athens with an understanding that they had entered a different stage in their lives. While they did not yet know the specific codes of behavior to which they would soon be subject, students did appreciate that they were expected to have new loyalties to their teachers and that certain actions, like brawling or kidnapping, were acceptable when done to demonstrate these loyalties. What is more, Libanius illustrates that, even though these values were antithetical to what was commonly accepted outside of the scholastic environment, it was recognized that one's status as a student made honorable behaviors out of those that were normally criminal.[13] While youths were students, normally unacceptable behaviors like brawling and throwing parties could be positive activities. In short, students arrived at school expecting to live according to a different set of values.

In Athens, at least, this sense that the arriving student had entered a new stage in his life was confirmed ritually when he first came to the city. When the student arrived, he was forced to swear an oath to study under a specific teacher. This oath was either "coerced" (as in the case of Libanius) or given willfully (as

Eunapius experienced).[14] Following the oath, the ritual initiation of the student began. After agreeing to study under a teacher, the student "is mocked by all who wish to do so, with the intention of reducing the conceit of the newcomers, and bringing them to submission. . . . Next, he is conducted in procession through the market place to the bath" (Gregory Nazianzen, *Or.* 43.16).[15]

The procession was something of a production that was designed to be quite frightening to the student involved.[16] "All the novices, both advanced and beginning students, were led to the public bath. And those of their number who were of the right age and ready for the *tribōn* (a special cloak) were pushed to the front of the crowd by those scholars who were leading them. Then, while some rushed forward and blocked their way, others pushed them from behind. And all of those who blocked them screamed, 'Stop! Stop! Do not bathe!' " (Olympiodorus of Thebes, frg. 28)

This process seems to have been a rather rough affair and may have included some physical violence against the new student. Eunapius, who was quite ill when he arrived in Athens, was initiated later than his compatriots. When this was done, the older students who initiated him were instructed by their professor to "refrain from all mockery and teasing, and scrub him as if he were my son" (*VS* 486). Other new students, presumably, were "scrubbed" much more harshly. Whatever the form of these initial rites, once the students managed to process into the bathhouse, they were "washed, dressed, and received the right to wear the *tribōn*" (Olympiodorus, frg. 28). When the bath was completed, Gregory Nazianzen says, the students "allowed (the initiate) to enter, presented him with his freedom, and received him after the bath as an equal" (*Or.* 43.16).

Leaving aside the religious parallels to this cleansing bath, the significance of this ritual as a welcoming to the community of students is clear. The new arrival, who had just formally agreed to join the school by swearing an oath, was first treated as an outsider and mocked as an inferior member of the community. He was also threatened with violence (if not actually beaten). When this experience was complete, he was led in a procession to the Agora baths[17] and only then admitted fully into the community. This initiation ritual, which began with the scorn of the new arrival and ended with his acceptance into the community, both illustrates the transition of the student into a new stage in life and distinguishes his new self from his past identity.

This ancient process of student initiation has a remarkable similarity to modern scholastic initiation rituals. When describing such things, scholars tend to see three stages of initiation,[18] including an initial phase of separation during which the initiates are reminded of their distinction from the full members of the group. In the Athenian setting, this stage includes both the initial swearing of an oath to study under a professor and the subsequent sustained mockery the student must endure. Next comes something of a liminal phase during which initiates are left to anticipate some fearful challenge that they must overcome before joining the group. For Athenian students, this phase is represented by the procession to the bathhouse. Finally, a ritual of reincorporation occurs during which the initiate is fully welcomed into the group. In Athens this would have been the ceremony during which the student receives his *tribōn*. Ultimately, the effects of this process in both the ancient and modern environment are clear. The initiated students understand that they have left behind their past and, to some degree, their past identities as well.[19]

Once initiated, the Athenian student became a part of the school, and to signify this, he was expected to wear the *tribōn* when in public.[20] He also began to participate in activities with others in the school. His relationships to the other members of his school, however, were defined by a rather rigid hierarchy. The professor of the school sat at the top of this hierarchy, and below him were his most advanced students, the senior students described by Olympiodorus. These were more like modern graduate students and often doubled as assistant teachers.[21] Below them was the crop of less-advanced students. They formed the *choros* of the professor, a sort of student body that was bound both to one another and to the service of the professor.[22] This corps of students was organized according to seniority and led by a designated student leader.[23] Not surprisingly, the first-year students were at the bottom of the hierarchy, and hazing was not uncommon. In fourth-century Athens, for example, it was common to gang up on first-year students whenever they argued an intellectual point. Indeed, the arguing could get so fierce that Gregory Nazianzen once felt compelled to break with student protocol in order to help his friend Basil win such an argument (*Or.* 43.17). Almost 150 years later, a similar scenario is known to have played out in the law schools of Berytus (Zacharias Scholasticus, *Vit. Sev.* 47).[24]

While a student entered this defined scholastic hierarchy at the bottom, this arrangement was neither wholly unwelcoming nor unfamiliar. The professor was a trusted figure on whom students were taught to depend. In fact, it was common for teachers and students alike to see their relationship in familial terms. Libanius speaks of himself as a father to his students, and Synesius describes his teacher, the philosopher Hypatia, as his mother.[25] In a more practical way, a student could call on his teacher for support if he was arrested (Eunapius, *VS* 483).[26] He could also ask for the professor to use his influence to convince government officials to give his family special treatment (Libanius, *Ep.* 359). A young man could even sometimes convince his teacher to ask for a raise in his allowance (*Ep.* 428).

A student's relationship with his professor was important, and in the ideal if not in actual practice, a student was expected not only to be loyal to his professor but to manifest this loyalty whenever possible. Students cheered their professor when he gave a public lecture,[27] avoided the public lectures of other professors when so instructed,[28] and even clubbed the students of particularly hated rivals.[29] In fact, Libanius' comparison of fealty to a professor with loyalty to one's homeland is exaggerated but not wholly misleading, and it illustrates the basic level on which this identification with a teacher was supposed to operate (*Or.* 1.19).

While student-professor relationships were, at least in theory, character-ized by respectfulness and mutual gestures of loyalty, student relationships with their classmates were far closer. Eunapius, for example, describes how the rhetorician Prohaeresius lived with his classmate Hephaestion and became so close to him that they even shared a *tribōn* (*VS* 483). Although the students were generally older in a philosophy school, the relationships between them were just as intimate if not more so. Synesius, for example, bemoaned the lack of such companionship in a letter to his fellow student Herculianus: "It is not without fear that I remain helplessly alone without anyone with whom to share my philosophic frenzy. . . . Leaving aside your holy soul, next to what other kindling can I rub to produce the shining child of reason? Who will be so able to powerfully call forth a hidden spark which loves to conceal itself and show forth a brilliant fire?" (*Ep.* 139)

This personal intimacy was fostered by a curriculum that emphasized the value of close friendships and taught students the skills to successfully maintain such relationships.[30] Nevertheless, these relationships also were sustained by other less savory communal activities. The kidnapping of students, the brawl-ing, and the partying with classmates have all been described above.[31] What is important about such things, however, is not that ancient students were a wild bunch (which they were), but that in most cases these actions were performed as a part of a group. Although these fights did not usually involve all of the students in the school, the punishment of these riots makes clear that they were seen as actions taken on behalf of the entire school. Eunapius describes the aftermath of one particular street battle between the *choroi* of the professors Julianus and Apsines (*VS* 483). When a complaint about the violence was filed by students of Apsines, the proconsul of Achaea ordered the arrest, not just of the students involved, but of the entire school of Julianus, including the teacher himself. The idea behind this collective punishment seems to be that the school as a whole shared responsibility for the violence because it had been motivated by the interests of the *choros* and the professor it served.

As this incident suggests, student violence was actually an expression of loyalty that was reserved for only the most advanced students. Libanius, for example, describes something called "the Great Riot" that involved all Athenian students in a major street brawl. He makes a point of indicating that even the most junior members of the school (who were normally not involved) partici-pated in the fighting (*Or.* 1.21).[32] Libanius' description seems to suggest that this was an exceptional case and that under normal circumstances only the more advanced members of the *choros* would engage in such fights. This normally deviant behavior, then, not only showed loyalty to the school, but it also com-municated a student's high position within the scholastic hierarchy.

In spite of these rituals, the process of integration into the student body of an ancient school was not nearly as successful as one might presume. The overwhelming majority of students in the Roman Empire did not attend elite schools or travel to elite educational centers. Among the select group of students who were educated in elite centers, many were unable to complete their training for financial or other reasons.[33] In addition, student loyalty was often a problem. It was not uncommon for students to shift from professor to professor in pursuit of a cheap, yet still high-quality education.[34] Even among those students who stayed and completed their study under one professor there were the occasional students who sullenly refused to participate in such group activities. Libanius, who proudly counted himself among that group, was thought disrespectful and ostracized by his classmates for his bad attitude.[35]

With all of these exceptions noted, one can still accept Libanius' youthful idea that scholastic life in a major educational center required students to adopt a set of behaviors that differed dramatically from those they displayed at home. It is important to realize, however, that these behaviors were shaped by relationships, values, and rituals specific to the scholastic environment. A student arriving in Athens, for example, would undergo a dramatic initiation into the community of scholars that illustrated his new status. When the initiation was complete, he would be given the privilege of publicly displaying his acquired status, and while a student, he would be expected to do so at all times.[36] This ritual initiation signified a new stage in the student's life, but it also marked the beginning of his integration into the *choros* of the school. This process combined moderate hazing with public displays of loyalty to the professor; and in its course, many students developed close bonds with each other and deep affection for the school.[37]

These first stages of student life would have had two significant effects on the student and his conception of self. First, the student was taught to value new relationships with peers and adults who did not share his familial and regional background. In both the curriculum (with its emphasis on friendship) and the communal activities of the school, a student was taught to be positively disposed to the new people with whom he was associating. Separated from the relatively closed social networks within which he was raised, this meant that he was often inclined to take a more open-minded view of ideas that were widely accepted within the school. This would have been especially true if the student was young and the new ideas were those of an individual who occupied a high position in the scholastic hierarchy. Second, and of equal importance, the student learned that in a scholastic setting normally unacceptable behaviors were acceptable if they either enhanced his integration into the group or furthered the group's interest. Consequently, the acceptability of behaviors was now evaluated according to new criteria, and activities that had been frowned upon at home could, in a scholastic setting, be seen as acceptable if not even virtuous.

Religious Values and the Student Self

To this point, our discussion has highlighted only how the student identity, as constructed in the first years of schooling, caused students to engage eagerly in behaviors that they would not normally deem acceptable. It should not be surprising, then, that this peculiar student self-identity could have implications for religious behavior as well. One of the most concise illustrations of this danger is Gregory Nazianzen's description of the religious environment encountered by fourth-century Athenian rhetorical students: "Athens is harmful to the soul and this is of no small consequence to the pious. For the city is richer in those evil riches—idols—than the rest of Greece and it is hard not to be carried along and led away with their devotees" (*Or.* 43.21). Gregory makes it clear that Athens was a difficult place for Christian students because it was an environment in which paganism was still functioning. At the same time, the real danger came from the possibility that students would be carried away by this religious atmosphere. Although overstated, there is good reason not to disregard Gregory's concern. The peculiar culture of the scholastic environment emphasized friendship with one's classmates and made it clear that activities done collectively by these students were generally acceptable even if they would not be tolerated outside of school.

While Gregory merely suggests that this environment put pressure on Christian students to participate in pagan religious activities, two later sources provide a clearer glimpse of how a student's self-identity could be torn between loyalty to his comrades and loyalty to his faith. The best description of this personal conflict comes from a segment of Zacharias Scholasticus' *Life of Severus*, which describes life at a law school in Berytus in the 490s. Zacharias introduces his readers to John, "nicknamed the Fuller." This man was probably a law student and came from an Egyptian Christian family. While in Berytus, he fell in with a group of students who experimented with pagan and magical rituals.[38] On certain occasions they would assemble and carry out these rites. According to Zacharias, one night this ring assembled to sacrifice one of John's slaves. The slave escaped and told one of John's Christian acquaintances about the affair. Soon a group of Christians (including Zacharias) confronted John. In obvious shock, John told them that this magical experimentation was motivated by his love for a woman and thanked God for delivering him "from the servitude and error of demons. He declared he was, in fact, a Christian and the son of Christian parents but he had erred and had worshipped idols" (*Vit. Sev.* 62). Zacharias and his friends accepted John's tearful apology, prayed with the repentant Christian, and went off in search of his compatriots.

John's story of coming to Berytus as a Christian and falling in with a group of fellow students who were experimenting with paganism was not unique. Severus, the future bishop of Antioch, described a scene in which such experimentation was common: "I know many of the young men who devoted themselves to Roman law in that turbulent city, that is Berytus, and they went off to [Tripoli] to pray and speedily left their vain erudition and way of life and purified their minds of Hellenic myths."[39] This speech, which was intended to emphasize the power of the shrine of St. Leontius, also makes it clear that pagan religious experimentation was common in the law schools of Berytus. Indeed, despite his descent from a prominent bishop and his own future career in the church,[40] Severus admits in this speech that he too was swept up in the general mood of religious experimentation and toyed with paganism while a law student.

For John, Severus, and probably even many of Gregory's associates in Athens, the religious experimentation they engaged in was not much different from hazing or ritualized violence. It was an activity that was very much a product of the particular social atmosphere of the school, and as such, it was acceptable only within a scholastic setting. The willingness to engage in such experimentation, like the willingness to punch a stranger in the nose for studying under the wrong teacher, was an attribute of the student's self-identity *as a student*. It was inconsistent with his religious self-definition outside of school and, when he left the peculiar environment of the intellectual center, it was likely that these elements were disregarded, perhaps with some embarrassment at their ever having been his in the first place.[41]

Nevertheless, for some students, this religious experimentation triggered a tension between their self-identity as a student and their religious self-definition.[42] For those who chose to remain in a scholastic environment, this tension could even result in conversion. I began with ancient descriptions of the conversion of three people, all intellectuals, from Christianity to paganism. Ammonius Saccas' conversion was certainly tied to his study of philosophy, but beyond that no details are available. We are slightly better informed about the Alexandrian intellectuals Epiphanius and Euprepius.[43] Like John the Fuller and Severus, Epiphanius and Euprepius were born Christians and became acquainted with paganism through their association with pagans, but unlike the two law students, they did not see this pagan experimentation as a youthful indiscretion. It revealed a fundamental difference between the activities that characterized their student life and those that identified them as Christians. Instead of turning away from the experiences of student life that conflicted with their Christianity, they chose to alter their religious self-definition and embrace the behaviors they had experimented with in school.

It is at this point that the Christian concern with the pagan doctrinal content of ancient education should perhaps re-enter this discussion. While social and cultural factors that were peculiar to the academic environment made religious experimentation a plausible manifestation of the student self-identity, the choice to integrate this behavior into one's larger religious identity would likely not be made solely on the basis of peer pressure. Other elements contributed to such a choice. In some scholastic settings, this experimentation occurred within an academic hierarchy in which the most important people were practicing pagans. The grammarian Horapollon, for example, taught in Alexandria while Severus was a student there. He was an active pagan who encouraged interested students to worship with him (*Vit. Sev.* 15). Some teachers also combined pagan practice with teaching that conflicted with Christian doctrines. In the *Ammonius*, Zacharias Scholasticus classifies Ammonius Hermeiou as such a figure: "Ammonius is the teacher of Plato and Aristotle. . . . He is a clever man (who) corrupts the souls of youths and takes them away from God and truth . . . and raises the heavens to the same level as God, saying that the whole universe came about from one cause, was co-eternal with its creator, and would never perish" (lines 19–38).

Ammonius' teachings about the co-eternity of creation and the impossibility of a destruction of the universe were philosophically defensible points,[44] but they also conflicted with very basic Christian teachings. Ammonius was an authoritative figure, the dominant figure in his particular school,[45] and as such, students were expected to listen respectfully to his ideas. For many Christian students, and probably for most, Ammonius' classes represented nothing more than a basic introduction to philosophy.[46] For such students, the lasting impact of these teachings would have been minimal. Ammonius' teaching about the universe either would have been dismissed as irrelevant or would have represented a momentary intellectual experimentation that paralleled a student's ephemeral willingness to participate in pagan rituals.

For students who were struggling with the conflict between their student self-identity and their religious upbringing (like Epiphanius and Euprepius), teachings like those of Ammonius would have provided an authoritative, intellectually defensible support for their inclination to a new (and hitherto deviant) religious identity. This pull would have been especially strong if the student became convinced that he wanted either to spend his life teaching or to remain otherwise active in a scholastic environment.[47] If he chose to do so, he could never fully abandon the communal values of the schools that most other students dropped when they left school.

Christian Religious Activity in the Schools

The danger of deviant religious behavior among students is equally well illustrated by Christian religious activity in the schools. One type of activity, the composition of texts that attack uncomfortable doctrinal positions, was quite common.[48] While these could certainly affect wider perceptions of pagan teachers and possibly prevent students from studying under a professor, there is no reason to believe that such texts would have swayed the opinions of students already at a school. An attack on the skill of a professor, like that found in Zacharias Scholasticus' *Ammonius*, would have even less chance of success. In fact, it probably would have provoked incredulity or even violent opposition from among Ammonius' own students. In keeping with the custom of the scholastic environment, Ammonius' students would have been expected to remain loyal to their teacher and if necessary even fight for the reputation of his school. Indeed, in the *Life of Severus*, Zacharias describes the beating of a student named Paralius. He was set upon after he openly dismissed the wisdom of his teacher, denigrated the intelligence of a group of philosophers (including Ammonius), and attacked the pagan religious ideas this group of intellectuals advocated (*Vit. Sev.* 22–23).[49] His points against the philosopher were met, not with a reasoned reply, but with the violent response that one would expect from a properly loyal student of a slandered teacher.

Texts written to attack the basic competency of a teacher would not work particularly well in an environment where a fundamental part of many students' self-identity was their loyalty to their school. Christians, however, did employ more effective strategies that used specific elements of the properly developed student self-identity to combat the temptation to experiment with paganism. One such strategy was used in fifth-century Alexandria by a group called the *philoponoi*.[50] The role of *philoponoi* in the classrooms of Alexandria is known only through the *Life of Severus*, but its description of their activities is quite vivid. They encouraged students to think positively about Christianity and gave religious guidance to those who were receptive to them. Zacharias, who was himself a *philoponos* in the 480s, indicates that the methods of the *philoponoi* were systematic. First they talked to their classmates and found out something about their religious backgrounds. If they found someone who was anything short of a convinced Christian, the *philoponoi* would try to get him to read Christian literature that countered the pagan texts being taught in the schools (Basil and Gregory were apparently the favorites) (*Vit. Sev.* 48). They would then offer to give him instruction in the texts' meaning in a group setting.[51] From there, the group would draw him closer until they persuaded the individual to accept baptism and, possibly, to join them.

The *philoponoi* methods were effective not for doctrinal reasons but because they provided students with a communal environment in which they could study Christianity and Christian writings. They were a group of students bound by a scholastic friendship who were working together to re-affirm their Christian religious identity. Nevertheless, while their collective activities emphasized different things than the classroom teaching, they were not inherently disloyal to either the school or the professor. The *philoponoi* reading curriculum was made up largely of fourth-century authors—a sort of Christian "classics" program—that seems explicitly designed to emphasize Christian themes without bringing one's immediate loyalty to a current school or its teachings into question. The *philoponoi*, then, offered a particularly attractive package through which the student self, which was interested in communal activities and scholastic loyalty, could be made to complement one's previous religious identity. Indeed, the appeal of this package is suggested by the fact that the *philoponoi* seem to have attracted some pagan converts as well.[52]

Another approach that showed an equal sensitivity to the needs of the scholastic self was that taken by Origen almost 250 years before the *philoponoi*. Although Origen is on the early side of this study, his activities as a teacher are particularly relevant to any consideration of the religious implications of a student's self identity. Whereas the *philoponoi* program worked by having students reach out to one another in ways that were acceptable within the scholastic environment, Origen capitalized on the natural respect that a student had for a teacher to communicate a Christian message to students of philosophy.[53]

By the later stages of his life, Origen had become recognized as a powerful intellectual figure,[54] and he parlayed this fame into an effective protreptic teaching curriculum.[55] Origen understood philosophical explanation to be a gateway through which students could be led to Christianity.[56] For him, education became a method to bring about conversion, and the teacher became a type of missionary. Gregory, a student who joined Origen's circle while he taught in Caesarea, provides even more details about how Origen used philosophy to attract educated men to Christianity. Gregory came to Origen's school as a pagan with training in philosophy and law. Nevertheless, through daily philosophical discussions, Origen made Gregory begin to consider the Christian significance of pagan philosophy and ultimately produced a conversion in Gregory.[57]

By the end of this time with Origen, Gregory saw Origen as a teacher and accorded him the respect expected of a student. In fact, it has been argued that Gregory's *Address to Origen* was a goodbye speech composed to express his respect for his teacher as well as his gratitude for the instruction he received.[58] If this is a correct assessment of Gregory's intent, this speech was paralleled many times by the addresses pagan students gave when leaving their teachers.[59] Origen then succeeded in facilitating Gregory's conversion through his teaching. The doctrinal message, however, was couched in the language and institutions of traditional education. Consequently, Origen's success with Gregory resulted from the same peculiar mixture of professorial respect and intense doctrinal study that would make student conversion such a danger in fifth-century Alexandrian pagan schools.

The later Roman scholastic environment, with its unique combination of communal rituals and adolescent insecurity, created a particular set of challenges to the religious identity of young students. Some of this was inherent in a curriculum wholly comprised of pagan texts. Nevertheless, it seems that the most significant challenges students faced were not doctrinal in nature. A student who attended school in one of the most prestigious intellectual centers of the empire entered into a new social environment in which individual values and relationships were different. The distinction between scholastic life and one's previous existence was made clear when a student was first initiated into the student body and given the privilege of wearing a *tribōn*. The student's physical distinction from his prior appearance was matched by a new set of attitudes he was expected to display. Students were to respect the other members of their school and respond to any attempts to disparage the school or its head. They were encouraged to defend the institution's honor collectively, be it through acclamations when their professor gave a public performance or street fighting against the students of a scholastic rival. Perhaps encouraged by a curriculum that taught students how to maintain friendships, this activity helped particularly strong bonds to develop between some classmates.

While he was in school, a student's self was defined generally by his status as a student and specifically by his identification with a particular school. For many of those who studied in elite teaching centers like Athens, a great pride was attached to their ability to uphold the values of the student community. Consequently, when the youth of individual students combined with the general emphasis on collective action and the toleration of otherwise unacceptable activities, religious experimentation was not surprising. Although the Christian nature of most of our sources makes it difficult to know for sure, it seems that this experimentation was a product of the specific stimuli of the scholastic environment. But experimentation alone rarely resulted in conversion; the variable nature of both student religious identities and student personality types combined to make such conversions exceptional. The reason for this, it seems, lies in the process that helped new students understand what the scholastic community expected of them. While rituals demonstrating loyalty to a teacher and a cohort of students were significant, the rituals and activities that formally shaped a student's self-identity did not have any explicit religious content. Thus, while this unique environment fostered religious experimentation, such activity was an unintended (and officially unsanctioned) consequence of study. The student converts produced by this environment were welcomed by pagans, but one cannot imagine that they were particularly common.

NOTES

1. Frank Trombley's study of late paganism (*Hellenic Religion and Christianization* [2 vols.; Religions in the Graeco-Roman World 115; Leiden: Brill, 1993–94]) has illustrated how imprecise the line between paganism and Christianity can be. The later collection of essays edited by Polymnia Athanassiadi and Michael Frede, *Pagan Monotheism in Late Antiquity* (Oxford: Oxford University Press, 1999) also provides a series of insightful discussions about the overlap between pagan and Christian religious understandings. Like Athanassiadi and Frede, I have chosen to use the term "pagan" in this essay because, while an imperfect label, it remains the best category in which to place Romans who are neither Christian nor Jewish (cf. *Pagan Monotheism*, 4–7).

2. This was due, in large part, to the traditional nature of these curricula. Many of the standard teaching approaches were framed before the emergence of officially tolerated Christianity (e.g., the *progymnasmata* of Theon and Hermogenes). Consequently,

they were designed to teach students how to behave in a pagan religious environment (cf. Plutarch, *Mor.* 7E).

3. Choricius, *Laudatio Marciani* 1.4. See also Robert Kaster, *Guardians of Language: The Grammarian and Society in Late Antiquity* (The Transformation of the Classical Heritage 11; Berkeley: University of California Press, 1988), 80–81.

4. Basil, *Ad adulescentes* 4.4.

5. Julian's *Epistula* 61 (as numbered by Bidez-Cumont) describes the intended effects of his education law and is perhaps the best ancient statement attesting to this. It concludes with the statement "Any youth who wishes to attend the schools is not excluded; nor indeed would it be reasonable to shut out from the best way, boys who are still too ignorant to know which direction to turn or to compel them through fear to paganism . . . for we ought, I think, to teach but not punish the demented." Interesting as well is *Codex Justinianus* 1.11.10, a Justinianic law prohibiting pagans from teaching because of the possible negative effect their "dementia" could have on Christian students.

6. For the *Ammonius,* the latest edition is *Ammonio* (ed. M. Minniti Colonna; Naples: Tipolitografia "La Buona Stampa," 1973). On the text and its context, see Edward Watts, "An Alexandrian Christian Response to Neoplatonic Influence," in *Philosophy and Science in Late Antiquity* (ed. A. Smith, forthcoming).

7. See Rodney Stark, *The Rise of Christianity: A Sociologist Reconsiders History* (Princeton, N.J.: Princeton University Press, 1996), and John Lofland and R. Stark, "Becoming a World-Saver: A Theory of Conversion to a Deviant Perspective," *American Sociological Review* 30 (1965): 862–75.

8. See the concise discussion of Kaster, *Guardians,* 15. One sees a similar phenomenon in modern education: see Jacques Barzun, *The American University: How It Runs, Where It Is Going* (New York: Harper & Row, 1968), 65.

9. With education came an understanding of essential virtues like "what is honorable and what is shameful, what is just and what is unjust . . . how a man must bear himself in his interactions with the gods, with his parents, with his elders, with the laws, with strangers, with those in authority, with friends, with women, with children, and with servants" (Plutarch, *Mor.* 7E). On the role of education in shaping social relationships in late antiquity, see Peter Brown, *Power and Persuasion in Late Antiquity: Towards a Christian Empire* (Curti Lectures; Madison: University of Wisconsin Press, 1992), 35–41.

10. Raffaela Cribiore, *Gymnastics of the Mind: Greek Education in Hellenistic and Roman Egypt* (Princeton, N.J.: Princeton University Press, 2001), 41–43.

11. On student travel and the emergence of "international" intellectual centers, see Edward Watts, "Travel to School: What Was the Attraction?" in *Travel, Communication and Geography in Late Antiquity* (ed. Linda Ellis and Frank Kidner; Burlington, Vt.: Ashgate, 2004), 11–21.

12. Although some stayed with their teachers for decades, most students did not stay long. Indeed, of the 57 students of Libanius whose term of study is known, fully 35 dropped out by the end of their second year. On this, see Kaster, *Guardians,* 26–27.

13. This idea is eloquently illustrated by Augustine, *Conf.* 5.8: "Their recklessness is unbelievable and they often commit outrages that ought to be punished by law, were it not that custom protects them."

14. Libanius (*Or.* 1.16) describes the unpleasant experience of being abducted and held against his will. This happened despite the fact that Libanius had agreed to study under another teacher before he had departed for Athens. Himerius (*Or.* 48.37) also describes this phenomenon. For Eunapius' experiences, see *VS* 485–87.

15. This ritual is known as well from Eunapius, *VS* 486 and Olympiodorus of Thebes, frg. 28 = Photius, *Bibliotheca* cod. 80.177f.

16. Gregory describes the performance as "seeming very fearful and brutal to those who do not know it (but) it is to those who have experienced it quite pleasant and humane, for its threats are for show rather than real" (*Or.* 43.16).

17. I thank Neil McLynn for the identification of the baths mentioned by Gregory.

18. The fundamental study on this remains Arnold van Gennep, *The Rites of Passage* (trans. M. B. Vizedom and G. Caffee; 2d ed.; Chicago: University of Chicago Press, 1960). For these rituals as they relate to a modern scholastic setting, see Hank Nuwer, *Wrongs of Passage: Fraternities, Sororities, and Binge Drinking* (Bloomington: Indiana University Press, 1999), 53–56.

19. On this idea in a modern context, see Nuwer, *Wrongs*, 54, and Thomas Leemon, *The Rites of Passage in a Student Culture: A Study in the Dynamics of Transition* (Anthropology and Education Series; New York: Teachers College Press, Columbia University, 1972).

20. The necessity of wearing a student cloak while engaged in basic rhetorical study is suggested by Eunapius, *VS* 487. This was not only an Athenian convention. Heraclas in Alexandria was forced by his teacher to wear a *tribōn,* and once he began, it seems he continued to wear the garment whenever he engaged in intellectual pursuits (Eusebius, *Hist. eccl.* 6.19.12–14).

21. See Edward Watts, "City and School in Late Antique Athens and Alexandria" (Ph.D. diss., Yale University, 2002), 79–82, 114–20, and Cribiore, *Gymnastics,* 28–29.

22. See the good, if anachronistic, description of John W. H. Walden, *Universities of Ancient Greece* (New York: Scribner's, 1909), 296–98, and the more concise description of Cribiore, *Gymnastics,* 43. Other terms, like *fratria* (on which see Gregory Nazianzen, *Poema de se ipso* 2.1, 215), were also used.

23. The student leaders have different names in ancient sources. Their role in the school is not particularly clear nor is it evident that they were distinct from the upper-level students. Olympiodorus (frg. 28), for example, mentions that newly initiated students had to pay them a fee upon the commencement of their studies.

24. The page numbers for this text refer to Zacharias of Mytilene, *Sévère, patriarche d'Atioche, 512–218: Textes syriaques* (ed. and trans. Marc-Antoine Kugener; rev. ed.; PO 2; Turnhout, Belgium: Éditions Brepols, 1971). The translations are based on Kugener as well.

25. Libanius, *Ep.* 931, 1009, 1070, 1257. For a discussion of the term, see Paul Petit, *Les Étudiants de Libanius* (Études prosopographiques 1; Paris: Nouvelles Éditions latines, 1957), 35–36, and Synesius, *Ep.* 16.

26. This especially applied when a student was brought into court for something he did on his teacher's behalf.

27. Among many other references, see Eunapius, *VS* 483.

28. Libanius indicates that such a restriction was placed on Julian (*Or.* 18.13–14).

29. Libanius watched this happen to a classmate while he was a student (*Or.* 1.21).

30. See, for example, Plutarch, *Amic. mult.* 95C-F. An example of the teaching of friendship is found in Iamblichus, *VP* 33.

31. In addition to the description of Libanius (above), such behavior is alluded to by Himerius (*Or.* 4.9; *Or.* 69) and, in an Antiochene context, Libanius again (*Or.* 19).

32. Because they fought on behalf of their teachers, when the violence subsided, the teachers were punished instead of the students.

33. For the attrition rate of Libanius' school, see above. Family financial trouble was often the reason a student gave for abandoning his education. This was such a significant problem that funds were given to poor students by city governors (cf. Libanius, *Ep.* 319, 550, 552).

34. On this, see Augustine, *Conf.* 5.12; Libanius, *Or.* 43.8; and Cribiore, *Gymnastics,* 58–9. Interesting in this context is the earlier evidence from *P. Oxy.* 2190 as well as the discussion of Bruce Winter, *Philo and Paul among the Sophists* (SNTSMS 96; Cambridge: Cambridge University Press, 1997), 19–39.

35. Libanius describes his attitude and the reaction to it in *Or.* 1. 17.

36. Damascius, *Isid.* frg. 135 = Ath. frg. 59 B.

37. Scholastic loyalty is shown in many ways. These range from Synesius' personal affection for Hypatia to the financial gifts given to teachers by alumni (described by Apuleius, *Apol.* 23, and Damascius, *Isid.* frg. 158 = Ath. frg. 102).

38. Pierre Chuvin (*Chronicle of the Last Pagans* [Revealing Antiquity 4; Cambridge, Mass.: Harvard University Press, 1990], 112–13) seems to feel that, on the basis of his nickname, John was not a student but an itinerant soul who had decided to stay in Berytus and experiment with magic. While this is a possibility, his relationship with many students from the law schools and the speed with which he abandons magic when confronted seems to refute the impression that he was a non-student leader of this ring of magicians.

39. The homily is discussed in Trombley, *Religion,* 2:49–51, and G. Garitte, "Textes hagiographiques orientaux relatifs à S. Leonce de Tripoli: II. L' homélie copte de Sevère d'Antioche," *Le Muséon* 79 (1966): 335–86.

40. On Severus' family background, see *Vit. Sev.* 10–11.

41. One can note John the Fuller's profound shame and embarrassment at having been caught dabbling in paganism (*Vit. Sev.* 63). Unfortunately, we lack any reminiscence of student paganism that is not used rhetorically to highlight subsequent Christian piety.

42. Worth noting in light of this is a not-unproblematic study by Jeff Koon (*Types, Traits, and Transitions: The Lives of Four-Year College Students* [Berkeley: Center for Research and Development in Higher Education, 1974]). This study attempted to classify and assess the personality types of university students as well as their personal tendencies during their enrollment. One element on which he focused was the students' tendencies to identify with or react against "conventional society." His findings revealed that the "conventional" behaviors of many students were influenced by their studies, but only certain types of students consciously rejected these behaviors.

43. Damascius, *Isid.* frg. 100 = Ath. frg. 41.

44. Ammonius did indeed seem to accept these basic doctrines. Simplicius even tells us that Ammonius wrote a work about the beginninglessness of the cosmos (*in Ph.* 1363.8–12; *in Cael.* 271.18–21). For the larger philosophical significance of such discussions, see Richard Sorabji, *Time, Creation and Continuum: Theories in Antiquity and the Middle Ages* (Ithaca, N.Y.: Cornell University Press, 1983).

45. For the nature of his teaching position, see Watts, "City and School," 365–69.

46. Zacharias is a good example of such a student. *Vit. Sev.* 23–24 indicates that he was studying philosophy, probably on a basic level. Two years later, he had left the school and was studying law in Berytus. The opening exchanges of both the *Theophrastus* of Aeneas of Gaza and the *Ammonius* of Zacharias suggest that short-term study of philosophy was a common course for elite Christian students.

47. Such students could join the inner circle of a school. On the nature of a philosophical inner circle, see Watts, "City and School," 286–94; and Hans-Rudolf Schwyzer, *Ammonios Saccas, der Lehrer Plotins* (Geisteswissenschaften, Vorträge G260; Opladen: Westdeutscher Verlag, 1983), 36.

48. The nature of the attack depended on the type of audience that was to be reached. For a comparison of the strategies used by authors with a similar message but two different intended audiences, see Watts, "Christian Response."

49. Zacharias portrays this beating as motivated by religious concerns, but a violent response to a slanderous attack on one's teacher would have been expected of any loyal student.

50. This was a special student version of a more common Egyptian ecclesiastical institution. For more on the functions of the *philoponoi,* see Christopher Haas, *Alexandria in Late Antiquity: Topography and Social Conflict* (Baltimore: Johns Hopkins University Press, 1995), 238–40. See also Ewa Wipszycka, "Les confreres dans la vie religeuse de l'Egypte chrétienne," in *Proceedings of the Twelfth International Congress of*

Papyrology (Toronto: A. M. Hakkert, 1970), 511–25; and Pieter J. Sijpesteijn, "New Light on the *Philoponoi*," *Aeg* 69 (1989): 95–99.

51. The group setting and the curriculum the group followed is described in *Vit. Sev.* 53–54.

52. Paralius was one such pagan convert in Alexandria (*Vit. Sev.* 36–38).

53. Origen worked within the scholastic framework to facilitate the conversion of intellectuals like Heraclas: "While Origen was lecturing . . . some of the Greeks came to him to hear the word of God. The first of them was Plutarch . . . the second was Heraclas, the brother of Plutarch" (Eusebius, *Hist. eccl.* 6.3.1–2).

54. Porphyry indicates that Origen was indeed famous and that this reputation intrigued him enough that he attended one of Origen's public lectures. This incident is described by Eusebius, *Hist. eccl.* 6.19.5.

55. Origen taught him Christian interpretations of physics, astronomy, geometry, and ethics (*In Origenem oratio panegyrica*, 8–11). He did this, in Gregory's words, by "picking out and placing before us everything that was useful and true in each of the philosophers . . . (while) counseling us not to pin our allegiance to any philosopher, even if all men swear that he is all-knowing, but to attach ourselves only to God and the Prophets." (*Orig. or.*, 14–15). On this ordering of teaching, see Joseph W. Trigg, "God's Marvelous *Oikonomia*: Reflections of Origen's Understanding of Divine and Human Pedagogy in the *Address* Ascribed to Gregory Thaumaturgus," *JECS* 9 (2001): 28–29.

56. E.g., Origen, *Hom. Jer.* 15.2.8. On this idea, see Patricia Cox, *Biography in Late Antiquity: A Quest for the Holy Man* (The Transformation of the Classical Heritage 5; Berkeley: University of California Press, 1983), 94; and Pierre Nautin, "Origène Prédicateur," in *Origène: Homélies sur Jérémie 1–11* (ed. and trans. Nautin; SC 232; Paris: Cerf, 1976), 152.

57. Gregory Thaumaturge, *Orig. or.*, 6–8. The identification of this Gregory with the Thaumaturge has been questioned by P. Nautin, *Origène: Sa vie et son oeuvre* (Christianisme antique 1; Paris: Beauchesne, 1977), 161, 184. Against this, see Trigg, "*Oikonomia*," 29.

58. Trigg, "*Oikonomia*," 28.

59. On the type of speech Gregory gave, see August Brinkmann, "Gregors des Thaumaturgen Panegyricus auf Origenes," *Rheinisches Museum* n.f. 56 (1901): 55–76 (esp. 59–60).

CONTRIBUTORS

DAVID BRAKKE is Professor of Religious Studies and Adjunct Professor of History at Indiana University. He is author of *Athanasius and Asceticism* and *Demons and the Making of the Monk: Spiritual Combat in Early Christianity* and co-editor of *Reading in Christian Communities: Essays on Interpretation in the Early Church*. He serves as co-editor of the *Journal of Early Christian Studies*.

GEORGIA FRANK is Associate Professor of Religion at Colgate University in Hamilton, New York. Her research focuses on late antique Christianity, with an emphasis on lay devotional practices. She is author of *The Memory of the Eyes: Pilgrims to Living Saints in Late Antique Christianity*.

J. ALBERT HARRILL is Associate Professor of Religious Studies and Adjunct Associate Professor of Jewish Studies at Indiana University. He received his Ph.D. in New Testament and Early Christian Literature from the University of Chicago. He is author of *Slaves in the New Testament: Literary Social, and Moral Dimensions* and *The Manumission of Slaves in Early Christianity*.

SUSAN ASHBROOK HARVEY is Professor of Religious Studies at Brown University. She is co-author of *Holy Women in the Syrian Orient* and author of *Asceticism and Society in Crisis: John of Ephesus and the Lives of the Eastern Saints* and *Scenting Salvation: Ancient Christianity and the Olfactory Imagination*.

ESTHER MENN is Associate Professor at the Lutheran School of Theology at Chicago and an Instructor at the University of Chicago Divinity School. Her scholarly interests include the history of Jewish interpretation of the Bible, women in the Bible, and biblical narrative and poetry, including the Psalms. She is author of *Judah and Tamar (Genesis 38) in Ancient Jewish Exegesis: Studies in Literary Form and Hermeneutics*, as well as numerous articles in scholarly journals.

PATRICIA COX MILLER is the W. Earl Ledden Professor of Religion and Director of Graduate Studies at Syracuse University. Her works include *Biography in Late Antiquity: A Quest for the Holy Man, Dreams in Late Antiquity: Studies in the Imagination of a Culture, The Poetry of Thought in Late Antiquity: Essays on Imagination and Religion,* and *Women in Early Christianity: Translations from Greek Texts*.

Saul M. Olyan is Professor of Judaic Studies and Religious Studies at Brown University. He is author of four books, including *Biblical Mourning: Ritual and Social Dimensions,* and *Rites and Rank: Hierarchy in Biblical Representations of Cult,* and over thirty articles in the areas of Israelite religion, literature, and history, and the history of biblical exegesis. He is currently coordinating editor of the monograph series Brown Judaic Studies.

Michael L. Satlow is Associate Professor in Judaic Studies and Religious Studies at Brown University. He specializes in the study of early Judaism and is the author of *Tasting the Dish: Rabbinic Rhetorics of Sexuality* and *Jewish Marriage in Antiquity*. He has also written extensively on the historiography of ancient Judaism, the Dead Sea scrolls, and Jewish history and theology.

Jonathan Schofer is the Belzer Assistant Professor of Classical Rabbinic Literature at the University of Wisconsin, Madison. He is author of *The Making of a Sage: A Study of Rabbinic Ethics*. His work on ethics and self-cultivation also includes articles on rabbinic Judaism and early Confucianism, as well as a theoretical and methodological study.

Guy G. Stroumsa is the Martin Buber Professor of Comparative Religion and Director of the Center for the Study of Christianity at the Hebrew University of Jerusalem. He is author of *Barbarian Philosophy: The Religious Revolution of Early Christianity, Hidden Wisdom: Esoteric Traditions and the Roots of Christian Mysticism,* and *Mutations religieuses de l'antiquité.*

Peter T. Struck is Assistant Professor of Classical Studies at the University of Pennsylvania. He does his research on Greek and Roman theories of signs and interpretation. He is author of *Birth of the Symbol: Ancient Readers at the Limits of Their Texts.*

Edward Watts is Assistant Professor of History at Indiana University. He is author of *City and School in Late Antique Athens and Alexandria,* and the author of articles in *Journal of Roman Studies* and *Byzantium.*

Steven Weitzman is Associate Professor of Religious Studies, the Irving M. Glazer Chair in Jewish Studies, and Director of the Robert A. and Sandra S. Borns Jewish Studies Program at Indiana University. He is author of *Song and Story in Biblical Narrative* and *Surviving Sacrilege: Cultural Persistence in Jewish Antiquity.*

SUBJECT INDEX

Adam, 209–210: Christian interpretations of, 212; as cosmic being, 211–212; and eyesight, 166, 168; and the Fall, 167

Aelius Theon, 5

Akabya ben Mahalalel, 202, 215

allegory: Origen's use of, 21–22; Stoicism's use of, 117

Ambrose of Milan, 28: on bodily discipline, 151–152

Ammonius Hermeiou, 244

Ammonius Saccas, 234–235, 243

angels: body of, 202, 216n12

Anthony, 28

Antiochus Epiphanes, 98

Apophthegmata Patrum, 223

appetite: danger of, 132

Apuleius, 64n59

Aquinas. *See* Thomas Aquinas

Aristotle, 53–54: on dreams, 116–117; and sensory distrust, 123

Artaxerxes (Persian king), 74–76

Artemidorus, 8–9: on the cause of dreams, 116–117; and the dreamer, 113; and the religious self, 110–111, 113, 115; on the soul, 117; as source for daily life, 111–112; and Stoicism, 111, 117–118

asceticism, 27–28, 83–84, 88–89: and the body, 150–152; and community, 150–151; and demons, 191; and Evagrius, 226; and Scripture, 152; and sensory experience, 146, 151

Athanasius of Alexandria, 27–28: and *Life of Antony*, 191

Athens: religious atmosphere of, 242

Augustine of Hippo, 52: on paradise, 156; on the resurrection body, 155–156

Augustus, 56, 59

authorial voice, 64

Babylonian exile, return from, 41–43

Babylonian Talmud, 70

Bakhtin, Mikhail, 214

baptism, 60–63: and creation, 148; and knowledge, 148; in *kontakia*, 169; and sensory experience, 148

Bar-Kochva, Bezalel, 97

Barsunaphius of Gaza, 192

Basil of Caesarea: on creation, 147

bathing, 206

Berchman, Robert, 35n62

Berlinerblau, Jacques, 97

blindness: in *kontakia* 166–167, 172; and Satan, 173

body, 18, 20, 22–24, 27, 29: of angels, 202, 216n12; and asceticism, 150; beastly function of, 197, 202; care for, 205–207; and demons, 226; as discursively malleable, 198; and excrement, 203–204; and God, 148–149, 154; "grotesque" characterization of, 214–215; and identity, 78–84; as image of God, 204–205, 214; imagery for, 211; and knowledge, 154–155; as "lived" space, 198; as microcosm, 208–211, 213; in paradise, 157; parts of, 212; and prayer, 78–84; rabbinic understanding of, 198, 200, 213–215; and religious identity, 146–147; and religious knowledge, 141, 149; and ritual practice, 145; as salvific instrument, 150; and sexual activity, 207; and slavery, 54; and the soul, 18, 20, 22–24, 27, 157; as spatial location, 198; transformation of, 175. *See also* resurrection body

Bowerstock, Glen, 120n4

Boyarin, Daniel, 218n37

Branham, Joan, 100

Bright, John, 40

Brown, Peter, 6

Calvin, John, 52

Cassian, John, 192: and Michel Foucault, 222; and monasticism, 230–231

Cassius Dio, 56

Christ, Jesus: and body-as-instrument, 141; and dialogue, 171; faith of, 60–61; incarnation of, 185; and smell, 169

Christian teacher, 192: and disciple, relation to, 191; and obedience, 192; and pagan teacher, difference from, 190–191

Christological controversy: and sensory experience, 144

Chrysostom, John: and perception, 174

Cicero, 53, 57–58

circumcision: as identity marker, 87

Clement of Alexandria: and sensory experience, 142

clothing: and identity, 80–83

communal identity: and collective memory, 85, 90; and ethnicity, 84; and opposition, 86 conversion, 184, 234: catalysts for, 236; and education, 246; to paganism, 188, 235

Cox-Miller, Patricia, 100

cult of the saints, 28: and sensory experience, 143

custom: as "element" of dreams, 114

Cyril of Jerusalem: on the senses, 148

Daniel, 71, 87

David (King), 96

Davidman, Lynn, 48n2

Dawson, David, 35n61

Dead Sea Scrolls: on freewill offerings, 98

demons: in ascetic life, 191; and the body, 202, 226; categorization of, 223, 225; and "talking back," 223

Descartes, René, 119

Deuteronomy: compositional integrity of, 135, 138n7; and cultic worship, 125, 136; and God, 129–131; and Greek thought, 136–137; and idolatry, 123, 128, 139n10; and the "law code," 135; and memory, 132; and the Pentateuch, 126–131, 138n8; and religious experience, 136; and the self, 124; and the senses, 131; and sensory reform, 135; and the "spy episode," 126–127, 130; and wisdom texts, 125, 130

diet, 87–89: as educational discipline, 133–134

Dotham, Moshe, 102n1

dreams: categories of meaning, 112; and divination, 111, 115–117; and God, 111, 116–117; and Greek psychology, 116; interpretation of, 8–9, 112–114, 119; and language, 114; as part of the natural order, 117; private and public character of, 111; and the soul, 115–116

eating, 125: and hearing, 133; and ritual, 134; and the "sensory problem," 134

education: in cities, 236, 241; and conversion, 246; difficulties of, 235; and initiation rituals, 238–239; versus monasticism, 184; and religious behavior, 242; and religious experimentation, 242–244, 247; and religious identity, 245–246; and ritual, 237, 247; in Roman empire, 184; and the self, effects on, 7, 241; and self-identification, 235, 242–243, 247; as social marker, 236; and teacher, 190–191; and teaching, 190; traveling for, 236–237; utility of, 235. *See also* Christian teacher; schools

Eilberg, Howard, 200

Eleazar, 87

emotion: linguistic representation of, 40–41

ephebe: in dreams, 112

Ephrem the Syrian, 161n32: on the Christian life, 150–151; on creation, 147–148; on divided self, 149; on divine activity, 157; on the Eucharist, 149; on paradise, 154, 156–157

Epictetus, 57, 224

Epicurus: as spiritual master, 188

Epiphanius, 234, 243

eroticism: and monasticism, 228; and the self, 229

Essenes: and freewill offerings, 98

Esther Rabbah, 70

ethnicity: and communal self, 84

Eucharist: celebration of, 148–149; and sensory experience, 149

Eunapius, 238

Euprepius, 234, 243

Evagrius of Pontus, 192–193: on demons, 223; and informal meetings, 225; and *kephalaia* genre, 224; on listlessness, 227–228; and the monastic self, 225; and the self, 231; and self-disclosure, 223; and spiritual senses, 153, 161n39; on thoughts, 191, 231, 233n43

excrement: and mortality, 203–204

Exodus imagery, 41–44

eyesight, 18, 23–24, 28, 125–129, 138n9: and Adam, 168; and Deuteronomic "spy episode," 126–127, 130; and the Fall, 166; as highest sense, 156; and knowledge, relation to, 166; and Mary, 168; and Moses, 128; and sin, 128

Ezekiel, 46–47

Ezra, 71

family: and monks, 227–228; and self, 228

The Fathers According to Rabbi Nathan (*R. Nathan*): and the body, 200–202, 205; characterization of, 198–199; and creation, 201; and *2 Enoch* (Slavonic), 212; and humility, 202–204; and list, cosmic Adam, 209–213, 221n74; and list, regimen, 206–208; and other rabbinic literature, 199–200; and the self, care of, 206; textual history of, 199

Fine, Steven, 106n67

Foucault, Michel, 2, 6, 183: on self-disclosure, 222–223

freewill offerings, 96–97

Freud, Sigmund, 52

friendship, 240

Gallagher, Catherine, 17–18, 33n19

Geller, Stephen: on *Deuteronomy* and the self, 124; on *Deuteronomy* and wisdom texts, 130

gender relations, 75–76, 81; and votive offerings, 98

God: and body, 148, 154; and communal identity, 89; communication with, 118; and creation, 147; and dreams, 116–117; and hearing, 131; and Israel, relation to, 130; as king, 73–78, 82; as relational other, 72–73; sensory access to, 129; and solitude of status, 73; visual experience of, 127–128; voice of, 129–131, 136–137; and votive inscriptions, 91, 94–95, 99, 102; and votive offerings, 91, 94–95, 102

Godelier, Maurice, 95

Goldin, Judah, 216n9

Goodenough, Erwin R., 107n72
Goodman, Martin, 106n67
Greek and Roman religion, 110–111
Greenblatt, Stephen, 6, 17–18, 33n19
Gregory of Nazianzus, 239, 242
Gregory of Nyssa, 28, 147
Gregory Thaumaturgus, 246
Grottanelli, Cristiano, 95
guilt, 52

Hadot, Pierre, 6
Hammath Tiberias synagogue, 92–93, 103n22
Harvey, David, 198
hearing, 125, 129–132, 164, 171: and the
    Decalogue, 129
Hell: in *kontakia*, 171–175, 178n44
Heraclitus: and sensory distrust, 123
Holiness School, 46–47
Honorius, 93
Horapollon, 244
Horvat Susiya synagogue, 93
hospitality: and monasticism, 227

Iamblichus, 24
identity: in Roman empire, 184
idolatry, 73–74, 86: and the senses, 123, 138n5;
    and visual experience, 128
image of God: as the body, 204–205, 214; polit-
    ical charge of, 204, 206; rabbinic exegesis of,
    204–205
Isaiah (abba), 192

Jay, Gregory, 16
Jeremiah, 44–46
Jerome, 28: on sensory appreciation, 144–145
Jerusalem temple, 97–98
Jewish votive inscriptions, 9: function of, 95,
    101–102; and *euergesia*, 101–102, 106n60,
    108n93; and gifts, 93; and God, 91, 94–95, 99,
    102; and the Jerusalem temple, 99–100; in
    late antiquity, 100–102, 105n38; and non-
    Jewish inscriptions, 100–102, 108n94,
    108n96; in Palestinian synagogues, 92–93;
    and "people of the land," 94; public charac-
    ter of, 100–102; and rabbinic literature, 94;
    religious aspects of, 91, 95; representative of
    popular religion, 94–95; role of exchange in,
    95; in Second Temple Judaism, 99–100; ter-
    minology of, 92–94, 103n5; types of, thanks-
    giving, 94, 104n29; types of, conditional, 94–
    95
Jewish votive institutions: and freewill offer-
    ings, 96–97; popular character of, 97; reg-
    ulations of, 95–96; types of, 96
Jewish votive offerings: Diasporic, 98; func-
    tion of, 98–99; and the Jerusalem temple,
    97–98; and Judith, 97, 105n46. See *also* Jew-
    ish votive inscriptions *and* Jewish votive
    institutions

John of Antioch, 184
Josiah: and centralization of Israelite worship,
    135–136
Josephus, 86, 98
Judith, 71, 87
Julian, 248n5
Justin Martyr, 190

Kierkegaard, Søren, 52
kingship, 74–75
knowledge: and baptism, 148; and body, 154–
    155; of God, 149, 155; and monasticism, 191;
    sensory experience, based on, 146, 154–155;
    weakness of, 192
kontakia, 3: and baptism, 169; and Christ, cru-
    cifixion of, 171–175, 176n4; dialogue within,
    165; and liturgy, 165; as Scriptural interpreta-
    tion, 164–165; and speech, 169–170

language: in dreams, 114
law: as "element" of dreams, 113
Libanius, 183–184, 239–241: on being a student,
    237
Life of Aesop, 55–57, 64
Lieberman, Saul, 104n95
listlessness, 227–228
liturgy: as instruction, 174–175; purpose of,
    149; and sensory experience, 144–145
Lloyd, G.E.R., 136
Luther, Martin, 52
Lysimachus, 90n2

Marcus Aurelius, 15–16, 20, 225
marriage: between Christians and pagans, 142
martyrs/martyrdom, 28–29: and purification,
    141; and teachers, 190
Masoretic Text, 70, 71–72, 80, 84, 88
Mauss, Marcel, 2, 95
Maximos, 91–92
memory, 7–8: communal identity, 85, 90; and
    Deuteronomy, 132, 137; scripturalization of,
    85, 90; as sensory solution, 135
Midrash on the Psalms, 70
Mishnah, 97–98
Momigliano, Arnaldo, 185
monastic self: challenges for, 225–227; dis-
    closure of, 222; as embodied, 226; ideal of,
    230; and other monks, 229; and pride, 229;
    social nature of, 228
monasticism: as differentiated from magic,
    224; and education, as unique from, 184;
    emergence of, 143; and eroticism, 228; famil-
    ial opposition to, 229; and family, 228; and
    hierarchy, 230; and hospitality, 227; and
    knowledge, 191; and manual labor, 226; and
    the poor, 227; and the self, 223; and shame,
    227; and schools, 187; and temptation, 226;
    and wealth, 228
Mordecai, 88

mortality: imagery of, 203–204; as moral condition, 149; in *R. Nathan*, 203
Moses: and eyesight, 128; as mediator, 131, 137
musical instruments: in dreams, 112

Narcissus, myth of, 18
nature: in Artemidorus' thought, 120n6; as
"element" of dreams, 113
numerology: in dreams, 114

Onians, John, 24n67
Onias, 98
Origen of Alexandria, 23, 27–28, 31, 34n48,
35n54; and allegory, 21–22; and the body, 20,
22–23; and divided consciousness, 21; and
Incarnation, 22; and inner *logos*, 16; and love,
21; and Scripture, 21–23; and sense perception, 21; and sensory experience, 159n3; and
the soul, 20–23; as teacher, 246, 251nn53–55
Origenist controversy, 223

pain: and perception, 173
Palestinian synagogues, 92–93
Parable of the Talents: and Paul, 58
Parmenides of Elea: parallel to *Deuteronomy*,
136; and sensory distrust, 123, 136
Paul: anthropology of, 53, 59–61; and "apocalyptic drama," 61–62; and *auctoritas*, 58–63;
and authorial voice, 64; and baptism, 60–63;
and faith of Christ, 60–61; and guilt, 52; letters of, 185; and Parable of the Talents, 58;
and paraenesis, 62; and *prosōpopoiia*, 53–54,
59–60; and the self, 53, 59–61, 63; and slavery, 51–64; and Stoicism, 54, 56, 62; and textual first-person, 51–52, 62
Paulinus of Nola: and sensory appreciation,
145
perception: and pain, 173
Perpetua, 113–114
Perrone, Lorenzo, 192
personal appearance, 78–84
Philo of Alexandria: and sensory distrust, 123;
on votive offerings, 98
philoponoi: and educational methods, 245–246
Plato: on popular religion, 95, 104n28; and sensory distrust, 123
Platonism: 53, 60–61, 66n17
pleasure: and the soul, 142
Plotinus, 23–24, 27, 31: anthropology of, 18–19;
and the body, 18; and *ekstasis*, 153; and Narcissus, myth of, 18; and sense perception, 18–
19; and the soul, 15–16, 18–20; and spiritual
exercises, 19–20; and transcendence, 19–20
Plutarch: 33n23, 57–58, 64
pneuma, 118
political identity: and Artemidorus, 113
Polycarp, martyrdom of: and Christ's crucifixion, 141; as sacrifice, 141; and sensory experience, 140–141, 145

popular religion: and religious self, 110; and
votive offerings, 94–95, 97–99, 104n28
Possekel, Ute, 160n25
prayer: and Esther, 72; physical aspects of, 78–
84; and religious self, 71–72
Prayer of Esther: and the body, 78–84; and
communal identity, 84–86; date of composition, 71; and Esther's diet, 87–88; Esther's
paradoxical status, 77–78; and God, 72–75;
versus Hellenistic philosophical tropes, 77;
and identity, 70–71; and Jewish religiosity,
70–71; and kingship, motif of, 74–76 ordinariness of, 72; and power dynamics, 77; and
praise, motif of, 74; reflecting subordinated
self, 76–78; relation to larger text, 71; rhetoric of, 73; separation as ideal, 87–88; Septuagint version of, 70–72, 75, 80–83, 85–86,
88–89; various versions of, 70–72, 75
priesthood: and the spiritual master, 185; symbolic role of, 186
Price, Simon, 110
pride: in monasticism, 230
Proclus, 24, 31: and ritual, 27; and self, 25–26;
and sensible world, 25; and statues, 25–26;
and theurgy, 25
prophecy: in Israel, 185–186
prosōpopoiia, 52–54
Prudentius: on creation, 148; and smell, sense
of, 145
Pseudo-Hecataeus, 97
Pseudo-Macarius: on spiritual senses, 153
purification: and martyrdom, 141
Purim: establishment of, 84–85
Pythagoreanism: and contact with the divine,
189

Quintilian, 53

Rahab (the sea dragon), 43
Reddy, William M., 48n2
relic veneration, 28–30, 143, 145
religious self: and the body, 146–147; and God,
141; and sensory experience, 141
resurrection body: as instrument of knowledge, 154; and sense perception, 155
Ricoeur, Paul, 109
rites of initiation: and new identity, 238; in
schools, 241
ritual practices: and the body, 145; and Christian identity, 145; Christian versus pagan in
late antiquity, 145; in *Deuteronomy*, 134–135;
as sensory solution, 135. *See also* rites of
initiation
Roberts, Michael, 36n65
Roman empire: and Christianity, 143, 184; and
education, 184; and identity, 184
Roman votive inscriptions: and Jewish votive
inscriptions, 102
Romanos the Melodist: and blindness, 167; on

connection between self and senses, 167; dialogue of, 174; and deliberation, 174; and hymnal characters, 163; and hymnal interpretation, 167; and *kontakia*, 3, 164–165; and sense perceptions, rhetoric of, 163; and sense perceptions, reflection on, 165; and sense perceptions, "reeducation of," 164, 168; and senses, relation between, 168; and sensory experience, 165; and speech types, 169; on spiritual senses, 174–175; and vocal women, 169–170
Rosenwein, Barbara H., 48n2

sacraments: and oneness of being, 150. *See also* baptism; Eucharist
Sarah, 72
Schmidt, Leigh, 164
schools: and collective identity, 240; as family, 237; fights among, 240; initiation into, 238; and late antique Christianity, 187; and loyalty, 239, 241, 245; and monasticism, 187; and pagan sage, 189; and polemical texts, 244–245; and religious behavior, 244–246; social hierarchy within, 239; student/teacher relations, 239; and students, intimacy among, 240–241; and teacher, role of, 190–191; and teaching, role of, 190. *See also* Christian teacher; education
Scripture, 21–23: and communal memory, 85–86, 90; interpretation of, 204–205, 209; and suprasensory experience, 152; and *kontakia*, 164–165; and sensory images, 152
Second Isaiah, 41, 44, 46–47
self: as animated statue, 26–27; in antiquity, 16–17, 41, 47, 63–64; and Artemidorus, 114; and the body, 27, 78–84; care of, 206; within classes of experience, 113; communal self, 84–90; discipline of, 124, 126; as divided, 149; as divinity, 115–117; and dreams, 114; and eyesight, 18, 125–129; and family, 227–228; formation of, 1; grammatical meaning of, 69n57; and God, 118; Greek notion of, 109, 119n2; and group orientation, 227–228; and Hebrew Bible, 124; history of, 3, 124; and imagination of "place," 17–18, 31; and interiority, 72; linguistic representation of, 109; and materiality, 23–24, 31; nominalization of, 110; and *pneuma*, 118; and Prayer of Esther, 70–71; rabbinic representations of, 197; and Scripture, 21–22; in slaves, 5, 56–57, 63–64; spiritualization of, 22–23; structure of, 4; as subjected, 76–77; technologies of, 6; and textual first-person, 40–41, 44, 47, 51, 62; transformation of, 202; unity of, 185, 202, 213. *See also* monastic self; religious self; soul
Seneca: on the sage, 188–189
sense perception, 18, 21: and behavior, 133–134; and *Deuteronomy*, 123–139; and dialogue, 174; discipline of, 132; distrust of, 123–124;

127; and the divine, 166; and the Fall, 167; human-divine encounter, as foundation for, 157; and impressions, 118; and interiority, 163, 174; and Israel's religious life, 126; and knowledge of Christ, 169; and memory, 133; and pain, 173–174; problems of, 132; "reeducation" of, 164, 168; and resurrection body, 155; and Satan, 173; solutions to, 132, 134. *See also* sensory experience; spiritual senses
sensory experience, 3, 6: and baptism, 148; and Christian identity, 141; and Christian piety, 144, 146; as dangerous, 145–146; and early Christianity, 141–142, 145; and Eucharist, 149; and God, 148; and intermarriage, 142–143; and knowledge, 146, 154–155; and late antique Christianity, 141, 143; and misperception, 128; as narrative structuring device, 125–126; and paganism, 142; as redefining an event, 141; and religious identity, 158; and ritual distinction, 144, 146; and spiritual senses, 154. *See also* eating; eyesight; smell
sex: rabbinic estimate of, 207
Shamash: and votive inscriptions, 101
shame: and monasticism, 227
slave(ry), 51–64: in Aristotle, 53–54; and Esther, 76; Greek and Latin terms for, 54; as metaphor, 63; Roman ideologies of, 54–56; and Roman military culture, 62; and the self, 5, 56–57, 63–64; and somatic vocabulary, 54
smell, sense of: and Adam, 167; and Christ, 169; in *kontakia*, 170; and martyrdom, 141; and temptation, 142
Socrates: and *ekstasis*, 153; as spiritual master, 188
soul, 15–16, 18–23: in Artemidorus' thought, 115–117; and body, 18, 20, 22–24, 27, 157; as divinity, 115; and dreams, 115–116; and pleasure, 142; and *pneuma*, 118; as self in Graeco-Roman antiquity, 16–17, 119; and theurgy, 24–25; and volition, 115–118. *See also* self
speech: in *kontakia*, 169–170
"spiritual direction," 184–185, 187: and Christianity, 190; and pagan sage, 188–189; and pagan sage, divinization of, 189; and self, unity of, 185; and Talmudic sage, 186; and urban elites, 189–190
spiritual senses: 174–175
Stewart, Columbia, 161n39
Stoicism, 54, 56, 62: contrasted to Prayer of Esther, 77; and the divinatory soul, 117–118; and sage, as exemplum, 188–189
stylite saints, 152
suprasensory experience: and late antique Christianity, 152; philosophical models for, 153
synagogue: in late antiquity, 100; sacrality of, 99–100; in Second Temple Judaism, 99–100
Synesius, 239

Talmudic sage: role of, 186
Targumim, 70, 86
technê: as "element" of dreams, 114
temple of Atargatis: and votive inscriptions, 101
temptation: and monasticism, 226
Tertullian: on marriage, 142–143; on sensory experience, 142, 159n3
Thales, 136
Theodoret of Cyrrhus, 190
Theodosius II, 93
Theophilus of Alexandria, 223
Theophrastus, 95
theurgy, 24–25, 28–29
Thomas Aquinas, 52
time: as "element" of dreams, 114
Tobit, 71
transcendence, 19–20

Trinitarian controversy: and sensory appreciation, 144
type scenes: and Prayer of Esther, 79–84

Urbach, Ephraim, 217n18

Victricius, 28, 31: and body, 29; and eyesight, 28; and martyrs, 28–29; and relic veneration, 28–30; and ritual, 30
votive offerings, 91, 94–95, 102

wealth: and monasticism, 228
writing: as extending sensory experience, 131–132; and individual subjective experience, 40–41, 44

Zacharias Scholasticus: and conversion, 235, 242, 244–245

SOURCE INDEX

HEBREW BIBLE/OLD
TESTAMENT

Genesis
1.26–27   204
1.26–28   205
2.7   168, 203
3.7   166–167
3.19   203
6.9–8.22   176n4
9.6   204–205
9.6–7   205
31.13   98

Exodus
9.23   176n4
12.11   43, 49n13
12.33   49n13
14.23   42
15.1b–18   42, 49n11
15.16   42
20.18–19   129
20.19   131
35.4–5, 21–22   96
36.3–7   96

Leviticus
7.1–10, 16–18   96
7.16   105n46
22.18, 21   105n46
22.21–23   96

Numbers
13.27–28   126
14.10–22   127
14.22–23   127
14.36–37   126–127
15.2–13   96
15.3   105n46
29.39   105n46

Deuteronomy
1.21   129
1.21–39   138n9
1.22–40   125
1.25   126
1.27–28   126
1.29–33   127

1.34   127, 131
1.41   131
2.31   129
3.23–29   128
3.24–25   128
4.4–28.68   138n7
4.6   129
4.9   125, 127–128
4.10   129
4.11–12   127
4.12   125, 129
4.15   128
4.15–31   128
4.19   128
4.25–28   125
4.32   129, 211, 220n63
4.36   127–128
5.1   125
5.5   130–131
5.22–27   129–130
5.25   139n12
5.25–28   131
6.3   134
6.3, 4   125
6.3, 16   125
6.3–12   133
6.7–9   132
7.8   43
7.19   125
8.2–3, 16   125
8.3   133
8.7–14   133
8.10   134
8.11, 14   134
8.12   125
9.9, 18   125, 134
10.21   125
11.1–7   135
11.2–7   127
11.8–17   135
11.18–21   135
12.6   105n46
16.3   43, 49n13
23.13–15   203
26.1–11   134
26.5–9   139n14
26.9, 15   134
26.12   134

26.13–15   134
29.1–4   124
30.11–14   137

Joshua
2.1–24   178n37
10.26–27   176n4

Judges
4.21–22   176n4

1 Samuel
1.13–15   178n37

2 Samuel
7.23   43
15.7   105n39

1 Kings
8.39   49n5

2 Kings
6.25   203

1 Chronicles
28.9, 11–12, 17   96

Ezra
1.4, 6   50n18
2.68   97
7.15–16   97
9.5–15   71

Esther
1.11   79
1.23   79
2.1   75
2.6   85
2.7   77
2.9   83, 87
2.10   84
2.10, 20   78
2.12   80, 82
2.12–13   80
2.15   78
2.17   80, 87
2.18   80
3.1–6   88

3.8 — 88
3.10 — 75
4.1–3 — 82–83
4.1–8 — 84
4.4 — 83
4.8 — 82
4.11 — 72, 78
4.13 — 77
4.13–14 — 78
4.15 — 77
4.16 — 72, 82–83
5.1 — 71, 75, 77, 80, 82
5.4, 7–8 — 72
6.3 — 76
7.3–4, 6 — 72
7.4 — 86
7.9 — 76
7.10 — 176n4
8.5–6 — 72
8.7–14 — 88
8.8 — 74, 88
8.16 — 72
9.13 — 72
9.13–15 — 88
9.20–22, 26–29 — 85

Job
22.27 — 105n39
25.6 — 203
42.5–6 — 130

Psalms
7.10 — 220n60
22.26 — 105n39
50.14 — 105n39
54.8 — 96
56.13 — 105n39
61.9 — 105n39
65.2 — 105n39
66.13 — 105n39
76.12 — 105n39
115.5–7 — 138n5
116.14, 18 — 105n39
135.16 — 138n5
139.1–6, 23 — 49n5
141.2 — 144

Proverbs
30.8–9 — 132

Ecclesiastes
1.13 — 226
5.3 — 105n39
12.2 — 211
12.7 — 203

Song of Songs
4.1–8 — 220n65
4.4 — 211

5.8–6.3 — 220n65
5.9–6.3 — 220n65
7.1–7.10 — 220n65
7.8 — 211

Isaiah
14.11 — 203
19.21 — 105n39
40.3 — 49n9
42.16 — 49n9
43.16, 19 — 49n9
43.16–21 — 41–42
49.9, 11 — 49n9
51.10 — 49n9
51.9–11 — 42–43
52.11–12 — 43, 49n13

Jeremiah
1.10–12 — 45, 50n16
2.13 — 229n59
11.20 — 220n60
16.14–15 — 49n6
17.13 — 220n59
17.20 — 220n60
20.12 — 220n60
31.27–28 — 44–45, 47, 50n16

Ezekiel
4 — 203
42.22–23 — 46–47
47.13–48.29 — 50n19

Daniel
1.8–16 — 87
9.3–19 — 71

Hosea
11.10–11 — 49n6

Jonah
2.10 — 105n39

Micah
6.4 — 43

Haggai
2.9 — 44

APOCRYPHA AND
SEPTUAGINT

Psalms
118:131 — 223

Esther
2.2 — 80
2.9 — 82
2.12 — 82
2.13 — 80

2.15 — 80
2.18 — 80
2.20 — 89
4.2 — 83
4.8 — 85
4.11 — 74
7.4 — 86
8.4 — 74
8.11 — 89
10.9–12 — 72
13.4 — 89
13.5 — 89
13.9 — 73
14.1–2 — 79, 81
14.3 — 72–73, 84
14.3–4 — 84
14.5 — 84–85
14.5 (AT) — 74
14.5–7 — 85
14.5–11 — 84
14.6 — 86
14.6–12 — 86
14.7 — 86
14.7–10 — 85–86
14.8–9 — 74, 86
14.9 — 74, 86
14.10 — 74, 83, 86
14.10 (Addition C) — 74
14.11 — 74, 86
14.12 — 73
14.13 — 74, 86
14.14 — 72
14.15 — 87
14.16 — 87
14.17 — 87
14.17, 18 — 76
14.18 — 87
14.19 — 73
15.1 — 80–81
15.2 — 80
15.4 — 80
15.5 — 80
15.6 — 75
15.11 — 74
16.19 — 89

Baruch
3.35–38 — 177n24

Judith
4.14 — 97
9.9–14 — 71
12.2–4 — 87
16.18 — 97
16.19 — 105n46

2 Maccabees
6.18–31 — 87
9.16 — 105n48

3 Maccabees
3.17 106n49

Tobit
3.1–6, 12–15 71

NEW TESTAMENT

Matthew
3.16 141
4.1–11 223
5.46 191
7.6 20
7.14 226
15.21–28 178n37
15.27 170
23.9 191
25.15, 21–22, 24–27, 30 58
26.6–13 177n33

Mark
1.10 141
7.24–30 178n37
14.2–9 177n33

Luke
1.46–55 170
3.22 141
4.1–13 223
7.36–50 169
10.16 192
21.5 98
23.34 172–173
23.42–43 172

John
19.34 141

Romans
1.5–6 54
1.10–15 58
1.13 54
1.18–32 59
2.28 60
3.21–3 60
6.6–14 60
6.13 62
6.14 61
6.16–18 60
7.7–25 52, 59
7.14–25 60, 62
7.18–19 61
7.21–25 51
7.22–23 61
7.25 62
8.2 61
8.15 62
8.21 60
11.81 66

13.1–7 62, 68n51
15.15–16 54

1 Corinthians
1.18–25 190
6.20 61
7.23 61
8.9 59
9.4–6, 12, 18 59
15.51 154

2 Corinthians
3.1–3 59
4.16–18 68n44
4.18 223
12.2–4 152

Galatians
1.13–14 52
1.10 229
5.17 34n41

Philippians
3.4–6 52

PSEUDEPIGRAPHA

2 Enoch
30:8 221n69

DEAD SEA SCROLLS

4Q271 4 ii 13 106n56
4Q418 10 9–10 106n57
11Q19 xlvi, 13–18 203

JOSEPHUS AND
PHILO

Josephus, *Antiquitates judaicae*
4.72–73 106n54
8.195 105n47
12.35, 50, 58, 85, 249 105n48
13.78 106n49
15.394–395 97
17.151 105n47
17.265 98
18.19 98
18.312–13 98
19.294–295 106n49

Bellum judaicum
2.312–14 105n49
2.413 106n49
4.181 106n49
5.205, 562–563 106n49
5.210–212 106n50
6.335 106n52
7.44–45 98

7.45 98
7.428 98

Contra Apionem
1.199 97
2.48 105n49

Philo of Alexandria, *De decalogo*
35 123
133 98
147 123

Legatio ad Gaium
280 106n55
319 106n49

De somniis
1.252 98

De specialibus legibus
1.20 124
1.66 98
1.174 123
1.247 98
2.32–38, 115 106n55

De virtutibus
12 123

De vita Mosis
2.211–212 123–124

RABBINIC
LITERATURE

Mishnah
'Abot
3.1 217n16
5:1 219n44
Ketubbot
7:10 203
Middot
3:8 106n50
'Ohalot
1:8 220n67
Sanhedrin
4:5 219n45
Šeqalim
6:5–6 106n51

Tosefta
Ḥagigah
2:7 220n63
Megillah
2(3):14 106n64
2(3):16 99

Yebamot
8:7   218n26

Jerusalem Talmud
Megillah
3.2, 74a   106n63
Kil'ayim
9.4, 32b   104n25

Babylonian Talmud
'Arakin
15b   220n61
Baba Batra
12a   185
Berakot
57b   219n41
61a–b   220n67
Ḥagigah
11b   220n63
12a   220n63
16a   216n13
Ketubbot
77a   203
Pesaḥim
42a–b   219n41
Šabbat
151b   220n62
151b–152a   219n41
Sanhedrin
38b   220n63
Yebamot
63b   218n26
Yoma
18a–b   219n41
75b   217n13

Other Rabbinic Works
'Abot de Rabbi Nathan A
2   204
3   219n45
17   218n27
19   202–203
26   218n33
31   208–209, 220n60
33   220n60
37   201–202, 206
39   204
41   207
'Abot de Rabbi Nathan B
8   220n63
13   219n53
30   205, 218n27
32   217n16
43   216n11–12
48   207

Derek Ereṣ Rabbah
3:1   217n16
3:3   217n20
Derek Ereṣ Zuṭa
9:13   220n64
Genesis Rabbah
8:11   216n13
24:2   219n47
61:1   220n60
Exodus Rabbah
40:3   219n47
Leviticus Rabbah
18:1   217n16, 219n52, 220n62
20:2   220n63
34:3   218n28
61:1   220n67
Ecclesiastes Rabbah
1:4   220n66
12:1   217n16
12.2   220n62
Lamentations Rabbah
2:15   219n41
*Mekilta de-Rabbi Ishmael,
    Ba-Hodesh*
8   217n26
*Mekilta de-Rabbi Ishmael,
    Beshallah*
8   219n48
Pesiqta de Rab Kahana
12:1   220n63
Seder Eliyahu Zuṭa
12   216n13

APOSTOLIC
    FATHERS

Diognetus
5.8–10   141

Martyrdom of Polycarp
15.1–16.1   140

CLASSICAL AND
    ANCIENT
    CHRISTIAN
    SOURCES

Ambrose of Milan, *De fuga
    saeculi*
1.3   151

De Spiritu Sanctu
2.7   161n38

Apuleius, *Apologia*
23   250n37

Aristotle, *De divinatio per
    somnum*
463b12–15   117

Ethica nichomachea
8.11.6–7 (1161b)   53

Metaphysica
1.2   123

Politica
1.1–7 (1252a–56a)   53

Artemidorus, *Onirocritica*
1.2   113, 115, 117
1.3   113
1.6   116–117
1.8   113–114
1.9   113
1.17   120n6
1.27   120n6
1.38   120n6
1.42   120n6
1.44   120n6
1.54   112
1.56   112
1.66   120n6
1.76   112
1.79–80   120n6
2.17   112
2.29   114
2.32   114
2.54   113
2.66   120n6
3.24   114
3.28   114
4.2   113, 117
4.4   114

Athanasius of Alexandria,
    Contra Gentes
2.20–21   38n97
3.3–5   38n97
3.16–17   38n97

Epistula ad Marcellinum
33   232n8

Vita Antonii
15–16   195

Augustine of Hippo,
    Confessiones
5.8   248n13
5.12   249n34

De civitate Dei
14.11   154
22.17, 19, 20   155

22.24   155
22.29–30   156

De libero arbitrio
2.3.27–37   161n38

De Trinitate
9.6–7, 11, 15   161n38

Augustus, *Res Gestae*
34.3   56

Basil of Caesarea, *Ad adulescentes*
4.4   235

Homiliae in hexaemeron
1   147

Callistratus, *Descriptiones*
5.3   33n24

Cassius Dio, *Historiae Romanae*
55.3.5: 56

Choricius, *Laudatio Marciani*
1.4   235

Cicero, *De natura deorum*
2.72   118

Pro Caecina
51–52   57

Codex Justinianus
1.11.10   248n5

Codex Theodosianus
16.8.25   93

Cornutus, *De natura deorum*
35   118

Corpus inscriptionum iudaicarum
1.690   106n61
2.1441–1444   106n59

Cyril of Jerusalem, *Catecheses*
4.22   148

Damascius, *Vita Isidorii*
frag. 100   234, 250n43
frag. 135   249n36
frag. 158   250n37

Dorotheos of Gaza, *Vita Dosithei*
9   192

Egeria, *Itinerarium*
24–25   159n8

Ephrem the Syrian, *De fide*
14.5   148
18   160n21
81.9   148

De paradiso
7.12   157
8.9   162n43

Hymnae de virginitate
2.15   150–151
20.12   147
31.16   148
35.12   149
37.2   149

De nativitate
4.144–145   157

De nisibe
69.3, 5   149

Epictetus, *Dissertationes*
4.11.26–27   66n29

Enchiridion
12.2   57

Eunapius, *Vitae sophistarum*
483   239, 249n27
485–487   248n14
486   238, 248n15
487   249n20

Eusebius of Caesarea, *Historia ecclesiastica*
6.3.1–2   251n53
6.9.12–14   249n20
6.19.5   251n54
6.19.6–7   234
10.3–4   159n8

Evagrius Ponticus, *Ad Eulogium*
2.2   233n43
4.4   233n43
31.33   233n43

Antirrheticus
Preface 223, 226

1.3, 20, 33, 43, 44, 47, 52   232n12
1.3, 25, 29, 32, 40, 60   232n13
1.8, 10, 16, 62   232n17
1.10, 12, 47   232n19
1.14, 15, 19, 22, 26, 59, 65   232n12
1.21   227
1.28, 49   232n21
1.30, 36, 38, 39   232n25
1.48   226
1.56   232n14
1.57   226
1.58   232n22
1.61–63   227
1.63   225
2.1, 6, 9, 15, 19, 21, 23, 24   232n28
2.2, 4, 5, 8, 18, 28, 29, 43   233n29
2.7, 13, 16, 41   233n30
2.11, 23, 25, 45, 55, 63   232n15
2.14   228
2.31, 32, 36, 54, 56, 60   232n28
2.33, 42   233n29
2.35, 58   228
2.40   240
2.49   229
2.65   228
3.1   232n27
3.2, 26, 28, 56   232n17
3.3, 16, 17, 20, 22   232n27
3.4, 6, 8, 29, 56   232n18
3.5, 7, 9, 10, 27, 31, 37   232n20
3.12, 30, 33, 45   232n22
3.14   227
3.18, 46   228
3.22, 34   232n25
3.28, 57   232n21
3.38, 40, 43, 44, 47, 48, 58   232n20
3.25, 35, 54   232n19
3.46   223
4.15, 33, 36, 41, 49   232n15
4.22   232n15
4.25   224
4.39   224
4.42   228
4.52, 53, 56, 65   232n15
4.76   232n14
5.4, 6, 11, 13   233n31
5.5, 17, 20, 29, 31, 35, 39   233n31
5.14, 47, 49   233n32
5.28   232n21
5.34, 56   229
5.44   229

5.48, 51, 57   232n22
5.62–64   233n31
6.1, 28, 37   232n18
6.2, 30, 50, 55   233n33
6.5   233n32
6.6, 36   232n14
6.7, 39, 43–45, 53, 57   232n26
6.9   233n31
6.23   233n32
6.32   226, 232n14
6.46   229
7.2   233n32
7.1, 9, 10, 13, 29, 41   233n334
7.39   229
8.1, 2, 6, 14, 15, 30, 35, 39
     233n35
8.3, 5, 7, 13, 18, 25, 34   233n36
8.8   233n33
8.10, 20, 28   233n38
8.12   230
8.21, 23, 29, 41, 44, 49
     233n37
8.24, 47, 56   233n39
8.31   230
8.31, 33, 38, 42   233n32
8.37   229
8.43, 45, 48, 50, 55, 58
     233n35
8.53–54   230

Kephalaia Gnostica
1.33, 34, 36   161n39
2.35   161n39
3.29, 43, 76, 85   161n39
4.18, 21, 22, 25, 29, 68
     161n39
5.53, 58, 59, 78   161n39

Praktikos
51   232n28

Gregory of Nazianzus,
    Orationes
43.16   238, 248n16
43.17   239
43.21   242

Poema de se ipso
2.1, 215   249n22

Gregory of Nyssa, *De
    humani corporis fabrica*
2.1   147

In Canticum canticorum
1, 11, 15   161n38

Oratio Catechetica
37   161n28

Gregory Thaumaturgus, *In
    Origenem oratio
    panegyrica*
6–8   251n55
8–11   251n55
14–15   251n55

Himerius, *Orationes*
4.9   249n31
6.9   249n31
48.37   248n14

Hippocrates, *Epidemiae*
6.6.2   218n36

Homer, *Odyssey*
9.371–412   178n44

Iamblichus, *De Mysterium*
3.30   37n84
4.2   25
5.23   37n74–75

De vita Pythagorica
2   195n20

Isaiah of Gaza, *Ascetic
    Discourses*
1   195n36
6   191

Jerome, *Adversus
    Vigiliantium*
4–7   145

John Cassian, *Conferences*
1.22   192

John Chrysostom,
    Adversus Judaeos
6.7.2   106n68

*Catechesis ultima ad
    baptizandos*
1.13   179n55
2.9   179n56
2.9–10   179n55
2.17, 28   179n55
3.2.25   179n55
3.3.9–22   179n56
4.20   179n55

Justinian, *Digesta*
1.5.4.1   66n19
1.5.4.2–3   62

Edicta
1.3.2   66n19

Libanius, *Epistulae*
139   240
319   249n33
359   239
428   239
550   249n33
552   249n33
931   249n25
1009   249n25
1070   249n25
1257   249n25

Orationes
1.11   237
1.16   248n14
1.17   249n35
1.19   237, 240
1.21   240, 249n29
18.13–14   249n28
19   249n31
43.8   249n34

Marcus Aurelius,
    Meditationes
5.11   15

Maximus of Turin,
    Sermones
56   160n22

Olympiodorus of Thebes
fragment 28   238, 248n15,
     249n23

Origen of Alexandria,
    *Commentarii in
    evangelium Joannis*
1.8.44–45   34–35n50
32.27.338   21, 35n52

*Commentarius in
    Canticum*
Prol. 2   21, 161n38
Prol. 2.4   34n42
1.4   34n43, 161n38

Contra Celsum
1.48   34n43, 161n38
7.33   27
7.38   161n38

De principiis
3.3   21
3.4.1   20
3.4.4   34n41–42
3.6.6   35n60
4.2.4   35n54

Diologus cum Heraclide
13.3–6 20
14 21
16 34n42
16–22 34n43

Fragmenta in Psalmos 1–
150
1 35n61

Homiliae in Ezechielem
3.8 16, 34n42

Homiliae in Genesim
1.2 34n42
1.13 34n42
1.15 34n41–42
2.6 22

Homiliae in Leviticum
3.2 161n38
4.8 35n57

Homiliae in Lucam
8.2 34n48
8.3 16, 34n48
39.5 34n42

Philocalia
15.19.15–16 22
15.19.25–28 22

Paulinus of Nola, *Carmina*
14 159n10
14, 18, 21, 25, 33 159n8,
1559n12

Persius, *Satirae*
5.120–23 118

Petronius, *Satyricon*
117 66n27

Photius, *Bibliotheca*
cod. 80.177 248n15

Plato, *Leges*
905d–907d95

Plautus, *Mostellaria*
780 56 n.27

Plotinus, *Enneades*
1.1.1.1–3 15
1.1.4 32n2
1.1.13.1–3 16
1.6.5.50–58 18
1.6.8.26–28 19
2.3.9.31–32 33n25

4.3.8.5–6 32n4
4.3.12.5 20
4.3.26.54 18
4.8.1.1–11 32n12
4.8.2.23–27 18
4.8.2.43–45 18
4.8.2.46–49 18
4.8.4.15–18 33n25
4.8.8.1–6 32n12, 36n68
5.2.2.24–29 33n28
5.3.17.37–39 20
5.8.4.4–7 33n32
5.8.9.8–17 19
6.4.14.17 15
6.4.14.18–22 19
6.5.12.13–29 32n12
6.9.9.56 24
6.9.9.57–59 34n38
6.9.10.3 34n38

Plutarch, *Moralia*
7e 248n9
95c–f 249n30
511d–e 57
680c–682b 33n23

Porphyry, *Vita Plotini*
23 195n21

Priscianus, *De anima*
223.32 24

Proclus, *Eclogae de*
philosophia Chaldaica
5.8–11 26, 37–38n86

In Parmenides
847 26
948 25, 37n80

In Timaeus
1.51.25–31 26
3.155.18 37n86

Institutio theologica
prop. 57 25
prop. 140 37n79
prop. 142–143 37n79
prop. 144 25
prop. 145 25, 37n79, 37n82
prop. 190 37n81
prop. 211 37n80

Prudentius, *Cathemerinon*
11.61–76 160n22

Pseudo-Macarius,
Homiliae spirituales
33.1 153

Romanos the Melodist,
Hymnes
4.9 177n22
10.1 167
11.4 167
11.5 167
11.6 167
11.7 167–168
11.8 168
11.10 168
11.16 168
16.10, 14, 16, 17 177n20
17.1 166
17.2 166
17.3 166
17.4 166
17.5 166–167
17.7 166–167
17.8 166
21.prol.2 169, 178n39
21.1 169
21.1, 3, 7–12 177n20
21.3 169–170, 178n37
21.5 169
21.6 169, 178n36
21.7 178n37
21.8 170, 178n37
21.9 169
21.10 169
21.11 170, 178n49
21.12 169
22.2 165, 178n49
23.13 177n20
26.9–12 178n49
34.5 177n20
38.1 171
38.2 172
38.5 172
38.7 172
38.8 172
38.8, 13 176n4
38.9 172
38.10 172
38.11 172
38.14 172–173
38.16 173
38.18 173
46.3, 13, 17 177n20

Seneca, *Ad Lucilium*
2.19.2 188
5.52.3 194n18
6.1 189
9.87.19 189
15.50 189
15.51 189
18.109 189
94.40 195n22

Ad Marciam de consolatione
24.5   66n29

De beneficiis
3.20   66n29

Epistulae morales
37.1–2   66n27
124.13–14   118

Simplicius, *In Aristotelis de Caelo Commentarii*
271.18–21   250n44

In Aristotelis de Physica Commentarii
1363.8–12   250n44

Socrates, *Historica ecclesiastica*
6.3   193n2

Sozomen, *Historica ecclesiastica*
8.2   193n2

Synesius, *Epistulae*
16   249n25

Tertullian, *De idololatria*
15   159n4

Ad uxorem
2.5   142
2.8   142

Theodoret of Cyrrhus, *Historica ecclesiastica*
5.40   193n2

Theophrastus, *Fragmenta*
8   95

Valerius Maximus, *Factorum et dictorum memorabilium*
6.8.1–7   68n48

Victricius of Rouen, *De laude sanctorum*
1.18   29
3.11–42   39n118
7.1   30
7.12   29
7.39–40   29
8.15–16   29

8.19–22   29
8.25–40   29
9.15–16   28
9.30–31   29
10.1–5   28
11.27   39n115
11.46–50   29
12.1–8   29
12.25–33   30

Zachrias Scholasticus, *Ammonius*
19–32   235
19–38   244
357–60   235

Vita Severii
10–11   250n40
15   244
22–23   245
23–24   250n46
36–38   251n52
47   239
48   245
53–54   251n51
62   242
63   250n41